The Physical Self

From Motivation to Well-Being

Kenneth R. Fox, PhD
University of Exeter

Editor

Human Kinetics

To my parents, Angela and Eric, who showed me that
the journey is more important than the
destination.

Library of Congress Cataloging-in-Publication Data

The physical self : from motivation to well-being / Kenneth R. Fox,
   editor.
      p. cm.
   Includes bibliographical references and index.
   ISBN 0-87322-689-5
   1. Body image.   2. Physical education and training--Psychological
aspects.   3. Sports--Psychological aspects.   4. Self-esteem.
I. Fox, Kenneth R., 1949-   .
BF697.5.B63P48   1997
155.2--dc21   97-128
                                                                               CIP

ISBN: 0-87322-689-5
Copyright © 1997 by Kenneth R. Fox

Acquisitions Editor: Becky Lane; **Developmental Editor:** Marni Basic; **Assistant
Editors:** Sandra Merz Bott and Alesha G. Thompson; **Editorial Assistants:** Jennifer J.
Hemphill and Laura C. Majersky; **Copyeditor:** Joyce Sexton; **Proofreader:** Kathy
Bennett; **Indexer:** Mary Prottsman; **Graphic Designer:** Stuart Cartwright; **Graphic
Artist:** Tara Welsch; **Cover Designer:** Jack Davis; **Illustrator**: Jennifer Delmotte;
Printer: Braun-Brumfield

Printed in the United States of America   10 9 8 7 6 5 4 3 2 1

Human Kinetics
Web site: http://www.humankinetics.com/

United States: Human Kinetics, P.O. Box
5076, Champaign, IL 61825-5076
1-800-747-4457
e-mail: humank@hkusa.com

Canada: Human Kinetics, Box 24040,
Windsor, ON N8Y 4Y9
1-800-465-7301 (in Canada only)
e-mail: humank@hkcanada.com

Europe: Human Kinetics, P.O. Box IW14,
Leeds LS16 6TR, United Kingdom
(44) 1132 781708
e-mail: humank@hkeurope.com

Australia: Human Kinetics, 57A Price
Avenue, Lower Mitcham, South Australia
5062
(08) 277 1555
e-mail: humank@hkaustralia.com

New Zealand: Human Kinetics, P.O. Box
105-231, Auckland 1
(09) 523 3462
e-mail: humank@hknewz.com

CONTENTS

Preface   v

Introduction: Let's Get Physical   vii
     Kenneth R. Fox

PART I: PERSPECTIVES ON THE PHYSICAL SELF   1

Chapter 1   The Physical Self-System: 3
      A Mediator of Exercise and Self-Esteem
      Robert J. Sonstroem

Chapter 2   The Measurement of Physical Self-Concept: 27
      A Construct Validation Approach
      Herbert W. Marsh

Chapter 3   Cognitive Theories of Motivation   59
      and the Physical Self
      Stuart J.H. Biddle

Chapter 4   Reflections on the Socially Constructed   83
      Physical Self
      Andrew C. Sparkes

Chapter 5   The Physical Self and Processes in   111
      Self-Esteem Development
      Kenneth R. Fox

PART II: POPULATIONS AND PRACTICE   141

Chapter 6   Body Image, Exercise, and Eating Behaviors   143
      Caroline Davis

Chapter 7   Self-Esteem in Children and Youth: 175
      The Role of Sport and Physical Education
      James R. Whitehead and Charles B. Corbin

Chapter 8   Identity, Sport, and Youth Development   205
      Wolf-Dietrich Brettschneider and Rüdiger Heim

Chapter 9   Adolescent Weight Management and the   229
      Physical Self
      Angela Page and Kenneth R. Fox

Chapter 10   Disability, Identity, and Involvement in   257
      Sport and Exercise
      Claudine Sherrill

**Chapter 11 The Therapeutic Effects of Exercise on   287
             the Self**
             Nanette Mutrie

Index   315
About the Contributors   327
About the Editor   329

PREFACE

In the last two decades, there have been important developments in the field of self-concept research. One of the most crucial has been the recognition that *multiple* selves make up our total being. Although there have been many different attempts to express and document this multidimensionality, virtually all have made some reference to the importance of the *physical self*. For many theorists, the physical self has become the *major* component of our self-expression and interaction with the world, and it is seen to hold a key to our understanding of the total self. What we feel about our physical abilities and our appearance and how important these matters are to us determine our physical identities. The significance of this becomes apparent when we examine pertinent personal issues such as exercise and sport participation and performance, weight management, self-presentation strategies, and the ways in which people cope with injury, illness, disability, and aging.

Through my own research work in this field, I have become aware of the growing interest throughout the world in the physical self. Perspectives have converged from diverse origins that include the medical sciences, clinical and social psychology, sociology, physical education, and the exercise and sport sciences. To date, however, there has been no attempt to pull together the body of research that is central to our understanding of the physical self and its links with behavior. As a practitioner who remains involved in physical education, exercise, and sport promotion, the need for such a resource has become increasingly apparent to me.

This book provides a reflection on the recent explosion of interest in the physical self. To achieve this, I have been fortunate to have garnered the help of several of the leading researchers and speakers in this field of scholarship. They originate from six different countries and all are seasoned writers, several having produced well-known books of their own. They represent a range of perspectives and approaches, and there are strong contrasts to be made—for example, between the psychometric focus of some authors and the ideographic techniques of others. This has been a deliberate strategy on my part, as it is my belief and experience that no single method of investigation can provide a complete picture of the richness of human thought and behavior. Given this diversity, it is significant that common themes consistently emerge throughout the book, regardless of approach.

I have invited the authors to prepare a state-of-the-art summary, similar to a keynote presentation at an international conference. The assumption is that as less knowledgeable mortals we have respect for their experience and judgment and welcome their vision of where we are with regard to the particular issue they are presenting. Authors have been encouraged to editorialize and provide personal interpretations. The reader should keep this license in mind.

The book has been a dynamic journey. Regardless of the end product, the process has acted as a catalyst for conversations. Dialogue throughout has constantly thrown up new questions and challenges, and in this sense the field has already moved forward. I am forever indebted to the authors for laying their own sense of self on the line and allowing my probing editorial comments to stimulate debate and discussion with them. At the same time, as editor, I have worked hard with authors to produce a coherent package rather than a set of isolated offerings. The final product should be especially useful to a wide range of students, researchers, and professionals in the fields of education, health, and sport. Besides being of academic interest, the material is relevant to the design of clinical, educational, and health interventions.

My thanks go out to the authors for sharing their expertise; I look forward to years of continued interaction with them. In particular, my appreciation is extended to my mentor and friend Chuck Corbin, who has provided continued inspiration. I also thank Marni Basic, developmental editor, for her patience and professional guidance. Finally, I am indebted to my wonderful family—Linda, Robbie, and Gregory—for all the unconditional time and support they have given me as I was putting this volume together.

LET'S GET PHYSICAL

KENNETH R. FOX

Regardless of the extent to which we aspire to the spiritual, there is no way around the fact that we *are* physical entities. Our health and emotions are expressed through our bodies. Our desires and behaviors are enacted through our bodies. At the same time, our bodies place us on display to the senses of others and consequently make each of us public property. Sometimes we take advantage of this and use our bodies to display characteristics about ourselves that we want others to notice. We also search the bodies of others for signs of their persona and intentions. Given this accessibility of our bodies to others, it is easy to see why some researchers consider the physical self to be the *public self*. It is not surprising, therefore, that the appearance and capabilities of our body soon become apparent to us as we grow and learn, eventually forming a mental abstraction—the *physical self-concept*. It is difficult to find a topic of conversation that captures more attention, especially given the high profile afforded by society to related issues such as illness, fitness, sport, attractiveness, dieting, fashion, and our curiosity with anything that is physically out of the ordinary.

INVESTIGATING THE PHYSICAL SELF

Over the years, volumes of rhetoric and research that would require a lifelong jail sentence to fully absorb have expounded the nature and the implications of self-concept, self-esteem, and identity. However, it has taken the recent acceptance of multidimensionality of self to provide license to focus on a single element such as the physical self. With this has come the opportunity (as reflected by the title of the book) to begin to investigate the importance of the physical self (a) as a determinant or motivator of behaviors and (b) as a contributor to mental health and well-being.

This implies a two-directional flow of energy. Several motivational theories in psychology and sociology are built on the premise that the self and/

or its elements provide a stimulus that determines choice and persistence in a range of behaviors. Campbell's First Law of Human Behavior (1984), for instance, states, "Each human organism seeks to maintain or increase its sense of its own excellence" (xi). This motive, sometimes called the *self-enhancement hypothesis*, suggests that we constantly search for areas of life in which we can display our qualities. Conversely, we are likely to steer ourselves away from behaviors that carry a high risk of failure or discomfort. Our self-perceptions are clearly pivotal in such a lifelong mission, and the physical self is necessarily implicated in behaviors such as those involving fitness and health, weight management, sport and exercise participation, and recovery from injury or illness.

On the other hand, the rationale for educational, sport, exercise, and other health-related programs has been increasingly built around the enhancement of holistic health and mental well-being. The assumption is becoming popular that involvement in physical activities and improvement in skill, knowledge, fitness, or health will enhance self-perceptions. With increasing frequency in several professional quarters we hear claims that such changes generalize to improved self-esteem and well-being. This implies that certain behaviors or physical changes in the individual influence global mental constructs. This has been termed the *skill enhancement hypothesis*. Because of the wide array of changes that might take place, through the range of programs of involvement, perhaps a more encompassing term that implies the origin of change would be the *intervention hypothesis*.

These two hypotheses raise important research and practical questions that will figure throughout the book. Degrees of support will be provided for either hypothesis. However, several authors will make the case that it is the *reflexivity* of flow that is likely to provide the more complete explanation of the development and functionality of the physical self. There is a continual trade-off between life experiences and decisions that not only help shape the self, but in return direct future behaviors and lifestyles.

This book provides a comprehensive documentation of existing research into aspects of the physical self. It also attempts to extend horizons of both research and practice by addressing contentious or overlapping issues and introducing new ideas. It highlights the contrast in emphasis that has emerged from different disciplines. Researchers from physical education and exercise and sport science, for example, have focused heavily on perceived physical competencies and abilities. This has been applied to motivational issues concerned with participation and performance in sport and exercise. Furthermore, the belief has been widespread that programs designed for skill and fitness improvement can have a positive impact on self-esteem. On the other hand, sociologists have focused on identity formation and the broader context of the body and its appearance as a public representation of the self. Psychologists have dealt with a wide range of clinical issues regarding self-esteem and health. Sometimes the literature from these perspectives barely overlaps and it soon becomes clear that there is a case for greater integration.

Furthermore, the answer to understanding the physical self does not lie in a singular approach, and in recognition of this, a spectrum of research paradigms is represented in this book. All offer unique insight into the world of the physical self. Without a strong nomothetic and statistical perspective we would find great difficulty in identifying patterns among populations and deriving variables that are critical to determining differences among individuals. However, the dynamics and processes of change are often subtle and require a much more focused approach. More detailed qualitative work with individuals, particularly those who have experienced physical change through disability or illness, clearly provides an important route to furthering our understanding. Readers will naturally feel an affiliation to a singular perspective, as it is difficult to break away from our roots. This is particularly the case when language from both the positivistic and interpretive paradigms seems to be overtly designed to exclude rather than invite. However, readers are encouraged to remain open-minded and to explore the writings of authors from different perspectives.

Although authors from six different countries have contributed to this book, the content is largely built on research from the westernized cultures of North America, Europe, and Australasia. This has produced an unavoidable bias, and the reader should be aware of the potential for true cross-cultural differences. Not only is study of such differences interesting in its own right, but it may also provide a very insightful path into mechanisms and processes involved in the formation and development of the self.

ORGANIZATION OF THE BOOK

The book is presented in two parts. Part I brings together researchers who document the general advances in our conceptualization of the physical self that have taken place over the last 10 to 15 years. These contributors also suggest future research directions. It is appropriate that Bob Sonstroem should provide the first chapter of this book. More than 25 years ago, at a time when sport psychology was in its infancy and largely focused on motor learning or "skill acquisition," Bob Sonstroem saw the value of a social-psychological approach and developed one of the first models involving aspects of the physical self. He has continued to advance the field, and in his chapter he provides a historical context to his present work with physical self-perceptions and exercise.

A major step forward in this field was made by Shavelson, Hubner, and Stanton in 1976 when they provided an intuitively appealing and now well-known multidimensional model of self-concept. At the same time, with advances in statistical techniques such as structural equation modeling and with the greater capacity of computers, the opportunity has arisen to develop and test a range of theoretical models of self-concept. Herbert Marsh, a prolific education researcher, has applied his statistical expertise to the study of self-concept models and, more recently, the physical self-concept. In chapter 2, he convincingly outlines the importance of partnerships between developments in theory and instrumentation. He uses examples from his own extensive work and that of others to demonstrate the process of construct validation in instrument design and development.

The self is inextricably tied to motivation and behavior. Several theories have been developed to encompass this relationship, with the majority implicating elements of the self as precursors to choice and persistence in behaviors. Stuart Biddle is well known for his work in the motivational aspects of exercise and sport psychology. In chapter 3, he provides a comprehensive analysis of a range of contemporary self-based motivational theories that fall within the social cognitive framework. Throughout, he provides a useful interpretation of their relevance to sport, exercise, and other health-related behaviors.

Sociological and interpretative theorists have influenced visions and explanations of the self throughout the century, mainly through symbolic interactionism. Recently there has been a resurgence of interest in the body as a sociological entity. In chapter 4, Andrew Sparkes provides an insightful discussion of the role of the body in society and reminds us of the powerful social forces that constrain the self. Furthermore, Andrew enlightens us to life history research, which surely has tremendous scope for understanding the processes of change in identity and the self over time.

Although there have been important advances in our understanding of self-concept and its measurement, most of the empirical research in the last 10 years has been descriptive and nomothetic. We have been content with developing and modifying instruments and cross-sectionally applying them to a range of populations. We are now due for a further leap forward, and it is clear to me that this must take place in the area of processes and mechanisms involved in self-perception and self-esteem change. In chapter 5, I redress some assumptions about the self-system and attempt to provide a focus for future research.

Part II of the book provides greater access to specific issues that are inexorably linked with the physical self. Although there is certainly no absence of strong theoretical underpinnings in this section, there is a concentration on various populations, with children and youth quite heavily represented. This is intentional, as youngsters represent our greatest hope for change. Furthermore, many readers will be involved at some level in the education system and are responsible for designing and influencing exercise, sport, and health programs for young people.

One of the strongest themes to emerge through the book is the salience of perceptions of physical appearance in both the physical and global self-system. In chapter 6, Caroline Davis provides thorough and insightful coverage of the huge and diverse literature on body image, including her own extensive work. The influences on body image are explored in detail, and important links are developed with eating and exercise behaviors.

Physical educators and sport coaches have historically claimed that their programs have the potential for building "character" and self-esteem. However, explanations of mechanisms of self-perception enhancement have been notably absent, and empirical evidence until recently has been sparse. In chapter 7, Jim Whitehead and Chuck Corbin bring together their wealth of experience as physical educators and researchers to provide a strong theoretical rationale for the processes underlying children's self-esteem development in sport and physical education. This foundation is translated into practical pointers to guide curriculum design and teaching and coaching styles.

Adolescents face the tremendous challenge of developing a coherent and consistent identity. Sport and exercise participation and issues concerning appearance feature prominently in the culture of youth. In chapter 8, Wolf-Dietrich Brettschneider and Rüdiger Heim cleverly combine concepts from sociological and psychological literature, including their own research, to explain the relationship between the development of identity, sport involvement, and the adolescent physical self.

This theme is extended in chapter 9. As the cultural focus on the body has increased, it has acquired considerable social currency for young people. Feeling too fat has become a major source of concern for youngsters to the extent that for many it threatens their sense of self and well-being and leads to unhealthy dietary practices. Ironically, this is at a time when *actual* fatness among people in Western society, including youngsters, is rapidly increasing and already posing a serious health problem. In chapter 9, Angela Page and I analyze the psychology of adolescent weight management and its implications for health promotion.

Few if any researchers have as much wealth of experience and insight as Claudine Sherrill in the field of physical education and disability. Her extensive knowledge has been applied to produce a unique analysis of the way society views and addresses disability and the impact that this has on the self for individuals with disabilities. Particular attention is paid to sport; this not only is extremely valuable for program design for people with disabilities, but also provides a special arena for revealing critical pointers to some of the generic processes of self-development that currently remain speculative.

Increasingly, health professionals are realizing that psychological factors are important mediating and outcome variables in a range of medical interventions. In chapter 11 Nanette Mutrie, one of the leading researchers in the use of exercise as a therapy, provides a comprehensive overview of the field for us. In the process, attempts are made to identify potential mechanisms through which self-perception change might be stimulated.

TERMINOLOGY

A problem that has plagued this area of study is that of terminology. This problem is intensified by the diversity of disciplines that have influenced the field and the range of settings in which concepts are applied. Although there remains a great deal of conceptual overlap between constructs and terms in the literature, over the past 10 to 15 years, theoretical developments have stimulated a convergence and consensus, particularly in the area of social psychology. With the sanity of the reader in mind, throughout the development of this book the authors have been encouraged to try to work with a set of definitional guidelines for the commonly used terms.

Self-perceptions: An umbrella term that denotes all types of self-referent statements about the self, from those that are global to those that are specific in content.

Self-concept: The individual as known to the individual. This is a self-description profile based on the multitude of roles and attributes that we consider make up our self. Examples might be "I am a father," "I am a friend," "I am a golfer." Some theorists include evaluative statements within the self-concept, such as "I am a really talented golfer," whereas others exclude them.

Identity: The integration of beliefs, values, self-perceptions, and behaviors into a consistent, coherent, and recognizable self-package. It is more than a self-description—more akin to a self-theory. This term is used more frequently in the sociology literature, with some writers maintaining that an individual can have separate identities in different domains of life.

Self-esteem: The awareness of good possessed by the self (Campbell 1984, 9). This is a global construct that provides an overall statement of the degree to which an individual perceives himself or herself to be an "OK" person, dependent on whatever criteria that individual uses to determine "OK."

Self-worth: Essentially the same meaning as self-esteem.

Perceived competence: A statement of personal ability that generalizes across a domain such as sport, scholarship, or work.

Perceived ability: A more specific statement of competence restricted to a limited set of behaviors such as playing soccer, doing mathematics, or conducting relationships with similar-sex peers.

Body image: The mental representation an individual has of his/her body.

Body esteem: The value or worth an individual attaches to his/her body. Similar to self-esteem, it represents an overall judgment based on body criteria that the individual feels are important.

Self-efficacy: A statement of expectancy about one's ability to accomplish a specific task.

Self-confidence: A general term reflecting the degree to which an individual feels he/she is able to successfully meet the demands of a social context.

FINAL COMMENT

As is often the case, this book has raised as many questions as it has answered. However, given the large volumes of literature from several disciplines that have been used throughout the book, along with the presentation of research and ideas from different paradigms, it is encouraging to see common themes emerging and a consensus on many important issues. These are clearly visible with progression through the chapters. All that remains is to invite the reader to read on. I hope that the experience is as enlightening and stimulating for others as it has been for me.

REFERENCE

Campbell, R.N. 1984. *The new science: Self-esteem psychology*. Lanham, MD: University Press of America.

PART I

PERSPECTIVES ON THE PHYSICAL SELF

THE PHYSICAL SELF-SYSTEM: A MEDIATOR OF EXERCISE AND SELF-ESTEEM

ROBERT J. SONSTROEM

The past five years have brought a rejuvenation to the study of exercise and self-esteem. For this observer, much of this invigoration comes from the development of multidimensional physical scales (Fox and Corbin 1989; Marsh et al. 1994) and from the use of hierarchical systems of self-perceptions (Sonstroem, Harlow, and Josephs 1994). We tend to speak best about topics that we feel we know well. Therefore, in order to provide a historical perspective on recent work in this field, I will first present a chronological summary of my own investigative experiences.

AN EARLY PHYSICAL SELF-CONCEPT MEDIATOR

My initial approach to this content area years ago began with the tacit assumption that physical fitness was synonymous with self-esteem. Imagine my consternation when our first data showed that the two were practically unrelated across people (Neale, Sonstroem, and Metz 1969). The self-esteem literature at that time was just beginning to recognize smaller, more specific components of self-perception. Fortunately, we had employed an early form of the Estimation scale, a measure of perceived physical competence, in the study. While self-esteem was unrelated to exercise participation or physical fitness, estimation related moderately but significantly to physical activity participation, to physical fitness, and also to global self-esteem. So here a variable had been identified that mediated the association between fitness and self-esteem. It was a mental variable presumed to contain cognition and affect, and it provided a bridge between the physical world of activity and the psychological state of self-esteem. As to why global self-esteem and fitness should not be related across people, we need look no further than self-esteem theory itself. People strive to think well of themselves. Therefore they tend to rely on any perceived success, skill, or positive attribute as a basis for establishing, enhancing, or maintaining self-esteem. An orchestra conductor need not bench-press heavy weights or jog for long distances in order to have positive self-esteem. Success is critical in our society, and ultimately people will locate an area of perceived personal success that fosters favorable self-esteem.

Physical Estimation assessed personal evaluations of a broad variety of physical and sport skills and was featured in the Psychological Model for Physical Activity Participation (Sonstroem 1978) (see fig. 1.1). The model proposed that physical activity participation leads to increased physical ability (in this case, physical fitness), which produces psychological benefits that are reflected in self-esteem enhancement. However, self-esteem is influenced by exercise and increased fitness through the mediating influence of estimation. That is, increases in fitness lead to increases in perceived physical competence that are associated with concurrent increases in self-esteem. This type of path from external behaviors/successes to augmented internal self-esteem is labeled the skill development hypothesis of self-esteem (Marsh 1986).

Attraction in figure 1.1 represents interest in (attraction toward) vigorous physical activity. The model proposes also that perceived physical competence leads to a strong interest in vigorous activity and that these two

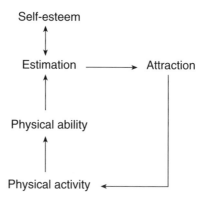

Figure 1.1   Psychological Model for Physical Activity Participation.

Reprinted, by permission, from R.J. Sonstroem, 1978, "Physical Estimation and Attraction Scales: Rationale and Research," *Medicine and Science in Sports and Exercise* 10: 101.

variables will predict subsequent exercise participation. In self-esteem parlance, this path from internal self-esteem or self-esteem components to congruent external behavior is labeled the self-development or self-enhancement hypothesis. We tend to engage in behaviors that increase or maintain positive self-esteem. It is believed that both skill development and self-enhancement processes occur repeatedly in the lives of people. The Psychological Model for Physical Activity Participation accommodates both skill development and self-enhancement paths and proposes that perceived physical competence serves as a bridge between external exercise and internal self-esteem.

Validity testing of the model, as with many psychological models, has relied on correlational rather than causative evidence. Studies have shown that scores on the Estimation scale are related to physical fitness scores (Sonstroem 1974, 1976, 1978), but few have attempted to show that increases in fitness lead to increases in estimation. Morgan (as reported in Sonstroem 1984, 134), however, found increased estimation scores in police officers after a 12-week conditioning program. Kowal, Patton, and Vogel (1978) showed increases in both fitness and estimation scores in 200 male soldiers after six weeks of basic training. The same effect was not obtained in 200 female soldiers. Sonstroem and Kampper (1980) used estimation scores obtained during the first week of school to predict those middle-school boys who subsequently would volunteer for fall athletic competition. This latter study supports the self-enhancement hypothesis of self-esteem.

While estimation and attraction scores have been significantly correlated with exercise self-reports (Fox, Corbin, and Couldry 1985; Sonstroem 1978), the Psychological Model for Physical Activity Participation has generally been ineffective at predicting adherence to exercise (Dishman, Sallis, and Orenstein 1985; Sonstroem 1988). Sonstroem (1988) has indicated that this inability may be caused by measurement shortcomings, particularly in the Attraction scale, rather than model ineffectiveness. Modern attitude measurement employs statements congruent with the attitude object in terms of target, action, context, and time as opposed to the broad, general attitude statement found in the Attraction scale.

Although the Estimation scale has demonstrated associations with important life adjustment variables (Sonstroem 1974, 1976) and has provided supportive evidence for the self-enhancement properties of perceived physical competence (Sonstroem, Harlow, and Salisbury 1993; Sonstroem and Kampper 1980), it lacks the psychometric development and discriminating ability of later inventories such as the Physical Self-Perception Profile (Fox and Corbin 1989).

THE EXERCISE AND SELF-ESTEEM MODEL

The majority of exercise and self-esteem studies have been designed to test the skill development hypothesis of self-esteem. The adjustment properties of self-esteem seem to be so universally accepted that inclusion of self-esteem in study designs has appeared to be a relatively straightforward way to document the salutary effects of exercise. In a review of 16 studies testing this proposition, Sonstroem (1984) concluded that exercise participation was associated with increases in subsequent self-esteem scores. Studies were so simplistic in design, however, that it remained impossible to determine how or why self-esteem enhancement might have occurred. The review recommended a variety of experimental procedures and the development and testing of models as ways of advancing knowledge in this area.

MODEL STRUCTURE

As a result, Sonstroem and Morgan (1989) proposed the Exercise and Self-Esteem Model as a self-system to explain how the effects of physical training generalize to global self-esteem (see fig. 1.2). The model is based on dimensions of perceived physical competence and self-acceptance that are generally postulated as two of the foundations involved in the establishment of favorable self-esteem (Harter 1985; Wells and Marwell 1976). Self-acceptance denotes personal regard and liking that people hold for them-

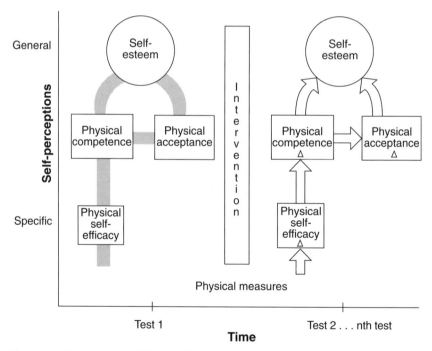

Figure 1.2 Exercise and Self-Esteem Model.

Reprinted, by permission, from R.J. Sonstroem, 1989, "Exercise and Self-Esteem: Rationale and Model," *Medicine and Science in Sports and Exercise* 21: 333.

selves and for their attributes irrespective of their levels of perceived competence.

The recency of the model has precluded tests of the self-acceptance dimension to date. Therefore, discussions in this chapter are limited to the competence dimension as shown in figure 1.2. The base of the model consists of objective evaluations of physical performance that might be enhanced through training, such as distance run in 12 minutes or the amount of weight lifted in one attempt. A sport study might employ physical measures such as number of base hits in a game or percentage of ground balls fielded successfully in practice. A self-efficacy statement specific to a physical measure represents the first self-perception variable. It provides the bridge from the physical to representations of the physical within the mind of the person. A self-efficacy is an expectation that at this moment one can successfully perform a particular task, such as field ground balls or run for distance. Social cognitive theory (Bandura 1977, 1986) has popularized self-efficacy and provided it with widespread applications to human functioning. High self-efficacy levels have been related to high levels of motivation, performance of more challenging tasks, setting of higher goals, and perseverance in reaching them (Schwarzer 1992). Self-efficacies indicate perceptions of mastery or competence at specific activities. The principle of reciprocal determinism states that success at tasks influences the further development of positive self-efficacies and that such enhanced self-efficacies influence the attainment of further successes.

Within the model, self-efficacies are believed to be closely related to perceived physical competence, defined as a self-evaluation of overall level of physical ability. Previous research employing estimation as a measure of perceived physical competence consistently found moderate to large associations between estimation and global self-esteem (Fox, Corbin, and Couldry 1985; Sonstroem 1974, 1978). Global self-esteem is retained in the model because of its recognized validity as an index of life adjustment.

The left portion of figure 1.2 illustrates the static hierarchical structure of the model. For example, it hypothesizes that global self-esteem (labeled "Self-esteem" in figure 1.2) should develop closer associations with perceived physical competence than with physical self-efficacy and that efficacy should develop stronger relationships with physical measures than does perceived physical competence. From the model's horizontal axis, which is included to represent change over time, we can see that increases in self-efficacies are hypothesized to cause increases in perceived physical competence that may lead to increases in global self-esteem. This represents another example of the skill development hypothesis.

MODEL VALIDATION

Model structure and hypothesized associations among elements were first examined under the conditions of a single testing session. Next, a longitudinal design with repeated measures was utilized to examine the interplay of model elements over time.

Internal Structure and Associations

Structure for the competence dimension of the Exercise and Self-Esteem Model was initially validated with a sample of middle-aged and older adults (mean age = 54.22, SD = 11.74) (Sonstroem et al. 1991). Subjects completed the Rosenberg Self-Esteem Scale (Rosenberg 1965) and the Global Self-Worth Scale (Messer and Harter 1986) as measures of global self-esteem. A study-revised Estimation scale assessed self-perceptions of a well-conditioned body, stamina, and strength and was partitioned into two scales (Physical Condition and Physical Doubt) by principal component analysis. The technique for self-efficacy assessment was similar to that employed in subsequent studies. The self-efficacy for walking scale consisted of 14 categories ranging from "walk for 1 minute" to "walk for 5 hours." Subjects estimated their degree of confidence (0% to 100%) in walking each of the distances. A strength of self-efficacy score was obtained by summing these percentages and dividing by the number of categories (14 in this case). This study contained scales for walking, stair climbing, and jogging.

Confirmatory factor analyses tested a variety of models considered to be possible in explaining responses to the seven scales (i.e., two self-esteem, two perceived physical competence, three physical self-efficacies). These analyses confirmed that the hypothesized measurement model provided the best fit (X^2 [df = 14, N = 145] = 25.22, p < .01). The Normed Fit Index and the Tucker-Lewis Index were both .94. Structural modeling analyses subsequently confirmed hypothesized associations within the Exercise and Self-Esteem Model as opposed to alternative associations. For example, the path between self-efficacies and perceived physical competence was significant, as was the path between perceived competence and self-esteem. However, as hypothesized by the model, the path from self-efficacies to self-esteem was not significant.

It was possible to administer a submaximal step test to 70 subjects. As predicted, Pearson rs calculated between the step test and two self-esteem measures were not significant (r = −.03 and r = −.13). Pearson rs calculated between the step test and the three self-efficacies were all significant and ranged from .38 to .47. These data validated structure and paths among variables as proposed by the Exercise and Self-Esteem Model.

Dynamic Associations

In a more recent study, path analysis was employed to examine the structure of the Exercise and Self-Esteem Model across a high school varsity swimming season and to test for the presence of both skill development and self-enhancement paths (Sonstroem, Harlow, and Salisbury 1993). Male swimmers (N = 93) were administered a test battery in November, January, and March that provided preseason, midseason, and postseason measurements, respectively. Swimmers indicated their best event and their best time for that event since the previous testing (labeled PERF in fig. 1.3). The test battery consisted of the Rosenberg Self-Esteem Scale, a study-revised Estimation scale, and a study-developed perception of swimming stroke skills scale (labeled SKILL). Perception of skills temporarily replaced self-efficacies for this study because swim performance is generally thought to rely on the conscious monitoring of strokes. Subjects evaluated themselves at each testing on starts, turns, arm stroke, leg stroke, and coordination of strokes. The five evaluations were summed to provide perception of skills. Social desirability (labeled SD) (Jackson 1984) was included in the battery because it has been reported as a frequent response contaminant in sport psychology research (Morgan 1978) and has often developed moderate to large associations with self-esteem.

The first column of figure 1.3 depicts the competence phase of the Exercise and Self-Esteem Model as operationalized for this swim study. Because social desirability is believed to associate more readily with abstract as compared to situation-specific self-perceptions, it was positioned between self-esteem and perceived physical competence in the hierarchy. The model

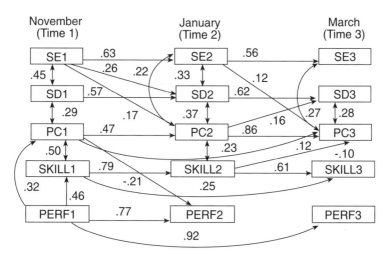

Figure 1.3 Longitudinal test of Exercise and Self-Esteem Model. (Values represent standardized coefficients.) Self-esteem (SE), social desirability (SD), perceived physical competence (PC), perception of swim skills (SKILL), and swim performance (PERF). Scores for November (1), January (2), and March (3).

Data from R.J. Sonstroem, 1993, "Path Analysis of a Self-Esteem Model Across a Competitive Swim Season," *Research Quarterly for Exercise and Sport* 64: 334-342. Reproduced with permission from the American Alliance for Health, Physical Education, Recreation and Dance, Reston, VA 22091.

outlined in figure 1.3 provided an excellent data fit across the three test times (X^2 [df = 41, N = 93] = 59.89, p < .028, root mean square residual = .043). Only significant paths are drawn in figure 1.3, and the relatively large number of them provides additional model validity. Few of these paths represented hypothesized skill associations, however. Exceptions included previous swim times (PERF), which significantly predicted both perception of skills and perceived competence (PC) scores in November. While January perception of skills scores predicted March perceived competence scores, the sign of the standardized regression coefficient (–0.10) was in the wrong direction.

The presence of few skill development paths (upward-moving diagonals) is surprising because the model was developed initially to delineate the manner in which self-esteem (SE) and perceived competence changed as a result of physical gains. Study swimmers significantly improved performance in 4 of 14 events across the time periods (significance was approached in 5 other events with Z scores > 1.50). Significant increases occurred in self-esteem at Time 2, in perceived physical competence at Time 3, and in perception of skills at Times 2 and 3. It would be easy to conclude (as studies have) that improved self-esteem and perceived competence had been caused by better swim times and enhanced feelings of mastery. Our model and analyses indicate that this was not true. Psychological change may have occurred because of many possible factors that have been discussed by Sonstroem (1984). In this connection it is helpful to recall the study of Jasnoski et al. (1981). They found that participants in college conditioning classes improved both in fitness and in perceptions of physical ability. However, correlations between changes in the two variables were nonsignificant, leading the authors to conclude that psychological enhancement was caused by other factors such as increased social support within the program. Interestingly, as later chapters in this book will note, although exercise interventions have been designed around the skill development model, physiological change, such as improved functional capacity, has been found to be remarkably unrelated to significant changes in global measures of well-being. The results of our swim study highlight the advantages of working within a model and utilizing appropriate tests of model hypotheses.

The absence of significant paths capable of explaining the significant increases in psychological scores is believed to be attributable, perhaps, to two related factors. A majority of these boys had been swimming in high school and in amateur competition for the previous five to eight years. Quite probably, self-perceptions as well as performance had stabilized. Since the amount of performance change was relatively small (median change = 2.9%), it may have been insufficiently powerful to influence psychological change. In 1984, Sonstroem summarized intervention research by concluding that change was generally limited to subjects initially lower in self-esteem or ability.

Besides demonstrating a very adequate model-to-data fit across three time periods, the study produced the following important conclusions:

1. The self-enhancement influence of higher-level components on those lower in the model was clearly shown. November self-esteem scores influenced January and March perceived competence scores. Figure 1.3 portrays, also, the significant influence of prior perceived competence scores on subsequent January swim times. Additionally, the association between January perceived competence scores and March swim times was in the proper direction ($p < .13$). These results, combined with those of Sonstroem and Kampper (1980), provide a new validity for perceived physical competence. It is able to predict subsequent physical performance.

2. Social desirability failed to significantly influence subsequent associations among self-esteem, perceived competence, perception of skills, or performance scores. This indicates that relationships among these variables were not causally influenced by social desirability motivation.

Model Expansion: EXSEM

The development of the Physical Self-Perception Profile (PSPP) (Fox and Corbin 1989) represents a major advance in the study of the physical self. As described in more detail in the next chapter, the investigators developed a general physical self-worth scale (PSW) subsuming four more specific scales of perceived sport competence (SPORT), physical condition (COND), attractive body (BODY), and strength (STREN). Multidimensional assessments of the physical self provide greater opportunities for developing discriminant validity and for increasing correspondence between a physical self-system and external criteria. The development of the PSPP offered the opportunity to replace the unidimensional perceived physical competence level of the Exercise and Self-Esteem Model with a multidimensional physical self-concept profile. This expanded model with multiple physical self components is referred to as EXSEM to distinguish it as an extension of the original Exercise and Self-Esteem Model containing a unidimensional perceived physical competence assessed by the Estimation scale of the Physical Estimation and Attraction Scale.

Adult females ($N = 216$, age $M = 38.4$, $SD = 16.2$), enrolled in aerobic dance classes in two cities (Providence, Rhode Island, and Washington, DC), completed the Global Self-Worth Scale (Messer and Harter 1986) assessing self-esteem and also completed the PSPP as well as self-efficacy measures for jogging, sit-ups, and dancing (Sonstroem, Harlow, and Josephs 1994). The PSPP had been validated earlier for a similar-aged sample (Sonstroem, Speliotis, and Fava 1992).

The hypothesized expansion of the competence dimension (see fig. 1.4) was tested against three alternative models. The model pictured in figure 1.4 proved to be superior to alternatives and demonstrated an acceptable data fit. The comparative fit index was .913, the parsimonious fit index was .840, and the root mean square residual was .047. A latent variable developed from the summation of the three specific self-efficacies is represented by EFF. All paths between variables were significant. Standardized regression coefficients are printed beside paths. The amount of variance explained by the model is enclosed within parentheses at the top of the latent variable. For example, EFF accounts for 15% of sport competence variance, and its regression coefficient is .39. Further validity for the model is provided by its accounting for 88.6% of the variation in PSW scores and by the large standardized coefficient between PSW and self-esteem. The fact that the model is able to explain 32.8% of self-esteem variance is notable and perhaps surprising if we think of the range of skills and attributes on which self-esteem can be established.

The standardized solution in figure 1.4 presents some interesting information about component relationships. While self-efficacies are able to explain 27.4% of the variation in perceived physical condition (COND) scores, they explain only 4.4% of variation in perceived bodily attractiveness (BODY) scores. Of the four subdomain scales, however, BODY exhibits the largest association with PSW.

We can infer that two forces are portrayed in figure 1.4. On the one hand, we have the agentive self-efficacies associating rather well with perceived

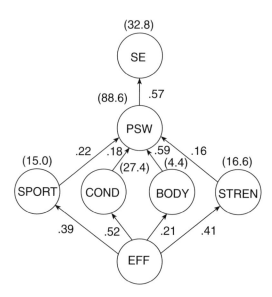

Figure 1.4 **Standardized Solution, Expanded Model. Values beside paths represent standardized regression coefficients. Values within parentheses represent variance percentages accounted for.**

Reprinted, by permission, from R.J. Sonstroem, L.L. Harlow, and L. Josephs, 1994, "Exercise and Self-Esteem: Validity of Model Expansion and Exercise Associations," *Journal of Sport and Exercise Psychology* **16**: 38.

sport competence, perceived physical condition, and perceived strength, but not perceived bodily attractiveness. On the other hand, we see perceived bodily attractiveness relating very strongly with overall physical self-worth and, eventually, global self-esteem. For practitioners, this could be considered to be somewhat defeating. The practice of sport and exercise appears more likely to influence attributes such as sport competence, fitness, and strength, but these seem to have less potential than attractiveness to develop strong associations with more global elements of the self. Many investigations have verified the extremely potent relationship between self-esteem and physical attractiveness (Harter 1990). Physical attractiveness represents an extremely interesting and perhaps confounding factor in research that examines the interplay among physical activity, the physical self, and psychological benefits. It is a topic that in itself has generated considerable research and will be the focus of further chapters in this book.

ASSOCIATIONS OF EXSEM WITH EXERCISE

Validity for a model or system can be developed by examinations of hypothesized relationships with external criteria. Our criterion variables for validation of the EXSEM as discussed in this section are limited to self-reports of exercise behavior. First, we will consider several studies that have examined direct associations between PSPP scores and activity self-reports. This will be followed by discussion of studies that have included self-efficacy measures.

ASSOCIATIONS WITH AN EXERCISE DICHOTOMY

Fox and Corbin (1989) classified 180 male and 175 female college students into exercise and nonexercise groups (see upper part of table 1.1). Discriminant function analysis successfully categorized 70.7% of the female sample and 70.4% of the males. As hypothesized, perceived physical condition represented the major predictor for both females and males.

The lower four rows of table 1.1 contain data from a study conducted by Sonstroem, Speliotis, and Fava (1992). Subjects were 149 females and 111 males (age $M = 44.1$, $SD = 11.6$). The ability of PSPP scales to predict exercise participation was again tested by discriminant function analysis. It should be mentioned that the discriminant function analyses reported here involved direct entry of all five PSPP scales whereas the Fox and Corbin analyses did not employ PSW as a predictor. The categorization of subjects into exercisers and nonexercisers was predicted by the PSPP scales with 88.6% accuracy in the case of females and 80.2% accuracy in the case of males. Obviously, these are extremely accurate predictions. The COND scale demonstrated the largest coefficients in all analyses.

Table 1.1	Physical Self-Perception Profile Prediction of Exercise by Discriminant Function Analyses: Two Studies				
Study	Criterion for exercise	Sex	Primary predictors	Canonical correlation coefficient (R)	Subjects correctly classified (%)
Fox and Corbin (1989)	Y or N	F M	COND = .95 COND = .87 SPORT = .78 STREN = .72	.47 .43	70.7% 70.4%
Sonstroem, Speliotis, and Fava (1992)	Y or N Degree	F M F M	COND = .97 COND = .88 COND = .89 COND = .89	.71 .64 .73 .64	88.6% 80.2% 59.1% 54.1%

Note: Criterion for exercise: Y = Yes, N = No; degree = scale of 1-5; primary PSPP predictors: COND = perceived physical condition, SPORT = perceived sport competence, STREN = perceived strength. Values under primary predictors are within function correlation coefficients.

ASSOCIATIONS WITH DEGREE AND TYPE OF ACTIVITY

Subjects were also placed into one of four degrees of exercise categories based on reports of exercise frequency and duration. Rows 5 and 6 of table 1.1 show that 59.1% of females and 54.1% of males were correctly classified by the PSPP (Sonstroem, Speliotis, and Fava 1992). There are several ways to interpret this degree of success. Since there are four possible activity categories, our degree of success should be approximately 25% by chance. However, this does not account for the actual size of categories. For example, in the female analysis there were 31 subjects in the second-to-highest activity group. This represents a base rate of 20.8% (i.e., 31/149 × 100) of the entire sample. A more valid standard for evaluating success posits that predictions across all categories should be above category base rates. Female category 3 was the only instance in the two analyses in which the PSPP prediction failed to better the base rate. The PSPP scales predicted 19.8% of group 3 membership correctly as compared to a base rate of 20.8%. These analyses attest to the sensitivity of the PSPP in predicting activity participation. Perceived physical condition was easily the most sensitive predictor of activity, with a coefficient of .89 in the two analyses. Size of the canonical Rs constitutes another measure of the degree of fit between self-perception components and exercise behavior. Squaring these coefficients indicates that 42.16% to 53.29% of the variance in either set of variables represents shared variance.

Fox and Corbin (1989) asked subjects to indicate the type of activity in which they participated. A canonical correlation was calculated between five activity types and four PSPP scales. Two significant functions were found for each sex. The first function denoted an athletic female in whom sport competence perceptions were linked with participation at ball sports. The second function linked perceived physical condition with calisthenics and aerobic exercise, indicative of the exercising female. For males, the first function related perceived strength, physical condition, and bodily attractiveness scores to weight training and calisthenics, possibly representing the male who is working out. The second function associated perceived sport competence with ball sports, again indicating athletic involvement.

STRUCTURAL MODELING ANALYSIS WITH EXSEM

Structural modeling presents the distinct advantage that one can control for measurement error while examining associations between variables. In the study of Sonstroem, Harlow, and Josephs (1994), subjects were asked how many aerobic classes per week they typically attended (DANCE) and how much time they averaged per week in exercise activities outside of class (EXERCISE). The ability of EXSEM to predict these two variables was tested by hypothesizing a downward or self-enhancement flow of influence in the model. Global self-esteem was presumed to influence PSW, which in turn would affect the four subdomains as represented by perceived sport competence, physical condition, bodily attractiveness, and strength. Paths were hypothesized from the subdomains to the latent variable, EFF. On the basis of theory by Shavelson, Hubner, and Stanton (1976) it was predicted that EFF would associate most strongly with dance and exercise behavior followed by the four subdomains. All proposed paths were tested for significance.

Structural modeling statistics again indicated a very adequate fit of data to the model. A comparative fit index of .911 and a root mean square residual of .047 were obtained. The model predicted 26.0% and 27.6% of dance and exercise behavior, respectively. However, only two (perceived physical condition and bodily attractiveness) of the five hypothesized activity predictors developed significant associations. A refined model was tested by dropping SPORT, STREN, and their nonsignificant paths from the model. For theoretical reasons, EFF was retained as a predictor. This refinement increased the correspondence between model and data slightly in that the comparative fit index was increased from .911 to .927. These results validate EXSEM as a predictor of physical activity and provide valuable information on the types of physical self-perceptions that are most closely associated with exercise. While perceived physical condition would be readily hypothesized as a leading predictor, the significant negative association between perceived bodily attractiveness and activity reports merits additional explanation.

Subjects in this study had also completed the Perceived Importance Profile (PIP) (Fox 1990). In this eight-item inventory, subjects are asked to report the importance of competence in each of the four subdomains to their overall sense of self. During data analysis it became apparent that subjects strongly valued the importance of an attractive body (importance $M = 3.30$ on a scale of 1 to 4). However, the mean evaluation of personal body attractiveness was only 2.50. This body discrepancy mean of –0.80 ($SD = .88$) can be compared with discrepancy means of 0.08, –0.38, and –0.14 for perceived sport competence, physical condition, and strength, respectively. A comparison between 41 women having the largest body discrepancies ($M = -2.12$) and the remainder of the sample found that these women exercised more often, were younger, and had lower self-esteem and PSW values than the rest of the group. These differences were all significant, as were the higher body importance values and lower perceived bodily attractiveness values of this high body-discrepant group. On the basis of the analyses described, it was concluded that exercise participation in adult female aerobic dancers is associated with positive feelings of personal physical condition but also with strong negative evaluations of body attractiveness in certain females.

FURTHER EVIDENCE FOR BODY AND EXERCISE ASSOCIATIONS IN WOMEN

These body discrepancy conclusions are supported elsewhere (Leveillee, Sonstroem, and Riebe 1994). Ultraexercisers (women who exercised more than six hours per week, $M = 12.75$, $n = 158$) displayed significantly larger body discrepancy and perceived physical condition scores than women who exercised six hours or less per week ($M = 4.00$, $n = 61$). The highly active group had significantly larger scores on the Drive for Thinness, Bulimia, and Body Dissatisfaction scales of the Eating Disorder Inventory (Garner, Olmstead, and Polivy 1983). However, their self-esteem and depression scores were not significantly different from those of women with less rigorous exercise habits. Somewhat less than 20% of this highly active group displayed bulimia scale scores indicative of the disease or of high risk for developing the disease. These data suggest that negative evaluations of their own bodies are extremely important motivators for exercise in some women. Unfortunately, it appears that these drives, at least in a minority of cases, may come to be associated with negative psychological characteristics and even psychopathology.

An extremely interesting multicultural study by Collins (1993) found that the opposite was the case for female Mexican university students. Their self-evaluations of bodily attractiveness (PSPP) were positively and significantly related to degree of both habitual and recreational physical activity. The conclusion was advanced that Mexican women view their bodies from a utilitarian/functional orientation. This is in contrast to American women, who are more likely to focus on the cosmetic aspects of their bodies, as documented in the study of Leveillee, Sonstroem, and Riebe (1994).

Given the strong association between self-esteem and perceived physical attractiveness, the relationship between exercise and the body seems to be critical to our understanding of the development and maintenance of women's self-esteem. A more complete discussion of this issue is provided by Caroline Davis in chapter 6. The broader issue of the impact of culture on body and the self is presented at length by Andrew Sparkes in chapter 4.

THE FACILITATIVE EFFECT OF COMPONENT IMPORTANCE ON BEHAVIOR PREDICTION

Theorists have proposed that self-esteem can be more accurately predicted by its components when the relative importances of components are mathematically added to the prediction (Coopersmith 1967; James [1890] 1963; Rosenberg 1965). Utilizing extensive analyses, Marsh (1986, 1993) failed to obtain support for the hypothesized combinations. Fox (1990) suggests that importance ratings from the PIP can be combined in traditional ways with PSPP components to predict physical self-worth. Marsh's (1994) research failed to support this hypothesis. More recently, Marsh and Sonstroem (1995) replicated these results. The latter study, however, provided some evidence that the prediction of external behavior, in this case exercise, may be improved by utilization of importance scores. Using Marsh's generalized multiple regression approach, which tested for the unique variance provided by variables, they found that the addition of importance ratings significantly improved the prediction of exercise provided by PSPP components. While the effect was relatively small, these data point to the interesting prospect of studying component importances in addition to self-perceptions in the prediction of target behaviors. Certainly there are strong theoretical reasons, based around the self-enhancement hypothesis, for believing that those self-evaluations that are personally important become manifested in appropriate behaviors.

THE ROLE OF SELF-EFFICACIES IN EXERCISE PREDICTION

The study of Sonstroem, Harlow, and Josephs (1994) was the first to predict physical activity with physical self-efficacies as well as perceived physical self subdomains. The fact that the subdomains developed the larger associations with exercise represents a limitation of this validating research.

Several factors may have contributed to this result. The general self-efficacy variable EFF, utilized for structural modeling purposes, may lack strong validity in terms of self-efficacy theory. This theory specifies a high degree of congruence between a self-efficacy measure and a behavior. Additionally, the investigators experienced difficulty in writing a self-efficacy statement that conveyed a skill essential to aerobic dancing. Self-efficacy for dancing was eventually operationalized by asking subjects to indicate how long they could dance without stopping. This item was seen as limited in terms of its ability to represent the many competence opportunities that attract women to aerobic dance. Furthermore, Marsh, Walker, and Debus (1991) question the ability of current self-efficacy assessment, which emphasizes cognitive processes only, to predict behavior as well as self-concept measurement, which involves both affective and cognitive processes.

Another attempt was made to examine associations between exercise and EXSEM elements by assessing university female ($n = 69$) and male ($n = 56$) students. Subjects completed the PSPP and self-efficacy scales for jogging and for weight lifting, and then indicated how many times per week they participated in these activities. On the basis of EXSEM theory, self-efficacies were entered first as a class and then subdomain scores were entered as a second class in the hierarchical multiple regression analyses. The top row of table 1.2 shows that self-efficacies significantly predicted jogging behavior ($p < .001$) in females. As hypothesized, self-efficacy for jogging (EFJOG) developed a larger standardized coefficient (.67) than self-efficacy for

Table 1.2 Self-Efficacies and Subdomains in the Prediction of Exercise by Hierarchical Multiple Regression

Dependent variable						Predictors					
	Sex	EFJOG	EFWL	R^2	p^a	SPORT	COND	BODY	STREN	p^b	Cum. R^2
JOGFR	F	.67	.03	.35	.001	.24	.06	-.08	-.14	.000	.41
JOGFR	M	.43	-.05	.14	.007	.00	.11	.10	-.08	.110	.18
WTTFR	F	.23	.39	.17	.001	.07	.46	-.17	-.09	.000	.33
WTTFR	M	.03	.49	.24	.001	-.16	.53	-.03	.18	.000	.41

Note: JOGFR = frequency of jogging; WTTFR = weight training frequency. Values beneath model components represent standardized regression coefficients. Predictors: EFJOG = self-efficacy for jogging; EFWL = self-efficacy for weight lifting; SPORT = perceived sport competence; COND = perceived physical condition; BODY = perceived body attractiveness; STREN = perceived physical strength; R^2 = regression coefficient; p^a = significance for efficacies; Cum. R^2 = multiple regression coefficient after adding subdomain predictors to the equation; p^b = significance for adding subdomains to the prediction.

weight lifting (EFWL) (.03). When entered second into the equation, the subdomains made a significant contribution ($p < .001$). The efficacies and subdomains, together, explained 41.3% of jogging participation. While efficacies significantly predicted jogging in males ($p < .007$), the addition of the subdomains failed to improve this association significantly ($p > .11$). Efficacies, first, and subdomains, second, significantly predicted weight training frequency in females and in males (rows 3 and 4, respectively, of table 1.2). The EXSEM was able to explain 33.3% of weight training variance in females and 41.2% in males. These analyses provide support for EXSEM in that (a) self-efficacies made significant contributions in all four analyses; (b) the appropriate self-efficacy developed the larger association with a congruent behavior in all cases; and (c) subdomains significantly increased the prediction of activity in three of the four analyses. An interesting conclusion is that young people appear to associate physical condition more with weight training than with jogging. This conclusion is supported by Pearson r as well as the regression analyses. However, the limitations imposed on conclusions by the small sample sizes in this pilot study must be recognized.

SUMMARY OF EXERCISE ASSOCIATIONS

It must be emphasized that the percentage of activity variance explained by PSPP and EXSEM associations represents very acceptable effect sizes when compared to values reported in the exercise participation and adherence literature. Meanwhile, adherence theorists have called for multifaceted and comprehensive approaches in solving the dilemma of adoption of and dropout from activity (Dishman, Sallis, and Orenstein 1985; Sallis and Hovell 1990). To date, very few personality variables have been employed. On the basis of the data presented in the preceding sections, it would seem that physical self components, as personality variables, would represent an excellent activity predictor to be employed along with social learning variables (Sallis, Hovell, and Hofstetter 1992) or the stages and processes of the Transtheoretical Model (Marcus et al. 1992).

Causation represents an added rationale for including self-esteem as an exercise predictor. Much of the previous exercise and self-esteem literature has examined the skill development rather than the self-enhancement aspects of self-esteem. It is easy to lose sight of an important reason why self-esteem is regarded as the premier psychological adjustment variable. Its ultimate validity resides in the fact that it is a powerful determinant in people's behavior (Felson 1984; Spears and Deese 1975). We tend to act as our conception of self dictates to us. At present, there is theoretical and correlational support for this proposition, but very little data supporting a causative claim. However, recent research testifies to the agency of self-esteem in health behaviors. It has been found to be an excellent predictor of stress reduction, diet, and exercise in 197 myocardial infarction survivors (Conn, Taylor, and Hayes 1992). Furthermore, personal self-systems and goals have been found to be important predictors of health behaviors assessed in the following week (Hooker and Kaus 1992).

Our research indicates that components of self-esteem are capable of influencing behavior. Sonstroem and Kampper (1980) found that estimation (of physical ability) scores predicted boys who would later enroll in after-school sports as opposed to boys who did not. The swim study already discussed (Sonstroem, Harlow, and Salisbury 1993) showed that November perceived physical competence scores predicted January swimming performance. When the evidence provided in this chapter relative to the agentive powers of physical self components is complemented by recent results identifying the role of component importance in exercise prediction (Marsh and Sonstroem 1995), the study of self-systems and physical component importances in predicting exercise becomes especially attractive.

THE PHYSICAL SELF AND LIFE ADJUSTMENT

The conclusion that components of the self can influence subsequent behavior in a manner similar to that seen with global self-esteem was an exciting revelation. What other attributes of self-esteem are components capable of exhibiting? A paramount value of global self-esteem is its recognized capacity to reflect favorable life adjustment. Therefore, a recent study set out to test the life adjustment correlates of the physical self (Egleston and Sonstroem 1993). Previously, estimation scores in adolescent males had been shown to be significantly associated with lack of neuroticism, lack of maladjustment, and lack of personality disorder even with the effects of social desirability and defensiveness controlled (Sonstroem 1976). The study of Egleston and Sonstroem (1993), involving 119 female and 126 male undergraduates, showed moderate to large inverse relationships between all five PSPP scales and depression, negative affect, and health complaints. The PSPP scores were positively related to possession of positive affect. Across both genders, 29 of the 40 PSPP zero-order coefficients with adjustment variables were significant. The independence of these associations was demonstrated when partial correlation was used to simultaneously control for the effects of self-esteem and two measures of social desirability. Twelve of these relationships remained significant, a result considerably better than chance. Shared variance estimates of these partial coefficients ranged to 15.21%, considered by Cohen (1977) to be a moderate effect size. These analyses meaningfully demonstrate that self-perceptions of physical competence, particularly perceptions of sport competence in males and evaluations of physical condition in females, are essentially related to favorable life adjustment. These relationships are statistically independent of global self-esteem and social desirability influences. It appears that, of itself, a positive physical self-concept is desirable and is inherently related to favorable life adjustment.

SUMMARY

The research reviewed in this chapter shows that people are able to distinguish among four levels of generality in attributing personal characteristics to the self. A path analysis exhibited model structure and variable associations that were reliable over time. Perceived physical competence proved capable of predicting subsequent athletic performance. It was shown that EXSEM variables were capable of developing strong associations with exercise participation. Use of the PSPP in conjunction with the PIP importance scales clearly showed that many women in the United States exercise because of dissatisfaction with their bodies. Additionally, the COND scale, as hypothesized, was shown to be the best PSPP predictor of activity in both adult females and males across several research studies. Components of the physical self developed significant associations with life adjustment variables that were independent of global self-esteem and social desirability.

The net effect of much of this research is to provide preliminary evidence that physical self components possess certain attributes that are generally ascribed to global self-esteem. One of these concerns the capacity to influence behavior. Secondly, favorable self-perceptions of one's physical assets are related to positive emotional adjustment in college students. This places the physical self-concept at a critical position in the relationship between physical self-systems and behavior. With skill development hypotheses, physical self-concept can serve to mediate effects to self-esteem or can serve as a valid outcome variable in and of itself. In self-enhancement research it seems capable of influencing behavior directly or indirectly through the mediation of self-efficacies.

DIRECTIONS FOR FURTHER WORK

Herbert Marsh in chapter 2 outlines the importance of adequate instrumentation for the development of this field of research and argues that theory and the development of measuring instruments should go hand in hand. The PSPP displays many recommended test characteristics. Initially, I respected its internal development. With each new data collection I remain pleased at the very satisfactory to excellent Cronbach alpha values indicative of high internal consistency. Item response scales range from 1 to 4. It is satisfying to almost always find subject means at or near a midrange level (scale medians = 2.5). As an example of this feature, researchers who wished to show increases in perceived physical condition and strength scores as the result of an intervention program would feel defeated at finding means of 3.8 on the pretest. Additionally, the PSPP has shown itself to be relatively unaffected by socially desirable responding as assessed by several different scales. Future users may wish to know that some investigators have claimed subject difficulty in understanding the alternative response format of the PSPP. This seems to be manifested especially in younger students and older adults and may have contributed to the uncharacteristically low alpha coefficients reported by Marsh et al. (1994).

It is exciting that Herbert Marsh has recently emphasized the study of the physical self. His Physical Self-Description Profile (PSDQ) item format appears capable of eliciting a valid and spontaneous response rather than one that relies more on studied cognitive reflection. The PSDQ, with its increased number of relevant scales, should develop increased knowledge of the physical self. In particular, its health and activity subdomains are well suited to advancing the study of exercise participation and adherence. The new PSDQ with its attractive potential should be utilized quickly in the United States. One of the first inquiries might be a comparison of cultural relationships between the nine components and both general physical self-concept and self-esteem. For example, Herb Marsh's Australian data in chapter 2 (see table 2.1) indicate that coordination bears the largest relationship among the nine subdomains to both general physical self-concept and self-esteem. Would data from the United States lead to similar conclusions for the same age group?

Harter's (1990) research documents physical appearance as the self component most closely associated with self-esteem across the life span in the United States. The major confounding variable accompanying EXSEM and PSPP research to date concerns the close associations between BODY and other scales, particularly PSW, COND, and SE. These can be interpreted in at least three ways:

1. An attractive body is synonymous with physical self-worth and self-esteem in the minds of people.

2. An attractive body is synonymous with health in the minds of people, and health is equivalent to physical self-worth.

3. Scale overlap may be caused partially by similar phrases referring to confidence or pride that are embedded in several items of each of the scales mentioned.

It must be recognized that the critical criterion defining what a scale actually measures is the item content of the scale rather than its name. While it will be interesting to compare responses to Attractive Body and Appearance scales of the PSPP and PSDQ, respectively, we should realize that they tap somewhat different constructs. The word "body" is included in all six PSPP BODY items, whereas the Appearance items of the PSDQ refer generally to good looks with no specific physical referent except the face. This suggests, for example, that we would not expect identical results when administering the two scales to adult female exercisers. Utilizing all of the PSPP and PSDQ scales with subsequent variance analyses should provide newer insights into the exercise process.

It is possible that further investigation into the BODY-PSW overlap in the PSPP may open additional vistas to us. We recognize competence and self-acceptance as two major dimensions of self-esteem (Harter 1985; Wells and Marwell 1976). The manifestation of dimensional differences can be seen in people who know that their sport competence is not of Olympic caliber or who realize that many people are stronger than they are. In terms of competence these people may rate themselves at a midrange level. Yet they recognize these attributes as their own, accept them, and like them. Their acceptance level of these attributes is high. This scenario could be contrasted with that of female exercisers we have studied who fail to accept their bodies, even after they have developed superb physical condition. We would think that extensive exercise has produced body characteristics that would receive at least fair ratings when evaluated objectively on a competence dimension. The fact that the BODY scale covaries with PSW and self-esteem may represent a condition in which all three scales load relatively higher on a self-acceptance as opposed to a competence dimension. This would imply a self-system that highlights competence at more specific, lower levels and rests on self-acceptance at higher, more general and integral levels.

It is hoped that this chapter has successfully traced the development of newer measures and models for studying the physical self-concept. Emphasis has been placed on presenting the newer information about the physical self that these measures and models have developed. Continued research is enthusiastically encouraged. We are closer to understanding realities of the physical activity experience.

REFERENCES

Bandura, A. 1977. Self-efficacy: Toward a unifying theory of behavioral change. *Psychological Review* 84: 191-215.

—. 1986. *Social foundations of thought and action: A social cognitive theory.* Englewood Cliffs, NJ: Prentice Hall.

Cohen, J. 1977. *Statistical power analysis for the behavioral sciences.* Rev. ed. New York: Academic Press.

Collins, I.T. 1993. Cultural differences in perceived physical competence, self-esteem, and gender traits in female university students. Master's thesis, University of Rhode Island.

Conn, V.S., Taylor, S.G., and Hayes, V. 1992. Social support, self-esteem, and self-care after myocardial infarction. *Journal of Health Behavior, Education, and Promotion* 16: 25-31.

Coopersmith, S. 1967. *The antecedents of self-esteem.* San Francisco: Freeman.

Dishman, R.K., Sallis, J.F., and Orenstein, D.R. 1985. The determinants of physical activity and exercise. *Public Health Reports* 100: 158-72.

Egleston, S.A., and Sonstroem, R.J. 1993. Life adjustment correlates of perceived physical competence. Paper presented at Annual Meeting, American College of Sports Medicine, June, Seattle, WA.

Felson, R.B. 1984. The effect of self-appraisals of ability on academic performance. *Journal of Personality and Social Psychology* 47: 944-52.

Fox, K.R. 1990. *The Physical Self-Perception Profile manual.* DeKalb, IL: Office for Health Promotion, Northern Illinois University.

Fox, K.R., and Corbin, C.B. 1989. The Physical Self-Perception Profile: Development and preliminary validation. *Journal of Sport and Exercise Psychology* 11: 408-30.

Fox, K.R., Corbin, C.B., and Couldry, W.H. 1985. Female physical estimation and attraction to physical activity. *Journal of Sport Psychology* 7: 125-36.

Garner, D.M., Olmstead, M.P., and Polivy, J. 1983. Development and validation of a multidimensional eating disorder inventory for anorexia nervosa and bulimia. *International Journal of Eating Disorders* 2: 15-34.

Harter, S. 1985. Competence as a dimension of self-evaluation: Toward a comprehensive model of self-worth. In *The development of the self,* ed. R.H. Leahy, 55-121. New York: Academic Press.

—. 1990. Causes, correlates, and the functional role of global self-worth: A life-span perspective. In *Competence considered,* ed. R.J. Sternberg and J. Kolligian Jr., 67-97. New Haven, CT: Yale University Press.

Hooker, K., and Kaus, C.R. 1992. Possible selves and health behaviors in later life. *Journal of Aging and Health* 4: 390-411.

Jackson, D.N. 1984. *Personality research form manual.* New York: Research Psychologists Press.

James, W. [1890] 1963. *The principles of psychology.* Reprint, New York: Holt, Rinehart, & Winston.

Jasnoski, M.L., Holmes, D.S., Soloman, S., and Aguiar, C. 1981. Exercise, changes in aerobic capacity, and changes in self-perception: An experimental investigation. *Journal of Research in Personality* 15: 460-66.

Kowal, D.M., Patton, J.F., and Vogel, J.A. 1978. Psychological states and aerobic fitness of male and female recruits before and after basic training. *Aviation, Space, and Environmental Medicine* 49: 603-8.

Leveillee, C.M., Sonstroem, R.J., and Riebe, D. 1994. Self-perception and eating disorder differences in routine and ultra adult exercisers. Paper presented at the Annual Meeting of the American College of Sports Medicine, June, Indianapolis.

Marcus, B.H., Rossi, J.S., Selby, V.C., Niaura, R.S., and Abrams, D.B. 1992. The stages and processes of exercise adoption and maintenance in a worksite sample. *Health Psychology* 11: 386-95.

Marsh, H.W. 1986. Global self-esteem: Its relations to specific facets of self-concept and their importance. *Journal of Personality and Social Psychology* 51: 1224-36.

—. 1993. Relations between global and specific domains of self: The importance of individual importance, certainty, and ideals. *Journal of Personality and Social Psychology* 65: 975-92.

—. 1994. The importance of being important: Theoretical models of relations between specific and global components of physical self-concept. *Journal of Sport and Exercise Psychology* 16: 306-25.

Marsh, H.W., Richards, G.E., Johnson, S., Roche, L., and Tremayne, P. 1994. Physical Self-Description Questionnaire: Psychometric properties and a multi-trait-multi-method analysis of relationships to existing instruments. *Journal of Sport and Exercise Psychology* 16: 270-305.

Marsh, H.W., and Sonstroem, R.J. 1995. Importance ratings and specific components of physical self-concept: Relevance to predicting global components of physical self-concept and exercise. *Journal of Sport and Exercise Psychology* 17: 84-104.

Marsh, H.W., Walker, R., and Debus, R. 1991. Subject-specific components of academic self-concept and self-efficacy. *Contemporary Educational Psychology* 16: 331-45.

Messer, B., and Harter, S. 1986. Manual for the Adult Self-Perception Profile. Denver: University of Denver.

Morgan, W.P. 1978. Sport personology: The credulous-skeptical argument in perspective. In *Sport psychology: An analysis of athlete behavior*, ed. W.F. Straub, 671-79. Ithaca, NY: Mouvement.

Neale, D.C., Sonstroem, R.J., and Metz, K.F. 1969. Physical fitness, self-esteem, and attitudes toward physical activity. *Research Quarterly* 40: 743-49.

Rosenberg, M. 1965. *Society and the adolescent self-image*. Princeton, NJ: Princeton University Press.

Sallis, J.F., and Hovell, M.F. 1990. Determinants of exercise behavior. *Exercise and Sport Sciences Reviews* 18: 307-30.

Sallis, J.F., Hovell, M.F., and Hofstetter, C.R. 1992. Predictors of adoption and maintenance of vigorous physical activity in men and women. *Preventive Medicine* 21: 237-51.

Schwarzer, R. 1992. Self-efficacy in the adoption and maintenance of health behaviors: Theoretical approaches and a new model. In *Self-efficacy: Thought control of action*, ed. R. Schwarzer, 217-43. Washington, DC: Hemisphere.

Shavelson, R.J., Hubner, J.J., and Stanton, G.C. 1976. Self-concept: Validation of construct interpretations. *Review of Educational Research* 46: 407-11.

Sonstroem, R.J. 1974. Attitude testing examining certain psychological correlates of physical activity. *Research Quarterly* 45: 93-103.

—. 1976. The validity of self-perceptions regarding physical and athletic ability. *Medicine and Science in Sports* 8: 126-32.

—. 1978. Physical Estimation and Attraction Scales: Rationale and research. *Medicine and Science in Sports* 10: 97-102.

—. 1984. Exercise and self-esteem. *Exercise and Sport Sciences Reviews* 12: 123-55.

—. 1988. Psychological models. In *Exercise adherence: Its impact on public health*, ed. R.K. Dishman, 125-54. Champaign, IL: Human Kinetics.

Sonstroem, R.J., Harlow, L.L., Gemma, L.M., and Osborne, S. 1991. Test of structural relationships within a proposed exercise and self-esteem model. *Journal of Personality Assessment* 56: 348-64.

Sonstroem, R.J., Harlow, L.L., and Josephs, L. 1994. Exercise and self-esteem: Validity of model expansion and exercise associations. *Journal of Sport and Exercise Psychology* 16: 29-42.

Sonstroem, R.J., Harlow, L.L., and Salisbury, K.S. 1993. Path analysis of a self-esteem model across a competitive swim season. *Research Quarterly for Exercise and Sport* 64: 335-42.

Sonstroem, R.J., and Kampper, K.P. 1980. Prediction of athletic participation in middle school males. *Research Quarterly for Exercise and Sport* 51: 685-94.

Sonstroem, R.J., and Morgan, W.P. 1989. Exercise and self-esteem: Rationale and model. *Medicine and Science in Sports and Exercise* 21: 329-37.

Sonstroem, R.J., Speliotis, E.D., and Fava, J.L. 1992. Perceived physical competence in adults: An examination of the Physical Self-Perception Profile. *Journal of Sport and Exercise Psychology* 14: 207-21.

Spears, W.D., and Deese, M.E. 1975. Self-concept as cause. *Educational Theory* 23: 144-52.

Wells, L.E., and Marwell, G. 1976. *Self-esteem: Its conceptualization and measurement.* Beverly Hills, CA: Sage.

CHAPTER 2

THE MEASUREMENT OF PHYSICAL SELF-CONCEPT: A CONSTRUCT VALIDATION APPROACH

HERBERT W. MARSH

In the psychosocial sciences, theory, measurement, empirical research, and practice are inexorably intertwined. The neglect of one will undermine the integrity of others. Ideally, validation is an ongoing process in which theory and practice are used to develop a measure; empirical research is used to test the theory *and* the measure; both the theory and the measure are then revised in the light of findings; new research is conducted to test these refinements; and theory and research are finally used to inform practice. Reality seldom matches this ideal. All too often, measures in the sport and exercise sciences (Ostrow 1990) and other social science disciplines are ad hoc endeavors that are not soundly based on theory, not systematically evaluated, and not refined on the basis of subsequent theoretical or substantive developments. Weak measures inevitably undermine research and theory evaluation, thereby limiting their contribution to practice.

A focus on a construct validation approach to the measurement of physical self-concept is consistent with calls from a growing number of sport/ exercise psychology and physical education researchers for the development of instruments specific to the physical domain (Nelson 1989). In this regard, Vealey (1986) claimed that significant advances in sport and exercise psychology research "await sport-specific conceptualization and measurement instrumentation" (222). In his review of sport and exercise tests, Ostrow (1990) reported substantial gains over the last 25 years, but emphasized that many tests are still "one shot assessments," lacking further development and refinement. More specifically, Gill, Dzewaltowski, and Deeter (1988) argued for the construction of multidimensional sport and exercise instruments based on theory, followed by item and reliability analysis, exploratory and confirmatory factor analysis, tests of convergent and divergent validity, and application in research and practice.

Self-concept, like many other psychological constructs, suffers in that *everybody knows what it is*, so that many researchers do not feel compelled either to provide a theoretical definition of what they are measuring or to evaluate the psychometric properties of responses to their measures. However, because self-concept is a hypothetical construct, its usefulness must be established through investigations of its construct validity. Construct validity research can be classified into *within-network* or *between-network* investigations. Within-network studies explore the internal structure of self-concept. They test, for example, the dimensionality of self-concept and may seek to show that the construct has consistent, distinct multidimensional components (e.g., physical, social, academic self-concept) or that a specific domain-like physical self-concept has multiple dimensions (e.g., strength, endurance, appearance, sports competence). Implicit in this aspect of construct validity is the possibility that a construct *is* multidimensional. Even if a construct is hypothesized to be unidimensional, however, it is important to test empirically this within-network assertion (i.e., to show that it is *not* multidimensional) as part of the construct validation process. Within-network studies typically employ empirical techniques such as factor analysis or multitrait-multimethod (MTMM) analysis. Between-network studies attempt to establish a logical, theoretically consistent pattern of relationships between measures of self-concept and other constructs. The resolution of at least some within-construct issues should be a logical prerequisite to conducting between-construct research, but until recently, between-network research has predominated.

STRUCTURAL MODELS OF SELF-CONCEPT

Marsh and Hattie (1996) described a variety of possible theoretical models of self-concept (see fig. 2.1) that have been derived largely through analogy with corresponding models of intelligence. They noted the relevance of issues such as the existence and relative importance of a general ability factor (i.e., Spearman's *rho*), multidimensional theories of intelligence (e.g., Thurstone's seven primary abilities), and hierarchical models that incorporated both general and multidimensional perspectives. Through recent years, these features have increasingly appeared in self-concept research.

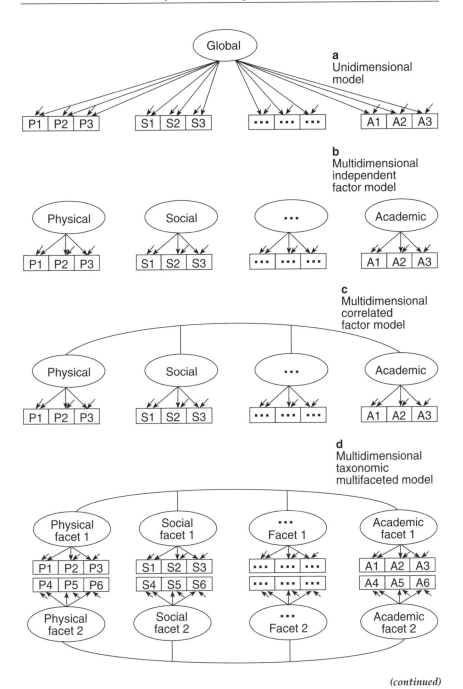

a
Unidimensional model

b
Multidimensional independent factor model

c
Multidimensional correlated factor model

d
Multidimensional taxonomic multifaceted model

(continued)

Figure 2.1 Structural models of self-concept derived from related models of ability and intelligence.

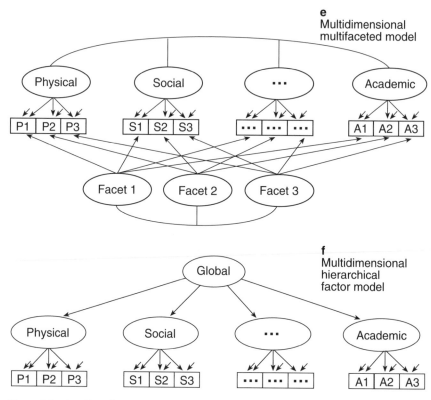

Figure 2.1 *(continued)*

UNIDIMENSIONAL MODEL

The unidimensional model, reminiscent of Spearman's two-factor intelligence model, suggests that there is only a general factor of self-concept or that a general factor dominates more specific factors (see fig. 2.1a). Some researchers (e.g., Coopersmith [1967]; Marx and Winne [1978]) argued that the multiple dimensions of self-concept were so heavily dominated by a general factor that the separate factors could not be adequately differentiated. However, further scrutiny revealed that this conclusion reflects problems in measurement and statistical analysis rather than supporting the unidimensionality of self-concept (Hattie 1992; Marsh 1990a; Marsh and Hattie 1996). Subsequent research has clearly established the multidimensionality of self-concept (see reviews in Byrne 1984; Marsh and Shavelson 1985; Shavelson and Marsh 1986), and there appears to be little or no support for the unidimensional perspective—implying that self-concept cannot be adequately understood if its multidimensionality is ignored.

INDEPENDENT AND CORRELATED FACTOR MODELS

Both the independent and correlated factor models represent self-concept as a multidimensional construct, but they differ in the degree to which the multiple dimensions are correlated. A strong version of the independent factor model requires all the factors to be absolutely uncorrelated (see fig. 2.1b), although it may be reasonable to posit a weak version of the model in which the factors are defined to be relatively uncorrelated. Apparently, no self-concept theorists have argued for the strong form of this model, although Soares and Soares (1977) and perhaps Marsh and Shavelson (1985) may be interpreted as supporting a weak version. Marsh and Hattie (1996), however, concluded that the correlated factor model (see fig. 2.1c) had received stronger support than the independent factor model.

MULTIFACETED, TAXONOMIC MODELS

Guilford's (1969) structure of intellect model was apparently the inspiration for the taxonomic model of self-concept proposed by Soares and Soares (1977). A unique aspect of Guilford's model is that the components of intellect reflect the intersection of two or more facets, each of which has at least two levels. There are a number of self-concept instruments that implicitly or explicitly posit a taxonomic or classification model. For example, the structural model underlying the design of the Tennessee Self Concept Scale (Fitts 1964) reflects a taxonomic model with three facets: a 5 (external frame of reference) $\times$ 3 (internal frame of reference) $\times$ 2 (positively/negatively worded items) design. The five levels of the external facet—physical, moral, personal, family, and social—are similar to the self-concept domains proposed in many subsequent instruments. In Fitts' schema, each of these domains could be manifested in relation to three internal frames of reference, the second facet in his test design: identity (e.g., what I am), satisfaction (e.g., how I feel about myself), and behavior (e.g., what I do or how I act). The third facet, based on the wording of the items, provides a control for various response biases and may or may not be substantively important. Bracken (1992) also based the design of his new Multidimensional Self Concept Scale on a three-facet taxonomic model that included self-concept domains, evaluative perspective (personal or other), and performance standards (absolute, ipsative, comparative, and ideal standards). At least implicitly, Fox's (1990) Physical Self-Perception Profile—considered in detail in this chapter—also used a multifaceted, taxonomic design in which each physical subdomain scale contained items reflecting process, product, and confidence. Neither Bracken nor Fox, however, formally evaluated this design aspect of their instrument or incorporated it into the instrument's scoring system.

Two forms of the multifaceted, taxonomic self-concept model are presented in figure 2.1. As depicted in figure 2.1d, there are eight factors representing all multiplicative combinations of four levels of the domain facet (i.e., the content domain typically considered in self-concept studies) by two levels reflecting a second facet. The second facet could reflect identity versus behavior responses as proposed by Fitts (1965), responses to positively and negatively worded items as emphasized by Marsh (1990a), or responses to items reflecting a personal or other perspective as emphasized by Bracken (1992). Figure 2.1e is an alternative representation of multifaceted, taxonomic data derived from confirmatory factor analysis (CFA) models of MTMM data. There are seven factors representing four levels of the domain facet and three levels reflecting a second facet. Both of these representations could be extended to have more levels in either of the two facets or to have more than two facets. Either model 2.1d or 2.1e could be appropriate when the design of an instrument is multifaceted. The main difference between the two is that model 2.1d assumes that each combination of levels from each facet forms a unique scale, whereas model 2.1e assumes that the physical scale incorporates items from all three facets. The choice between the two models may also be an empirical issue.

MULTIDIMENSIONAL, HIERARCHICAL MODELS

The multidimensional hierarchical factor model (see fig. 2.1f) in some respects incorporates each of the other models as a special case. As in the unidimensional, global factor model, it hypothesizes a global component at the apex of the hierarchy. Thus, support for the unidimensional factor model could also be interpreted as support for a hierarchical model in which the hierarchy is very strong. At the opposite extreme, support for the weak version of the multidimensional independent factor model could be interpreted as support for a hierarchical model in which the hierarchy is very weak. Only in the extreme cases in which correlations among the self-concept factors approach the reliabilities of the factors, or are consistently close to zero, would support for the hierarchical model be dubious. Support for the multidimensional correlated factor model automatically implies support for a hierarchical model. This flexibility of the hierarchical model, however, is both a strength and a weakness. It is a strength because it provides a broad framework for exploring the structure of self-concept. It is a weakness because the hierarchical model, at least at the level of abstraction considered thus far, may not be falsifiable. Hence, it is critically important that a priori hierarchical models of self-concept are specified in sufficient detail to enable them to be rigorously tested.

STRUCTURAL MODELS AND INSTRUMENT DEVELOPMENT

Historically, self-concept instruments typically consisted of a collection of self-referent items designed to broadly cover the domain of interest. Although factor analysis was used widely, the intent of such factor analyses was often to discover the important factors ex post facto. A long history of factor analytic research has demonstrated that this purely exploratory approach to factor analysis is typically ineffective. The emergence of structural models of self-concept has encouraged the development of instrumentation to measure specific, a priori factors. Wylie (1989) made this point in comparing instruments included in her 1974 and 1989 reviews of self-concept measures. In 1989 she noted that more recently developed multidimensional self-concept instruments were more likely to begin with an explicit theoretical basis for the domains they sought to measure than to rely on atheoretical, empirical approaches to identify the salient factors from a broad collection of items. In the a priori approach, it is possible to use factor analysis as a hypothesis-testing tool by evaluating the compatibility between the predicted and obtained factors. It is possible to use what is typically referred to as exploratory factor analysis (e.g., the principal components or principal axis factor analysis) to confirm a priori factors. However, the development of CFA and hierarchical CFA (HFCA) using statistical packages such as LISREL or EQS has allowed considerable freedom in specifying the model to be tested (e.g., the nontarget loadings are typically fixed to be zero). This recent approach to instrument development has eventually found its way into physical self-concept research that is reported later in this chapter.

THE SHAVELSON, HUBNER, AND STANTON MODEL AND MARSH/SHAVELSON THEORETICAL MODEL OF SELF-CONCEPT

The emphasis on between-construct research to the exclusion of within-construct research has been counterproductive. It appears to be one reason for the inconsistency in findings across self-concept studies reported in several reviews (e.g., Burns 1979; Shavelson, Hubner, and Stanton 1976; Wells and Marwell 1976; Wylie 1974, 1979). However, more recently the work of Shavelson, Hubner, and Stanton (1976), through the adoption of structural models, has stimulated great advancements in the field. These investigators systematically applied the construct validity approach to self-concept research in a classic review that had a profound influence on subsequent work. They provided a blueprint for constructing self-concept instruments, for designing within-network studies of the proposed structure of self-concept, for testing between-network hypotheses about relations with other constructs, and, eventually, rejecting and revising original construct definitions.

CONSTRUCT DEFINITION OF SELF-CONCEPT

Shavelson, Hubner, and Stanton (1976) began by developing a theoretical definition of self-concept. They integrated features of various definitions of self-concept to formulate their working definition. They described self-concept as a person's self-perceptions that are formed through experiences with and interpretations of his/her environment. They emphasized that self-concept is not an entity within the person, but a hypothetical construct that is potentially useful in explaining and predicting how a person acts. Consistent with this perspective, Shavelson, Hubner, and Stanton noted that self-concept is important as both an outcome and as a mediating variable that helps to explain other outcomes. Thus, for example, physical self-concept may be influenced by an experimental intervention involving sport, exercise, or a weight loss program. Alternatively, physical self-concept may function as a behavioral mediator of the influence of an intervention on subsequent exercise adherence.

Shavelson, Hubner, and Stanton identified seven critical features in their definition of the self-concept construct: (1) it is organized or structured; (2) it is multidimensional; (3) it is hierarchical, with perceptions of personal behavior in specific situations at the base of the hierarchy, inferences about self in broader domains (e.g., social, physical, and academic) at the middle of the hierarchy, and a global, general self-concept at the apex; (4) self-concept at the apex of the hierarchy is stable, but becomes increasingly situation specific and as a consequence less stable as one descends the hierarchy; (5) self-concept becomes increasingly multidimensional with age; (6) self-concept is both descriptive and evaluative—and these self-perceptions can be made against some absolute ideal (running a five-minute mile), against a personal, internal standard (a personal best), or against a relative standard based on comparisons with peers or the expectations of significant others; and (7) self-concept can be differentiated from other constructs.

Shavelson, Hubner, and Stanton (1976) offered one possible representation of this hierarchical model in which general self-concept appeared at the apex and was divided into academic and nonacademic self-concepts at the next level. Academic self-concept was further divided into self-concepts in particular subject areas. Nonacademic self-concept was divided into social, emotional, and physical self-concepts. Each of these was subdivided, with physical self-concept, for example, made up of physical ability and appearance. Lower levels of division were hypothesized for each of these specific self-concepts so that at the base of the hierarchy self-concepts were of limited generality, quite specific, and more closely related to actual behavior. The model, which is consistent with the one shown in figure 2.1f, provided a vital prototype for a new generation of multidimensional self-concept instruments that have had an important influence on the field. Furthermore, the review by Shavelson, Hubner, and Stanton outlined the logical, correlational, and experimental procedures that are fundamental for evaluating construct definitions. The application of some of the more advanced techniques is presented later in this chapter.

SELF-DESCRIPTION QUESTIONNAIRES

When Shavelson, Hubner, and Stanton first developed their model, there was only modest support for their hypothesized domains, and no single instrument considered in their review was able to differentiate among even the broad academic, social, and physical domains. In order to address these concerns, the Self-Description Questionnaire instruments were developed for preadolescent primary school students (SDQI), adolescent high school students (SDQII), and late adolescents and young adults (SDQIII). In the development of the SDQ instruments it was reasoned that within-network measurement issues should be resolved before between-network relationships were evaluated. Atheoretical and/or purely empirical approaches to developing and refining measurement instruments were rejected. Instead, the Shavelson et al. model was taken as the starting point for instrument construction, and empirical results were used to support, refute, or revise the instrument *and* the theory upon which it is based. Implicit in this approach is the presumption that theory building and instrument construction should be inseparable. In this sense the SDQ instruments have developed from both a strong empirical foundation *and* a clearly defined theoretical model.

The SDQ scales were posited on the basis of the Shavelson et al. model, item pools were constructed for each scale, and factor analyses and item analyses were used to select and refine the items eventually used to represent each scale. The three SDQ instruments demonstrated high internal consistency, and responses were stable, particularly for older children. For example, the stability of SDQIII scales measured on four occasions varied from a median of $r = 0.87$ for a 1-month interval to a median of $r = 0.74$ for intervals of 18 months or longer. Factor analyses of diverse samples differing in gender, age, country, and language have consistently verified the instrument's structure. Marsh (1989a) summarized factor analyses of more than 12,000 sets of responses from the normative archives of the three SDQ instruments, and the results indicated that the domains of self-concept are remarkably distinct (median rs among the SDQ scales vary between 0.1 and 0.2). Reviews of the SDQ instruments (Boyle 1994; Byrne 1984; Hattie 1992; Wylie 1989) suggest that in terms of their psychometric properties and evidence of construct validity, they are among the best multidimensional instruments available.

Consistent with the construct validation approach, SDQ research has provided support for the Shavelson et al. model but has also led to its subsequent revision. Thus, for example, the strong hierarchical structure posited by Shavelson, Hubner, and Stanton required self-concepts to be substantially correlated, but the low degree of observed associations implies that any hierarchical structure of the self-concept responses must be much weaker than anticipated. Complications such as these led to the Marsh/Shavelson revision (Marsh 1990a; Marsh, Byrne, and Shavelson 1988; Marsh and Shavelson 1985) of the original Shavelson, Hubner, and Stanton model. The Shavelson, Hubner, and Stanton and Marsh/Shavelson models prompted between-network research, primarily in the academic domains of self-concept, and eventually led to the construction of the Academic Self-Description Questionnaire, which measures multiple dimensions of academic self-concept (see Marsh 1990b, 1993a for further descriptions). On the basis of this research, Marsh (1990b, 1993a) argued that self-concept researchers and practitioners should measure self-concept at a level of specificity consistent with their research question as well as perhaps employing the more general measures of academic self-concept and esteem that are typical in much self-concept research.

THE SDQ PHYSICAL SCALES

The physical scales incorporated in the SDQs provided an early opportunity to investigate the differential effect of specific elements of physical self-perceptions. Factor analyses (e.g., Marsh 1990b) have consistently differentiated responses to the SDQ Physical Ability and Physical Appearance scales from each other and from academic, general, and other nonphysical components of self-concept. In an application of the *known group differences* approach to construct validation, Marsh and Jackson (1986) and Jackson and Marsh (1986) demonstrated that athletic participation by high school and young adult women was substantially related to physical ability self-concept, but much weaker associations were found with nonphysical areas of self-concept. Marsh and Peart (1988) demonstrated that physical fitness was substantially related to physical ability self-concept, modestly related to physical appearance self-concept, and unrelated to other areas of self-concept. In this study, subjects in competitive and cooperative aerobics interventions were compared; both groups experienced substantial increases in physical fitness compared to pretest scores and those of a randomly assigned control group. Consistent with a priori predictions, the cooperative intervention also led to an *increase* in physical ability self-concept, whereas the competitive intervention led to a *decline* in physical ability self-concept. Marsh, Richards, and Barnes (1986a, 1986b) demonstrated that participation in Outward Bound significantly enhanced those SDQ factors most relevant to the program, such as physical ability self-concept. Furthermore, the size and pattern of these effects were stable over an 18-month follow-up. Collectively, the factor analyses and the support for convergent and divergent validity demonstrate the overall construct validity of responses to the SDQ physical scales.

Although not based on SDQ responses, data from the Australian Health and Fitness Survey were used by Marsh (1993d) to relate academic and physical self-concepts to a diverse set of physical fitness indicators and to academic achievement. For a nationally representative sample of Australian boys and girls aged 9 to 15, physical self-concept was significantly correlated to a variety of components of physical fitness (but not academic achievement), whereas academic self-concept was substantially related to academic achievement (but not physical fitness). The size and specificity of these associations increased with age. As students grew older, physical and academic self-concepts became less correlated with each other and more correlated with physical fitness and academic achievement, respectively.

The design and development of the Self-Description Questionnaires and subsequent research have substantiated some important general features of the construct validation approach. It has been demonstrated that theory and instrumentation can progress in partnership. Use of the instrument has consistently supported the within-network relationships. Where this has not been the case, the underlying theoretical model has been modified accordingly. The between-network relationships have established the efficacy of differentiated elements of both academic and physical self-concepts. Within this framework, the remainder of this chapter will focus on research that has centered around the physical self-concept.

PHYSICAL SELF-CONCEPT MEASUREMENT: A BRIEF HISTORICAL PERSPECTIVE

Wylie (1974, 1989) evaluated a wide variety of self-concept measures. Her 1974 review revealed that at the time most self-concept instruments focused on global self-concept or self-esteem. Shavelson, Hubner, and Stanton (1976) evaluated five of the popular self-concept instruments: Brookover's Self-Concept of Ability Scale, Coopersmith's Self-Esteem Inventory, Gordon's How I See Myself Scale, the Piers-Harris Children's Self-Concept Scale, and the Sears' Self-Concept Inventory. Although several of these instruments contain items relating to physical skills and elements of physical appearance, Shavelson, Hubner, and Stanton found that different domains could not be distinguished so that none provided a clearly interpretable measure of physical self-concept. Self-perception change specific to a domain was therefore impossible to document. From a practical perspective, therefore, these older instruments appear to be of little value for sport and exercise psychologists.

Until relatively recently, therefore, there was little emphasis on the comprehensive measurement of self-concept in the physical domain. In 1990, Ostrow produced the *Directory of Psychological Tests in the Sport and Exercise Sciences*, which included psychological instruments, with reliability and validity information, from the sport and exercise literature published between 1965 and 1989. However, of the 175 instruments listed, only one-third had items based on a conceptual or theoretical framework, less than one-fourth reported factor analyses, and fewer than one-tenth showed evidence of extensive reference support. Although none of Ostrow's (1990) chapters specifically focus on physical self-concept, relevant instruments are reviewed in the chapters on body image and confidence.

BODY IMAGE MEASURES

Historically, interest in physical self-concept has been dominated by research into body image and its relation to global esteem. Wylie (1974) noted that Secord and Jourard's (1953) Body Cathexis Scale was one of the few instruments purporting to measure a specific aspect of self-concept that was important to global esteem yet distinct from it. Wylie noted that whereas responses to the instrument were reliable and related to some other constructs in the predicted direction, its convergent and discriminant validity had not been adequately explored. Wylie (1989) subsequently noted that the original instrument had been used only rarely since 1972 but that a revision called the Body Esteem Scale (Franzoi and Shields 1984) might be useful.

The 14 tests in Ostrow's (1990) chapter on body image "assess attitudes of individuals toward their body appearance, structure, and movement" and "body esteem and body satisfaction" (101). They are primarily idiosyncratic measures that have not been used widely, and there is only limited support for their psychometric properties or construct validity. Thus, for example, only 5 instruments appeared to have a theoretical basis for the construction of items and only 4 were supported by factor analyses. Attributes measured by these instruments included satisfaction with body parts, physical appearance, body size/weight, somatotypes, health, fitness/condition, movement, and physique anxiety. In addition to the traditional Likert-type items typically used in self-concept measures, a number of scales asked respondents to evaluate their satisfaction with each of a set of body parts (as in the Body Cathexis Scale) or to evaluate themselves in relation to silhouette figures varying in obesity or somatotype. The concept of body image and its contemporary measurement are further discussed by Caroline Davis in chapter 6.

PHYSICAL CONFIDENCE/COMPETENCE MEASURES

The 19 tests in Ostrow's (1990) chapter on confidence "assess perceptions of movement confidence, confidence in physical fitness, and perceptions of sport competence" and "self-efficacy in relation to sport performance and physical ability" (135). Instruments referred to in this chapter are somewhat stronger in that 11 seemed to have a theoretical rationale for the construction of items and 12 were supported by factor analyses. Five of these instruments are specific to a particular sport, and many produce only a single scale score. Whereas most emphasize physical competence, several also measure some aspect of physical appearance, enjoyment of or attraction to physical activity, fear of injury or harm, and components of physical condition.

Sonstroem's (1978; also see Ostrow 1990) Physical Estimation and Attraction Scales (PEAS) and the theoretical model on which they were based have had considerable impact on sport psychology research as discussed in chapter 1. The PEAS were designed to measure two global components called estimation (e.g., I am stronger than a good many of my friends; It is difficult for me to catch a ball) and attraction (Sports provide me with a welcome escape from present-day life; I love to run). In the development of the PEAS, Sonstroem and his colleagues assessed reliability, factor structure, and within- and between-network components of construct validity. The appeal of the PEAS stems in part from interest in Sonstroem's model of physical activity participation from which the instrument was derived. The evaluation of the PEAS must be considered within an appropriate historical context. It represented an early attempt to combine instrument development with model building. At the time the instrument was being developed in the late 1960s and early 1970s, there were no comparable measures in the physical domain, and there was little emphasis on specific components of physical self-concept. Few researchers in the sport sciences were using factor analysis at all, and recent advances in the application of this technique were obviously not available. Whereas the PEAS may not be the instrument of choice today, it has historic significance in that its research incorporated many of the features of the construct validity approach advocated in this chapter, was heuristic, and provided an important basis for subsequent research.

MULTIDIMENSIONAL INSTRUMENTS INCORPORATING PHYSICAL SCALES

Wylie (1989) identified several multidimensional self-concept instruments containing a measure of one or more components of physical self-concept that can be differentiated from other specific domains of self-concept and general self-concept. She reviewed the set of three SDQ instruments discussed earlier that contain Physical Ability and Physical Appearance scales.

Wylie also evaluated Harter's (1985) Self-Perception Profile for Children, which contains Athletic Competence and Physical Appearance scales. She reported good factor analytic support for the five specific domains, but questioned the logic of excluding the general scale from the factor analysis. Wylie also suggested that Harter's rationale for using a nonstandard response scale in order to avoid social desirability responding was not logically or empirically convincing. She indicated that there had been no MTMM studies comparing Harter's instrument with others and was also critical of Harter's use of discrepancy scores.

Other multidimensional instruments containing physical scales that were not reviewed by Wylie include the Self-rating Scale (Fleming and Courtney 1984) measuring physical ability and physical appearance; the Song and Hattie test (Hattie 1992) measuring physical appearance; and the Multidimensional Self Concept Scale (Bracken 1992), which has a physical scale that includes physical competence, physical appearance, physical fitness, and health. The Tennessee Self Concept Scale (Fitts 1965) also purports to measure physical self-concept. This physical self subscale was widely used in earlier sport and exercise research. In their review and empirical evaluation of this instrument, Marsh and Richards (1988) found distinguishable physical components reflecting health, neat appearance, physical attractiveness, and physical fitness. However, Marsh and Richards argued that physical scores combining and confounding such a wide range of differentiable physical components should be interpreted cautiously (also see similar comments by Fox and Corbin [1989]).

THE DEVELOPMENT OF MULTIDIMENSIONAL PHYSICAL SELF-CONCEPT INSTRUMENTATION

The greatest steps forward recently in physical self-concept research have been facilitated by the development of multidimensional physical self-concept scales. Three such instruments are the Physical Self-Perception Profile (PSPP) (Fox 1990; Fox and Corbin 1989), the Physical Self-Concept Scales (PSC) (Richards 1987), and the Physical Self-Description Questionnaire (PSDQ) (Marsh et al. 1994). Each of these instruments has been developed in tandem with a structural model of self-concept. Although evaluations of the structure of the PSPP and PSC have relied primarily on exploratory factor analysis, it is clear that the intent was to confirm the existence of a priori factors. Factor analyses of PSDQ responses have relied primarily on CFA, and research will be presented to demonstrate advantages of the use of CFA.

PHYSICAL SELF-PERCEPTION PROFILE

The PSPP is the strongest multidimensional physical self-concept instrument in Ostrow's (1990) directory. Fox (1990) and Fox and Corbin (1989) provided a brief overview of theoretical and empirical research leading to the development of the instrument. The PSPP was based substantially on research by Harter (1985, 1986) and Shavelson, Hubner, and Stanton (1976). Fox noted that broad measures of physical competence and physical appearance are used to represent the physical domain in the Shavelson, Hubner, and Stanton model but saw the need for measures that provided a more complete depiction of perceptions in the physical domain. Fox argued, consistent with a hierarchical model (see fig. 2.1f), that self-perceptions can vary from one level to another: the superordinate (global self-esteem), domain (physical), subdomain (sport competence), facet (soccer ability), subfacet (shooting ability), and state (I can score this penalty). This theoretical base guided the PSPP design, provided a means of evaluating the construct validity of PSPP responses, and may be heuristic in characterizing factors from other physical self-concept instruments.

Fox (1990) began by determining the most important components of physical self-concept by reviewing previous research and collecting open-ended responses from university students about the important components of the physical self. This form of content validation is a particular strength of the PSPP. On the basis of this preliminary work and exploratory factor analyses, Fox eventually posited five scales: Sport (athletic ability, ability to learn sport, confidence in sport); Condition (condition, stamina, fitness, ability to maintain exercise, confidence in exercise setting); Body (attractive physique, ability to maintain an attractive body, confidence in appearance); Strength (perceived strength, muscle development, confidence in situations requiring strength); and Global Physical Self Worth (general feelings of pride, satisfaction, happiness, and confidence in the physical self). Within each scale, items were designed to reflect product (good at sport), process (learn sport skills slowly), and perceived confidence (confidence in sport), implicitly representing a multifaceted, taxonomic model (see fig. 2.1).

In an adaptation of the format used in Harter's (1985) self-concept instrument, each item consisted of a pair of contrasting statements ("Some people feel that they are not very good when it comes to playing sports" *but* "others feel that they are really good at just about every sport"). Respondents select which statement is most like them and then indicate whether it is "really true of me" or "sort of true of me" so that responses vary along a four-category response scale. This structured alternative format is intended to reduce social desirability responding, a problem which has plagued self-esteem research in the past. This was supported in the developmental work that revealed nonsignificant weak correlations between all subscales and individual items with the short version of the Crowne-Marlowe Social Desirability Scale. However, Wylie (1989) questioned the rationale and empirical support for Harter's original claims. There is also evidence that this format can be confusing for some respondents (Marsh and Gouvernet 1989; see Sonstroem, chapter 1).

Fox used factor analysis extensively in the development and refinement of the PSPP. He found good support for the four PSPP subdomain factors and a reasonably similar factor pattern for males and females. Internal consistency measures of reliability (.80 to .92) were good, and the stability coefficients over a two- to three-week interval varied from .74 to .89. Through partial correlation techniques, Fox also found that elements of the hierarchical structure were well supported. In further construct validation research, Fox (1990) related PSPP responses to various self-reports of physical activity as already summarized in chapter 1.

Fox and Corbin (1989) modestly referred to their research as "development and preliminary validation" (408). Particularly in comparison to most instruments in the sport and exercise field that were reviewed by Ostrow (1990), the development of the PSPP is exemplary. Fox (1990), however, emphasized that the construct validation of instruments is never completed and noted a number of directions for further research. From this perspective, it is disappointing that apparently so little construct validity research has emerged since the initial publication (Fox 1990; Fox and Corbin 1989) of the instrument. However, Sonstroem has reported his and his colleagues' recent work involving the PSPP (e.g., Sonstroem, Harlow, and Josephs 1994; Sonstroem, Speliotis, and Fava 1992). I briefly note some directions for further research based on suggestions by Fox (1990), Fox and Corbin (1989), and Marsh and Redmayne (1994), which are specific to the PSPP, and on the general criteria proposed by Hattie (1992), Shavelson, Hubner, and Stanton (1976), and Wylie (1974, 1989). My intent is primarily to illustrate additional aspects of the construct validity approach, but I hope also to stimulate further research that builds on the strong beginning provided by the authors of the PSPP.

1. In addition to the PSPP, Fox (1990) developed the Perceived Importance Profile (PIP) to measure the importance placed on each subdomain of the physical self with regard to more global feelings of worth. This featured a proposed alternative *personalized* hierarchical model, based on Harter's work (1986), in which relations between each tier of the hierarchy depend on the importance of a particular domain. Although Fox (1990) did not actually test this model, Marsh (1986, 1993a, 1993e) argued that the theoretical rationale and empirical support for Harter's model were weak. In subsequent research, Marsh (1994b) found no support for Harter's model with PSDQ responses and corresponding importance ratings, or with PSPP and PIP responses (Marsh and Sonstroem 1995). These results appear to undermine the notion of a personalized hierarchical model and suggest that further research is required on the role of importance in self-concept formation.

2. Fox (1990) specifically noted that the PSPP was developed for and validated with U.S. university students, so that its use with other popula-

tions without further modifications may be unwarranted. Even within his target population, Fox provided only preliminary support (based on separate exploratory and confirmatory factor analyses for each gender) for the generalizability of the factor structure over gender. The most appropriate statistical technique for evaluating the generalizability of factor structures over groups is a multiple group confirmatory factor analytical test of factorial invariance. This statistical technique is appropriate for testing the invariance of responses for groups differing in age, gender, background (Marsh 1993b, 1994a; Marsh and Hocevar 1985), or nationality (Marsh and Byrne 1993).

3. Fox and Corbin (1989) provided preliminary support for the hierarchical structure of PSPP responses based on patterns of correlations and partial correlations. Although these are relevant, stronger tests are available through the application of HCFA (Marsh 1987; Marsh and Shavelson 1985).

4. More generally, there has been only preliminary and limited construct validity research relating PSPP responses to other constructs such as profiles of health-related physical fitness, physical activity, health problems, physical self-concept inferred by significant others (teachers, parents, peers, coaches), exercise maintenance, and experimental interventions. For each criterion, emphasis needs to be placed on both convergent and divergent validity.

In summary, the PSPP along with the initial construct validity research presented by Fox (1990) and Fox and Corbin (1989) was exemplary in relation to other physical self-concept instruments that had been reported in the literature. However, there is more work to be done, including the directions for further construct validity research that Fox (1990) noted in the PSPP test manual as well as suggestions offered here. It is hoped that this chapter will stimulate further construct validity research with the PSPP that follows up the rich, heuristic, theoretical framework presented in the test manual.

PHYSICAL SELF-CONCEPT SCALES

Richards (1987) argued that physical self-concept instrumentation has been ill defined and poorly developed. For this reason he developed the PSC as a short, easily completed instrument that measured multiple dimensions of physical self-concept appropriate for males and females over the age of 12. Based on the Marsh/Shavelson model, on the SDQ instruments, and on a review of the physical self-concept literature, the PSC was initially developed to define eight a priori factors. In the process of development, items were revised according to four criteria: internal consistency item analysis, stability over time, a well-defined factor structure, and a factor structure that was consistent over gender and age. As a consequence of this revision, seven factors were retained (body build, appearance, health, physical competence, strength, action orientation, and overall physical satisfaction) and a total score that was the sum of the seven scales. Each scale consisted of five items, and responses to each item were on the eight-category true-false scale used with the SDQIII.

Richards (1987) summarized psychometric properties of PSC responses based on four groups (total N = 800): adolescent males and females (mean age 13.9) and young adult males and females (mean age 21). Across gender and age, coefficient alpha estimates of reliability were consistently high (> 0.80), and test-retest correlations over approximately three weeks approached the internal consistency estimates. Furthermore, Richards demonstrated that the PSC factor structure was very robust over gender and age, with every PSC item loading at least 0.6 on the factor that it was intended to measure (target loadings) and no more than 0.3 on any other factor (nontarget loadings).

Richards (1987) used 3500 PSC responses from subjects who ranged in age from 10 to over 60 years to document the stability of physical self-concept across age groups. He also summarized the effects of attending the 26-day Outward Bound Standard Course for young adults and the 10-day Outward Pack-and-Paddle course for young adolescents. He used a short time series design in which participants completed the PSC three weeks prior to the start of the course (T1), on the first day of the course (T2), and at the end of the course (T3). Consistent with a priori predictions, there was a slight decline in physical self-concept between T1 and T2 for young adult males and females, apparently due to pre-program apprehension. Richards found that this slight decline before the start of the program was followed by a substantial increase between T2 and T3. These findings are supported by previous research in the Outward Bound setting with the SDQIII (see Marsh, Richards, and Barnes 1986a, 1986b).

The PSC instrument appears to be remarkably successful in relation to its intended goals of providing a short, multidimensional estimate of physical self-concept whose psychometric properties are robust over gender and age. Hence, it is disappointing that the research summarized here is only described in one unpublished conference paper (Richards 1987). Even more than PSPP research, PSC research has focused on within-network components of construct validity such as reliability and factor structure. Whereas the results provide good evidence for the generalizability of the psychometric properties over gender and age, stronger tests are possible with CFA tests of invariance like those suggested for the PSPP. Although the gender and age differences and the Outward Bound intervention effects provide limited support for the construct validity of the PSC responses, there is considerable scope for further work. Furthermore, although there is clear support for the a priori PSC scales, some idiosyncrasies in the scales may influence their interpretation. These issues are addressed in detail by Marsh et al. (1994).

PHYSICAL SELF-DESCRIPTION QUESTIONNAIRE

The PSDQ is a 70-item test designed to measure nine specific components of physical self-concept (strength, body fat, activity, endurance/fitness, sports competence, coordination, health, appearance, flexibility), global physical self-concept, and global esteem. The theoretical rationale for the PSDQ is based on the Marsh/Shavelson self-concept model and previous SDQ research. The PSDQ scales reflect some scales from the SDQ instruments (Physical Ability, Physical Appearance, and Self-Esteem), scales from the earlier version of the PSDQ presented by Marsh and Redmayne (1994), and an attempt to parallel components of physical fitness identified in Marsh's (1993b) CFA of physical fitness indicators from the Australian Health and Fitness Survey. Each PSDQ item is a simple declarative statement, and subjects respond with a six-point true-false response scale. The instructions, response format, and layout of the instrument are based on the widely used SDQII instrument (Marsh 1992). The PSDQ is designed for adolescents at least 12 years of age, but it should also be appropriate for university students and adults. Here I summarize research describing the development and testing of the PSDQ factor structure, tests of the construct validity of PSDQ responses in relation to external criteria, and an MTMM study of responses to the PSDQ, PSPP, and PSC instruments.

Marsh and Redmayne (1994) used a preliminary version of the PSDQ in a small study of high school girls ($N = 105$). They reported good coefficient alpha estimates of reliability for all scales (.84 to .92) and an exploratory factor analysis that identified each of the six a priori scales. They then used CFA and HCFA to relate the six physical self-concept scales to four physical fitness measures (static strength, balance, shuttle run, and sit-and-reach) from Fleishman's Basic Fitness Tests (1964) and the 12-minute run. Confirmatory factor analysis clearly identified the scales from the preliminary PSDQ, and HCFA identified a hierarchical component of physical self-concept. Endurance, strength, and flexibility self-concepts were all significantly correlated with matching components of physical fitness, and scores on the general Physical Ability scale were substantially correlated to most of the fitness scores. As predicted, physical appearance was not substantially correlated with fitness indicators. Balance self-concept, however, was not substantially correlated with objective indicators of balance, calling into question the usefulness of this scale. In a subsequent hierarchical model, second-order components of physical fitness and physical self-concept were substantially correlated ($r = .76$). These results provided preliminary support for the factor structure of the instrument, for a hierarchical model of physical self-concept, and perhaps for the convergent and discriminant validity of responses to the instrument in relation to multiple dimensions of physical fitness.

Marsh et al. (1994) tested the 11-scale version of the PSDQ described earlier with two samples of high school students. Sample 1 consisted of 315 Australian Outward Bound participants. Sample 2 consisted of 385 students from a high school in metropolitan Sydney. Students in Sample 1 also completed the PSPP and PSC instruments. Coefficient alpha estimates of reliability for PSDQ responses were consistently good for males and females in both samples (0.82 to 0.96).

Confirmatory Factor Analysis

Confirmatory factor analysis was used to test the *simple structure* a priori model in which each measured variable was allowed to load only on the factor that it was intended to measure. As recommended for analyses of SDQ responses (e.g., Marsh 1990b, 1992), all factor analyses were conducted on item-pair responses: The first two items in each scale were averaged to form the first item-pair, the second two items were averaged to form the second item-pair, and so forth. This resulted in three or four item-pair indicators for each PSDQ scale. Item-pair scores are more reliable and contain less idiosyncratic variance as the responses to item-pairs tend to be more normally distributed, and the ratio of the number of measured variables to the number of respondents is improved. The Tucker-Lewis Index was used to evaluate goodness of fit along with an evaluation of the parameter estimates and other fit indexes (for further discussion see Marsh, Balla, and McDonald 1988; McDonald and Marsh 1990). The Tucker-Lewis Index varies along a 0-to-1 continuum in which values greater than 0.9 are typically taken to reflect an acceptable fit.

As mentioned earlier, when parallel data exist for more than one group (e.g., males and females), CFA provides a particularly powerful test of the equivalence of solutions across the multiple groups (see Marsh 1994a). The researcher is able to fit the data, subject to the constraint that any one parameter, any set of parameters, or all parameters are equal (i.e., invariant) in the multiple groups. Typically, the minimal condition for factorial invariance is the invariance of the factor loadings across groups, but tests for the invariance of factor correlations, factor variances, and uniquenesses that reflect measurement error are also of interest.

Marsh et al. (1994) evaluated factorial invariance over gender on the basis of responses from both samples ($N = 415$ males and 285 females). When no invariance constraints were imposed, the fit of the model was somewhat better for females than for males. The imposition of the equality of factor loadings for the male and female solutions resulted in no change in the Tucker-Lewis Index, providing particularly strong support for this aspect of factorial invariance. The most important aspect of this solution, perhaps, was the large factor loadings (0.74 to 0.92, median = 0.87), indicating that the

PSDQ factors were well defined. Consistent with the moderately larger reliability estimates for females than for males, uniquenesses (measurement error) were slightly higher for males (median = 0.28) than for females (median = 0.25). Gender differences in the pattern of correlations among the 11 PSDQ traits were typically small. In summary, the results of this analysis indicated that the a priori PSDQ model was able to fit the data well for both males and females and that the solutions for males and females were similar (see Marsh et al. 1994 for further discussion).

Relations to External Criteria

In subsequent, unpublished research, 258 high school students in Years 7 to 10 from Sample 2 of the study by Marsh et al. (1994) completed additional materials as baseline measures for a physical activity intervention. These data are used to test the construct validity of PSDQ responses in relation to external criteria. Although a full presentation of the results is beyond the scope of this chapter, a summary illustrates some important general points.

In the "what do you look like" task, students were asked to choose, from nine silhouettes varying in body fatness (based on Stunkard, Sorenson, and Schulsinger 1983), the one that best represented their actual body and the one that best represented their ideal body. Consistent with predictions, actual body and the actual-ideal body discrepancy were substantially related to the PSDQ Fat scale, with the discrepancy score producing the highest correlation. Ideal body was not highly correlated with any PSDQ scales. This is consistent with the notion that self-concept is affected by both self-perceptions and the standards against which the self-perceptions are evaluated. Although not a focus of this chapter, it is also interesting to note that females had substantially higher scores on the PSDQ Body Fat scale and more demanding body ideals (in the direction of being slender) than males, but did not differ significantly from males in terms of actual body scores. Furthermore, the scores on the PSDQ Body Fat scale were substantially related to objective measures of body fat based on weight, girths, and a seven-site skinfold test, indicating that perceptions have some foundation in reality. There was a modest correlation between PSDQ Physical Appearance and actual body, actual-ideal body, and objective body fat (particularly for women) in comparison to the results achieved with PSDQ Body Fat. This provides strong support for the separation of the broader-based physical appearance and body fat components of physical self-concept on the PSDQ.

Four components of participation and adherence to a regular program of physical activity (actual participation, barriers to participation, benefits of participation, commitment to participation) were all more strongly related to the PSDQ Physical Activity scale than to other PSDQ scales. Two field indicators of endurance fitness were most strongly associated with the PSDQ Endurance/Fitness scale, but were also substantially related to the PSDQ Body Fat, Sports Competence, Coordination, Flexibility, and General

Physical Self-Concept scales. Two strength tests were significantly correlated with the PSDQ Strength scale, but, particularly for females, were as
highly correlated with sports competence. Performance/dynamic strength
tests were significantly related to PSDQ Sports Competence, but correlations with PSDQ Strength were surprisingly low. Blood pressure was
modestly related to PSDQ Body Fat. Consistent with predictions, the
sit-and-reach test was more highly correlated with the PSDQ Flexibility
scale than with any other PSDQ scale. Whereas no a priori predictions were
made for lung capacity, results show that it was more strongly related to
PSDQ Strength and, to a lesser extent, Sports Competence.

It had been predicted that PSDQ Sports Competence would be correlated
with the performance/dynamic strength measures, but it was also significantly correlated with physical activity levels, endurance fitness, and even
lung capacity. This suggests that the PSDQ Sports Competence scale may be
measuring a more general component of physical self-concept.

Whereas PSDQ Coordination was not predicted a priori to be highly
correlated with any of the external criteria, not surprisingly it was modestly
correlated with most of the physical performance tests (e.g., long jump, beep
test, 1.6k run, basketball throw) that apparently involve some degree of
coordination. It is also interesting to note that PSDQ Coordination was
modestly correlated with physical activity and components of participation
and adherence to exercise programs. The highest of these correlations was
with barriers to participation (negative relationship), suggesting that
self-perceptions of physical coordination may be an important measure to
consider in exercise adherence models.

In summary, in nearly all cases, the external criteria were more strongly
related to the specific PSDQ scales to which they were most theoretically
related than to other PSDQ scales, to general physical self-concept, or to
general esteem. This provides good support for the construct validity of
PSDQ responses in relation to a wide variety of external criteria. The PSDQ
is a new instrument, and considerable further work is needed to fully
establish its construct validity. Nevertheless, the initial results are very
encouraging.

MULTITRAIT-MULTIMETHOD ANALYSIS
COMPARING PSPP, PSC, AND PSDQ RESPONSES

Not surprisingly, given the level of specificity of physical self-concept, there
seems to be considerable overlap in the factors measured by the PSPP, PSC
and PSDQ. It is, however, important to formally pursue this observation
with an MTMM analysis of relations among responses to the instruments.
The MTMM design is perhaps the most widely used paradigm specifically
developed to assess convergent, discriminant, and construct validity. The
general reviews of self-concept measurement by Wylie (1974, 1979) and

Shavelson, Hubner, and Stanton (1976) emphasized the central role of MTMM analyses in the construct validation of self-concept responses. Multitrait-multimethod analyses also reveal potential problems in the interpretation of scale scores based on the label that is attached to them by their author or other researchers. Thus, for example, the Jingle Fallacy assumes that two scales with the same label measure the same construct, and the Jangle Fallacy assumes that two scales with different labels measure different constructs. Given the prevalence of the MTMM design in self-concept research and, more generally, in most areas of psychological measurement, it is surprising that the technique has not been used more widely in sport and exercise research. The research of Marsh et al. (1994) summarized here is apparently the first MTMM study of multidimensional physical self-concept instruments.

PREDICTED RELATIONS AMONG THE PSPP, PSC, AND PSDQ

In MTMM analysis, correlations between matching scales (i.e., the strength scales from the three instruments) should be systematically higher than correlations between nonmatching scales. On the basis of a preliminary content analysis of the items from the three instruments, which also provides information relevant to their content validity, Marsh et al. (1994) derived a priori predictions about which scales from the different instruments were likely to be matching (also see subsequent discussion of table 2.1).

Relations Between PSDQ and PSPP

There is a reasonable correspondence between the PSPP Strength, Sports, and Physical Self Worth scales and the PSDQ Strength, Sports, and General Physical Self Concept scales, respectively. Each of the remaining two PSPP scales apparently combines distinguishable components of physical self-concept that are reflected by separate PSDQ scales. Items from the PSPP Condition scale (e.g., "take part in some form of regular vigorous physical exercise," "ability to maintain regular exercise and physical condition") reflect the PSDQ Physical Activity scale but also the PSDQ Endurance scale (e.g., the PSPP item "maintain a high level of stamina and fitness"). Items from the PSPP Body Attractiveness scale (e.g., "have an attractive body," "admired because their physique or figure is considered attractive," "bodies do not look in the best of shape") are likely to be most closely related to the PSDQ Physical Appearance scale although this scale may also be related to the PSDQ Body Fat scale.

Relations Between PSDQ and PSC

There is a reasonable correspondence between the PSC Strength, Appearance, Health, and Competence scales and the PSDQ Strength, Appearance,

Health, and Coordination scales. Although the label of the PSC Competence scale does not directly match that of the PSDQ Coordination scale, the PSC items (e.g., "I am physically uncoordinated" and "My natural coordination and agility are good") apparently do. The PSC and PSDQ Activity scales and, to a lesser extent, the PSC Body and the PSDQ Body Fat scales also appear to be reasonably similar. The PSC Activity scale (e.g., "I dislike sports and physical activity" and "I like to keep out of games, sports, and other physical activities") actually reflects avoidance of activity which may be different from the PSDQ Activity scale. The PSC Body scale reflects primarily body "shape and proportion" rather than body fat per se. Hence, the content of the PSC Body scale is more closely related to that of the PSPP Body scale than to the PSDQ Body Fat scale. The PSC scale measuring satisfaction (e.g., "I would like to be more physically able," "I would like to be more physically attractive," and "I would like to have better coordination and agility") reflects a desire to be different in each of the other components, in contrast to the PSDQ General Physical Self Concept scale, which measures generalized perceptions of physical competence.

Relations Between PSC and PSPP

The PSC Strength and Body scales appear to be similar to the PSPP Strength and Body scales. The PSPP Physical Self Worth scale is more similar to the General Physical Self-Concept scale from the PSDQ than it is to the PSC Satisfaction scale. Whereas no other PSC and PSPP scales are clearly matching, the PSPP Condition scale is expected to be related to the PSC Activity scale, and the PSPP Sports Competence scale is expected to be related to the PSC Competence (coordination) scale.

OBSERVED RELATIONS BETWEEN PSDQ, PSPP, AND PSC RESPONSES

Although Marsh et al. (1994) considered a variety of complex CFA models derived from the MTMM literature (Marsh 1988, 1989b, 1993c), their initial model provided a good overview of the results. In this a priori model, it was hypothesized that PSDQ, PSPP, and PSC responses could be explained in terms of 23 latent constructs reflecting the scales each instrument was designed to measure: 11 PSDQ factors, 5 PSPP factors, and 7 PSC factors. This restrictive, a priori solution provided a reasonable fit to the data (Tucker-Lewis Index = 0.902), but it is also relevant to evaluate the parameter estimates (see Marsh et al. 1994 for a presentation of the actual parameter estimates).

Factor loadings reflect the relation between each measured variable and a latent construct—the *validity* of the measured variable. Because all 71 factor loadings were large (0.67 to 0.90; median = 0.80), there was good support for this aspect of the factor solution for all 23 factors. Factor loadings for the PSDQ (0.67 to 0.90; median = 0.83) were somewhat higher than those for the PSC (0.65 to 0.87; median = 0.80) and the PSPP (0.67 to 0.79; median = 0.74). Similarly, measurement error tended to be smaller for the PSDQ responses than for the PSC and particularly the PSPP responses, as was also reflected in corresponding coefficient alpha estimates of reliability (PSDQ: 0.82 to 0.92, median = 0.88; PSC: 0.77 to 0.88, median = 0.85; PSPP: 0.77 to 0.79, median = 0.77). The major focus of this presentation, however, is the correlations among the 23 latent variables (see table 2.1).

In MTMM analyses (Campbell and Fiske 1959; Marsh 1988) it is typical to evaluate convergent and discriminant validity and method effects by comparing convergent validities (correlations between matching traits), heterotrait-heteromethod correlations (correlations between different scales measured by different instruments), and heterotrait-homomethod correlations (correlations among nonmatching scales from the same instrument). Large convergent validities support the convergent validity of the responses, whereas discriminant validity is supported when convergent validities are larger than other correlations. Method effects are inferred when heterotrait-heteromethod correlations involving a particular method approach 1.0 or are higher than heterotrait-heteromethod correlations. Thus, for example, the large correlations among the PSPP scales in this Australian sample (correlations of .65 to .89; see table 2.1) may call into question the divergent validity of responses to these scales.

Table 2.1 differs from a traditional MTMM matrix in two ways. First, correlations represent relations among latent constructs that are appropriately correlated for measurement error instead of correlations among simple scale scores that contain measurement error and that may not reflect the underlying factor structure. Hence many of the limitations in inspecting MTMM matrices based on scale scores are no longer relevant (see discussion in Marsh 1993c; Marsh and Hocevar 1988), greatly facilitating the interpretation of the MTMM data. Second, the same set of traits is not measured by each of three instruments. Whereas there is an unambiguous matching of some of the scales in the three instruments (e.g., the three Strength scales), earlier discussion suggested that this is typically not the case. Hence, there is a certain degree of subjectivity in determining which correlations should be considered the *convergent* validities. These features complicate interpretations, but perhaps represent a realistic problem in a relatively new area where the intended scales from independently designed instruments are unlikely to be strictly parallel.

Based on the earlier predictions, the 167 correlations between the 23 latent constructs were classified into three a priori categories: 9 convergent validities in which the scales were most closely matched (superscripted *a* in table 2.1), 6 convergent validities in which the scales were less closely matched (superscripted *b*), and the remaining 152 (heterotrait-heteromethod)

Table 2.1 Confirmatory Factor Analysis of Three Physical Self-Concept Instruments: Factor Correlations Among 23 Trait Factors

Trait Factors	PSDQ											PSPP					PSC						
	1	2	3	4	5	6	7	8	9	10	11	12	13	14	15	16	17	18	19	20	21	22	23
PSDQ (Marsh)																							
1. STRG	1.00																						
2. BFAT	.05	1.00																					
3. PACT	.56	.24	1.00																				
4. ENDR	.56	.39	.68	1.00																			
5. SPRT	.64	.36	.76	.72	1.00																		
6. CORD	.56	.46	.70	.57	.78	1.00																	
7. HEAL	.21	.27	.24	.18	.25	.37	1.00																
8. APPR	.39	.45	.34	.38	.50	.58	.14	1.00															
9. FLEX	.42	.36	.51	.58	.47	.62	.31	.34	1.00														
10. GPSC	.50	.60	.57	.50	.65	.77	.36	.64	.50	1.00													
11. ESTM	.47	.56	.49	.50	.60	.66	.58	.60	.56	.74	1.00												

PSPP (Fox)

	1	2	3	4	5	6	7	8	9	10	11	12	13	14	15	16	17	18	19	20	21	22	23
12. STRG	.86[a]	.20	.52	.51	.62	.50	.23	.39	.34	.47	.41	1.00											
13. BODY	.42	.61[b]	.36	.46	.49	.53	.14	.68[b]	.37	.67	.51	.65	1.00										
14. COND	.49	.45	.73[b]	.70[b]	.68	.58	.20	.38	.45	.60	.51	.67	.71	1.00									
15. SPRT	.58	.38	.69	.69	.86[a]	.67	.25	.47	.45	.59	.55	.69	.89	.85	1.00								
16. GPSW	.54	.51	.57	.60	.64	.62	.24	.54	.45	.81[a]	.68	.73	.82	.85	.86	1.00							

PSC (Richards)

	1	2	3	4	5	6	7	8	9	10	11	12	13	14	15	16	17	18	19	20	21	22	23
17. STRG	.90[a]	.02	.48	.43	.56	.47	.16	.36	.31	.42	.46	.79[a]	.41	.40	.51	.50	1.00						
18. BODY	.46	.68[b]	.46	.53	.58	.60	.22	.65	.44	.74	.63	.46	.81[a]	.60	.61	.70	.46	1.00					
19. PACT	.44	.23	.66[b]	.53	.62	.54	.36	.18	.33	.37	.45	.40	.22	.58	.63	.48	.38	.35	1.00				
20. COMP	.52	.33	.57	.56	.69	.84[a]	.32	.57	.59	.59	.62	.51	.49	.50	.70	.65	.59	.64	.58	1.00			
21. HEAL	.25	.10	.25	.22	.28	.37	.83[a]	.18	.23	.32	.42	.21	.12	.20	.31	.22	.15	.23	.41	.41	1.00		
22. APPR	.34	.33	.34	.29	.43	.52	.18	.88[a]	.25	.58	.51	.33	.61	.33	.41	.49	.41	.64	.15	.54	.21	1.00	
23. PSAT	.28	.38	.32	.38	.41	.38	.20	.33	.30	.39	.38	.36	.39	.41	.55	.42	.31	.42	.32	.44	.14	.26	1.00

Note: STRG = strength; BFAT = body fat; PACT = physical activity; ENDR = endurance/fitness; SPRT = sports competence; CORD = coordination; HEAL = health; APPR = appearance; FLEX = flexibility; GPSC = general physical self-concept; ESTM = esteem; COND = condition; GPSW = general physical self-worth; COMP = competence; PSAT = physical satisfaction. All coefficients vary between 0 and 1. Scales from different instruments that are predicted to be most highly correlated (i.e., the convergent validities in MTMM analysis) are bolded. Each variable was allowed to load on only the factor that it was designed to measure, and all other factor loadings were constrained to be zero (see Marsh et al. [1994] for factor loadings and further analyses).

[a]Convergent validities between scales predicted a priori to be most closely matched. [b]Convergent validities between scales predicted a priori to be less closely matched.

Note: Table adapted from part of table 4 in Marsh et al. (1994).

correlations among nonmatching constructs. There was good support for convergent validity in that the correlations in the first category (0.79 to 0.90, median = 0.84) and the second category (0.61 to 0.73, median = 0.68) were all substantial. Further support for construct validity came from the fact that correlations in the first category were systematically larger than those in the second category. There was also good support for discriminant validity in that the remaining 152 correlations (0.02 to 0.74, median = 0.44) were smaller than all convergent validities in the first category and smaller than most of the convergent validities in the second category.

The results of this MTMM analysis provide good support for the construct validity of physical self-concept as well as several of its underlying elements. Furthermore, the availability of three multidimensional instruments has allowed a detailed comparison of content and compatibility. This type of detailed analysis provides unique insight into the intricacies of item and scale design and content and into the way wording is interpreted by the population under scrutiny. This in turn can only enhance future instrument design in an area that is still in its early stage of development.

Directions For Further Research

As opposed to the situation for self-concept research in general, there does not seem to be a plethora of dubious and untested physical self-concept instruments. Nevertheless, it is important to identify and establish those that are of good quality. Desirable features based on suggestions by Hattie and Marsh (1996), Ostrow (1990), Shavelson, Hubner, and Stanton (1976), Wylie (1974, 1989), and the dictates of good measurement include a priori scales derived from defensible theoretical models; evaluation of irrelevant response determiners, bias, and method effects; evidence of the relative unidimensionality of scales; and support for the internal consistency, reliability, and stability of responses. Further requirements are CFAs that support the a priori dimensionality and design of the instrument, MTMM studies of relations with existing instruments, and further evidence of convergent and discriminant validity in relation to appropriate external criteria (e.g., theoretically relevant constructs, known group differences, experimental interventions, structural equation models of causal ordering). Instruments should be accompanied by a test manual providing a clear statement of the appropriate uses and limitations of the instrument, information on how to interpret test scores, and suitable norms where available. Because none of the physical self-concept tests considered here is able to meet these stringent demands, much work remains to be done.

Although physical self-concept measurement has recently made great strides, there is still too little research to claim with confidence that the domains measured by the PSDQ, PSC, and PSPP include all the relevant components of physical self-concept. Conversely, more research is needed to establish that all the domains on the various instruments are important to measure. In all likelihood, there can be no fully adequate answers to these questions. Instead, the most appropriate domains are likely to vary depending upon the population, the particular context, the concerns of a particular researcher, and the nature of the research application.

Between-network research in the measurement of physical self-concept has not progressed very far. It has been appropriate to focus initially on within-network concerns such as the structure of physical self-concept; however, it is now time for research to move beyond these concerns. This is not to say that all the within-network issues have been resolved, but further exploration of between-network issues will clarify directions for within-network research. From this perspective, it is important for researchers to relate multidimensional physical self-concept measures such as those described here to a much wider variety of external validity criteria than have been considered so far. It is also important for researchers to evaluate physical self-concept elements as outcome measures and mediating variables in theory-driven experimental interventions and longitudinal research. There are several examples of this type of self-concept research in educational psychology (e.g., Marsh 1990a, 1993a). It is encouraging to see that recent research featured throughout this book, by a range of research teams, provides good examples of emerging and relevant work in sport and exercise psychology.

REFERENCES

Boyle, G.J. 1994. Self-Description Questionnaire II: A review. *Test Critiques* 10: 632-43.

Bracken, B.A. 1992. *Multidimensional Self Concept Scale*. Austin, TX: Pro-Ed.

Burns, R.B. 1979. *The self-concept: Theory, measurement, development and behaviour*. London: Longman.

Byrne, B.M. 1984. The general/academic self-concept nomological network: A review of construct validation research. *Review of Educational Research* 54: 427-56.

Campbell, D.T., and Fiske, D.W. 1959. Convergent and discriminant validation by multitrait-multimethod matrix. *Psychological Bulletin* 56: 81-105.

Coopersmith, S.A. 1967. *The antecedents of self-esteem*. San Francisco: Freeman.

Fitts, W.H. 1965. *Tennessee Self Concept Scale: Test booklet*. Nashville, TN: Counsellor Recordings and Tests.

Fleishman, F.A. 1964. *The structure and measurement physical fitness*. Englewood Cliffs, NJ: Prentice Hall.

Fleming, J.S., and Courtney, B.E. 1984. The dimensionality of self-esteem: II: Hierarchical facet model for revised measurement scales. *Journal of Personality and Social Psychology* 46: 404-21.

Fox, K.R. 1990. *The Physical Self-Perception Profile manual*. DeKalb, IL: Office for Health Promotion, Northern Illinois University.

Fox, K.R., and Corbin, C.B. 1989. The Physical Self-Perception Profile: Development and preliminary validation. *Journal of Sport and Exercise Psychology* 11: 408-30.

Franzoi, S.L., and Shields, S.A. 1984. The Body Esteem Scale: Multidimensional structure and sex differences in a college population. *Journal of Personality Assessment* 49: 173-78.

Gill, D.L., Dzewaltowski, D.A., and Deeter, T.E. 1988. The relationship of competitiveness and achievement orientation to participation in sport and nonsport activities. *Journal of Sport and Exercise Psychology* 10: 139-50.

Guilford, J.P. 1969. *The nature of human intelligence*. New York: McGraw-Hill.

Harter, S. 1985. *Manual for the Self-perception Profile for Children*. Denver: University of Denver.

—. 1986. Processes underlying the construction, maintenance and enhancement of self-concept in children. In *Psychological perspectives on the self*, ed. J. Suls and A. Greenwald, vol. 3, 136-82. Hillsdale, NJ: Erlbaum.

Hattie, J. 1992. *Self-concept*. Hillsdale, NJ: Erlbaum.

Hattie, J., and Marsh, H.W. 1996. Future directions in self-concept research. In *Handbook of self-concept*, ed. B.A. Bracken, 421-63. New York: Wiley.

Jackson, S., and Marsh, H.W. 1986. Athletic or antisocial: The female sport experience. *Journal of Sport Psychology* 8: 198-211.

Marsh, H.W. 1986. Global self-esteem: Its relation to specific facets of self-concept and their importance. *Journal of Personality and Social Psychology* 51: 1224-36.

—. 1987. The hierarchical structure of self-concept and the application of hierarchical confirmatory factor analysis. *Journal of Educational Measurement* 24: 17-19.

—. 1988. Multitrait-multimethod analyses. In *Educational research methodology, measurement and evaluation: An international handbook*, ed. J.P. Keeves, 570-80. Oxford: Pergamon Press.

—. 1989a. Age and sex effects in multiple dimensions of self-concept: Preadolescence to adulthood. *Journal of Educational Psychology* 81: 417-30.

—. 1989b. Confirmatory factor analyses of multitrait-multimethod data: Many problems and a few solutions. *Applied Psychological Measurement* 13: 335-61.

—. 1990a. Confirmatory factor analysis of multitrait-multimethod data: The construct validation of multidimensional self-concept responses. *Journal of Personality* 58: 661-92.

—. 1990b. A multidimensional, hierarchical self-concept: Theoretical and empirical justification. *Educational Psychology Review* 2: 77-172.

—. 1992. *Self-Description Questionnaire II: Manual*. Sydney: Publication Unit, Faculty of Education, University of Western Sydney.

—. 1993a. Academic self-concept: Theory measurement and research. In *Psychological Perspectives on the self*, ed. J. Suls and A. Greenwald, vol. 4, 59-98. Hillsdale, NJ: Erlbaum.

—. 1993b. The multidimensional structure of physical fitness: Invariance over gender and age. *Research Quarterly for Exercise and Sport* 64: 256-73.

—. 1993c. Multitrait-multimethod analyses: Inferring each trait/method combination with multiple indicators. *Applied Measurement in Education* 6: 49-81.

—. 1993d. Physical fitness self-concept: Relations to field and technical indicators of physical fitness for boys and girls aged 9-15. *Journal of Sport and Exercise Psychology* 15: 184-206.

—. 1993e. Relations between global and specific domains of self: The importance of individual importance, certainty, and ideals. *Journal of Personality and Social Psychology* 65: 975-92.

—. 1994a. Confirmatory factor analysis models of factorial invariance: A mutifaceted approach. *Structural Equation Modeling* 1: 5-34.

—. 1994b. The importance of being important: Theoretical models of relations between specific and global components of physical self-concept. *Journal of Sport and Exercise Psychology* 16: 306-25.

Marsh, H.W., Balla, J.R., and McDonald, R.P. 1988. Goodness-of-fit indices in confirmatory factor analysis: The effect of sample size. *Psychological Bulletin* 102: 391-410.

Marsh, H.W., and Byrne, B.M. 1993. Do we see ourselves as others infer: A comparison of self-other agreement on multiple dimensions of self-concept from two continents. *Australian Journal of Psychology* 45: 49-58.

Marsh, H.W., Byrne, B.M., and Shavelson, R. 1988. A multifaceted academic self-concept: Its hierarchical structure and its relation to academic achievement. *Journal of Educational Psychology* 80: 366-80.

Marsh, H.W., and Gouvernet, P. 1989. Multidimensional self-concepts and perceptions of control. Construct validation of responses by children. *Journal of Educational Psychology* 81: 57-69.

Marsh, H.W., and Hattie, J. 1996. Theoretical perspectives on the structure of self-concept. In *Handbook of self-concept*, ed. B.A. Bracken, 38-90. New York: Wiley.

Marsh, H.W., and Hocevar, D. 1985. The application of confirmatory factor analysis to the study of self-concept: First and higher order factor structures and their invariance across age groups. *Psychological Bulletin* 97: 562-82.

—. 1988. A new procedure for analysis of multitrait-multimethod data: An application of second order confirmatory factor analysis. *Journal of Applied Psychology* 73: 107-11.

Marsh, H.W., and Jackson, S.A. 1986. Multidimensional self-concepts, masculinity and femininity as a function of women's involvement in athletics. *Sex Roles* 15: 391-416.

Marsh, H.W., and Peart, N. 1988. Competitive and cooperative physical fitness training programs for girls: Effects on physical fitness and on multidimensional self-concepts. *Journal of Sport and Exercise Psychology* 10: 390-407.

Marsh, H.W., and Redmayne, R.S. 1994. A multidimensional physical self-concept and its relation to multiple components of physical fitness. *Journal of Sport and Exercise Psychology* 16: 45-55.

Marsh, H.W., and Richards, G.E. 1988. The Tennessee Self Concept Scales: Reliability, internal structure, and construct validity. *Journal of Personality and Social Psychology* 55: 612-24.

Marsh, H.W., Richards, G., and Barnes, J. 1986a. Multidimensional self-concepts: The effect of participation in an Outward Bound program. *Journal of Personality and Social Psychology* 45: 173-87.

—. 1986b. Multidimensional self-concepts: A long-term follow-up of the effect of participation in an Outward Bound program. *Personality and Social Psychology Bulletin* 12: 475-92.

Marsh, H.W., Richards, G., Johnson, S., Roche, L., and Tremayne, P. 1994. Physical Self-Description Questionnaire: Psychometric properties and a multitrait-multimethod analysis of relations to existing instruments. *Journal of Sport and Exercise Psychology* 16: 270-305.

Marsh, H.W., and Shavelson, R.J. 1985. Self-concept: Its multifaceted, hierarchical structure. *Educational Psychologist* 20: 107-25.

Marsh, H.W., and Sonstroem, R.J. 1995. Importance ratings and specific components of physical self-concept: Relevance to predicting global components of self-concept and exercise. *Journal of Sport and Exercise Psychology* 17: 84-104.

Marx, R.W., and Winne, P.H. 1978. Construct interpretations of three self-concept inventories. *American Educational Research Journal* 15: 99-108.

McDonald, R.P., and Marsh, H.W. 1990. Choosing a multivariate model: Noncentrality and goodness-of-fit. *Psychological Bulletin* 107: 247-55.

Nelson, J.K. 1989. Measurement methodology for affective tests. In *Measurement concepts in physical education and exercise science*, ed. M.J. Safrit and T. M. Wood, 271-95. Champaign, IL: Human Kinetics.

Ostrow, A.C. 1990. *Directory of psychological tests in the sport and exercise sciences.* Morgantown, WV: Fitness Information Technology.

Richards, G.E. 1987. *Outdoor education in Australia in relation to the Norman Conquest, a Greek olive grove and the external perspective of a horse's mouth.* Outward Bound School: Tharwa, ACT Australia. Paper presented at the 5th National Outdoor Education Conference, January, Perth, Western Australia.

Secord, P.F., and Jourard, S.M. 1953. The appraisal of body-cathexis: Body cathexis and the self. *Journal of Consulting Psychology* 17: 343-47.

Shavelson, R.J., Hubner, J.J., and Stanton, G.C. 1976. Validation of construct interpretations. *Review of Educational Research* 46: 407-41.

Shavelson, R.J., and Marsh, H.W. 1986. On the structure of self-concept. In *Anxiety and cognitions*, ed. R. Schwarzer, 305-30. Hillsdale, NJ: Erlbaum.

Soares, L.M., and Soares, A.T. 1977. *The self-concept: Mini, maxi, multi.* Paper presented at the annual meeting of the 1977 American Educational Research Association, April, New York.

Sonstroem, R.J. 1978. Physical Estimation and Attraction Scales: Rationale and research. *Medicine and Science in Sports* 10: 97-102.

Sonstroem, R.J., Harlow, L.L., and Josephs, L. 1994. Exercise and self-esteem: Validity of model expansion and exercise associations. *Journal of Sport and Exercise Psychology* 16: 29-42.

Sonstroem, R.J., Speliotis, E.D., and Fava, J.L. 1992. Perceived physical competence in adults: An examination of the Physical Self-Perception Scale. *Journal of Sport and Exercise Psychology* 10: 207-21.

Stunkard, A.J., Sorenson, T., and Schulsinger, F. 1983. Use of the Danish Adoption Registry for the study of obesity and thinness. In *The genetics of neurological and psychiatric disorders*, ed. S. Kety, 115-20. New York: Raven Press.

Vealey, R.S. 1986. Conceptualization of sport-confidence and competitive orientation: Preliminary investigation and instrument development. *Journal of Sport Psychology* 8: 221-46.

Wells, L.E., and Marwell, G. 1976. *Self-esteem: Its conceptualization and measurement.* Beverly Hills, CA: Sage.

Wylie, R.C. 1974. *The self-concept.* Rev. ed. Vol. 1. Lincoln, NE: University of Nebraska Press.

—. 1979. *The self-concept.* Vol. 2. Lincoln, NE: University of Nebraska Press.

—. 1989. *Measures of self-concept.* Lincoln, NE: University of Nebraska Press.

CHAPTER 3

COGNITIVE THEORIES OF MOTIVATION AND THE PHYSICAL SELF

STUART J.H. BIDDLE

The notion of the self, in general or physical terms, is clearly central to any discussion of decision-making in physical activity, sport, and health contexts and is closely related to motivated actions. One way to view the link between self-esteem and behavior is through the *self-enhancement hypothesis* (discussed by Sonstroem, chapter 1). This maintains that people are motivated to action in areas of their lives in which they are likely to experience positive feelings of competence and esteem. The reverse is true as well; that is, low domain-specific self-esteem or perceived competence is likely to reduce motivation in related activities. This chapter will address issues from the contemporary motivation literature that are consistent with or relate to the self-enhancement view. In particular, I will discuss the role of self-perceptions, particularly self-perceptions of ability, with reference to motivation in sport, health-related exercise, and other health behaviors.

ELEMENTS OF HUMAN MOTIVATION

The study of human motivation has been central to psychology since its earliest days and has developed through many different perspectives (see Weiner 1992). Maehr and Braskamp (1986) state that "most motivational talk arises from observations about variation in five behavioral patterns, which we label direction, persistence, continuing motivation, intensity, and performance" (3). *Direction* is the first indicator of motivation, as it implies that a choice has been made. Decision-making therefore becomes central to understanding motivation. In the context of exercise, for example, the basic choice exists of whether to exercise or not or which form of activity to take up. These decisions are related to self-perceptions since choices can be made that reinforce personal perceptions of competence or contribute, through the adoption of an identity, to the central core of self. This is consistent with group behavior and *social identity theory* (Tajfel 1981), according to which people are motivated to see themselves and the groups to which they belong as different from, and better in comparison to, other people and groups (Fiske and Taylor 1991; also Sparkes, chapter 4).

The second motivation factor of Maehr and Braskamp (1986), *persistence*, refers to the degree of sustained concentration or involvement in one task. Persistence, and hence motivation, might be inferred about someone who walks to work instead of taking the bus. Lack of persistence is implied when the walker gives up after five minutes and takes the first available bus. Persistence is also a reflection of choice, that is, decision-making, and can act as an indicator of achievement and so again may be congruent with the self-enhancement view of self-esteem. In addition, such choices may be made to enhance self-presentational aspects of the self: "I want to be seen walking to work as this confirms my identity (to me and others) that I am an active person."

Continuing motivation is seen when people regularly return to a task after a break. Indeed, Maehr and Braskamp (1986) suggest that "it is almost as if a certain tension exists when a task is left incomplete; the person simply cannot leave it alone" (4). There is some evidence that a few individuals feel highly committed in this way to structured exercise (see Veale 1987)—the so-called phenomenon of *exercise dependence*. At a more moderate level, many people report "feeling good" from exercise and less good when they have missed exercise for several days. In addition, a strong sense of identity invested in an activity such as a sport will lead to negative feelings when that person is unable to continue involvement. In a debate about boxing in the United Kingdom, the father of boxer Johnny Owen, a professional who died as the result of a knockout in a fight, said that he still believed boxing should be allowed to continue. One reason he cited was that it had given his son a real sense of identity. This would appear to be a powerful motivator, therefore, since in this case it is present even in the face of physical injury or even death.

Behavioral intensity is another indicator of motivation. This is important in relation to the debate about how much exercise is enough for health gains, since moderate forms of exercise may require less intense levels of motivation. One could argue that the more one has invested one's identity and self in an activity, the higher will be the motivational intensity. This may be congruent with Csikszentmihalyi's (1975) investigations of highly motivated behavior in people who invest far more time in an activity than would seem to be warranted by the external rewards offered. Motivational intensity may also be correlated with unhealthy behaviors such as steroid use or obsessive or pathogenic weight control practices (Leary, Tchividjian, and Kraxberger 1994).

Finally, Maehr and Braskamp (1986) refer to *performance* as an indicator or outcome of motivation, although this is more problematic than the other indicators and is not a pure measure of motivation. The inference of motivation, they suggest, is made when performance cannot be explained simply in terms of competence, skill, or physiological factors.

STAGES OF MOTIVATION

The analysis of motivation components by Maehr and Braskamp (1986) suggests that the construct of motivation is complex. In addition, one should also view motivation in terms of its role in the temporal location of behavior patterns and action. In other words, motivational processes may differ when one is attempting to *initiate* a health behavior in comparison with, say, *maintaining* the same behavioral pattern or resuming the behavior after a substantial period of cessation. This view is consistent with the Transtheoretical Model of Stages of Change in psychotherapy and, more recently, health and exercise research (see Prochaska and Marcus 1994), as well as with models attempting to explain the determinants of exercise (Biddle 1992; Sallis and Hovell 1990).

COGNITIVE MOTIVATION THEORIES IN A HISTORICAL CONTEXT

The study of human motivation has shifted a great deal over time. Initial perspectives emphasized people's motivation more in terms of mechanistic processes or drives. Weiner (1992) describes such views as encompassing the *machine metaphor* according to which behaviors are largely involuntary and predetermined, fixed, and routine and are described in terms of energy transmission. Should the "machine" be out of balance, movement takes place to restore the balance. Such theoretical perspectives include psychoanalytic, ethological, sociobiological, drive, and gestalt theories of motivation, and these were particularly popular until the mid-1950s (Weiner 1992).

As drive-based theories waned in popularity, motivational psychologists increasingly adopted an expectancy-value orientation, or what Weiner (1992) has described as the *God-like metaphor*. Humans are seen to be "all-knowing," to be fully informed about possible behavioral options, to have complete rationality, and to be able to calculate "their most hedonic course of action" (159) by assessing the *expectation* of success and the *value* placed on success. This approach included theories of achievement motivation such as that advocated by Atkinson and his colleagues, locus of control theories, and attribution theories. This paradigmatic shift is also clearly seen in exercise and sport psychology (Biddle 1994) and the social psychological study of health (Stroebe and Stroebe 1995).

Even more recent perspectives in motivation research recognize that human beings are not perfectly rational decision makers and that their information-processing capacities are more limited than sometimes acknowledged. Weiner therefore extended the God-like metaphor to *person as judge*—a label he attached to more recent ideas often labeled the *social cognitive perspective*, although the distinction between some expectancy-value and social cognitive approaches is not always clear. Bandura (1986) says that in the social cognitive view, people are "neither driven by internal forces nor automatically shaped and controlled by external stimuli" (18). In other words, people evaluate their behaviors, cognitions, and environmental events in a reciprocal way (reciprocal determinism) and from this information anticipate future consequences. The self is central to this. For instance, Bandura (1986) discusses the importance of self-regulatory and self-reflective aspects of behavior in his approach:

> Another distinctive feature of social cognitive theory is the central role it assigns to self-regulatory functions. People do not behave just to suit the preferences of others. Much of their behavior is motivated and regulated by internal standards and self-evaluative reactions to their own actions. (20)

By this process, people evaluate their actions, often against some expectation or desire, and then modify their actions accordingly. For example, some people will be motivated to enact weight control behaviors if they perceive a discrepancy between what they are currently like and what they want to be. This provides an alternative view to the traditional stance of the self-enhancement model of self-esteem positing that people are drawn to behaviors in which they have a high expectation of displaying competence. In this case, perceived competence is not high, but the desire to *improve* competence or appearance seems sufficient to provide motivational energy.

The self-reflective elements of Bandura's social cognitive approach can also be used to explain human action. People analyze and reflect on their experiences and actions, and within the context of this chapter, an important aspect is self-reflection of competence. This operation of meta-cognition is recognized through Bandura's seminal work on self-efficacy, which will be discussed in more detail later. As Bandura (1986) says:

> Among the types of thoughts that affect action, none is more central or pervasive than people's judgments of their capabilities to deal effec-

tively with different realities. It is partly on the basis of self-percepts of efficacy that they choose what to do, how much effort to invest in activities, how long to persevere in the face of disappointing results, and whether tasks are approached anxiously or self-assuredly. (21)

SELF-BASED THEORIES OF MOTIVATION

Dominant theories of motivation—through which self-perceptions of ability have been a central feature in the contemporary sport and exercise literature—are those based on the constructs of competence motivation, achievement goals, self-efficacy, and perceptions of personal control (Thill and Brunel 1995). Some time ago, Ken Fox and I documented the importance of such theories in determining approach and avoidance tendencies in exercise (Biddle and Fox 1989). It is possible to locate such approaches within self-perception hierarchies such as those discussed by Marsh in chapter 2.

DOMAIN-GENERAL SELF-PERCEPTIONS AND MOTIVATION

The present chapter will consider motivation theories within such a framework by first dealing with theories that address motivation at the level of *domain-general* self-perceptions. Such theories are based around the assumption that individuals develop a global view of themselves and their abilities or adequacies within a domain. Such constructs are hypothesized to have predictive powers that generalize across behaviors within the domain. An example to be used here is perceived sport competence or sport ability, which represents a self-statement about a set of related behaviors (sports) that are defined by the individual. I shall then focus on *domain-specific* self-perceptions. These can be found at lower levels in self-perception hierarchies and are related to quite specific behaviors. Finally, perspectives on motivation through personal control, autonomy, and self-determination will be discussed.

COMPETENCE MOTIVATION THEORY

Attempts at explaining human behavior through an individual's desire to seek situations in which he or she can display competence is not new in psychology. White's (1959) seminal paper on *effectance* (competence) motivation argued against the mechanistic explanations of the time in favor of a more cognitive approach. A comprehensive, and more contemporary, interpretation of competence motivation has been offered by Harter (e.g., Harter 1978), who developed White's theory in several ways. First, she conceptualized competence as multidimensional by specifying domains of competence perceptions, such as scholastic and athletic competence, and developing measuring instruments for their assessment. She has shown that these domains become more differentiated and more complex with age as the range of behaviors and experiences facing the individual diversifies. Second, Harter related self-perceptions of competence to motivational orientations and perceptions of control.

Harter's theory suggests that individuals are motivated in achievement domains in which their competence can be demonstrated, particularly if they also feel intrinsically oriented toward that area and see themselves as having an internal perceived locus of control. Successful mastery attempts under such conditions are associated with positive emotion and low anxiety.

Many sport psychologists have followed the lead of Harter and tested her theory, or in most cases, the competence elements of her theory, in physical activity settings. Harter's theory predicts that those high in perceived physical competence will be more likely than others to participate in physical activity and sport. Such a relationship has been found (see Weiss 1987 for a summary of this research). Furthermore, similar concepts of physical competence have been used in the Psychological Model of Physical Activity Participation and in construct validation of the Physical Self-Perception Profile, discussed by Sonstroem (see chapter 1). Although in general only a moderate relationship has been found between perceived competence and measures of sport and exercise involvement, the strength and attraction of Harter's theory center on psychometrically sound and developmentally based instruments for the testing of her model. But it is surprising how research that has enthusiastically embraced this approach has neglected important elements of the model. Only parts of the model, such as motivational orientation or domain-specific perceptions of competence, have been tested against behavior and related variables. Also, the testing of Harter's theory in sport settings has been centered almost exclusively on children and youth in North America, and the cross-cultural validity of the theory has not received a great deal of attention.

GOAL PERSPECTIVES THEORY: DIFFERENTIAL DEFINITIONS OF SUCCESS AND ABILITY

Maehr and Nicholls (1980) influenced the thinking of many researchers interested in achievement-related constructs and behaviors, and in particular those in the field of education. Such an approach has been readily adopted by sport psychologists (see Duda 1993). In rejecting many of the assumptions of Atkinsonian achievement motivation theory, Maehr and Nicholls (1980) argued that success and failure are not concrete events. They are psychological states consequent on perception of reaching or not reaching goals.... It follows that, if there is cultural variation in the personal qualities that are seen to be desirable, success and failure will be viewed differently in different cultures. (228)

Maehr and Nicholls (1980) defined three types of achievement motivation: *ability-orientated* motivation, *task-orientated* motivation, and *social approval-orientated* motivation. Ability-orientated motivation is seen when "the goal of the behavior is to maximize the subjective probability of attributing high ability to oneself" (237). This has been modified in sport psychology to refer to *ego* goal orientations in which success is defined as the demonstration of superiority in comparison to others (Duda 1993).

In task-orientated motivation, according to Maehr and Nicholls (1980), "the primary goal is to produce an adequate product or to solve a problem for its own sake rather than to demonstrate ability" (239). This is the *task* goal orientation (Duda 1993). Finally, social approval goals are also recognized and are defined by Maehr and Nicholls as "conformity to norms or virtuous intent rather than superior talent" (241-42). Social approval orientation has been investigated less than the other two types of goals (see Whitehead 1995). Maehr and Braskamp (1986) have now developed the notions of goals into a more comprehensive social cognitive theory of motivation known as *personal investment theory* (see Duda 1993). In short, goal orientations refer to personal definitions of success in contrast to statements of competence that are acquired by a predetermined set of questionnaire items.

Three interrelated areas of goals and competence perceptions have now been studied in the context of physical activity and motivation, and these shed light on important processes of self-perceptions in the physical domain. These are (a) the relationships between individual differences in goal orientations and motivational constructs such as intrinsic motivation and perceptions of competence; (b) the links between situational achievement cues, such as group or classroom climate, and motivational responses; and (c) underlying belief structures and goals.

Individual Differences in Goal Perspectives

The psychological correlates of the task and ego constructs have been widely studied in sport (see Duda 1993). There is now consistent evidence that task or mastery goals in physical activity settings can be motivationally adaptive, as the construct is consistently associated with the application of effort and the belief that effort is the key determinant of success. On the other hand, ego orientation tends to be associated with beliefs that ability is the main determinant of success and that ability is relatively stable. Surprisingly, few studies have investigated behavioral choice as a function of goals (see Whitehead 1995).

My colleagues and I have argued elsewhere (e.g., Fox et al. 1994) that given the lack of a correlation between task and ego orientations, *goal profiles* should be studied. These incorporate combinations of task and ego goals, such as high ego/low task or low ego/low task, and are more meaningful for explanation of motivation at the individual and group level. Fox et al. (1994) found that in young adolescents, high task/high ego and high task/low ego groups were most motivated, in comparison with low task/high ego and low task/low ego groups, when asked about sport in general. Goudas, Biddle, and Fox (1994a), in a study of motivation following a specific physical fitness task, found that children in the high task/low ego group had the most motivationally adaptive profile. These studies suggest, therefore, that a high task orientation is motivationally supportive, either on its own or in combination with a high ego orientation. A high reliance on ego involvement and an absence of mastery goal setting seems to be motivationally weak.

Of particular significance here is the relationship between task and ego dominance and perceived competence or ability. Fox et al. (1994) found that children low in both task and ego goal orientations had significantly lower perceived sport ability. This represents an amotivated group that tends to be dominated by girls, whereas for the high task/high ego group, boys strongly outnumbered girls. One reason for this gender bias could be associated with socialization and personal identity, since it is often believed that it is more important for boys than for girls in our society to demonstrate "competence," however construed, in physical activity settings.

The theory suggests that those who are heavily ego involved are likely to be motivated as long as they are able to convince themselves that they have high competence. In support of this, Fox et al. (1994) found that the children with low perceived competence who were heavily reliant on ego goals appeared to enjoy sport less and to be less involved in sport than the two high task groups. There were no differences between the children high in perceived competence in the high ego/low task group and the other groups. More children with low to moderate perceived ability were found in the high task group than in the high ego group.

The findings from such research have made it clear that a further dimension needs to be added to the basic tenet of competence motivation. Building on Harter's theory, it is not simply how competent individuals feel that is important in the explanation of motivation, but the basis on which they have arrived at their competence judgment.

Goal Perspectives and Situational Factors

The interactions between individual goal orientations and the goals that appear to be dominant in the social setting are likely to be important motivational determinants in some exercise, sport, and educational settings. Ames (1992) refers to the *motivational climate* in the school classroom, and these concepts have been applied to goal perspectives in physical education (PE) classes, sport teams, and exercise classes. A mastery climate is based on some or all aspects of the following: defining success in terms of individual progress and improvement, valuing effort, evaluating participants through their effort and progress, viewing mistakes as part of learning, and allowing choice (Ames 1992; Biddle et al. 1995).

Papaioannou (1994) has reported on the development of a scale to assess Greek adolescents' perceptions of the motivational climate of their PE classes. His factor analytic approach revealed two higher-order classroom climate factors of "learning" (mastery) and "performance." The students' perceptions of a learning climate in PE were associated with higher levels of intrinsic interest and positive attitudes. In summarizing his research, Papaioannou (1995) stated, "The findings . . . suggest that the adoption of a high learning- and low performance-oriented environment is the most appropriate in order to maximize motivation and achievement for children of all levels of ability" (266).

Extending Papaioannou's work, my colleagues and I have reported on the development of scales, in both English and French, assessing PE class climate (Biddle et al. 1995) and have also found that a mastery class climate is predictive of intrinsic motivation and interest. For example, in PE classes of 12- to 14-year-olds in England, intrinsic interest and intentions were predicted in an activity reported as intrinsically interesting (football/ netball) by individual goal orientations (task predicted directly but ego predicted indirectly through perceived competence) and by perceived autonomy. Perceptions of class climate were indirectly predictive of motivation. However, for an activity that the children reported as being less intrinsically interesting, such as gymnastics (perceptions of competence were the same as for other sports), motivational variables were predicted directly by perceptions of a mastery climate. This suggests that for students in situations not initially interesting to them, a mastery climate can be particularly important to motivation.

Using the same rationale as for the individual goal profiles, we found that classes perceived as high in both mastery and performance climate were most motivational (Goudas and Biddle 1994); this contrasted with Papaioannou's (1995) assertion that high mastery (learning) but low performance is optimal. As for individual goals, though, it is likely that a high-mastery climate, either singly or in combination with a high-performance climate, is motivationally adaptive, but that the exact conditions and individuals under study will determine the precise relationship.

Conceptions of Ability and Goal Orientations

An important issue is to investigate how and why various goal orientations or profiles are developed. Dweck and Leggett (1988), for example, suggest that academic goals are related to underlying beliefs about the nature of intelligence. For example, those believing that intelligence is relatively fixed are more likely to adopt a performance (ego) goal, whereas others who believe that intelligence is more changeable will be predisposed to a learning (task) goal. This has some intuitive appeal, but little evidence has been produced beyond some exploratory data (Dweck and Leggett 1988), and initial efforts of mine, with colleagues in France and England, to find parallels in sport have met with mixed results (Sarrazin et al. 1996).

We first replicated Dweck and Leggett's (1988) method, with some modifications, by studying the relationship between goal choice and notions of the incremental nature of sport ability (Sarrazin et al. 1996). A small difference was noted between children choosing a learning (task) goal and those preferring a performance (ego) goal such that the former were more likely to believe that sport ability was incremental or changeable. However, the results were less clear than those shown by Dweck and Leggett (1988) for classroom settings.

In a follow-up study with French school students, we extended the notion of conceptions of sport ability to include several dimensions such as the belief that sport ability was the product of learning, was a "natural gift," was stable, and the like. Results were clearer than in the earlier study, demonstrating a relationship between a task orientation and beliefs that sport ability is incremental and is the product of learning. An ego goal orientation was associated with beliefs that sport ability is stable and perceived more as a "natural gift." These results support those of Duda et al. (1992), who found that task orientation was associated with the belief that effort produced sport success, whereas an ego goal orientation was correlated with beliefs that ability was important for sport success.

The identification of socialization influences, or precursors, of goal orientations is an important research issue requiring additional work. Results so far suggest that adaptive motivational goals are associated with beliefs concerning the priority of effort over ability, and of ability conceptions that stress change and control. Whether such notions are central to exercise and sport motivation requires further testing, but this appears to be an area of great potential.

Assessment of Perceptions of Competence

Perhaps a more critical question raised by goal perspective theory concerns how we assess perceived ability or competence. Because the theory clearly demonstrates that people are able to experience and measure their personal competence on contrasting criteria, this should be reflected in the scales used in research to assess competence. For example, for individuals who are highly task oriented and who have little interest in how they rate among peers (ego orientation), measures that rely on social comparison may have little relevance or salience.

It would appear that more account needs to be taken of the recent advances in achievement goal orientations such as those described in this chapter. At present, perceived competence scales may confound the issue of ego- versus mastery-based competence, in effect reducing their precision and validity. Researchers interested in self-perception instrument design should look into the possibility of developing scales that accommodate the range of criteria that may contribute to perceptions of success in sport, exercise, and health.

EXERCISE SELF-SCHEMATA: EXERCISE IDENTITIES

Perhaps one mechanism by which generalized notions of competence and identity relate to more domain-specific self-perceptions in the physical domain is through self-perceptions that personalize competence and allow the development of domain-specific identities (see also Brettschneider and Heim, chapter 8). Much of the linking between physical self-perceptions and motivation has emphasized the role of generalized beliefs and perceptions in health behavior and actions. One approach currently favored in contemporary social psychology is that of information processing guided by *self-schemata*. Fiske and Taylor (1991) define a schema as "a cognitive structure that represents knowledge about a concept or type of stimulus, including its attributes and the relations among those attributes" (98). Such knowledge is gained through experience, and schemata are thought to guide the way we retrieve, select, and interpret information.

Kendzierski (1994) has applied this construct to exercise through work on exercise self-schemata and has defined three main types of individuals:

1. *Exerciser schematics* describe themselves in terms of being an exerciser, being active, etc. and rate these constructs as important to their own self-image.

2. *Nonexerciser schematics* view exercise/physical activity descriptors as clearly not applying to them, but rate these descriptors as important to their self-image.

3. *Aschematics* do not rate exercise/physical activity descriptors as particularly descriptive of them and do not view these descriptors as important to their self-image.

Interventions using this approach, however, are not clear. Do we attempt to develop positive associations with exercise and self-image such that the development of exercise self-schemata promotes the likelihood of greater exercise? Or is it only through positive exercise experience, and presumably greater importance attached to this aspect of the self, that the self-schemata develop? Perhaps the answer is both, running parallel with self-esteem theory. Kendzierski (1994) argues that experience is a necessary but not sufficient condition for schemata development and that exercise self-schemata are not merely a reflection of exercise experience.

The notion of exercise self-schemata is an interesting one and fits well with the current discussion. In particular, it directs our attention beyond perceived competence within a domain and locates the self more completely within the domain's social contexts. For instance, current clothing fashion includes much more sport/leisure wear than in the past. Whether this will encourage the development of exercise self-schemata remains to be seen. It would appear more likely to do so than would be the case if these types of clothes were very unfashionable.

There is further scope for combining the notion of domain identities and self-schemata as they may represent a broader combination of self-attitudes and values that are closely linked with the social contexts built around sport and exercise settings. Simple measures of competence may miss this important link. One way forward may be to integrate this approach with the hierarchical self-esteem model of physical self-perceptions, particularly with respect to the perceived importance of subdomains of physical self-worth.

DOMAIN-SPECIFIC SELF-PERCEPTIONS AND MOTIVATION

So far, in the effort to understand motivation, theories based on relatively more generalized competence perceptions have been discussed. However, it is important in addition to appraise the role of more context-specific self-perceptions in motivated behavior.

SELF-EFFICACY THEORY: MOTIVATION AND CONFIDENCE

Confidence has been identified at the anecdotal and empirical level as an important construct in exercise and health motivation. Statements associated with self-perceptions of confidence are particularly commonplace in studies on exercise and sport.

Basic Tenets of Self-Efficacy Theory in Exercise

Physical self-efficacy is seen as a central construct in the exercise and self-esteem model of Sonstroem and Morgan (1989) (see fig. 1.2). Using the notion of a hierarchy, Sonstroem and Morgan place efficacy within the model as a lower-order specific construct that represents the "lowest generality level of the competence dimension." They state, "Self-conceptions at this level should be the most accurate and the most readily influenced by environmental interactions" (333). This concurs with Bandura's notions of self-efficacy. Sonstroem and Morgan's model proposes that physical self-efficacy is the first cognitive link between higher-order psychological constructs and actual behaviors. Also, with the direction of arrows shown in the model, an assumption is that behavioral outcomes influence self-efficacy, and onward to more global constructs of competence and self-esteem. In contrast to the self-enhancement hypothesis of the self-esteem/motivation relationship, this has been termed the *skill development hypothesis*, which suggests that positive experiences in specific domains will enhance self-efficacy and eventually generalize to higher-order self-constructs. However, at this interface, self-efficacy theory would also support the reciprocal nature of the relationship between efficacy perceptions and behavior by stating that motivation to take part in behaviors will not occur in the absence of self-efficacy—a statement that fits with the self-enhancement hypothesis.

Bandura (1986) defines self-efficacy as "people's judgements of their capabilities to organize and execute courses of action required to attain designated types of performances." He explains, "It is concerned not with the skills one has but with judgements of what one can do with whatever skills one possesses" (391). Of particular importance for motivation is the belief that one can carry out the task or behavior. Consequently, Bandura distinguishes between *efficacy expectations* and *outcome expectations*. The former are associated with beliefs that one can execute the behavior, for example, take part in regular exercise. Outcome expectations, on the other hand, are beliefs that the behavior will lead to certain outcomes, such as weight loss or fitness gain. It could be argued that outcome expectations will be more closely associated with perceptions of control, since some health/fitness outcomes are less controllable as products of exercise (e.g., body fat) than participation in the process of exercise (i.e., taking part).

Bandura has also identified key sources of efficacy information such as prior success, imitation and modeling, verbal and social persuasion, and perceptions of internal physiological states. Clearly, perceptions of past successes and failures will partly determine efficacy expectations, although the attributions given for success and failure will also be influential. Stable attributions for success and controllable attributions for failure may be adaptive for expectations and efficacy perceptions (Biddle 1993). In addition, efficacious individuals are more likely to make "positive" or motivationally adaptive attributions for their outcomes (McAuley 1991).

Self-efficacy may also be developed through imitation and modeling processes. Observing others succeed or fail could affect subsequent efficacy beliefs, particularly if the individual has little or no prior experience to draw on. Interestingly, Bandura (1986) suggests that social comparison information is important in self-efficacy beliefs. However, whether this is true about health-related exercise in comparison to competitive sport, for instance, is difficult to say. Although confidence may be associated with certain self-presentational processes, such as social physique anxiety (Leary 1992), it could be argued that health-related exercise is less likely to evoke social comparison than some other situations. Nevertheless, even casual observers of public exercise behaviors such as street jogging, public swimming, or exercise classes are likely to conclude that self-presentation, through feelings of inhibition, could be a major source of motivational variation. The following constructs are just some of those listed in Leary's (1995) book *Self-Presentation*: physical appearance, gestures and movement, public self-consciousness, weight, appearance and physique anxiety, and modesty. Clearly, there is great potential for using such constructs in furthering our understanding of physical activity and efficacy perceptions.

In relation to social physique anxiety, Hart, Leary, and Rejeski (1989) propose that people high in such anxiety, in comparison to those not anxious, "are likely to avoid situations in which their physique is under scrutiny of others (e.g., swimming in public) . . . avoid activities that accentuate their physiques (including aerobic activities that might be beneficial to them) . . . and attempt to improve their physiques through a variety of means, some of which may be harmful (e.g., fasting)" (96). Further testing of the social physique anxiety construct in health contexts, along with other self-presentational factors, is warranted. For example, data from the Allied Dunbar National Fitness Survey in England (Sports Council/Health Education Authority 1992) showed that concerns about lack of sport competence were major barriers to participation in physical activity. How generalizable such feelings are remains to be seen. For some individuals, feelings of "not being the sporty type" may generalize across many different physical activities, whereas for others they may affect only one or two specific pursuits. Indeed, most physical activities such as sports occur in such public settings that self-presentational issues are hard to ignore. Coupled with this is the widespread social acceptance and admiration of physical expertise. In view of this, social anxiety in physical activity contexts is likely to be common, since people are more likely to experience social anxiety when they are motivated to make a desirable impression on others but have low feelings of self-efficacy about being able to do so. There appears to be considerable scope for hypothesizing links between measures such as self-presentation and social physique anxiety and the domain-general level of identity, self-schemata, and physical self-worth.

Another point on vicarious processes in self-efficacy concerns the use of certain types of individuals in promoting exercise to nonexercisers or to certain groups, such as persons who are obese. It is common in the mass media to use elite sport models or models displaying high levels of fitness or physique/figure development. Bandura (1986) contends that vicarious influences such as modeling are more likely to have an influence when the individual has some empathy with the model. On the other hand, anecdotal evidence suggests that elite models are "interesting" and "motivational." This needs to be resolved if effective use of models is to be made in exercise promotion. Indeed, in our research my colleagues and I found that older patients referred into an exercise program by their family doctor were more confident when exercising with similar individuals. They also reported feeling uncomfortable when around young vigorous exercisers (Biddle, Fox, and Edmunds 1994).

Verbal and social persuasion sources of self-efficacy have not been studied much in exercise. However, certain exercise situations, such as structured classes with exercise leaders, are likely to influence efficacy perceptions through these sources of information. In other situations, persuasion may be less important. The social marketing approach to exercise may be one way forward here (see Donovan and Owen 1994). Indeed, verbal strategies have been the mainstay of several health promotion campaigns, although increasing self-efficacy has not always been the mechanism targeted. A recent campaign in England is aimed at redefining exercise for health for the public. The popular notion that exercise has to be strenuous, vigorous, or even skillful is being replaced with messages of more moderate lifestyle-related exercise with the view that self-efficacy for exercise can be increased and activity made more accessible.

Finally, Bandura proposes that perceptions of internal physiological states, such as heart rate, are also important sources of self-efficacy. However, findings on the influence of physiological information have been inconsistent in the sport performance literature on self-efficacy (see Feltz 1988), and this topic has been largely unstudied in connection with exercise efficacy. Research is needed to link self-efficacy with concepts such as perceived and preferred exertion, pain and soreness sensations, and the capability people have of self-monitoring physical exertion during exercise. Certainly there is a need to ease some people's fears concerning the acute effects of exercise on their body as well to place a priority on ease and comfort at the beginning of an exercise program.

Summary of Findings on Self-Efficacy in Exercise and Health

Although self-efficacy is just one part of Bandura's (1986) social cognitive theory, most of the studies investigating self-efficacy in exercise and health have done so without regard to the broader issues of the theory. Early studies often investigated patients in rehabilitation settings such as coronary heart disease clinics (Ewart 1989). However, more recently self-efficacy has been included in studies investigating nonpatient groups (see McAuley and Courneya 1993). For example, self-efficacy has been shown to predict walking in a large adult sample contacted by mail (Hofstetter et al. 1991), has predicted exercise change over time in a large community sample (Sallis et al. 1992), and has discriminated adherers from dropouts in an exercise weight loss program (Rodgers and Brawley 1993).

In summary, self-efficacy has consistently predicted involvement in physical activity and is often a better predictor of actions or intentions than similar theoretical frameworks. However, the role of efficacy perceptions across different health, exercise and activity settings, age groups, and people with varying exercise experience has not been fully determined and is a priority for future work in this field. "Self-efficacy has proven to be a very powerful behavioral determinant in many studies, and its inclusion in theories of health behavior, therefore, is warranted" (Schwarzer 1992, 223).

Measurement of Self-Efficacy and the Link Between Self-Perceptions and Motivation

As general motivational theories have progressively been applied to sport, exercise, and health behaviors, there arises the opportunity to reflect and improve on measurement instruments. To date, studies have been inconsistent in their approaches to measuring self-efficacy, which can vary along the dimensions of *magnitude, strength,* and *generality*. Most studies have used assessments of the strength of self-efficacy, with only a few assessing magnitude or generality. This suggests that self-efficacy in exercise research is currently limited in its scope, and a call to broaden the measurement protocol in such studies seems appropriate. In particular, the need to assess how well self-efficacy beliefs generalize between different physical activity settings is important, as this would provide a means of investigating the directional influence between specific and general perceptions in the self-perception hierarchy.

In addition, it has always been argued by Bandura and others (e.g., McAuley 1992) that self-efficacy needs to be assessed in relation to specific behaviors if increased magnitude of behavioral prediction is to be attained. Generalized perceptions of confidence are not the same as perceptions of efficacy. Similar to the situation with the attitude-behavior correspondence issue in social psychology, the utility of self-efficacy is likely to be greater when measures correspond closely to the behavior in question, such as jogging three times per week, rather than with use of a general reference such as "exercise." This confirms the importance of the self-perception hierarchy used as the conceptual and operational base for Fox's (1990) Physical Self-Perception Profile. For this reason, one must question the assumptions underpinning the Physical Self-Efficacy Scale of Ryckman et al. (1982). Their rationale for developing such a scale was based on the need for measuring self-efficacy for exercise in preference to more global measures of self-concept. However, they too have assessed only generalized perceptions of physical ability and "self-presentation confidence," and not self-efficacy as defined by Bandura.

Assessing self-efficacy in any meaningful way requires the behavior to be associated with effort, potential barriers, and behavioral self-regulation. In other words, habitual behaviors, such as brushing the teeth, are likely to be unrelated to feelings of efficacy, whereas physical exercise and other "effortful" health behaviors may be highly associated with efficacy beliefs since they involve planning, effort, and barriers.

Finally, caution needs to be exercised in the use of self-efficacy perspectives. Many have argued that self-determination underpins intrinsically motivated behavior. It does not necessarily follow, therefore, that feelings of efficacy are associated with feelings of autonomy. Indeed, expectations of efficacy, in some situations, may actually be controlling, for example, through coercion (see Deci and Ryan 1987, 1991). Domain-specific perceptions of efficacy and competence, therefore, must also account for recent perspectives on intrinsic motivation and self-determination. Such perspectives probably straddle the self-perception hierarchy rather than being appropriate to only specific or general perceptions.

Self-Determination and Intrinsic Motivation

It is generally acknowledged that the shift toward the study of a cognitive perspective on motivational needs began with White's (1959) paper on effectance motivation. White suggested that human beings have a basic need to interact effectively with their environment. He reviewed a wide range of studies and argued convincingly that operant theories could not account for behaviors such as mastery attempts, curiosity, exploration, and play. For all these and other similar activities, there seems to be no apparent external reward except for the activity itself; such activities have been termed intrinsically motivating.

An alternative approach was taken by DeCharms (1968). He argued that self-determination is a basic human need and that consequently individuals will be optimally and intrinsically motivated when they perceive themselves to be the "origin," or to be in control, of their own behavior. DeCharms (1968) used Heider's concept of perceived locus of causality (PLOC) to describe individuals' sense of autonomy or self-determination. Perceived locus of causality refers to the perception people have about the reasons they engage in a particular behavior. People with an internal PLOC feel that they are initiators or originators of their behavior. On the other hand, people feeling that their actions are initiated by some external force are said to have an external PLOC. External and internal PLOC are seen as mutually exclusive, and they represent opposite ends of a continuum. According to DeCharms, people are more likely to be optimally and intrinsically motivated when they have an internal PLOC. This may well be associated with higher levels of self-esteem, since feelings of control are thought to be worthwhile and free of tension whereas low control can be a determinant of depressive affect and negative self-perceptions. Similarly, internal PLOC may also be related to stronger feelings of personal identity and investment.

Cognitive evaluation theory (CET) (Deci and Ryan 1985) has reconciled the two conceptions of White and DeCharms by postulating that variations in individuals' feelings of competence and perceptions of locus of causality (autonomy) will produce variations in intrinsic motivation. In the 1970s, several studies showed that providing individuals with rewards for their participation in an already interesting activity often led to a decrease in intrinsic motivation (see Deci and Ryan 1985), although recent meta-analyses have suggested a more complex relationship (Cameron and Pierce 1994; Rummel and Feinberg 1988; Wiersma 1992).

It was theorized that the decline in intrinsic motivation was due to a shift in PLOC. Individuals who had an internal PLOC for performing an activity shifted their locus of causality to a more external orientation when they received a reward, and consequently their intrinsic motivation decreased. Intrinsic motivation can also be affected by changes in perceptions of competence.

Therefore CET can be summarized in three propositions offered by Deci and Ryan (1985). Proposition I states that "any event that facilitates the perception of an internal locus of causality for an activity will tend to enhance intrinsic motivation for that activity" (16). The role of perceived competence in the promotion of intrinsic motivation is captured by Proposition II, which states that "any event that enhances perceived competence will tend to enhance intrinsic motivation" (17). Proposition III emphasizes the phenomenological nature of the first and second propositions by arguing that events can be perceived as informational, controlling, or amotivating and that it is not the events per se that affect intrinsic motivation but rather their meaning as perceived by the individual. Informational events are those events that are perceived to convey feedback about one's competence within the context of autonomy. Controlling events are those perceived as applying pressure for a particular way of thought or behavior. Finally, amotivating events are those events that do not carry any feedback about competence or autonomy.

Cognitive evaluation theory was developed into the broader self-determination theory (SDT) (Deci and Ryan 1985; see also Whitehead and Corbin, chapter 7) in an attempt to suggest how we can facilitate interest toward tasks that may be uninteresting in the first instance. Deci et al. (1991) argue that individuals are inclined to internalize activities that are not initially interesting if these activities are useful for effective social functioning.

Deci and Ryan (1985) have linked the internalization concept to that of extrinsic and intrinsic motivation. In contrast to their earlier formulations, in which these two motivational types were regarded as mutually exclusive, the authors proposed a continuum along which different types of extrinsically and intrinsically regulated behavior can be located between external motivation and intrinsic motivation (see fig. 7.1; Whitehead and Corbin, chapter 7). Some have also proposed three types of intrinsic motivation: intrinsic motivation to know, to accomplish, and to experience stimulation (see Fortier et al. 1995 for details). Self-determination theory deals with the process of internalization and the way in which people transform regulation by external contingencies into regulation by internal processes. Hence, movement from extrinsic to intrinsic motives is likely to be reflective of greater perceptions of autonomy (Goudas, Biddle, and Fox 1994b; Whitehead 1993).

Self-determination theory may provide a vital missing link in the connections between self-esteem and behavior, especially where the self-enhancement hypothesis does not seem to directly apply. As mentioned earlier in this chapter, there are some behaviors that do not appear to be driven by perceptions of high competence. A clear example is provided by an overweight person who joins aerobic exercise classes in order to lose weight with the goal of improving appearance. In order to develop competence or adequacy in one aspect of self (appearance), the person is prepared to invest in a behavior that may not produce an immediate payoff in terms of experiencing competence (exercise) and may even carry a cost in the exposure of low competence or high embarrassment and anxiety. In SDT, this behavior is at least in part extrinsically driven. Similarly, coercion of patients by medical personnel to exercise in order to reduce risk of coronary heart disease can be regarded as extrinsic. The relationship between external motivation of this kind and future intentions is often low. The need for exercise is reduced if weight loss is achieved, or if weight loss does not take place, the individual loses enthusiasm. On the other hand, if in the process of losing weight, individuals begin to regard themselves as "exercisers" to the point that exercise is becoming an essential part of their identity, the chances of continuing exercise will be much higher, even perhaps under circumstances of low success.

Self-determination theory holds considerable promise for explaining an individual's personal relationship with behaviors such as sport and exercise. Similar to goal orientations theory, it also makes clear that level of perceived competence by itself provides a restrictive picture for the explanation of behavior. There are many behaviors in health and other areas in which feelings associated with autonomy may be as important as, or more important than, competence. Individuals who have successfully lost weight often report greater feelings of control over themselves and their lives. Similarly, exercisers may feel good about themselves through the mechanisms of autonomy rather than competence. There are many joggers out there (including me!) who have minimal levels of jogging competence but feel good about the efforts to self-regulate in terms of activity, fitness, and weight management. The focus in the past on competence, while important, has been simplistic. The combination of competence, autonomy, and sense of identity appears to be critical to understanding motivation and the relationship between achievement and self-esteem (for an extension of this discussion as applied to children and youth, see Whitehead and Corbin, chapter 7).

CONCLUSIONS AND ISSUES FOR FUTURE RESEARCH

Contemporary sport and exercise psychology research has placed a great deal of faith in cognitive approaches to motivation. In this chapter I have discussed how these popular theories are related to the theme of this book—the physical self and related self-perceptions. Most of the time the approach adopted was consistent with the self-enhancement view of self-esteem, in which perceptions of competence or ability are pivotal. However, examples have been presented that demonstrate that this approach has its limitations in that many people persist in their behaviors in spite of their lack of competence.

It should be recognized that the self-perception hierarchy, from global self-perceptions to state-specific and differentiated perceptions, applies to the analysis undertaken in this chapter. As Sonstroem and Morgan (1989) propose in their extension of their Exercise and Self-Esteem Model, perceptions of efficacy are closely linked to actual behaviors. On the other hand, there are some higher-order theories of competence motivation, self-perception, and identity that are important in understanding motivation for health and physical activity. This hierarchical organization could form the basis for a clear formulation of overlapping motivational theories.

The conceptual overlap between the various motivational constructs discussed is clear to see, and while one could argue that this might be positive (at least we are talking about the same kinds of things), it can also be a problem in terms of communication. One way to look at this may well be through a *proximal-distal approach*. Motivation—a proximal determinant of behavior—may be underpinned through more deep-rooted, possibly more distal, factors such as identity development, self-consistency, or self-presentation and impression management. This is speculative, as there are likely to be exceptions, but it is one way to view the complex interactions between physical self-perceptions and subsequent motivated behavior in physical activity and other health contexts.

Finally, it should be recognized that the commonalities between constructs and theories discussed here should be used as points of convergence rather than divergence. Exercise and health social psychologists, such as Brawley (1993) and Maddux (1993), have already argued this by specifying where the similarities are between various theories and how these similarities can be used to good effect. Given this overlap, it may be futile to pit theories against each other to see whether a few extra percentage points of variance can be explained by one over the other. In short, greater cooperation rather competition between approaches is required in order for theoretical and practical progress to be made.

ACKNOWLEDGMENT

I am grateful to the editor, Ken Fox, for his most helpful and insightful comments, not only on earlier drafts of this chapter but also in the context of our collaborative research, some of which is reflected here.

REFERENCES

Ames, C. 1992. Achievement goals, motivational climate and motivational processes. In *Motivation in sport and exercise*, ed. G.C. Roberts, 161-76. Champaign, IL: Human Kinetics.

Bandura, A. 1986. *Social foundations of thought and action: A social cognitive theory*. Englewood Cliffs, NJ: Prentice Hall.

Biddle, S.J.H. 1992. Adherence to physical activity and exercise. In *Physical activity and health*, ed. N. Norgan, 170-89. Cambridge: Cambridge University Press.

—. 1993. Attribution research and sport psychology. In *Handbook of research on sport psychology*, ed. R.N. Singer, M. Murphey, and L.K. Tennant, 437-64. New York: Macmillan.

—. 1994. Motivation and participation in exercise and sport. In *International perspectives on sport and exercise psychology*, ed. S. Serpa, J. Alves, and V. Pataco, 103-26. Morgantown, WV: Fitness Information Technology.

Biddle, S.J.H., and Fox, K.R. 1989. Exercise and health psychology: Emerging relationships. *British Journal of Medical Psychology* 62: 205-16.

Biddle, S.J.H., Fox, K.R., and Edmunds, L. 1994. *Physical activity promotion in primary health care in England*. London: Health Education Authority.

Biddle, S.J.H., Cury, F., Goudas, M., Sarrazin, P., Famose, J-P., and Durand, M. 1995. Development of scales to measure perceived physical education class climate: A cross-national project. *British Journal of Educational Psychology* 65: 341-58.

Brawley, L.R. 1993. The practicality of using social psychological theories for exercise and health research and intervention. *Journal of Applied Sport Psychology* 5: 99-115.

Cameron, J., and Pierce, W.D. 1994. Reinforcement, reward, and intrinsic motivation: A meta-analysis. *Review of Educational Research* 64: 363-423.

Csikszentmihalyi, M. 1975. *Beyond boredom and anxiety*. San Francisco: Jossey-Bass.

DeCharms, R. 1968. *Personal causation*. New York: Academic Press.

Deci, E., and Ryan, R. 1985. *Intrinsic motivation and self-determination in human behavior*. London: Plenum Press.

—. 1987. The support of autonomy and the control of behavior. *Journal of Personality and Social Psychology* 53: 1024-37.

—. 1991. A motivational approach to self: Integration in personality. In *Nebraska symposium on motivation.* Vol. 38, *Perspectives on motivation,* ed. R.A. Dienstbier, 237-88. Lincoln, NE: University of Nebraska.

Deci, E., Vallerand, R.J., Pellétier, L., and Ryan, R. 1991. Motivation and education: The self-determination perspective. *Educational Psychologist* 26: 325-46.

Donovan, R.J., and Owen, N. 1994. Social marketing and population interventions. In *Advances in exercise adherence,* ed. R.K. Dishman, 249-90. Champaign, IL: Human Kinetics.

Duda, J.L. 1993. Goals: A social-cognitive approach to the study of achievement motivation in sport. In *Handbook of research on sport psychology,* ed. R.N. Singer, M. Murphey, and L.K. Tennant, 421-36. New York: Macmillan.

Duda, J.L., Fox, K.R., Biddle, S.J.H., and Armstrong, N. 1992. Children's achievement goals and beliefs about success in sport. *British Journal of Educational Psychology* 62: 313-23.

Dweck, C., and Leggett, E. 1988. A social-cognitive approach to motivation and personality. *Psychological Review* 95: 256-73.

Ewart, C.K. 1989. Psychological effects of resistive weight training: Implications for cardiac patients. *Medicine and Science in Sports and Exercise* 21: 683-88.

Feltz, D.L. 1988. Self-confidence and sports performance. *Exercise and Sport Sciences Reviews* 16: 423-57.

Fiske, S.T., and Taylor, S.E. 1991. *Social cognition.* New York: McGraw-Hill.

Fortier, M.S., Vallerand, R.J., Brière, N., and Provencher, P.J. 1995. Competitive and recreational sport structures and gender: A test of their relationship with sport motivation. *International Journal of Sport Psychology* 26: 24-39.

Fox, K.R. 1990. *The Physical Self-Perception Profile manual.* DeKalb, IL: Office for Health Promotion, Northern Illinois University.

Fox, K.R., Goudas, M., Biddle, S.J.H., Duda, J.L., and Armstrong, N. 1994. Children's task and ego goal profiles. *British Journal of Educational Psychology* 64: 253-61.

Goudas, M., and Biddle, S.J.H. 1994. Perceived motivational climate and intrinsic motivation in school physical education classes. *European Journal of Psychology of Education* 9: 241-50.

Goudas, M., Biddle, S.J.H., and Fox, K.R. 1994a. Achievement goal orientations and intrinsic motivation in physical fitness testing with children. *Pediatric Exercise Science* 6: 159-67.

—. 1994b. Perceived locus of causality, goal orientations, and perceived competence in school physical education classes. *British Journal of Educational Psychology* 64: 453-63.

Hart, E.A., Leary, M.R., and Rejeski, W.J. 1989. The measurement of social physique anxiety. *Journal of Sport and Exercise Psychology* 11: 94-104.

Harter, S. 1978. Effectance motivation reconsidered: Toward a developmental model. *Human Development* 21: 34-64.

Hofstetter, C.R., Hovell, M.F., Macera, C., Sallis, J.F., Spry, V., Barrington, E., Callender, L., Hackley, M., and Rauh, M. 1991. Illness, injury and correlates of aerobic exercise and walking: A community study. *Research Quarterly for Exercise and Sport* 62: 1-9.

Kendzierski, D. 1994. Schema theory: An information processing focus. In *Advances in exercise adherence,* ed. R.K. Dishman, 137-59. Champaign, IL: Human Kinetics.

Leary, M.R. 1992. Self-presentational processes in exercise and sport. *Journal of Sport and Exercise Psychology* 14: 339-51.

—. 1995. *Self-presentation: Impression management and interpersonal behavior.* Dubuque, IA: Brown & Benchmark.

Leary, M.R., Tchividjian, L.R., and Kraxberger, B.E. 1994. Self-presentation can be hazardous to your health: Impression management and health risk. *Health Psychology* 13: 461-70.

Maddux, J.E. 1993. Social cognitive models of health and exercise behavior: An introduction and review of conceptual issues. *Journal of Applied Sport Psychology* 5: 116-40.

Maehr, M.L., and Braskamp, L.A. 1986. *The motivation factor: A theory of personal investment.* Lexington, MA: Lexington Books.

Maehr, M., and Nicholls, J.G. 1980. Culture and achievement motivation: A second look. In *Studies in cross-cultural psychology*, ed. N. Warren, vol. 2, 221-67. London: Academic Press.

McAuley, E. 1991. Efficacy, attributional, and affective responses to exercise participation. *Journal of Sport and Exercise Psychology* 13: 382-93.

—. 1992. Understanding exercise behavior: A self-efficacy perspective. In *Motivation in sport and exercise*, ed. G.C. Roberts, 107-27. Champaign, IL: Human Kinetics.

McAuley, E., and Courneya, K.S. 1993. Adherence to exercise and physical activity as health-promoting behaviors: Attitudinal and self-efficacy influences. *Applied and Preventive Psychology* 2: 65-77.

Papaioannou, A. 1994. Development of a questionnaire to measure achievement orientations in physical education. *Research Quarterly for Exercise and Sport* 65: 11-20.

—. 1995. Motivation and goal perspectives in children's physical education. In *European perspectives in exercise and sport psychology*, ed. S.J.H. Biddle, 245-69. Champaign, IL: Human Kinetics.

Prochaska, J.O., and Marcus, B.H. 1994. The Transtheoretical model: Applications to exercise. In *Advances in exercise adherence*, ed. R.K. Dishman, 161-80. Champaign, IL: Human Kinetics.

Rodgers, W.M., and Brawley, L.R. 1993. Using both self-efficacy theory and the theory of planned behaviour to discriminate adherers and dropouts from structured programs. *Journal of Applied Sport Psychology* 5: 195-206.

Rummel, A., and Feinberg, R. 1988. Cognitive Evaluation Theory: A meta-analytic review of the literature. *Social Behavior and Personality* 16: 147-64.

Ryckman, R.M., Robbins, M.A., Thornton, B., and Cantrell, P. 1982. Development and validation of a Physical Self-Efficacy Scale. *Journal of Personality and Social Psychology* 42: 891-900.

Sallis, J.F., and Hovell, M.F. 1990. Determinants of exercise behavior. *Exercise and Sport Sciences Reviews* 18: 307-30.

Sallis, J.F., Hovell, M.F., Hofstetter, C.R., and Barrington, E. 1992. Explanation of vigorous physical activity during two years using social learning variables. *Social Science and Medicine* 34: 25-32.

Sarrazin, P., Biddle, S.J.H., Famose, J.P., Cury, F., Fox, K.R., and Durand, M. 1996. Goal orientations and conceptions of the nature of sport ability in children: A social cognitive approach. *British Journal of Social Psychology* 35: 399-414.

Schwarzer, R. 1992. Self-efficacy in the adoption and maintenance of health behaviours: Theoretical approaches and a new model. In *Self-efficacy: Thought control of action*, ed. R. Schwarzer, 217-43. Bristol, PA: Taylor & Francis.

Sonstroem, R., and Morgan, W.P. 1989. Exercise and self-esteem: Rationale and model. *Medicine and Science in Sports and Exercise* 21: 329-37.

Sports Council/Health Education Authority. 1992. *Allied Dunbar National Fitness Survey: Main findings.* London: Sports Council/Health Education Authority.

Stroebe, W., and Stroebe, M.S. 1995. *Social psychology and health.* Buckingham, England: Open University Press.

Tajfel, H. 1981. *Human groups and social categories: Studies in social psychology.* Cambridge: Cambridge University Press.

Thill, E.E., and Brunel, P. 1995. Cognitive theories of motivation in sport. In *European perspectives on exercise and sport psychology*, ed. S.J.H. Biddle, 195-217. Champaign, IL: Human Kinetics.

Veale, D. 1987. Exercise dependence. *British Journal of Addiction* 82: 735-40.

Weiner, B. 1992. *Human motivation: Metaphors, theories and research*. Newbury Park, CA: Sage.

Weiss, M.R. 1987. Self-esteem and achievement in children's sport and physical activity. In *Advances in pediatric sport sciences*, ed. D. Gould and M. Weiss, 87-119. Champaign, IL: Human Kinetics.

White, R. 1959. Motivation reconsidered: The concept of competence. *Psychological Review* 66: 297-333.

Whitehead, J. 1995. Multiple achievement orientations and participation in youth sport: A cultural and developmental perspective. *International Journal of Sport Psychology* 26: 431-52.

Whitehead, J.R. 1993. Physical activity and intrinsic motivation. *The President's Council on Physical Fitness and Sports. Physical Activity and Fitness Research Digest* 1 (2): 1-8.

Wiersma, U.J. 1992. The effects of extrinsic rewards in intrinsic motivation: A meta-analysis. *Journal of Occupational and Organizational Psychology* 65: 101-14.

CHAPTER 4

REFLECTIONS ON THE SOCIALLY CONSTRUCTED PHYSICAL SELF

ANDREW C. SPARKES

It is the exterior territories, or surfaces, of the body that symbolize the self at a time when unprecedented value is placed on the youthful, trim and sensual body.... In the affluent West, there is a tendency for the body to be seen as an entity which is in the process of becoming; a *project* which should be worked at and accomplished as part of the *individual's* self-identity. (Shilling 1993, 3-5)

The work of Shilling (1993) on "body projects" and Giddens' (1991) recent analysis of self-identity have highlighted the ever-increasing intimacy of the relationship between the self and the physical body throughout the life span in contemporary Western cultures. In this chapter, I explore and develop the work of these scholars by considering how the dominant body stories, or narratives, available in a culture shape not only who we think we are but also who we think we can become.

BODY, SELF, IDENTITY, AND THE INDIVIDUAL

"The body, therefore, is the prime symbol of the self, and the prime determinant of the self" (Synnott 1993, 2). There seems to be little agreement about the meaning of terms such as *self* and *identity*. Given this general lack of consensus I will make no attempt to define these terms. Instead, my purposes in this chapter are best served by providing a brief overview of how the relationships between the body, self, identity, and the individual have been addressed by particular scholars and sociological schools of thought. The recent work of Giddens (1991) provides a useful starting point. Giddens argues that the current period of high modernity (or postmodernity, as others might call it) is characterized by uncertainty and pervaded by a radical doubt—a doubt that insists that knowledge about what bodies are takes the form of hypotheses that are, in principle, always open to revision and may need at some point to be abandoned. Giddens (1991) suggests that in such a situation, individuals engage in a reflexive project of the self that consists of sustaining coherent yet continuously revised biographical narratives as they are forced to negotiate lifestyle choices among a diversity of options. Therefore, for Giddens, the body is not just a physical entity that is possessed but is an action system. Its practical immersion in the interactions of daily life is seen as an essential part of sustaining a coherent sense of self-identity in the context of life politics at both the local and global level.

Giddens (1991) further emphasizes that in the conditions of high modernity, bodies and the self become increasingly coordinated within the reflexive project of self-identity, as the body becomes more immediately relevant to the identity the individual promotes. However, Giddens points out that in high modernity, with its ongoing pluralization of milieu, settings, and locales in which competence is expected to be displayed, the maintenance of a coherent self-identity (of linking feelings of being at home in one's body and the personalized narrative) can become problematic. This problem of coherence is intensified for those who claim the emergence of a postmodern subject in contrast to the Enlightenment subject, or a sociological subject.

THE ENLIGHTENMENT SUBJECT AND THE SOCIOLOGICAL SELF

According to Hall (1992), the Enlightenment subject was based on an individualistic conception of a person as a fully centered, unified individual, endowed with the capacities of reason, consciousness, and action. Such individuals had a *center*, an inner core, which first emerged when the subject was born and unfolded with the person, remaining essentially the same—continuous or *identical* with itself—throughout the person's life span. The essential center of the self was the person's identity. In contrast, reflecting the growing complexity of the modern world along with the influence of symbolic interactionists like G.H. Mead and C.H. Cooley, the concept of the sociological self acknowledges that the inner core of the subject is not autonomous and self-sufficient, but formed in relation to *significant others.* In this view, identity is formed in the *interaction* between self and society. The subject is still taken to have an inner core or essence that he or she thinks of as the "real me," but this is formed and modified in a continuous dialogue with the cultural worlds "outside" and the identities they offer.

THE POSTMODERN SELF

Hall (1992) emphasizes that as we move toward the 21st century, the subject previously experienced as having a unified and stable identity is becoming fragmented. It is composed not of a single identity but of several, often contradictory and unresolved, identities. At the same time, Hall argues that the identities that made up the social landscapes "out there," which enabled our subjective conformity with the objective "needs" of the culture, are themselves breaking up because of rapid structural and institutional change. Consequently, Hall suggests, the very process of identification through which we project ourselves into our cultural identities becomes more open ended and problematic as identity becomes a movable feast. Therefore, "If we feel we have a unified identity from birth to death, it is only because we construct a comforting story or 'narrative of self' about ourselves" (277).

For postmodernists, any notion that the self exists as a separate, atomized, autonomous, and identifiable object is rejected as ideological, obsolete, or both. We now live in what Baudrillard (1983) calls an electronic, high-tech, media-orchestrated cyberculture. Consequently, Escobar (1994) suggests, cyberculture embodies the realization that we increasingly live and make ourselves in techno-biocultural environments structured by novel forms of science and technology that continually transform our sense of reality and consciousness. This has led Gergen (1991) and Gottschalk (1993) to talk of a saturated, overpopulated, and multiphrenic self resulting from a rapid expansion in the roles we consciously or unconsciously play as we experience the vertigo of unlimited multiplicity and a cacophony of potentials.

The value of the postmodern stance is to accentuate the problems that people encounter when they have to participate in pluralistic, multiethnic societies with varied lifestyles. The postmodernists' claims that the self is socially constructed, emergent and plural, and in a state of crisis cannot easily be ignored. But this is a long way from claiming that the self has disappeared completely and that the concept of a core of self has nothing to offer, as many postmodernists would suggest (Shalin 1993). One is able to acknowledge that the self with its connected identities is not something given once and for all, but is an ongoing accomplishment, without advocating the conceptual death of the self. This is particularly so if people are viewed as complex sign systems and texts of meaning that are culturally embedded. Here, as Schwalbe (1993) notes, acquiring identities is the process of acquiring sign values or, more simply, the process whereby the person becomes a complex sign: "These signs, which can be manifested in speech, posture, dress, body type, and so forth, evoke responses in others, and in the individual as s/he reflects on him or herself" (335).

Of course, as Schwalbe (1993) is quick to point out, this process of signification is extremely complex. For example, individuals can signify in multiple ways simultaneously; when they function as signs they can elicit any number of unintended responses; the meanings that individuals have as signs are greatly influenced by the context; and because ambiguity is inescapable, there can be no one true meaning of an individual as a sign. What this all means is that while the self cannot disappear, identities can and do. The latter happens when the signs that give meaning to a person lose their signifying force. Imagine if body size/shape were no longer taken to signify anything about a person's character. Then the signs that are read off the body about character would be defunct, as would the identities *fat* and *thin*. Therefore, as Schwalbe argues, "Identities can change or disappear, or come into being, as quickly as any kind of sign. As this happens, as people come to signify different things, the self changes" (335).

How we come to understand our bodies as sign systems and how we come to read them as scripts are, in turn, closely related to the stories or narratives available within any given culture. For Shotter (1993), within the shifting terrain of the postmodern world, the narrative resources available to people in making sense of their lives have increased, thus expanding the genres available. These increased narrative resources provide greater space and opportunities for crafting who we want to be and who we can be. However, as Shotter acknowledges, this increased resourcing is not equitably distributed. Some people have greater ease of access to some narratives than others within a political economy of developmental opportunities that limits who or what people can become: "We cannot just position ourselves as we please; we face differential invitations and barriers to all the 'movements' (actions and utterances) we might try to make" (6-7). Therefore, as the storied identity and self get constructed and reconstructed, a paradox appears that revolves around the issue of stability and change. If the self-contained coherent self is, as postmodernists argue, an *illusion* that people actively create, then this illusion seems necessary to make our way in, and make sense of, the world. This having been said, the impact of such an illusion is very real in its consequences in terms of how people relate to themselves and others.

THE SOCIALLY CONSTRUCTED BODY

From a social constructivist stance the physical body, and the senses, are essentially storied and eminently social. Indeed, as Synnott (1992, 1993) argues, the body *is* socially constructed and has no intrinsic meaning. In this sense, the one word *body* can signify very different realities and perceptions of reality as cultures create meanings of their own that can vary dramatically over time. As Synnott (1993) comments: "Each new age seems to create and re-construct the body in its own image and likeness; yet at any given time there are likely to be many paradigms of the body: competing, complementary, or contradictory. And no doubt the re-definitions of corporeality will continue in the twenty-first century" (36-37).

One indicator of the various and ever-changing constructions of the body (and therefore the embodied self) consists of the metaphors that have been attached to the body in different historical periods. Whether we think of the body as a tomb, a temple, an enemy, a machine, or the self makes a big difference in how we lead our lives and treat our bodies. This being the case, it is interesting to note that the constructions of the body in the 20th century have been dominated by notions of the *mechanical body* and the *body beautiful*. For Synnott (1993), the philosophical and political construction of the body during this period has been intertwined with scientific constructions (especially those of medical science) that have served to reinforce mechanistic and material constructions of the body. For example, in view of the rapid growth of plastic and reconstructive surgery, the body is no longer seen as "given" (meaning, traditionally, a gift from God), but is now taken to be plastic, to be molded and selected at need or whim by those who are financially well off. The body is not only plastic; it is also bionic, and artificial parts such as cardiac pacemakers and titanium hips are now regularly implanted. The body is also communal and interchangeable in its parts; organ transplants are now commonplace. Increasingly the body is engineered. Advances in our knowledge about genetic coding and the rise of gene therapy have led to talk of "designer babies." The body may now also be chosen—selected from a wide range of possibilities in sperm and ovum bank catalogues. These choices draw upon a range of new reproductive technologies that include in vitro fertilization, artificial insemination, surrogate motherhood, and embryo freezing.

Such capabilities, while apparently indicative of a movement toward a cyberculture, raise a host of ethical problems about the body and humanity that require urgent attention. They also clearly signal how the body has increasingly become a project in which appearance, size, shape, and even content are potentially open to reconstruction in line with the designs of its owner. As Shilling (1993) notes, treating the body as a project does not necessarily entail a full-time preoccupation with its wholesale transformation, although there is this potentiality. However, he argues, it does involve individuals' being conscious of and actively concerned about the management, maintenance, and appearance of their bodies. This involves a practical recognition of the significance of bodies, both as personal resources and as social symbols that give off messages about a person's self-identity.

In contemporary society there is now a diverse range of body projects on offer. This means that the body can be constructed in almost as many ways as there are individuals. As a consequence, in a pluralistic society, no consensus of meaning regarding the body can be expected since constructions will reflect the values not only of the culture, but also of the subculture and of specific individuals. Of course, as indicated earlier, this does not mean that people are free to choose just any kind of body project. The manner in which the body is constructed does not exist in a social or political vacuum but within systems of meaning (or discourses) that are imbued with power. That is, some constructions come to be more equal than others, some come to be more legitimate than others, and some get to be promoted above others. For example, nondisabled bodies are promoted over disabled bodies, and thin bodies are promoted over fat bodies in many Western cultures.

As Scott and Morgan (1993) point out, to construct some bodily feature or process is to describe it in a certain way, or to lay social emphasis on some aspect of the body is in some measure to exercise control or constraint. Likewise, to regulate or to exercise control over a body or bodies is to see these bodies in a particular way and to privilege certain understandings or constructions as against others. This is a normative process that highlights the manner in which the individual body is intimately linked to the social body. For example, seemingly individual characteristics such as a person's physical appearance, style, taste, manners, and bodily deportment are not merely personal idiosyncrasies but are highly influenced by sociocultural norms linked to social class, gender, and ethnicity. Similarly, the ways in which the state undertakes the surveillance and control of bodies is linked to how, in turn, individuals come to self-regulate and discipline their bodies in terms of exercise and dietary regimes.

Indeed, for Foucault (1977, 1979), the body is the ultimate site of political and ideological control, surveillance, and regulation that since the 18th century has been the focal point for the exercise of disciplinary power (see Smart 1985; Turner 1984). By this he means that through the body and its behaviors, various state apparatuses such as medicine, the educational system, psychiatry, and the law have come to define the limits of behavior. These apparatuses not only record the activities of populations but also punish those bodies that violate established boundaries, and thereby render bodies docile, productive, and politically and economically useful. In the following sections, I want to develop some of these points by looking at a few of the dominant story lines that operate to shape the development of individual body projects in the context of the wider society.

INDIVIDUAL BODY PROJECTS AND CONSUMER CULTURE

To begin to understand the notion of private, individualized bodies that dominates our thinking today we need to revisit the Renaissance as it began in Italy during the 14th century. According to Synnott (1992), it was during this period that physical beauty began to be appreciated for its own, secular sake rather than as a rung on the ladder to God as in the view that had prevailed in earlier Christian times. The secularization of the body was linked to growing standards of refinement that began to define more and more instinctive and natural behaviors, for example spitting, as indelicate and unmannerly. Synnott suggests that these new notions of civility began to privatize the body so that people increasingly distanced themselves from bodily functions and the body itself—their own and those of other people. Drawing upon the work of Elias (1982) on the civilizing process, he attributes these changes in the discourse on, and the living of the body to the rise of individualism during the Renaissance and, more specifically, to the breakdown of group identities as defined by feudalism and the church.

The notion of the body as personal and private gathered pace following the Renaissance, and it now saturates contemporary consciousness. In relation to this, Shilling (1993) also draws upon the works of Norbert Elias and Pierre Bourdieu to suggest that the increased individualization and privatization of bodies in modern society tend to leave people alone with their bodies "investing more time and effort in their monitoring, control and appearance" (125). Much of this investment is in the pursuit of what Featherstone (1991) calls "the look." For him, the vast range of dietary, slimming, exercise, and cosmetic body maintenance products currently produced, marketed, and sold points to the significance of appearance and bodily preservation within late capitalist society that encourages the individual to adopt instrumental strategies to combat deterioration and decay. Here, the prime purpose of the maintenance of the inner body becomes the enhancement of the appearance of the outer body.

This "look," according to Kirk (1993), works around dominant definitions of appropriate body shape and physical attractiveness in which slenderness and high muscle tone or definition are important. This is especially so where the body is presented as a symbol of health, success, and wealth. Kirk points out that since the 1950s a cluster of ideas centering on body shape have been tightly interwoven as the dangers of consumerism and sedentariness, and its links to heart disease, have been popularized on a mass scale. In this context, body shape has become a critical sign of success, control, and personal worthiness while fatness has increasingly become a metaphor for ugliness, indulgence, greed, and sloth. In a similar fashion, Featherstone (1991) points out that in consumer culture those who can get their body to approximate the idealized images of youth, health, fitness, and beauty have a higher economic exchange value than those who cannot, or do not wish to, match such idealized images.

The values previously described, and stylized images of the body, are themselves constructed and circulated via advertisements, the popular press, television, and motion pictures. In all of this, Featherstone (1991) points out that the popular media constantly emphasize the cosmetic benefits of body maintenance—a term that indicates the popularity of the machine metaphor for the body. Featherstone continues. Here, like cars and other consumer goods, the body requires servicing, regular care, and attention to preserve maximum efficiency. Consequently, people tend to transform free time into maintenance work. This has the effect of imposing even greater demands on the individual and makes the monitoring of the current state of bodily performance essential if people are to get the most out of life: a hectic life that increases the need for *human servicing*.

As part of this body maintenance and servicing, a range of technologies or "disciplines" are invoked, such as diet, exercise, chemicals, and surgery, that are aimed predominantly at physical transformation. Here the rewards for ascetic body work cease to be spiritual salvation or even improved health, but become an enhanced appearance and a more marketable self. The pursuit of this goal leads to a preoccupation with fat, diet, and slenderness that in turn functions as a powerful *normalizing* strategy ensuring the production of "docile bodies" (Foucault 1977). These bodies are self-monitoring and self-disciplining, sensitive to any departure from social norms, and are constantly striving for self-improvement and transformation in the service of these norms.

FRAMING THE SELF AND BODY—THE IDEOLOGY OF INDIVIDUALISM

People come to understand their bodies within consumer culture. In doing so they come to understand their exchange value in the order of things, and with this their sense of self and their self-esteem are formed. Importantly, these understandings are developed within a cultural system that contains a range of ideologies including mesomorphism, healthism, youthism, and lifestylism (Colquhoun 1991; Crawford 1980; Featherstone 1987; Kirk and Colquhoun 1989; Sparkes 1991; Tinning 1990). At the heart of these lies the dominant ideology of individualism that pervades Western cultures. It works as a system of beliefs that is central to the process of producing meanings and ideas in our society relating to issues such as the body, health, wealth, and poverty.

According to Naidoo (1986), the essential core of individualism rests upon the belief that individual free choice is both an accurate account of the status quo and the most desirable goal to aim for in social affairs. However, individualism is a complex concept and there are many strands operating within its boundaries that contain a range of ambiguities. In this regard, Tinning (1990) suggests that while most of us would have little quarrel with the apparent concerns of individualism for individual autonomy, independence, and equality of opportunity, we might be more concerned that the ideology of individualism supports the questionable notion that an individual is fully and solely responsible for his or her own actions and life situation. That is, individualism as a meta-theory contains, and actively promotes, the age-old notion that individuals—rather than social structures, subcultures, or other forces—are ultimately responsible for their status in systems of social inequality (Smith and Stone 1989). Such a view now permeates our thinking.

Individualism would channel people to see things like body shape and health as operating along similar lines. Accordingly, everyone has the opportunity to adopt an active and healthy lifestyle, to work out and reach the slim, trim, taut, and terrific body shape. Indeed, governments now exhort people to take responsibility for maintaining personal bodily health. Likewise, current health promotion campaigns focus on the individual by associating the so-called lifestyle diseases with individual behaviors (Sparkes 1991). The rationale behind such campaigns is that the incidence of illness will be diminished if the members of the population can be persuaded to exercise greater control over their bodily deportment. To achieve this control, or so the rhetoric goes, people require information about the risks associated with "bad" behaviors so that they can be encouraged by a range of initiatives to adopt "good" behaviors. What kind of information is provided, how this information is presented, and what gets defined as good and bad behaviors are rarely problematized (Lupton 1994).

Within an individualistic framework, the individual unconsciously exerts disciplinary power both over others and over the self through self-regulation. Those who do not self-regulate are often viewed with moral indignation and at times with open hostility by those who do. As part of this process, those who do not meet the societal ideals of self-regulation often internalize feelings of anxiety and guilt about their apparent lack of self-control. This is particularly so in relation to body shape and health. Here, individualism asserts, those who do not have slim, healthy bodies must have chosen not to. Therefore, they have only themselves to blame for the consequences. In its crudest form this becomes victim blaming of the worst kind. Of course, this is not to deny the value of individual free choice, or to deny that people can take responsibility for their own health. However, dangers arise when the emphasis on the personal gets divorced from the social framework that gives it meaning. As Hyland (1988) comments:

> For many such "victims" the appeal to autonomy is false and insincere for it diverts attention away from the class, gender, and racial inequalities which, for a large proportion of the population makes real choice impossible. More importantly, this approach displays a willful disregard for epidemiological evidence which clearly demonstrates that health and illness are socially constructed . . . and that individual lifestyles pale into insignificance beside the structural inequalities which militate against healthy living. (26)

Here it is important to realize that blaming is a social construct, a reflection of a world view, social stereotypes, and political biases, that have always combined to allow some groups in society to pass moral judgment on the misfortune of others. As Nelkin and Gilman (1988) point out, in situations of anxiety, locating blame is in effect a strategy of control that defines normality and establishes the boundaries of healthy behavior and appropriate social relationships. They note that several categories of blame can be found in popular discourse. For example, some diseases have been attributed to particular racial groups or social stereotypes, to individual lifestyle, and to immoral behavior.

In contemporary society, issues of lifestyle have been of central importance and form a crucial link between individualism, victim blaming, and the politics of diversion. In combination, these operate to deflect attention away from the broader social structures that limit individual power and shape the choices available to people in different sections of society regarding how their bodies are treated, developed, and used by themselves and others (Ingham 1985). Developing such thoughts, Shilling (1993) points to the irony of the situation currently confronting people in Western cultures that although their health is threatened increasingly by global dangers, they are exhorted ever more to take individual responsibility for their bodies by engaging in strict self-care systems, and thereby seek solace in their individual bodies. It has been suggested by some that this retreat to the body as an island of security in the face of a recalcitrant outside world is part of a more wholesale movement toward the narcissistic cultivation of bodily appearance.

THE PERFORMING BODY AND THE SELF

According to Lasch (1980), a narcissistic type of individual began to emerge in the 1920s when a new relationship was constructed between the body and the self. These individuals are excessively self-conscious, chronically uneasy about their health, afraid of aging and dying, and constantly searching for flaws and signs of decay; they attempt to sell their selves as if their personalities were a commodity and are haunted by fantasies of omnipotence and eternal youth. In relation to this development, Featherstone (1991) emphasized the importance of the rise of consumer culture, as described earlier, which approximately coincides with the emergence of the culture of narcissism. As a result, he suggests, a new conception of self has emerged, revolving around the performing self, that places greater emphasis upon appearance, display, and the management of impressions. This increased recognition of the significance of bodies, both as personal resources and as social symbols that give off messages about a person's self-identity, firmly locates the performing self within Shilling's (1993) notion of body projects. As Giddens (1991) notes, "Consumer capitalism, with its efforts to standardize consumption and to shape tastes through advertising, plays a basic role in furthering narcissism. . . . Hence all of us, in modern social conditions, live as though surrounded by mirrors; in these we search for the appearance of an unblemished, socially valued self" (172).

Recent changes that have taken place in the material aspects of daily life, involving the restructuring of social space, have provided an environment that facilitates the display of the body and the importance that this displaying has for the lives of individuals. This point was emphasized by Goffman (1959) in his classic book *The Presentation of Self in Everyday Life*, which focused on how people, during everyday interaction with others, perform roles and present their selves in different ways depending upon the audience and the context.

Not to display in the appropriate manner according to the context can have drastic consequences. For example, it can mean the difference between being accepted into a social group and being rejected or excluded from the group. It can mean the difference between having our sense of self confirmed and having it denied by significant others in our life. It can lead people to have what Goffman (1963) called *stigmatized* identities. As early as in ancient Greece the term stigma was taken to refer to bodily signs that supposedly exposed something unusual or bad about the moral status of a person. More than ever, as Goffman outlines, the body is one of the key sources of stigma in a contemporary society that places so much attention on the performing body. As a sign system the body is highly visible and announces itself to everybody, even though it can be concealed under clothes. It is open to many readings and categorizations. Within this process "normality" gets defined and anything that falls outside is marginalized and stigmatized. As Morris (1993) points out in relation to the prejudice and discrimination experienced by people with disabilities, "Our difference is measured against normality and found wanting. Our physical and intellectual characteristics are not 'right' nor 'admirable' and we do not 'belong'" (16).

In a similar fashion, Bovey (1989) has shown how other bodily features such as the condition of being fat can lead to persecution and discrimination in everyday life. In short, in a physicalist society that celebrates the performing self, being physically "different" is likely to invoke a whole range of biases and prejudices in other people. This having been said, it needs to be made clear that stigmas are not a reflection of inherent weaknesses in a person's body or character. They are social labels created by the reactions of others (usually defined by the dominant or majority groups) in a society. Those who fail to live up to people's expectations and stereotypes about "normal" physical appearance and behavior tend to get disqualified from full social acceptance. In this way the process of stigmatization tells us as much about the "normal" others as it does about the stigmatized person. It also tells us a great deal about how notions of normality within any given society are constructed over time and how this process acts as a particular form of social control.

Having said all this, we cannot escape the importance of the performing body as a sign system, as a way of representing ourselves to others. Ultimately, Featherstone (1991) concludes, "Individuals may of course choose to ignore or neglect their appearance and refuse to cultivate the performing self, yet if they do so they must be prepared to face the implications of this choice within social encounters" (192).

The performing self is constructed along social class lines. That is, different classes and class fractions tend to develop distinct orientations toward their bodies that result in the creation of various bodily forms. In relation to this, Shilling (1993) has provided an interpretation and elaboration of the works of Bourdieu (1978, 1984, 1986). Bourdieu recognizes the unfinishedness of the body, the fact that the body is a project, and notes that acts of labor are required to turn bodies into social entities. These acts can influence how people develop and hold the physical shape of their bodies and learn how to present their bodies through styles of walk, talk, and dress. These body techniques are not natural; rather they represent highly skilled and socially differentiated accomplishments that people start to learn early in childhood. Therefore, for Bourdieu, the performing body as it develops bears the imprint of an individual's social class via the interrelation between the individual's social location, habitus, and taste. These factors are taken to perpetuate the different relationships that social groups have toward their bodies and how they represent themselves, and are central in guiding the lifestyle choices that people make.

With regard to social class differences in orientations to the body, Shilling (1993) points out that the working classes tend to develop an instrumental relationship with their body because, as a matter of necessity, they have little free time. Consequently the body becomes a means to an end, which impacts upon how bodies get treated in daily life and the kinds of sport and leisure activities chosen in time not spent working. There are also gender divisions within the working class. Shilling (1993) points out that the double burden of waged and unwaged work faced by many wives and mothers means that they tend to develop an even more instrumental relationship to their bodies than men. Working-class women tend to have little time at all for sport/leisure activities apart from those that are compatible with work. Therefore these women often develop orientations to their bodies that are strongly marked by the need to earn money and service the needs of the household.

In contrast, Shilling (1993) argues, the dominant classes have more time and resources to treat the body as a project in certain ways. These classes are less concerned than others with producing a large, strong body and more concerned with reproducing a slim body better suited to a world in which, for them, economic practice is closely linked to the presentation of the self. Orientations to the body become increasingly more finely differentiated within the dominant classes; for example, the upwardly mobile middle classes often engage in fitness training for its own sake. Likewise, women tend to be encouraged more than men to develop their bodies as objects of perception for others. In short, the work of Bourdieu suggests that different social classes produce distinct bodily forms and, most importantly, that there are substantial inequalities in the symbolic values accorded to particular bodily forms.

THE GENDERED-SEXUAL BODY

Masculinity and femininity are not inherent in the body; they are definitions given socially to certain characteristics. That is, "masculine" and "feminine" are social realities rather than biological realities. Indeed, the social process of categorization that begins during infancy in relation to gender construction often contradicts the bodily bases on which the categorization rests. Accordingly, we learn to be what men and women are supposed to be in our society.

In what follows, I want to focus on some of the social or disciplinary practices that produce the recognizable female body in many Western cultures and the manner in which this has implications for female identity and subjectivity. One powerful category that women quickly become aware of relates to body size and shape, according to which Bartky (1988) states, they aim "to produce a body of a certain size and general configuration" (64). As mentioned earlier in this chapter, the fashionable female body is taut and slim. Conversely, massiveness, power, or abundance is met with distaste and moral damnation. As Bovey (1989), drawing on her own experiences, comments:

> Being fat is about knowing it. It is about a round-the-clock awareness that the fat person's body overflows the strict boundaries imposed on it by Western social and cultural norms. To be a fat woman is to carry a double burden, for woman are expected to conform to a more rigorous and stereotyped aesthetic ideal. . . . Being fat is about experiencing hatred and contempt. (1)

Not surprisingly, dieting becomes an important discipline for regulating body size and shape in relation to cultural norms that reflect the particular aesthetic standards of the time. In this regard, as Bordo (1990) argues, the evidence is overwhelming that women in our culture are more tyrannized by the contemporary slenderness ideal than men, as they typically have been by beauty ideals in general. Women and girls are more prone than men to see themselves as "too fat" and are more likely to engage in crash dieting, laxative abuse, and compulsive exercising, and they are far more vulnerable to eating disorders than males. For Bordo, this preoccupation with fat, diet, and slenderness is one of the most powerful normalizing strategies of the 20th century operating to ensure the production of self-monitoring and self-disciplining docile bodies. Talking of her own early preoccupation with the size of her body, Kissling (1992) recalls, "I considered myself to be fat regardless of my weight and believed that my body was something that I had to get control over. This control usually took the form of food restrictions and diets. I no longer remember the age at which I went on my first diet; it was before my first menstrual period" (136).

The body fascism and tyranny of slenderness that women in particular are subjected to in Western cultures links to a second category of disciplinary practices identified by Bartky (1988). This focuses on bringing forth from the body of women a specific range of gestures, postures, and movements that revolve around constriction, grace, and "a certain eroticism restrained by modesty" (68). In this context, as Therberge (1992) observes, the gendering of exercise (as well as diet) plays a crucial part: "Although both men and women exercise, the meaning and aim of these activities may differ, and there is a set of activities (classes, videos, etc.) for women alone that concentrate on form, appearance, and feminization" (126). The aerobics boom during recent years provides a case in point. According to Warrick and Tinning (1989), as a recreational activity, aerobics is group based and noncompetitive. It is available to varying age groups and is equated with fitness, physique improvement, and social interaction. Furthermore, it involves movements incorporating rhythm, grace, coordination, and flexibility. It would seem that aerobics is the epitome of the culturally acceptable type of feminine female activity. However, as Warrick and Tinning are quick to point out, aerobics participation is not without its problems, since it can liberate *and* oppress women with respect to their perception of their own bodies. They comment:

> On the one hand the potential for exercise to enhance self and body image and cathexis has been well documented. . . . On the other hand the subculture of aerobics, with its emphasis on body weight and shape control, tends to reinforce the cult of slenderness which for many women is a source of anxiety, frustration and oppression. (8)

Different forms of physical activity have various symbolic meanings for women, meanings that have deep historical roots (see Hargreaves 1994; Lenskyj 1986; Mangan and Park 1987; Scraton 1992). In this regard, Coakley (1978) has noted some general principles relating to the ways in which certain forms of sport are deemed suitable or not suitable for women based on the specific kind of physical activity involved. For example, it is not appropriate for women to engage in contests in which the resistance of the opponent is overcome by bodily contact, the resistance of a heavy object is overcome by the direct application of bodily force, or the body is projected into or through space over long distances or for extended periods of time. In contrast, it is wholly appropriate for women identified with the more favored levels of socioeconomic status to engage in contests in which the resistance of a light object is overcome with a light implement, the body is projected in or though space in aesthetically pleasing patterns, the velocity and maneuverability of the body are increased by the use of some manufactured device, or a spatial barrier prevents bodily contact with the opponent in face-to-face forms of competition.

Given that Coakley was writing in the 1970s, it might be expected that things have changed dramatically to reflect the "new" liberated and active image of women in the 1990s unfettered by gender assumptions. Unfortunately, this does not seem to be the case. For example, while it remains acceptable for women to play tennis or gymnastics, it is less acceptable for women to become wrestlers, boxers, power lifters, or shot and discus throwers. Indeed, women engaging in the latter activities are often subjected to a range of negative comments, prejudices, and biases that operate to question their sexuality and demean their performances as active women. As Woods (1992) argues, "to be athletic is to be equated with masculinity and masculine women are labelled as lesbian. Therefore, athletic women are stereotyped as lesbian" (91).

Griffin (1992) illustrates the various effects of the power of the lesbian label to intimidate. In particular, it leads many heterosexual and lesbian sportswomen and physical educators to distance themselves from the lesbian image by embracing traditional standards of femininity and cultivating high-profile heterosexual images, in ways that support a heterosexist and homophobic culture (Griffin and Genasci 1990; Lenskyj 1991; Sparkes 1994b). In this regard, Hargreaves (1994) has provided a number of important insights into the process of image making and the sexualized female body in the domain of sports, reflecting the prevalence of images of women's bodies in Western culture, and into the ways in which these operate to reproduce a system of *dominant heterosexuality*.

For example, Hargreaves notes how body presentation that makes more visible the form and sexuality of the female body has become increasingly noticeable in particular female sports. To return to the point made earlier about "feminine-appropriate" activities that confirm the popular image of femininity and demonstrate its essential difference from popular images of sporting masculinity, this is particularly so with activities that emphasize balance, coordination, flexibility, and grace such as gymnastics, ice skating, and synchronized swimming. In this regard, the favored images produced by the media play a crucial role. Likewise, Duncan (1990) has illustrated how the photographic images of female athletes in the media put them in glamour poses, ignoring their skills of performance and highlighting their sexuality. In so doing, these images turn the athletes into objects of desire and envy as unambiguously sexual women.

Media images are incredibly important in shaping the gendered scripts made available to people. These images do not, however, work alone; rather they are interlinked with other sites of cultural reproduction that reinforce the dominant script. For example, Scraton's (1992) research into the practices and policies of physical education (PE) in British secondary schools demonstrates that deep-rooted assumptions about femininity relating to the categories of physical ability/capacity, motherhood, and sexuality—assumptions that have historically underpinned the provision of physical activity for girls in schools—remain firmly entrenched today. These assumptions and images of femininity that prevail in contemporary PE are seen to shape not only what is made available to young women during curricular and extracurricular time, but how it is organized and also how it is taught. Such social practices provide powerful messages to young women (and young men) about themselves and their relationship to their own bodies and the bodies of others.

It would seem that while the overt forms of instruction about techniques of being female and feminine have altered as conceptions of gender have shifted, the body stories and scripts available to women remain limited (Hill and Brackenridge 1989). In particular, many women remain constrained by representational codes that position them as passive vehicles of display and the object of "the look." As Craik (1994) points out with regard to fashion, this look is structured by the normative male gaze to make women appear "as objects of desire and repositories of pleasure" (46). This, in turn, relates to the third category of disciplinary practices noted by Bartky (1988), which is directed to "the display of the body as an ornamented surface" (70). The appropriate use of makeup and the choice of clothing can be understood here as disciplinary practices that, in combination with the others previously discussed, act to achieve a feminine embodiment and feminine subjectivity. Consequently, the body becomes a site on which feminine cultural ideals can quite literally be manufactured. As Betterton (1987) argues, "Paintings, advertisements, pornography, and fashion are all practices which produce particular ways of seeing the feminine body" (9).

Of course, this is not to say that the practices do not go uncontested or that they are not available for manipulation and transformation. For example, in discussing the kinds of body work that women have conventionally been expected to carry out in our society, Miller and Penz (1991) point to the restrictive danger of accounts that locate this body work entirely within male discourses of domination and that rehearse only the dominant patriarchal meanings of body work. They argue that these meanings do not exhaust the possibilities. The management of appearance need not inevitably be in the service of male desire, since body work can be used to protest against and challenge the dominant social order. It is to one such challenge, and its attendant contradictions, that I now turn.

CHALLENGES TO THE DOMINANT BODY ORDER

"Female body-building makes an unashamed display of the feminine physique, and creates radical notions of the female body, beauty and sexuality" (Hargreaves 1994, 168). This is particularly so with regard to highly developed muscularity that in the past has been reserved for male bodies, muscles having always symbolized and represented the embodiment of masculine power. Consequently, the image of the heavily muscled female bodybuilder remains threatening as it is difficult to assimilate into the taken-for-granted "natural" categories that structure everyday life and as it challenges conventional constructions of gender and the basis for sexual differentiation. As Mansfield and McGinn (1993) note, "This image is clearly not safe enough for consumption yet, even (or should it be especially) in the market of fitness products" (52).

In the world of professional bodybuilding this creates representational problems for those (predominantly men) who control the sport and for those females who compete. This is clearly illustrated in the study by Mansfield and McGinn (1993), who focus on the different meanings that bodybuilding has for men and women, and the manner in which the available discourses within bodybuilding act to constrain the latter and incorporate them into a socialization process that "makes them safe" for consumption (also see Klein 1993). Within the world of bodybuilding, gendered discourses operate to define "acceptable" levels of muscularity for women, and those who achieve too great a muscular mass just don't win competitions. Hargreaves (1994) emphasizes this point by giving details of the guidelines for assessing the female physique provided in 1984 by the *International Federation of Body Builders Constitution and Rule Book for Judges, Athletes and Officials:*

> The judge must bear in mind that he or she is judging a woman's body-building competition and is looking for the ideal *feminine* physique. Therefore, the most important aspect is shape, a feminine shape. The other aspects are similar to those described for assessing men, but in regard to muscular development, it must not be carried to excess where it resembles the massive musculature of the male physique. (cited in Hargreaves 1994, 275)

Although, as Hargreaves (1994) points out, in 1993 the International Federation of Body Builders changed its guidelines and professional rules for assessing the feminine physique, it still protected the right of the judges to make subjective assessments according to their preferred definitions of femininity. The new guidelines suggested that women should be encouraged to develop as much muscle mass as possible as long as this development conformed to the accepted standards of bodybuilding aesthetics, that is, symmetry, shape, proportion, definition, etc. Therefore, just as in 1984, the focus of assessment remains on the extent of muscularity that is acceptable for the female frame. These notions of feminine shape act to impose narrow definitions of femininity and sexuality, and further function to marginalize and mask alternatives.

Accordingly, both Nead (1992) and Hargreaves (1994) acknowledge the contradictory position that female bodybuilders find themselves in with regard to being simultaneously empowered and manipulated. As muscular women they do challenge the "natural" order of gender, but their sport is characterized as one that produces a distorted masculine body upon which stereotyped symbols of femininity can be imposed. Furthermore, to become muscular they must adhere to strict (often health damaging) diets in order to reduce their body fat and enhance muscle definition. This process eliminates breast definition, and in order to balance the dual demands of muscle and sex appeal (in male terms), some female bodybuilders are undergoing reconstructive surgery and having silicon breast implants in order to artificially meet the criteria they will be judged on in competition (MacNeill 1988). Hargreaves also adds that when the woman with a muscular body adorns herself with the accoutrements of mainstream femininity, for example by wearing a bikini, putting ribbons in the hair, and wearing makeup, then she is making a statement that overrides her athletic image. That is, often in female bodybuilding, idealized femininity and sexuality are prior to and more significant than muscularity and athleticism.

Therefore, the potential to blur the conventional definitions of gendered identity for female bodybuilders certainly exists; but these efforts are counteracted and resisted by, for example, the images of the muscular male body found in bodybuilding advertisements that, as visual and narrative texts, represent the male muscular body as a "naturalized" embodiment of power, authority, and masculine superiority. An analysis by White and Gillett (1994) of advertisements in *Flex*, a leading bodybuilding journal, illustrates how the bodybuilding discourse promotes the muscular body as a powerful endorsement of a culture built on male domination. This is done by foregrounding the muscles as signifiers of dominant masculinity in such a way as to undermine the potential legitimacy of alternative body images, and at the same time reinforcing the subordinate status of women and counterhegemonic masculinities.

Despite the tensions and contradictions that have been outlined in relation to female bodybuilding, it is important to emphasize that this activity does provide a potential site of resistance to dominant stories that conventionally define the appropriate female body. Female bodybuilders do provide some space for the emergence of differing versions of the self that reject conventional standards of feminine beauty. As a consequence, in examining the play of meaning attached to female bodybuilding, Miller and Penz (1991) warn against emphasizing the restrictive patriarchal uses of this concept since it can also be used to broaden women's possibilities by providing a window of opportunity that they discursively exploit to their own ends as an act of resistance.

FUTURE RESEARCH ON THE STORIED BODY AND SELF

For the body, despite its apparent immediacy, is never knowable in direct, unmediated ways. Instead, we know it through its discourses, the many meanings and senses that have accrued with it. (Miller and Penz 1991, 148)

Throughout this chapter, I have attempted to develop Shilling's (1993) notion of body projects and link this with the reflexive project of the self that Giddens (1991) suggests is a central characteristic of Western cultures. I have argued that the linkage between the two is through the production, reproduction, and transformation of life stories or narratives. According to McAdams (1985), identity is a life story. For him the problem of identity is the problem of arriving at a life story that makes sense (provides unity and purpose) within a sociohistorical matrix that embodies a much larger story. A person's world establishes parameters for life stories so that identity is truly psychosocial. That is, the life story is a joint product of person and environment. In a sense, the two write the story together.

In recent years there has been a resurgence of interest in the relationship between stories or narratives and the life as lived (Riessman 1993; Widdershoven 1993). For example, Bruner (1987) talks of life as narrative. He is particularly interested in the self-narratives, or autobiographies, that we construct about ourselves as part of a continuing interpretation and reinterpretation of our experiences that are part of the process of "life making." Bruner suggests that the ways of telling stories and the ways of conceptualizing that go with them become so habitual that they finally become recipes for restructuring experience itself and for laying down routes into memory. All of this not only guides the life narrative up to the present but also directs it into the future.

It would seem that the stories we are told, and the stories we learn to tell, about ourselves and our bodies are important in terms of how we come to impose order on our embodied experiences and make sense of events and actions in our lives (Kaskisaari 1994; Kosonen 1993; Silvennoinen 1993, 1994; Sparkes 1996; Tiihonen 1994). As individuals construct past events and actions in personal narratives they engage in a dynamic process of claiming identities and constructing lives. How individuals recount their histories (what they emphasize or omit) has a direct bearing on what they can claim of their lives.

Just as we can think of storied lives, so we can think of storied bodies and storied selves. In doing so, particular analytical lenses become available for exploring the relationships between the embodied self and the wider society that structures and shapes the stories available to particular individuals and groups. Or, in Bruner's (1987) terms, we can begin to interrogate the recipes that a culture provides for the construction of autobiographical narratives. For example, the work of Gergen and Gergen (1993) clearly illustrates how bodies are gendered in autobiographies. The narratives will also be framed in relation to other social categories that people can occupy in terms of age, social class, race and ethnicity, physical ability, and sexual orientation. Therefore, if indeed we do live our lives within frameworks of meaning that invite or constrain, celebrate or oppress, then there is a need to interrogate the dominant story lines that frame the physical self and its associated identities and to tease out how our understandings of who we are, and who we might be, are culturally located. This exploration into the physical self as storied should avoid deterministic views that provide little scope, or hope, for individual or social change. Rather, it should seek to understand better the socially constructed nature of the body and self via cultural stories and narratives so that these can be challenged and changed over time. As I have indicated in this chapter, this is no easy task, but at least the potential is there.

In exploring this potential a range of issues need to be considered. For example, people can and do create self-consistency in the face of a multiplicity of available selves and body projects across the life span. This raises the issue of *how* we recognize the diversity of selves that we are able to project in social situations and at the same time maintain at least some continuity of self across social situations and across time. Issues are also raised with regard to how people get to change their stories to create a different sense of self and identity. This is particularly so when body projects are interrupted or thrown irretrievably off course so that the self we thought we were, and acted to maintain along with a variety of related identities, no longer makes sense in a new context. Here, an obvious example is provided by the identity dilemmas faced when individuals experience chronic illness or when sportsmen or sportswomen suffer serious injuries that prematurely terminate their sporting careers. How do people accommodate and make sense of such fateful moments and turning points in their life stories? What impact does such an event have on the life story as told before the injury or illness, and how does the newly constructed story impact on the future life of the individual? What stories are available within the wider culture for individuals to draw upon in this reconstruction? Are such stories empowering or oppressive? Do they lead to an improved quality of life, a positive self-image, and hope for the future, or the reverse?

These questions are of no small importance. For example, in a study of the identity dilemmas of chronically ill men, Charmaz (1994) indicates that many men do not have the narrative resources available to develop a different story line for their lives following illness and instead cling to stories that attempt to recapture the past self.

> Before men learn these new ways of preserving self, many of them assume that they will recapture *the* past self, or explicitly aim to do so. Here, they aim to reclaim the same identities, the same lives that they had before illness. Nothing else will do. For these men, their "real" selves are and must be only the past self. . . . They lapse into invalidism and despondency if they cannot recapture their past selves. . . . Attempting to recapture the past self has its pitfalls when all valued social and personal identities remain in the irretrievable past. Being unable to measure up to the past self results in further preoccupation with it, and heightens identity dilemmas. (Charmaz 1994, 278-79)

Charmaz (1994) then argues that for many men, as the distance increases between their past self (now reconstructed in memory in idealized form) and present identities, the former valued identities collapse and new ones are viewed as negative. Significantly, with each identity loss due to chronic illness, the preservation of valued past "masculine" identities becomes increasingly difficult. This is particularly so, Charmaz argues, when men draw upon the existing cultural logic that currently defines masculinity as they try to make sense of their altered selves and situations. In a similar fashion, Young, White, and McTeer (1994) speak of disempowered masculinity in relation to male athletes who experience injury. They note that such experiences as unwanted weight gain or loss, feelings of ostracism, and depleted personal worth force many athletes to recognize, perhaps for the first time, that the physical body and its talents are integrally tied to the self and relationships. The authors add, "For men who conceive of sport in a principally gendered fashion, then, injury has consequences for the masculine self" (187).

As part of a multidisciplinary quest to gain a greater understanding of how people make sense of fateful moments and turning points in their lives such as the occurrence of illness and injury, and how these events impact upon their sense of self, several research traditions from various paradigms have a contribution to make (Sparkes 1992). Here it is interesting to note that Kleiber and Brock (1992), in a quantitative study of the effect of career-ending injuries on the subsequent well-being of elite college athletes, concluded that interpretive forms of inquiry would be required in the future to more fully determine the subjective impact of injury on the lives of athletes. In keeping with what has been advanced throughout this chapter, they suggest that for the injured athletes in their study, a career in sport was central to an unfolding life story, a story in which the presumed conclusion had been dramatically altered. Their views support the use of narrative approaches to understanding a person's experience of illness and injury, involving both an unpleasant sense of disruption of the body and a threat to the integrated sense of self that the person has constructed over time.

Others have also made a strong case for the use of narrative studies in understanding the subjective experiences of illness and injury on the sense of self (Brock and Kleiber 1994; Kleinman 1988; Sparkes in press, 1996). With this in view, the following are some questions that researchers into the self might need to consider in the future:

1. How do men and women positioned in associated social categories (e.g., temporarily able-bodied/disabled; working/middle/upper class; heterosexual/bisexual/lesbian/gay; white persons/persons of color; active/nonactive) come to know, construct, and understand their bodies and sense of self? Do different people have equal opportunities to tell the same life stories, or are they restricted to separate spheres? How do people come to accept some story lines for their lives but reject others?

2. What are the dominant narratives or stories that influence self-identity and structure the lives of various groups? What are the politics of such storytelling and narrative construction? What are the processes that lead some narratives to be privileged, foregrounded, and institutionalized while others are suppressed, marginalized, or silenced?

3. If men and women do inscribe their lives differently, what might be the consequences of these differences for their own lives—for example, in terms of physical and psychological health and feelings of self-worth?

4. What are the key turning points, fateful moments, or critical incidents in a life that stabilize or fracture, change, or integrate the self, and how do people react and adjust to and cope with these moments? For example, in relation to interrupted body projects, what are the conditions that shape whether a person will construct a positive identity or sink into depression?

5. How can the dominant, traditional narratives and stories that reflect cultural trends and shape the repertoire of life story possibilities be challenged? How can alternatives be created that enable people to alter the trajectories and experiences of their lives so that they can create novel body-self relationships?

To address such questions, we require research forms that can deal with the reflexive project of the self and the constant updating of the biographical narrative as a lifelong process. Traditional forms of psychological inquiry into conceptions of self, which have been concerned with the individual as a stabilized entity, have had limited success in addressing these questions, and a number of theoretical spaces remain. For Gergen and Gergen (1983), the research concern has been triadic, leading researchers to develop instruments for assessing self-esteem, to examine a range of formative influences, and to explore the behavioral implications of possessing various levels of self-esteem. However, much of this research has been both mechanistic and synchronic. Consequently it has tended to ignore the individual's capacity to actively shape the configuration of self and to deny the potential of the individual for reflexive reconstruction of self-understanding. The traditional view also fails to document the individual's understanding of him or herself as a historically emerging being, and yet the view of the self at any given moment is fundamentally linked to the past of the individual as part of a reflexive project.

In order to build on the insights provided by traditional psychological approaches to understanding the self, there is a need to integrate interpretive sociological and psychological perspectives that focus on the ways in which individuals actively develop their sense of self, via narratives and storying, as constructive agents in social life. Such an approach would be specifically concerned with the individual's active construction of a personal history. The analysis provided would be reflexive and diachronic—concerned with states of active becoming as opposed to passive being. In this context, a life history approach to understanding would appear to have some value. According to Plummer (1983), Sparkes (1994a, 1994b, 1995), and Sparkes and Templin (1992), this approach has a number of strengths:

1. Its focus on self stories and personal experience narratives provides powerful insights into the subjective reality of individuals and the manner in which they interpret their own lives and the world around them over time.

2. While much of social science, in its quest to impose order upon the social world, glosses over central moments in lives that revolve around indecision, confusions, contradictions, ironies, critical incidents, fateful moments, and turning points, the life history approach takes these seriously in order to understand how they are played out in everyday life as past experiences interact with and shape the present and the future. Consequently, life history research is able to give important insights into the construction and reconstruction of the self as a dynamic process.

3. The life history approach attempts to focus on the totality of the biographical experience. This perspective constantly addresses and interlinks biological bodily needs, immediate social groups, personal definitions of the situation, and historical change in the life of the individual and the outside world.

4. As individuals move through their lives they move persistently through history and social structures. Life history research has the potential to move constantly between the changing biographical history as told by individuals in their stories and the social history of their life span. That is, a life history cannot be told without constant reference to historical change. This central focus on change is a major strength of life history research.

5. Life history research has the capability to bestride the micro-macro interface. In studying a life history the researcher considers its historical context and the dialectical relationship between self and society as individuals come to terms with the imperatives of social structures. Therefore, from a collection of life histories that are grounded in personal biography and self-narratives, the possibility emerges for discerning what is general across cases in order for links to be made with macro theories. That is, the life history locates the life story or narrative of self in a wider sociohistorical, economic, and political context.

Together the strengths of life history research, by itself or in suitable combination with other modes of inquiry, offer the potential to provide insights into how a person's identity and sense of self are constructed and how these develop and change over time. The use of life history research could further assist us in understanding how and why certain stories of the body are told as they are and, perhaps most importantly, might enable us to create new stories in the future.

ACKNOWLEDGMENTS

I would like to thank Ken Fox (Exeter University) for his patience and editorial guidance, and Chris Shilling (Southampton University), Martti Silvennoinen (University of Jyväskylä), and Mark Sudwell (Exeter University) for their critical comments on an earlier draft of this chapter. A special thanks to Kitty, Jessica, and Alexander Sparkes for the stories they share with me on a daily basis and for the insights they have provided me into how the body gets storied and restoried over time.

REFERENCES

Bartky, S. 1988. Foucault, femininity and the modernization of patriarchal power. In *Feminism and Foucault: Reflections on resistance*, ed. I. Diamond and L. Quinby, 61-86. Boston: Northeastern University Press.

Baudrillard, J. 1983. The ecstasy of communication. In *The anti-aesthetic: Essays on postmodern culture*, ed. H. Foster, 111-59. Port Townsend, WA: Bay Press.

Betterton, R. 1987. *Looking on: Images of women in the visual arts and the media*. London: Pandora.

Bordo, S. 1990. Reading the slender body. In *Body/politics: Women and the discourses of science*, ed. M. Jacobus, E. Fox Keller, and S. Shuttleworth, 83-112. London: Routledge & Kegan Paul.

Bourdieu, P. 1978. Sport and social class. *Social Science Information* 17: 19-40.

—. 1984. *Distinction: A social critique of the judgment of taste*. London: Routledge & Kegan Paul.

—. 1986. The forms of capital. In *Handbook of theory and research for the sociology of education*, ed. J. Richardson, 241-58. New York: Greenwood.

Bovey, S. 1989. *Being fat is not a sin*. London: Pandora.

Brock, S., and Kleiber, D. 1994. Narrative in medicine: The stories of elite college athletes' career-ending injuries. *Qualitative Health Research* 4 (4): 411-30.

Bruner, J. 1987. Life as narrative. *Social Research* 54: 11-32.

Charmaz, K. 1994. Identity dilemmas of chronically ill men. *The Sociological Quarterly* 35 (2): 269-88.

Coakley, J. 1978. *Sport in society.* Boston: Times Mirror/Mosby.

Colquhoun, D. 1991. Health-based physical education: The ideology of healthism and victim blaming. *Physical Education Review* 14 (1): 5-13.

Craik, J. 1994. *The face of fashion: Cultural studies in fashion.* London: Routledge & Kegan Paul.

Crawford, R. 1980. Healthism and the medicalization of everyday life. *International Journal of Health Services* 10 (3): 365-89.

Duncan, M. 1990. Sports photographs and sexual difference: Images of women and men in the 1984 and 1988 Olympic Games. *Sociology of Sport Journal* 7: 22-43.

Elias, N. 1982. *The civilizing process.* Oxford: Blackwell.

Escobar, A. 1994. Welcome to cyberia: Notes on the anthropology of cyberculture. *Current Anthropology* 35 (3): 211-23.

Featherstone, M. 1987. Leisure, symbolic power and the life course. In *Sport, leisure and social relations,* ed. J. Horne, D. Jary, and A. Tomlinson, 113-38. London: Routledge & Kegan Paul.

—. 1991. The body in consumer culture. In *The body: Social process and cultural theory,* ed. M. Featherstone, M. Hepworth, and B. Turner, 170-96. London: Sage.

Foucault, M. 1977. *Discipline and punish: The birth of the prison.* London: Penguin.

—. 1979. *The history of sexuality.* Vol. 1. London: Penguin.

Gergen, K. 1991. *The saturated self.* New York: Basic Books.

Gergen, K., and Gergen, M. 1983. Narratives of the self. In *Studies in social identity,* ed. T. Sarbin and K. Scheibe, 254-73. New York: Praeger.

—. 1993. Autobiographies and the shaping of gendered lives. In *Discourse and lifespan identity,* ed. N. Coupland and J. Nussbaum, 28-54. London: Sage.

Giddens, A. 1991. *Modernity and self-identity.* Cambridge: Polity.

Goffman, E. 1959. *The presentation of self in everyday life.* Harmondsworth, England: Penguin.

—. 1963. *Stigma.* Harmondsworth, England: Penguin.

Gottschalk, S. 1993. Uncomfortably numb: Countercultural impulses in the postmodern era. *Symbolic Interaction* 16 (4): 351-78.

Griffin, P. 1992. Changing the game: Homophobia, sexism and lesbians in sport. *Quest* 44: 251-65.

Griffin, P., and Genasci, J. 1990. Addressing homophobia in physical education: Responsibilities for teachers. In *Sport, men and the gender order,* ed. M. Messner and M. Sabo, 211-21. Champaign, IL: Human Kinetics.

Hall, S. 1992. The question of cultural identity. In *Modernity and its futures,* ed. S. Hall, D. Hell, and T. McGrew, 374-425. Cambridge: Polity.

Hargreaves, J. 1994. *Sporting females.* London: Routledge & Kegan Paul.

Hill, J., and Brackenridge, C. 1989. "My body's a complete wreck." The contribution of PE to physical confidence. *Physical Education Review* 12 (2): 147-57.

Hyland, T. 1988. Values and health education: A critique of individualism. *Educational Studies* 14: 23-31.

Ingham, A. 1985. From public issue to personal trouble: Well-being and the fiscal crisis of the state. *Sociology of Sport Journal* 2: 43-55.

Kaskisaari, M. 1994. The rhythmbody. *International Review for Sociology of Sport* 29 (1): 15-23.

Kirk, D. 1993. *The body, schooling and culture.* Victoria, Australia: Deakin University.

Kirk, D., and Colquhoun, D. 1989. Healthism and physical education. *British Journal of Sociology of Education* 10 (4): 417-34.

Kissling, E. 1992. One size does not fit all, or how I learned to stop dieting and love my body. *Quest* 43 (2): 135-47.

Kleiber, D., and Brock, S. 1992. The effect of career-ending injuries on the subsequent well-being of elite college athletes. *Sociology of Sport Journal* 9: 70-75.

Klein, A. 1993. *Little big men: Bodybuilding subculture and gender construction.* New York: State University of New York.

Kleinman, A. 1988. *The illness narratives.* New York: Basic Books.

Kosonen, U. 1993. A running girl: Fragments of my body history. In *On the fringes of sport*, ed. L. Laine, 16-25. Sankt Augustin, Germany: Academia Verlag.

Lasch, A. 1980. *The culture of narcissism.* London: Abacus.

Lenskyj, H. 1986. *Out of bounds: Women, sport and sexuality.* Toronto, Ontario: Women's Press.

—. 1991. Combating homophobia in sport and physical education. *Sociology of Sport Journal* 8: 61-69.

Lupton, D. 1994. *Medicine as culture.* London: Sage.

MacNeill, M. 1988. Active women, media representations, and ideology. In *Not just a game: Essays in Canadian sport sociology*, ed. J. Harvey and H. Cantelon, 195-213. Ottawa, ON: University of Ottawa.

Mangan, J., and Park, R., eds. 1987. *From "fair sex" to feminism.* London: Frank Cass.

Mansfield, A., and McGinn, B. 1993. Pumping iron: The muscular and the feminine. In *Body matters*, ed. S. Scott and D. Morgan, 49-68. Lewes, England: Falmer.

McAdams, D. 1985. *Power, intimacy, and the life story.* Homewood, IL: Dorsey Press.

Miller, L., and Penz, O. 1991. Talking bodies: Female body-builders colonize a male preserve. *Quest* 43 (2): 148-63.

Morris, J. 1993. *Pride against prejudice: Transforming attitudes to disability.* London: Women's Press.

Naidoo, J. 1986. Limits to individualism. In *The politics of health education*, ed. S. Rodmell and A. Watt, 17-37. London: Routledge & Kegan Paul.

Nead, L. 1992. *The female nude: Art, obscenity and sexuality.* London: Routledge & Kegan Paul.

Nelkin, D., and Gilman, S. 1988. Placing blame for devastating disease. *Social Research* 55: 361-78.

Plummer, K. 1983. *Documents of life.* London: Unwin Hyman.

Riessman, C. 1993. *Narrative analysis.* London: Sage.

Schwalbe, M. 1993. Goffman against postmodernism: Emotion and the reality of the self. *Symbolic Interaction* 16 (4): 333-50.

Scott, S., and Morgan, D. 1993. Introduction. In *Body matters: Essays in the sociology of the body*, ed. S. Scott and D. Morgan, viii-xi. Lewes, England: Falmer.

Scraton, S. 1992. *Shaping up to womanhood: Gender and girls' physical education*. Milton Keynes, England: Open University.

Shalin, D. 1993. Modernity, postmodernism, and pragmatic inquiry: An introduction. *Symbolic Interaction* 16 (4): 303-32.

Shilling, C. 1993. *The body and social theory*. London: Sage.

Shotter, J. 1993. Becoming someone: Identity and belonging. In *Discourse and lifespan identity*, ed. N. Coupland and J. Nussbaum, 5-27. London: Sage.

Silvennoinen, M. 1993. A model for a man—tracing a personal history of body-awareness. In *On the fringes of sport*, ed. L. Laine, 26-32. Sankt Augustin, Germany: Academia Verlag.

—. 1994. To childhood heroes. *International Review for Sociology of Sport* 29 (1): 25-30.

Smart, B. 1985. *Michel Foucault*. London: Routledge & Kegan Paul.

Smith, K., and Stone, L. 1989. Rags, riches, and bootstraps: Beliefs about the causes of wealth and poverty. *Sociological Quarterly* 30: 93-107.

Sparkes, A. 1991. Alternative visions of health-related fitness: An exploration of problem-setting and its consequences. In *Issues in physical education*, ed. N. Armstrong and A. Sparkes, 204-27. London: Cassell.

—. 1992. The paradigms debate: An extended review and a celebration of difference. In *Research in physical education and sport: Exploring alternative visions*, ed. A. Sparkes, 9-60. Lewes, England: Falmer.

—. 1994a. Life histories and the issue of voice: Reflections on an emerging relationship. *International Journal of Qualitative Studies in Education* 7 (2): 165-83.

—. 1994b. Self, silence and invisibility as a beginning teacher: A life history of lesbian experience. *British Journal of Sociology of Education* 15 (1): 93-118.

—. 1995. Living our stories, storying our lives, and the spaces in between: Life history research as a force for change. In *The qualitative challenge: Reflections on educational research*, ed. T. Tiller, A. Sparkes, S. Karhus, and F. Dowling Naess, 77-112. Bergen, Norway: Caspar Forlag.

—. 1996. The fatal flaw: A narrative of the fragile body/self. *Qualitative Inquiry* 2(4): 463-494.

—. In press. Performing bodies, illness, and the death of selves. *Auto/Biography*.

Sparkes, A., and Templin, T. 1992. Life histories and physical education teachers: Exploring the meanings of marginality. In *Research in physical education and sport: Exploring alternative visions*, ed. A. Sparkes, 118-45. Lewes, England: Falmer.

Synnott, A. 1992. Tomb, temple, machine and self: The social construction of the body. *British Journal of Sociology* 43 (1): 79-110.

—. 1993. *The body social: Symbolism, self and society*. London: Routledge & Kegan Paul.

Therberge, N. 1992. Reflections on the body in the sociology of sport. *Quest* 43 (2): 123-34.

Tiihonen, A. 1994. Asthma—the construction of the masculine body. *International Review for Sociology of Sport* 29 (1): 50-62.

Tinning, R. 1990. *Ideology and physical education: Opening Pandora's box*. Victoria, Australia: Deakin University.

Turner, B. 1984. *The body and society*. Oxford: Basil Blackwell.

Warrick, R., and Tinning, R. 1989. Women's bodies, self-perception and physical activity: A naturalistic study of women's participation in aerobics classes, Part 1. *Australian Council for Health, Physical Education and Recreation National Journal* (September): 8-12.

White, P., and Gillett, J. 1994. Reading the muscular body: A critical decoding of advertisements in Flex magazine. *Sociology of Sport Journal* 11: 18-39.

Widdershoven, G. 1993. The story of life: Hermeneutic perspectives on the relationship between narrative and life history. In *The narrative study of lives*, ed. R. Josselson and A. Lieblich, 1-20. London: Sage.

Woods, S. 1992. Describing the experience of lesbian physical educators: A phenomenological study. In *Research in physical education and sport: Exploring alternative visions*, ed. A. Sparkes, 90-117. Lewes, England: Falmer.

Young, K., White, P., and McTeer, W. 1994. Body talk: Male athletes reflect on sport, injury, and pain. *Sociology of Sport Journal* 11: 175-94.

CHAPTER 5

THE PHYSICAL SELF AND PROCESSES IN SELF-ESTEEM DEVELOPMENT

KENNETH R. FOX

For many years self-esteem research has been restrictively descriptive. Studies have been directed at the documentation of group differences in self-esteem, and the establishment of relationships between self-esteem and achievements in settings such as work, school, and sport. Furthermore, self-esteem has been used as a positive endpoint of intervention programs in a range of educational and health settings. Unfortunately, during much of this *initial phase* of contemporary self-esteem research, a rather simplistic view of the self as a unidimensional construct was adopted (Wylie 1979). For those interested in the physical domain, this resulted in measurement instruments that clouded rather than clarified matters. Little of value that was specific to the physical aspects of self could be teased out, with the result that the processes underpinning the interactions between the self and physical behaviors such as sport and exercise remained a mystery.

More recently, we have seen several crucial developments, representing a *second phase* of self-esteem research, much of which has already been outlined in this book (in particular see Marsh, chapter 2). Multidimensional models of the self have been operationalized, and of tremendous significance has been the emergence of the physical self as an entity that plays an integral part in the structure of the whole self but is also open to independent inquiry. Developments in physical self-perception instrumentation have produced much richer profiles (e.g., Fox and Corbin 1989; Marsh et al. 1994; Whitehead 1995) that are proving capable of characterizing groups or individuals, documenting links between the physical self and related behaviors, and mapping self-perception change more precisely.

Although Phase 2 has made a significant impact, it has remained largely descriptive. It is time to put a hold on our descriptive advances, as we are in danger of missing the important point made by Harter (1996): "For investigators to merely describe the self-theory or the self-concept, as a function of age, gender, ethnicity, social group etc. is to miss the very processes through which it comes to be constructed." A *third phase*, which has to be considered the most critical, is required: one that will focus more directly on the *mechanisms of change* involved in the self-system. With regard to the physical domain, little is known about how individuals integrate aspects of their physical selves into their self-systems, how the physical self is modified through physical life experiences, or how the physical self mediates the effect of behaviors and their outcomes on self-esteem. The range of responses that individuals have to their bodies seems almost as varied as the array of body shapes, sizes, and abilities that are apparent in any crowd. Many of these responses seem anomalous and are not easily explained. For example, an individual who acquires a physical disability may come to see her condition as an opportunity to display courage and mastery, rather than defeat and depression, resulting in higher self-regard than might have been originally experienced. In contrast, an avid aerobic exerciser who has worked hard toward a slim and fit body may remain as dissatisfied with her appearance as on the day she started, even though she appreciates that there have been positive changes. Individual differences in reaction to sport injury, serious illnesses, puberty, the aging process, sexuality, and behaviors such as competitive sport or weight loss are clear yet unexplained. Although several reviews of studies addressing the effects of exercise on mental well-being have concluded that mastery and enhanced self-esteem may be implicated (e.g., Berger and McInman 1993; Boutcher 1993; Sonstroem 1984; see also Mutrie, chapter 11), examples are emerging in which the reverse may be true. In some instances involvement in exercise, sport, or dieting can become obsessive, frustrating, compensatory, counterproductive, or even addictive. In summary, it is fair to say that we are not much wiser about the processes than we were in 1984 when Sonstroem stated, "At this time it is not known why or in what manner exercise programs affect self-esteem, or which people are responsive" (150).

Given that the self is a very complex and intricate system of emotions and cognitions that is entangled with a life history of experiences, simple solutions are unlikely. However, much is at stake here. In Western societies at least, the body, its appearance, its capabilities, and its capacity to portray messages about and on behalf of the self, has recently been thrust into greater prominence. With this social shift, the physical self has become increasingly akin to the *public self* (see Harter 1990) as an item of consumption and social currency. More than ever, the body has become inexorably entangled with the whole self, and it has become increasingly difficult for individuals or researchers to ignore its social significance. In addition, there is a strengthening belief among agencies as diverse as health, education, and commerce that involvement in exercise and sport has an impact that stretches beyond the physical to the enhancement of life quality and mental well-being. In short, the physical self is becoming increasingly critical to human functioning. This chapter therefore calls for process-oriented research and presents some concepts and assumptions regarding the self that are central to forwarding our understanding of the role of the physical self in the dynamics of self-esteem change.

THE SELF-SYSTEM AND SELF-ESTEEM

It is impossible to speculate about processes of integration and change without returning to some of the traditional roots regarding the self, its structure, and its function. Volumes of literature in disciplines as diverse as philosophy, psychology, sociology, and theology are available on this topic, and any single account can provide only a sampler of the literature. Baumeister (1987), for example, has made a brave attempt to analyze historical biographies and records to provide an assessment of the role and nature of the self through the recent centuries. He provides a convincing argument that concurs with the contemporary sociological literature (see Sparkes, chapter 4) suggesting that the self has never been more problematic in its salience to people's lives. With liberation has come choice (sometimes taken as a responsibility) and a chance to break away from labels of class, culture, and religion that were once imprinted at birth. Greater opportunities have been made available for the development of individual identities, but on the other hand the increased array of potential selves on offer can promote identity confusion. It seems that never before has understanding the self been so difficult, not only for individuals themselves, but for psychotherapists and researchers.

Harter (1996) provides an excellent account of early self-concept approaches that have stood the test of time and are still contributing substantially to contemporary thinking. At the heart of most theses on the nature of the self is the notion of a *self-system*. Individuals are absorbed in a lifelong project to validate their sense of self. To provide an analogy, the self-system could be likened to a personal corporation with a managing director at the helm, the objective being to emerge from life's dealings with a healthy bank balance. Most writers recognize the existence of the *self director* or the *organizing self* who is the hub of the self-system and takes responsibility for the information processing and lifelong adjustments necessary to meet the needs of the self.

SELF-DIRECTION

The notion of a self director was evident in the early writings of James (1892), who distinguished between the "I" or the self as subject and the "Me" as the self as object. The "I" was the active agent of change and, working within a personal theory of selfhood, was responsible for a range of organizational tasks aimed at the achievement of the best possible result for the self. The "Me" was the sum of self-knowledge and provided the basis of the self-concept. The idea of the self-concept as "the individual as known to the individual" (Murphy 1947, 996) is now widely accepted. It can include a multitude of descriptors or beliefs about the self, for example the roles played in life as in father, son, student; a range of personal competencies and adequacies in different domains of life, such as job competence, success as a parent, physical appearance, and athletic ability; and other personal descriptors, for example personality traits like honesty, resilience, or moodiness. One of the tasks of the self director is to organize these experiences and attributes into a coherent structure. This is compatible with the notion of self-theory (Epstein 1973, 1991), self-schemata (Markus 1977; Markus and Wurf 1987), and organismic integration (Deci and Ryan 1991). The self-concept also has dynamic and developmental elements and can be described as a curriculum vitae or biography of the self. To some extent, identity theorists (Erikson 1968; Marcia 1980; Stryker 1987) have best accommodated the concept of the evolving self as they have focused on continuity and consistency and also have included personal value systems.

The self director is therefore seen as an active information processor and decision maker. The degree to which this is conscious or unconscious is a matter for debate. Psychotherapists generally emphasize the existence of deeper and more tacit levels of influence (Guidano 1986). Whatever the case, the items to appear on the curriculum vitae are likely to be selectively determined to produce a version that fits best with the aspirations and personal theory of the self. Some events and information will be played down and others built up. Self-serving biases and strategies such as these are now well documented (see Blaine and Crocker 1993) and are regarded as a positive characteristic because their use, particularly following successful events, is mainly found in those who are high in self-esteem.

It must be said at this point that not all scholars are convinced about the capacity or even the existence of a directing core of self. Following the lines of Cooley (1902), some theorists (see Hall 1992) maintain that the self is merely a constitution of the multiple social roles and reflections of the increasingly multifaceted world that we occupy. Their argument implies that there is little coherence or consistency between these facets and that an overall self-theory has little predictive value. Certainly the empirical work of Marsh (1987) suggests that hierarchical structuring of self is weak, particularly through late adolescence as the self becomes more differentiated. Some caution is in order, however, as his hierarchies are based largely on self-ratings of competencies. Some theorists (Kelly 1955; Markus 1977; Stryker 1987) would suggest that higher-order abstractions or self-schemata, such as consistency in guiding beliefs, principles, personality characteristics, or interpersonal response style, may be more critical than perceived abilities in defining the self as it matures.

This does not rule out the influence of reflected appraisal and social interaction on the self. The salience of the presence of others is confirmed by the literature on self-presentation (Baumeister 1993). Creating an impression seems to be a strong motive and implies that the self's public relations department is constantly in action (Leary 1992, 1995). This has major implications for the physical domain, where the dominance of appearance is already confirmed (Fox 1990; Harter 1990) and notions such as social physique anxiety (Hart, Leary, and Rejeski 1989) have already received support. These are points that are easily forgotten when we attempt to measure self-concept, and an important area for study is the extent to which the physical self is tied up with impression management and the degree to which it functions as the *public face* of the self.

SELF-ESTEEM

An important question is raised by the role of self-esteem in the self-system, particularly as it has received at least as much empirical and conceptual attention as the self-concept. James (1892) regarded self-esteem as an overall measure of success of the self-system. He believed that the success of the system was best reflected by a cost-benefit analysis along the lines of how well goals and aspiration had been achieved. This ratio of personal successes to pretensions has been operationalized by Harter (see Harter 1990, 1993) as the degree of perceived competence in a range of life domains in relation to the perceived importance of each competence. However, there have been other interpretations of the nature and determinants of self-esteem, several of which will be described later. Some believe that self-esteem is not the result of an audit of the credits and debits of the self-concept but a summation of all the positive aspects of the self, while others see it as unconditional on achievements and as a result of the integrity or harmony of the self.

Self-esteem is perhaps best described as an overall judgment made by the directing self of how well the self is doing. Throughout this book, a simple definition provided by Campbell (1984) has been preferred—"the awareness of good possessed by self" (9). This definition carries two important properties. First, it allows the individual to use whatever criteria in the self-theory are personally salient to determine *worth*. The term "good" does not necessarily have moral connotations but is based on the value system of the individual. A criminal, for example, might take pride in how well he plies his trade. Second, Campbell's definition provides a global summary that allows the individual to combine this salient content through personally weighted combinations. It therefore presents a holistic and phenomenological statement of the self. This approach, which avoids situation-specific responses, has been used in several of the contemporary measures such as the Rosenberg Scale (1965) and, more recently, in Harter's General Self-Worth subscale in her range of self-perception profiles (Harter 1985) and the General Self-Worth subscale of the Self-Description Questionnaires (Marsh 1992).

Since the days of James, self-esteem has become one of the most widely used psychological constructs in both the academic literature and the popular press. It is seen by many as the best indicator of the well-being of the self-system; it is frequently used as an index of mental health as it carries properties of emotional adjustment (Baumeister 1993), general coping with life (Brown 1993), and life satisfaction and well-being (Diener 1984).

SELF-DIRECTION TASKS

In order to produce a system that carries integrity and success, the self director is faced with two basic tasks: self-enhancement and self-consistency (Brown 1993).

Self-Enhancement

Many authorities have endorsed the idea that self-enhancement is a basic law of human behavior (Baumeister 1991; Campbell 1984; Maslow 1954; Tesser 1988). Brown (1993) describes self-enhancement processes as driven by a need to feel *competent, worthy, and loved by others*. Recently, Deci and Ryan (1996) have also emphasized a need for *competence, relatedness, and self-determination*. This line of thinking is clearly based on the self as functioning on hedonic principles. Actions can be altruistic, as seen, for example, when an individual dedicates unconditional time under dangerous circumstances in a famine-ridden or war-torn territory. However, such behavior is seen as desirable by the individual as it satisfies an important personal need and produces positive feelings about the self. Several self-enhancement strategies have been recognized. Some examples follow.

1. Directing the self toward life domains that yield a high possibility for success and positive affect (Harter 1990; Maehr and Braskamp 1986; White 1959)

2. Discounting the importance of and withdrawing from domains that tend to produce failure, lack of success, and negative affect (Harter 1990, 1993)

3. Shaping attributions for events in order to present the self-concept in the best possible light; expecting success and taking credit for it while

being surprised at failure and treating it as a learning experience (see Blaine and Crocker 1993)

4. Self-affirmation and self-verification when the self is under threat (La Ronde and Swann 1993; Tice 1993)

5. Maximizing social approval and support (Harter 1996)

A key to understanding the functionality of the physical self within the self-system requires an understanding of such processes, particularly as the tangibility and visibility of the physical self increase its salience.

Self-Consistency

Brown (1993) describes the second task as a drive toward self-consistency and stability (Epstein 1973; Lecky 1945). The existence of such strategies have been known for some time and have provided the basis of identity theory (Erikson 1968; Stryker 1987). Self-consistency allows the development of feelings of unity, uniqueness, independence, predictability, and control that provide a framework on which the self can organize and make sense of its interactions with life.

The integration of the physical self may be especially problematic. First, it is difficult to hide or ignore. Second, it is subject to critical changes throughout the life span, particularly at puberty, menopause, and during older age, and therefore has to be constantly reappraised. If physical appearance or physical abilities (the external self) are not consistent with the inner representation or aspirations of the self, then a sense of dissonance will be present that is a potential source of low self-esteem. This may be tied up with the notion of self-acceptance, which will be addressed later.

REFLEXIVITY AND RECIPROCITY

The two self-directing tasks just described are essentially interwoven, but they differ in their focus. Self-enhancement processes involve the self as an active agent, making the best of its strengths and experiences. Self-consistency motives are oriented to establishing and affirming the stability and coherence of the self under external and internal threat. Some sociologists refer to the *reflexivity* of the self (Giddens 1991) whereby the self is continuously but gradually revising its structure in response to the outcomes of behaviors. Guidano (1986), a psychotherapist, refers to the "integration of lifespan oscillations" (319) that occurs when the self is willing to modify its identity in response to intense informational challenges. Reciprocally, the self attempts to steer toward domains and behaviors that produce a high yield. The self therefore constantly buffers between the impact that experiences have on self-knowledge (reaction) and guiding behavior (action).

The degree to which each of these processes is dominant within an individual is of interest. Some people may tend to plan and be more proactive, while others may remain in a reactive or passive mode. These states or traits may be related to locus of control (Rotter 1990), the former being associated with internality and the latter with externality. It would seem that for people with an internal locus of control there is greater potential for high self-esteem: This individual is capable of organizing and making the best of the environment, in contrast to the reactive subject whose exposure to random environmental events may cause problems with self-consistency and identity.

Similarly, there will be some settings and events that force the self into the reactive mode as the situation cannot be adequately accommodated through cognitive strategies such as self-serving bias. This may be particularly the case for younger people whose self-concept is still developing or for individuals facing the consequences of a major life event such as divorce, job loss, a debilitating accident, or serious ill health. In such cases the process of change might be accelerated and thus more readily accessible for study.

To adequately address the constantly adjusting self and self-system, a dynamic perspective is required. Clearly, a better understanding of the operation of such processes of adjustment and manipulation within the physical domain is important. For example, are changes in body weight or shape required before the self can experience benefits from an exercise program? Are changes in the nature or structure of the self (identity) at a deep level required in order for such interventions to have a lasting effect? Is any lasting effect mediated by increased motivation and thus mainte-nance of the behavior?

HIGH VERSUS LOW SELF-ESTEEM

Some insight into the nature of change might be possible through compar-ing and contrasting individuals with high and low self-esteem in their reactions to events. For example, it is possible that success in self-directing tasks can distinguish between those with high and low self-esteem. People with low self-esteem tend to have the following characteristics:

1. They are neutral rather than negative in self-esteem. This is so because they are less likely to declare strong positive aspects of themselves and also less likely to disconfirm negative aspects but have a strong desire to experience self-worth (Baumeister 1993).

2. They have less well-defined self-knowledge and are unsure and confused about their self-concept. As a result, they are highly respon-sive to external cues; this makes them more malleable under threat or pressure (see Campbell and Lavallee 1993).

3. They tend to have simpler and fewer independent elements to their self-concept. The result seems to be fewer opportunities to self-affirm

when their self-concept is under threat (Linville 1985; Spencer, Josephs, and Steele 1993).

4. They seem to have more areas producing deficits in their self-concept as indicated by a mismatch (discrepancies) between level of perceived competence and the importance or aspirations attached to those competencies (Harter 1990).

5. They may perceive that they have social support but that it is conditional upon their achievements (Harter 1993, 1996).

Low self-esteem can therefore be seen as a defect in the use of self-enhancement strategies rather than a deep sense of self-disregard. People with low self-esteem understandably are highly protective and defensive about the few positive attributes they perceive themselves to have, and may even be prepared to denigrate others on those attributes in order to boost the significance of their own achievements. They tend to approach behaviors with conservatism and caution as they hate to experience further disappointment. Consequently, they are directed more to avoiding failure and are suspicious of success (see Blaine and Crocker 1993), being less likely to employ self-serving biases. They may also live out the success of others as this provides an opportunity to avoid responsibility for failure.

Brown (1993) suggests that for people with high self-esteem, the desire for self-enhancement does not conflict with their need for self-consistency. These individuals perceive that they have many positive attributes and are able to build a coherent identity around them. In contrast, people with low self-esteem are torn between the need for feeling positive self-regard through self-enhancement and their drive for consistency; the latter need, which is exaggerated by their sense of self-confusion and fragility, forces them toward maintaining a consistent self-concept even when much of it is perceived as negative. This notion is confirmed by Harter's work (1993), which has clearly indicated that those with low self-esteem are much less likely to let go of domains where they perceive a discrepancy between low competence and high importance of success. Individuals with high self-esteem tend to withdraw or discount, and invest their time elsewhere. It is possible that people with low self-esteem feel that they simply have few alternative places to go.

People who have low self-esteem are more reluctant and less able to change their self-concept and less likely to experience self-enhancement. This seems to represent a self-perpetuating downward spiral and reversal may require professional assistance. Psychotherapists, for example, frequently address low self-esteem in their work with individuals. However, it is rare that research on interventions in the physical domain have targeted people with low self-esteem. This is surprising because reviews of exercise programs with children (Gruber 1986) and adults (Berger and McInman

1993; Sonstroem 1984) have indicated that such individuals have shown greatest improvement. If health promoters are to establish cost-effective programs, they should be targeting the most needy and most responsive. Although influencing self-enhancement processes for those low in self-esteem may initially be difficult owing to a tendency toward resistance to change, should the right formula be found, the payoff could be high. Currently, we know very little about the circumstances that might bring this about because we rarely focus on this group in our research.

CONSTRAINTS ON THE SELF

Given the range of strategies on offer, we might expect that all people could find a way of experiencing positive self-esteem as they progressed through life. As this is not the case, we might be tempted to look for personality characteristics that predispose to low self-esteem such as pessimism, neuroticism, vulnerability, or low resilience (see Werner 1989). There may be a strong case for looking at such initial trait differences, and some authors have recently included variables of this kind in their studies (see Davis, chapter 6).

There are also political and social constraints facing the self that may be more problematic for some individuals than for others. Such constraints were described in detail by Sparkes in the preceding chapter. Societies and cultures set down patterns of existence that do not allow individuals total freedom to choose their own route toward self-consistency and identity formation. By definition, cultures and groups have membership requirements—social laws and traditions that place pressures on the self to conform through appearance, abilities, and behavioral characteristics. This has important implications for our understanding of people's self-esteem. Before we can adequately explain the level of self-regard of an individual and how it has been achieved, we have to address (a) the dictates and values of the pervasive culture to which the person belongs, (b) the degree to which the individual aspires to those dictates, and (c) the way the person rates himself or herself on those dictates.

The degree to which a person's values may be detached from the main culture may also be very important. A nonconformer may be granted the qualities of "individuality," a strong frame of mind, and/or leadership qualities. On the other hand, there is a chance that she might be labeled as an outcast, an eccentric, or an incompetent who is inadequate for group membership. The person who is an avid conformer may be seen as a slave to fashion, as a victim of coercion, or as lacking in substance or character. Furthermore, individuals may reject the pervasive culture and aspire to countercultures or subcultures with quite different sets of rules.

Whether or not an individual aspires to an internally developed set of values, the pervasive cultural marketplace, the demands of alternative groups, or some combination of these is crucial to understanding both self-concept and self-esteem. In all cases, the outcome must be dependent on what the individual *aspires* to achieve and the extent to which those achievements have been fulfilled. Thus we return to James' formulation of self-esteem--that of the ratio of success over pretensions. Without such an analysis, we cannot expect to understand complex issues as diverse as those of the athlete facing a career-threatening injury, the adolescent girl who aspires to be even thinner than she is, the obese person attempting exercise for the first time, the average person's reluctance to exercise, the compulsive exerciser who is reluctant to cut down, the coronary rehabilitation patient who chooses not to exercise, the recreational sport participant who is detrimentally overcompetitive, or other general issues of health such as drug taking. This matter is closely related to the work on perceived importance that will be described later in the chapter.

THE PHYSICAL SELF AND SELF-ESTEEM

With the recognition of the multidimensionality of self came the opportunity to investigate the physical self as an entity in its own right. Aspects of the physical self such as perceived physical competence and appearance had been considered, but given the potential of the body to influence both self-esteem and behaviors, Fox and Corbin (1989) sought to delineate the constitution of the physical self in more detail. Through content analysis of open-ended responses and factor analytic techniques, they developed the Physical Self-Perception Profile (PSPP). This instrument features scales around sport competence, attractiveness, physical condition, and strength. In addition, a physical self-worth scale was developed to test the hypothesis that content and experiences in the physical domain were combined in some personal formula to produce a sense of physical self-esteem, in a manner similar to that for global self-esteem.

The content of the instrument has been verified in a wide range of populations including, for example, senior high school and college students in the United States (Curby 1995; Fox and Vehnekamp 1992), college students in the United Kingdom (Page et al. 1993), middle-aged males (Sonstroem, Speliotis, and Fava 1992), and obese males and females attending treatment (Fox and Dirkin 1992). Modified versions for younger children (Welk, Corbin, and Lewis 1995; Whitehead 1995) and older adults (Chase 1991) have produced similar structures. Of particular significance here is the invariant emergence of physical self-worth as a mediator of the relationship between physical self-perception content and self-esteem. On its removal, relationships (usually in the region $r = 0.2$-0.5) are extinguished or dramatically reduced as are relationships among the subdomains. The relationship between physical self-worth and self-esteem has consistently been in the region of $r = 0.6$, which is quite sizable given the potential of nonphysical attributes to contribute. These relationships that have been established using partial correlation analysis have also been supported by structural equation modeling (Ebbeck 1992; Sonstroem, Harlow, and Josephs 1994). Furthermore, perceptions in the four subdomains have typically explained 65% to 75% of variance in physical self-worth, suggesting that the culturally pervasive content is adequately represented.

Physical self-worth therefore seems to emerge as a valuable indicator of the general well-being of the individual in the physical domain. Interesting recent work by Sonstroem and Potts (1996) has provided evidence that physical self-worth has valuable life adjustment properties that are independent of self-esteem. Positive relationships were obtained with indicators of mental health with the effect of self-esteem and social desirability statistically controlled. This clearly requires further study, but its substantiation would suggest that physical self-worth itself may be a useful target of exercise, sport, and physical education interventions (see Fox 1992b).

PHYSICAL APPEARANCE AND SELF-ESTEEM

The availability of the body for the display of valued characteristics makes it particularly central in many people's lives. Children have already begun to rate themselves on a range of appearance factors by the age of 11 and have formed an opinion of whether or not they have an attractive appearance. Our own data (see Page and Fox, chapter 9, table 9.2) have shown that even single features such as height, fatness, facial features, hair, and fashionable clothes become increasingly emotive subjects in childhood and consistently relate to self-esteem.

Similarly, throughout the many studies with the PSPP, the construct of bodily attractiveness has dominated physical self-worth. Correlations have generally been in the region of $r = 0.7$; these findings closely mirror those of Harter (1993), who reports correlations between appearance and global self-esteem as typically between $r = 0.7$ and 0.8.

The importance of the body to self is apparent through self-presentation strategies (Leary 1995), and this is evident in the sport and exercise setting (Leary 1992). Testimony is seen in the willingness of individuals to undergo unhealthy or expensive practices such as acquiring a suntan or undergoing cosmetic surgery in order to look attractive (Leary, Tchividjian, and Kraxberger 1994). Adolescent risk taking, steroid usage among bodybuilders, and the use of maladaptive eating behaviors in adolescent girls in order to be slim can also be viewed in these terms.

The cultural derivation of this dominance is also becoming increasingly apparent. Initial evidence from Portugal and Spain with the PSPP suggests that in those countries attractiveness is qualitatively different from attractiveness in the general culture of the United States. Furthermore, Collins (1993) concluded that a stronger appearance-exercise relationship among females in Mexico versus those in the United States was found because Mexican females see their bodies functionally as opposed to cosmetically. Such cultural differences require much further exploration.

In short, the salience of judgments about appearance in relation to self-regard among different cultural groups represents one of the most robust self-concept findings that we have and probably holds a key to our understanding of self-esteem processes in general. The body and its appearance have become a focal point of social interaction, sexuality, functionality, and health as well as carrying a multitude of membership labels, so its current significance in both sociology and psychology is perhaps not surprising.

It seems that the evidence is now sufficiently strong to warrant investigation of physical appearance as a higher-order construct that subsumes several other factors and that is similar to the notion of the public self as suggested by Harter (1990). The construct might be expected, for example, to show significant links with the social, sexual, and functional self. These are unavoidably brought together through the presence of the body in social settings and form a basis on which the attractiveness, confidence, and abilities of the individual are judged in the social world. It seems that concerted efforts could be made to combine sociological and psychological approaches to such issues to better explain the pressures on different cultural groups and individuals and the strategies by which they come to terms with this aspect of the self.

PHYSICAL COMPETENCE AND SELF-ESTEEM

Evaluative statements that refer to competencies have dominated multidimensional models and instruments. The exceptions are physical appearance factors (which are probably better described as attributes) and social acceptance. Harter (1996) has found that after perceived appearance factors, perceptions of social acceptance have produced the next strongest correlations with self-esteem. Competencies in scholastic, work, and sport domains take third place. Emotional factors such as mood stability, and personal constructs such as maturity, integrity, honesty, and reliability have received much less attention.

Certainly physical competence has dominated measurement in the physical domain. The Physical Self-Description Questionnaire (PSDQ) (Marsh et al. 1994) has five physical competence subscales, one activity subscale, one health subscale, and two subscales tapping appearance. The PSPP (Fox 1990) uses three competence subdomains and one appearance subscale. Harter's profiles (1985, 1988) include scales for physical appearance and athletic competence.

Physical competencies in general have revealed low to moderate correlations with self-esteem (in the region of $r = 0.15$-0.4). On current evidence, those who espouse the benefits of improvement of physical competence, sport skills, and aspects of fitness as a route to the promotion of self-esteem have to be slightly disappointed. Although elements of physical competence have shown improvements through interventions, these have not necessarily resulted in more global changes. In addition, perceived competence changes are not necessarily reflected in actual changes in physical skill or fitness (see Mutrie, chapter 11). Furthermore, some exercise studies using the PSPP have indicated changes in physical self-worth and self-esteem without changes in underlying subcomponents of physical competence (Mutrie and Davison 1994; Page et al. 1994), with one intervention study actually showing a decline in the physical self-worth of boys (Crocker et al. 1994). These confused findings show that the relationships among actual physical change, perceived physical change, and global aspects of self are far from straightforward. A thorough analysis of the many recent studies, including the many unpublished theses and dissertations, that have used multidimensional physical self-perception instruments is required as a starting point. Until we begin to unravel patterns of change in interventions, the conditions under which changes occur, and the types of individuals who are responsive or unresponsive, we are unlikely to identify the critical processes in operation.

There may be several explanations for the fact that competence and self-esteem relationships are lower than might be expected in the physical domain. Competencies themselves may merely provide information regarding achievement and in themselves have no motivational significance. Achievement goal theory (see Biddle, chapter 3; Duda 1992) suggests that there are at least two ways to conceptualize competence or ability. Even contemporary measures such as the PSPP and the PSDQ have not taken this into consideration, so competence scores are confounded. Some validity, as far as relationships with self-esteem are concerned, may have been lost. However, in contrast to the situation with physical appearance factors, which are culturally demanding, the self is faced with the choice of an array of competencies in a range of contrasting domains. This may allow greater scope for the use of self-enhancement strategies, allowing competencies that are weak to be ignored, thus weakening their impact and relationship with self-esteem.

PERCEIVED IMPORTANCE AND SELF-ESTEEM

Consistent with the organizational capacity of the self, and the drive toward self-enhancement, is the use of self-serving bias toward areas that yield a high payoff of success and away from failure. This "pick and mix" principle is consistent with the postulates of a host of authorities (Harter 1985, 1990; James 1892; Kelly 1955; Markus and Wurf 1987; Rosenberg 1965; Tesser

1988). The most commonly suggested strategy is the attachment of importance weights to elements of the self-concept. As discussed earlier, these are influenced by a combination of personal and cultural values. Harter (1990, 1993, 1996) presents evidence from several sources to show that individuals attribute different levels of significance or relevance to different aspects of themselves.

In particular, Harter has promoted the concept of *discounting* as a self-enhancement strategy whereby individuals attach a low importance weight to those domains where low competence is perceived. This in effect would prevent shortfalls in competence from impacting on self-esteem. Those unable to discount domains in which they exhibit low competence would be liable to *importance-competence discrepancies*. Those who successfully discount would have a higher *congruence* between their importance and competence ratings across domains. Harter and her colleagues have provided different levels of supportive evidence across a range of populations to substantiate the impact of these concepts on self-esteem.

First, Harter demonstrates that competence in domains rated as important is more highly related to self-esteem ($r = .70$) than competence in those domains seen as unimportant ($r = .30$). Second, discrepancy scores (subtracting perceptions of competence from its perceived importance in domains perceived to be high in importance) have produced a graded relationship across levels of self-esteem, with those individuals experiencing the highest levels of discrepancy having the lowest self-esteem. Third, higher importance-competence correlations exist for those who have higher levels of self-esteem as they are able to attach the appropriate level of importance to their competence in order to achieve self-enhancement.

The construction of the Perceived Importance Profile (PIP) (Fox 1990) to accompany the PSPP allowed similar investigations to be conducted with constructs within the physical domain. Across a range of populations, including children, adolescents, competitive athletes, and obese and older adults (some from different countries), patterns of results similar to those of Harter and her colleagues have been found. For example, the low mean perceived sport competence score of females has consistently been accompanied by low mean ratings of importance—compatible with the discounting hypothesis. However, ratings of importance of body attractiveness remain high even though the attribute is scored low on average, producing a high discrepancy. The explanation for this is that certain criteria are so culturally dominant that most individuals are unable to override any inadequacies. Physical appearance provides the strongest case. Discrepancy scores in those domains considered important produce the same graded relationship with physical self-worth and self-esteem. Furthermore, importance-competence correlations are progressively higher in those who have higher physical self-worth. This is accompanied by a similar but weaker trend shown for self-esteem (see table 5.1).

Table 5.1 Importance-Competence Correlation Coefficients for Levels of Physical Self-Worth and Self-Esteem

	Physical self-worth			Self-esteem		
	Low	Med	High	Low	Med	High
Females (n = 178)						
Sport	.28	.49	.81	.58	.55	.78
Condition	.58	.48	.79	.76	.74	.56
Strength	.42	.59	.62	.48	.44	.60
Body	.05*	.14*	.09*	.13*	.36	-.04*
Males (n = 187)						
Sport	.59	.81	.64	.54	.71	.78
Condition	.35	.61	.56	.60	.60	.79
Strength	-.02*	.42	.71	.07*	.31	.72
Body	-.28*	.13*	.49	-.03*	.07*	.67

*Not significant at p = 0.05 level.

Reprinted with permission from K.R. Fox, 1990, *The Physical Self-Perception Profile Manual*, (DeKalb, IL: Office for Health Promotion, Northern Illinois University).

Note: Sport = perceived sport competence; Condition = perceived physical condition; Strength = perceived physical strength; and Body = perceived body attractiveness.

Examination of these correlations reveals that the grading is greatest for those domains in which discounting is more culturally permissible, as in sport and strength for females. The body subdomain for females shows little importance-competence congruence for any level of physical self-worth, and only the males with high physical self-worth and high self-esteem show significant correlations. There is even a tendency for males with low self-esteem to rate their bodies as important if they perceive low body attractiveness. These males also find it difficult to match their perceived strength with an appropriate level of importance.

The concept of perceived importance has therefore revealed some interesting relationships at the group and individual level that are generally supportive of specific self-enhancement strategies in the physical domain. Certainly, the findings are compatible with the evidence presented by Brown (1993) suggesting that those low in self-esteem tend to cling to some domains, even when they produce negative evaluations, in order to maintain self-consistency.

Research with the PSPP suggests that perceived importance concepts are worthy of further investigation, particularly when the individual is the unit of analysis. As indicated in her summary, Harter (1996) agrees: "For educational and clinical purposes, however, it is critical that one examine individual profiles since often the hierarchies of competence and importance are idiosyncratic, in very meaningful ways."

However, Marsh (1986, 1993, 1994; Marsh and Sonstroem 1995) through a series of thorough investigations has consistently failed to find support for the validity of weighted importance-competence combinations in the prediction of self-esteem. Marsh has applied a range of formulations across the content of domains in his multidimensional model and has found that the level of prediction of self-esteem has not increased over that obtained through competence ratings alone. This is a serious finding given the strength of theoretical support for the concept of perceived importance across psychology and sociology. One explanation is that the formulations used by Marsh and Sonstroem (1995) in their test of the PSPP and PIP did not appear to fully match those originally proposed by Harter or those in the PSPP manual (Fox 1990, 15). If the discounting hypothesis is taken into account, *only* those domains deemed high in importance by the individual should be included in any analyses, but it seems that all subdomains were used. Furthermore, the use of competence × importance cross products in a generalized multiple regression approach confounds the importance-competence relationship.

However, there are probably inadequacies in the measurement of importance. The two-item PIP subscales have rarely produced high alphas, and it is unlikely that they are able to adequately capture the abstract and subtle nature of the construct of importance to self-esteem. The competencies included in the PSPP were chosen because they emerged as important for a large percentage of the population, so there may be a ceiling effect for some elements. Physical appearance especially suffers from an invariance effect as it is rated high by almost everyone and its value in prediction is thereby curtailed. It is probably time for research to develop more direct and intensive techniques.

Already some alternative methods have become available. Harter, Marold, and Whitesell (1991) have used self-portraits with adolescents whereby the more central elements of self-concept can be differentiated from the more peripheral. Schema theory (Markus and Wurf 1987) emphasizes personally important domains and holds considerable promise. Kendzierski (1994) has adapted this approach to investigate exercise schematics; and Brewer, Van Raalte, and Linder (1993) have used the theory to operationalize athletic identity and have correlated the construct with perceived sport importance from the PIP ($r = .42$). In chapter 9, Page and Fox have broadened the concept of importance into centrality in their discussion of body image and weight management. Kelly's construct theory also appears to be highly related, and now that repertory grid computer software is available, data collection with larger numbers is more feasible, making findings more generalizable. In short, the concept of perceived importance should remain alive and kicking. It can be found in many theoretical guises and should continue to be investigated through a range of methods and techniques.

ALTERNATIVE CONTRIBUTORS TO SELF-ESTEEM

The chapter to this point has largely focused on the role that our perceived competencies and attributes play in our sense of worth. While the strengths of associations between constructs such as physical appearance and self-esteem cannot be ignored, there are important anomalies that still require explanations. For instance, it is not difficult to find people who retain high self-esteem even under what many of us would consider conditions of adversity or disadvantage, such as physical disability or extreme poverty. Equally, there are many examples of people who seem to have everything in terms of talents, friendship, and possessions but who are self-deprecating or even prone to suicidal ideation. Alternative contributors and mediators of self-esteem have been suggested that warrant consideration in future research.

A point that often seems to be neglected is that competence and attributes were included as only one element among others in early self-concept formulations. In Epstein's (1973) hierarchical model, higher-order factors included general competence, but also moral self-approval, power, and love-worthiness. Coopersmith's (1967) dimensions of self-evaluation included competence, virtue, power, and significance (social success and acceptance). It may be fruitful to consider how experiences in the physical domain can influence some of these other broader-based constructs. Similarly, the relationship between perceived competence and identity is worthy of exploration. The motivational consequences of sport competence may be weaker than the identity of being "sporty," which has broader connotations entailing the embracing of membership in a sport culture. Additionally, there are several overlapping theories of self-esteem formation that suggest that a reliance on competence and attributes may even be detrimental to self-worth.

UNCONDITIONAL SELF-WORTH

The notion that personal worth is a given aspect of life and not something to be earned or proved provided the mainstay of Rogers' client-centered therapy (1951). The focus of this approach was the *realization* rather than earning of self-esteem. Lockhart (1989) applied this theme to the physical domain. She maintained that actual worth is implicit and available to all individuals. Self-esteem was simply a case of unconditional and evaluation-free acceptance by the individual. Lockhart implied that self-worth built around beauty, achievement, and acquisitions is likely to be superficial, unstable, unnecessary, and in the long run counterproductive as it cannot be indefinitely maintained. She concluded that realization of worth is based on knowing that the love and regard of others is unconditional, on celebrating personal uniqueness, and on accepting that life has inherent meaning and purpose. Certainly the first element is substantiated by the work of Harter and colleagues (Harter 1993; Harter, Marold, and Whitesell 1991) demonstrating the low self-esteem and suicidal ideation of adolescents who perceive that the support of their parents is conditional on their achievements.

TRUE VERSUS CONTINGENT SELF-ESTEEM

Recently, Deci and Ryan (1996) have described *contingent self-esteem* as a construct based on meeting external standards of excellence or living up to interpersonal expectations. A person with contingent self-esteem relies heavily on social comparison, is therefore ego involved, and experiences self-esteem only when successful in life's interactions. Thus such a person is constantly driven to proving him or herself, is prone to narcissism and self-obsession, is conscious of a need for favorable self-presentation, is rarely satisfied, and functions in a "keep up with the Joneses" mode. Deci and Ryan conclude, "To the extent that attaining such a goal determines a person's self-esteem, one can well imagine that the person will use whatever means are available to match the standards, including rationalization, self-deception, and other defensive processes that have been linked to less positive mental health" (32). Such a basis to self-esteem is fragile. There will always be people with higher levels of competence; and self-esteem would radically shift when reference groups change, for example when one moves from the state to the national level of competition or changes jobs or schools. Also, for physical competencies and appearance there is an inevitable absolute decline or deterioration with aging.

Conversely, Deci and Ryan maintain, *true self-esteem* is more secure and stable. They hold that true self-esteem is reflected in agency, proactivity, and vitality but see the route to the true self as self-determination. They comment, "True self develops as one acts volitionally (i.e., autonomously), experiences an inner sense of efficacy (i.e., competence), and one is loved (i.e., feels related to) for who one is rather than for matching some external standard" (33).

It is easy to paint a picture of a culture that is absorbed in a selfish mission of self-confirmation, social approval seeking, and metaphorical and literal trophy collection. Certainly at present in some Western societies, there seems to be evidence that contingent self-esteem is more the norm than the exception. However, the questions at this point concern whether different forms of self-esteem can be measured, whether they can be acquired, whether they can exist in differing degrees in people, and what their short- and long-term consequences are.

SELF-DETERMINATION

Deci and Ryan (1991, 1996) maintain that in order to feel self-determined, people must feel that their successes are truly their own. Although perceived competence may be important for self-esteem, the *source* of motivation and energy underlying an achievement may be more powerful. Extrinsic motives, such those arising from a doctor instructing a patient to exercise and lose weight, are not integrated into the self-system and do not contribute to autonomy, but work to create a self-esteem that is contingent and conditional on adequacy. Intrinsic motives, on the other hand, are integrated into and compatible with the person's identity and therefore have the capacity to be truly self-enhancing and self-confirming at the same time.

Deci and Ryan (1996) summarize evidence that links intrinsically motivated behaviors positively to mental health and negatively to measures of anxiety and depression. Individuals who have a high degree of self-determination would feel that they have less to prove, would be better equipped to handle adversity as their sense of self is not on the line, would be less enamored of status and power over others, and would have more capacity for supporting others. Extrinsic aspirations produce the reverse pattern.

Examples of externally regulated behaviors abound in the physical domain. Sport performance in children may be motivated by the desire to acquire the support and love of parents or to impress peers (Horn and Weiss 1991); exercise is often driven by a desire to look good; people invest in cosmetic surgery in order to remain young looking; and in elite sport, motivation is often dominated by a desire for status and financial gain. The thesis of Deci and Ryan would suggest that in all these cases, there has not been full integration of the behavior into identity and that therefore contingent rather than true self-esteem will be the result.

In contrast, there are early signs that sport or exercise participation can help people feel self-determined. Sherrill (see chapter 10), for example, discusses the *growth through adversity hypothesis*, which describes how wheelchair athletes seem to capitalize on their capacity to adapt through mastery challenge. Empowerment and feelings of control over the body have been frequently reported by patients (particularly females) on weight loss and exercise regimes (Biddle, Fox, and Edmunds 1994; Fox 1992a; Wilfley and Brownell 1994). Actual weight loss and fitness change seem to be secondary in importance.

Common to these reports is the notion that the *process* rather than the *products* of participation has provided an important contribution to positive self-regard, with the likely mechanisms being mastery gain or self-determination. This clearly ties the achievement goal and organismic integration theories together in a potential partnership in self-esteem research. Furthermore, should these processes be further supported by research there are important implications for the way we design and evaluate programs in sport, exercise, health, and weight management. There would have to be a radical shift away from outcome to process objectives, from subject dependence to independence, and from "white-coated" instruction to partnership. The reader is referred to Fahlberg and Fahlberg (1990) and Miller and Rollnick (1993) for discussion of clinical approaches designed to increase autonomy.

SELF-ACCEPTANCE

Self-acceptance is probably closely related to the concept of conditional and unconditional self-esteem. The self-accepting person is fully aware of his/her strengths and weaknesses but still has a high personal regard. Wylie (1974) defines self-acceptance as "respecting oneself, including one's admitted faults" (127). Self-accepting people could rate themselves low on competencies or attributes in self-perception profiles but still rate themselves quite high on self-esteem or physical self-worth scales.

Self-acceptance has been adopted as a cornerstone to the campaigns of several organizations, such as "No Man's Land" and "Big Is Beautiful," that address the problem women face in dealing with the cultural pressures to be slim and attractive. It has also been a key issue in some of the fundamental approaches to therapy (Rogers 1951).

The concept has been applied to the physical domain by Sonstroem and Morgan (1989; see Sonstroem, chapter 1) through their exercise and self-esteem model. They hypothesize the existence of physical acceptance as a domain-specific construct that focuses heavily on the body and its appearance. They operationalize it as "the degree of satisfaction with various parts or processes of the body" (343). The construct was included on the basis that self-perceptions and satisfaction with the body are known to be related to self-esteem and that individual aspects of body acceptance may be responsive to changes in weight, fitness, or skill initiated through program involvement. However, since its initial conception, the physical acceptance aspect of the model has remained untested and the mechanisms of self-acceptance are unknown in the physical domain.

It must also be recognized that previous work (Shepard 1979) suggested that self-description and self-acceptance are highly related, indicating that acceptance of inadequacies is not a widespread phenomenon. It may be that absence of self-acceptance is a particular characteristic of some groups. For example, Sherrill (see chapter 10) has provided evidence that wheelchair athletes, although high on self-regard, score lower than able-bodied groups on self-acceptance dimensions of the Personal Orientation Inventory. Certainly lack of body acceptance or body dissatisfaction seems to be a major problem for a large percentage of women and a potential source of low self-esteem. In some cases, this remains a problem for some women even when there has been substantial investment in exercise and positive body changes have been acknowledged.

Given its potential impact on self-esteem, it is possible that strategies to increase self-acceptance could be introduced into interventions in the physical domain in much the same way that they have been a feature in counseling in other areas. There is sufficient evidence to warrant the development of instrumentation that allows a more complete analysis of the role of self-acceptance in the physical domain. However, the issue may be more complex than presented by Sonstroem and Morgan (1989), as there may be problems locating acceptance in relation to the real, ideal, or fantasized self (see discussion by Harter 1996). In addition, satisfaction as an indicator (as suggested by Sonstroem and Morgan [1989]) may overconstrain the construct. A more profound level of acceptance may be present—for example, individuals may have the capacity to accept limitations and at the same time prevent those limitations from interfering with self-regard even though they remain somewhat dissatisfied. However, this is an empirical question that requires careful instrument development and well-conducted studies.

IMPLICATIONS FOR FUTURE RESEARCH

Although the last decade has seen an upsurge in the quality and quantity of research into the physical self, in order to progress into a third phase it is necessary to take stock of some of the limitations of our achievements. The following observations are offered:

1. The development of physical self-perception profiles has been vitally important. With the luxury of two widely used profiles available and more studies constantly reported, there are now sufficient data to warrant a comprehensive review that should include unpublished data, theses and dissertations, and abstracts. This will provide an updated view of emerging patterns and provide a sounder basis for the next step forward.

2. Profiles are useful only to the extent that they represent the normative self-perceptions of the population of interest. This representation can be achieved only by regular iterative content analysis using open-ended questionnaires, interviews, and observations with a representative sample of the population. Users should not blindly apply instruments to new populations, as the content might be inappropriate. For example, Chase (1991) wished to extend the applicability of the PSPP to an older population;

through open-ended analysis this led to the replacement of the conditioning and strength scales by a functionality scale and to the addition of a health scale. Without initial and updated checks on the centrality of content to the value system of the population, there is a danger that we develop a statistically neat set of items that may relate well to specific behaviors but have limited relevance to the way people establish their self-esteem.

3. The major drawback with profiles is that even within a well-defined culture, they assume that values are pervasive and accepted by all individuals in the population. Although aspects of appearance such as slimness for females and muscularity and height for males seem to influence a large percentage of the population, they do not influence everyone. Also we know that some subcultures adopt quite different sets of values and criteria on which to judge themselves. We cannot study the links between self-perceptions of competence and self-esteem in a valueless vacuum. Ironically, the acceptance or nonacceptance of the cultural norm may reveal quite a lot about people and their degree of resilience or individuality. The assessment of perceived importance has been an initial attempt to address this problem and has demonstrated its ability to differentiate individuals on their self-esteem. However, it has not improved the predictability above that obtained with competence information alone, and this raises a question about the limitations of its measurement. New approaches are needed and personal constructs, self-schemata, priority ratings, and centrality indexes may provide fruitful alternatives.

4. A confounded vision of competence has been used in perception profiles. There is sufficient evidence from the goal perspectives (see Duda 1992) and self-determination theories (see Deci and Ryan 1996) to indicate that competence and adequacy ratings tell only part of the story. As important is the process by which competence was arrived at. Mastery and autonomy may be just as critical determinants of self-esteem as level of perceived ability. Future attempts to assess competencies and attributes should also address the degree of autonomy and mastery accompanying each. Appearance or athletic ability, for example, may be perceived as a natural gift or as a product of personally motivated hard work and dedication. It is possible that autonomy could be included as an extra facet in self-perception hierarchies.

5. Currently, self-esteem measures do not seem to be capable of distinguishing between different foundations to self-esteem. For example, individuals who do not rate their capacities and abilities as outstanding could still report high self-esteem if they were self-accepting or did not base their worth on such criteria. On the other hand, persons who are highly driven to compete, achieve, and demonstrate superiority and who have developed a complex set of self-biasing strategies could also report high self-esteem under frequent success conditions. Yet, according to Deci and Ryan these

two types of individuals would be quite different in their behaviors and value systems. It may be necessary to develop new self-esteem measures that incorporate factors such as self-esteem swings after failures and that directly tap the degree to which a person feels that his or her self is dependent on competencies and attributes. The functioning and measurement of physical self-worth may also need to be reappraised in the light of these principles.

6. Until we know more about the processes of global self-esteem change, those interested in charting the impact of interventions and programs should consider a range of assessments. These might include specific measures of those competencies or attributes that might be expected to be most responsive to the intervention. However, physical self-worth is important as it seems to reflect changes at a higher level and may carry mental well-being qualities of its own. In addition, measures that reflect other potential routes to change in self-esteem, such as autonomy and control, social acceptance, self-acceptance, centrality, and importance, might be included at both the global and the specific level. Furthermore, the individual should be the unit of study rather than the group, as there may be very different responses across people; those with initially low self-esteem should be a priority.

7. A normative and structural approach will give us a broad picture across populations. However, in most cases through the process of reflexivity and adjustment, self-esteem change may typically be quite slow, subtle, and intricate—and the outcome of several stages of reflection and iteration. Approaches are required that will (a) provide a richer source of information and (b) allow an ongoing analysis of change. Qualitative methods such as the case study or life history method are likely to be particularly informative (see Sparkes, chapter 4). In particular, critical cases might be chosen of people who are faced with adjustments to their self-system after serious accidents, successful and unsuccessful weight loss, recovery from serious sport injury or a coronary event, or rapid success in sport. The thesis underlying this approach is the accelerated rate of change and perhaps the more overt display of mechanisms of self-concept and self-esteem adjustment.

SUMMARY

The physical self is undoubtedly a powerful element of the self-system. A third phase of contemporary self-esteem research is required that focuses more directly on the processes of self-esteem formation and change and the role of the physical self in the self-system. Closer links between psychological and sociological theory have been suggested. The self cannot be studied in a social vacuum, as personal and cultural values and aspirations play a pivotal role. Normative multidimensional models and instruments have been useful as a baseline, but are limited in that they extract self-evaluative reactions on a range of fixed competence/adequacy criteria. Such models are better equipped to study the commonalities than the differences among people, and their fine-tuning through further study is not likely to produce major advances in understanding the mechanisms of change. Furthermore, the focus has been heavily on competencies and attributes. The key to understanding self-esteem variability and change may be found in the way life events eventually influence higher-order constructs and self-schemata such as love-worthiness, self-determination, and social acceptance. The notion of self-acceptance and unconditional self-regard, evident in earlier theories of psychotherapy, has been revived as an alternative view to self-esteem development. Furthermore, the dominance of perceived appearance has not been fully recognized, and its role as a superordinate construct similar to the notion of a public self warrants attention.

Single snapshots of the self will provide only limited insight. Approaches are required that are capable of assessing the dynamics of self-esteem change. The study of people who have been forced to redress their self-concept through dramatic life events may prove to be particularly fruitful.

The potential payoff from more focused study of the physical self and self-esteem change is high. Not only is this topic understudied and of tremendous academic interest, but it holds considerable practical relevance for the design of effective interventions in exercise, sport, rehabilitation from injury and illness, and the increasing problem of weight loss and management.

REFERENCES

Baumeister, R.F. 1987. How the self became a problem: A psychological review of historical research. *Journal of Personality and Social Psychology* 52 (1): 163-76.

—. 1991. *Meanings of life*. New York: Guilford.

—. 1993. Understanding the inner nature of self-esteem. In *Self-esteem: The puzzle of low self-regard*, ed. R.F. Baumeister, 201-18. New York: Plenum Press.

Berger, B.G., and McInman, A. 1993. Exercise and the quality of life. In *Handbook of research on sport psychology*, ed. R.N. Singer, M. Murphey, and L.K. Tennant, 729-60. New York: Macmillan.

Biddle, S.J.H., Fox, K.R., and Edmunds, L. 1994. *Physical activity promotion in primary health care in England*. London: Health Education Authority.

Blaine, B., and Crocker, J. 1993. Self-esteem and self-serving biases in reactions to positive and negative events: An integrative review. In *Self-esteem: The puzzle of low self-regard*, ed. R.F. Baumeister, 55-86. New York: Plenum Press.

Boutcher, S. 1993. Emotion and aerobic exercise. In *Handbook of research on sport psychology*, ed. R.N. Singer, M. Murphey, and L.K. Tennant, 799-814. New York: Macmillan.

Brewer, B.W., Van Raalte, J.L., and Linder, D.E. 1993. Athletic identity: Hercules' muscles or Achilles heel? *International Journal of Sport Psychology* 24: 237-54.

Brown, J.D. 1993. Motivational conflict and the self: The double bind of low self-esteem. In *Self-esteem: The puzzle of low self-regard*, ed. R.F. Baumeister, 117-30. New York: Plenum Press.

Campbell, J.D., and Lavallee, L.F. 1993. The role of self-concept confusion in understanding the behavior of people with low self-esteem. In *Self-esteem: The puzzle of low self-regard*, ed. R.F. Baumeister, 3-20. New York: Plenum Press.

Campbell, R.N. 1984. *The new science: Self-esteem psychology*. Lanham, MD: University Press of America.

Chase, L. 1991. Physical self-perceptions and activity involvement in the older population. Ph.D. diss., Arizona State University.

Collins, I.T. 1993. Cultural differences in perceived physical competence, self-esteem, and gender traits in female university students. Master's thesis, University of Rhode Island.

Cooley, C.H. 1902. *Human nature and the social order*. New York: Scribner.

Coopersmith, S. 1967. *The antecedents of self-esteem*. San Francisco: Freeman.

Crocker, P., Chad, K., Humbert, L., and Graham, T. 1994. The effects of a 10-week jump rope program on physical self-perceptions of grade nine students. *Journal of Sport and Exercise Psychology* 16 (suppl.): S44.

Curby, D. 1995. An analysis of the Physical Self-Perception Profile when administered to high school students. *Medicine and Science in Sports and Exercise* 27 (suppl.): S212.

Deci, E.L., and Ryan, R.M. 1991. A motivational approach to self: Integration in personality. In *Nebraska Symposium on Motivation*. Vol. 38, *Perspectives on motivation*, ed. R. Dienstbier, 237-88. Lincoln, NE: University of Nebraska.

—.1996. Human anatomy: The basis for true self-esteem. In *Efficacy, agency, and self-esteem*, ed. M. Kernis, 31-49. New York: Plenum Press.

Diener, E. 1984. Subjective well-being. *Psychological Bulletin* 95: 542-75.

Duda, J.L. 1992. Motivation in sport settings: A goal perspective approach. In *Motivation in sport and exercise*, ed. G.C. Roberts, 57-92. Champaign, IL: Human Kinetics.

Ebbeck, V. 1992. The structure of self-esteem in relation to the physical domain: An examination of hierarchical organization and directionality. *Proceedings of the Annual Conference of the American Alliance for Health, Physical Education, Recreation and Dance*. Reston, VA: American Alliance for Health, Physical Education, Recreation and Dance.

Epstein, S. 1973. The self-concept revisited or a theory of a theory. *American Psychologist* 28: 405-16.

—. 1991. Cognitive-experiential self-theory: Implications for developmental psychology. In *Self-processes and development: The Minnesota Symposium on Child Development*, vol. 23, ed. M.R. Gunnar and L.A. Stroufe. Hillsdale, NJ: Erlbaum.

Erikson, E. 1968. *Identity, youth, and crisis*. New York: Norton.

Fahlberg, L.L., and Fahlberg, L.A. 1990. From treatment to health enhancement: Psychosocial considerations in the exercise components of health promotion programs. *Sport Psychologist* 4: 168-79.

Fox, K.R. 1990. *The Physical Self-Perception Profile manual*. DeKalb, IL: Office for Health Promotion, Northern Illinois University.

—. 1992a. A clinical approach to exercise in the markedly obese. In *Treating the severely obese patient*, ed. T.A. Wadden and T.B. Van Itallie, 354-81. New York: Guilford.

—. 1992b. Physical education and self-esteem. In *New directions in physical education: Towards a national curriculum*, vol. 2, ed. N. Armstrong, 33-54. Champaign, IL: Human Kinetics.

Fox, K.R., and Corbin, C.B. 1989. The Physical Self-Perception Profile: Development and preliminary validation. *Journal of Sport and Exercise Psychology* 11: 408-30.

Fox, K.R., and Dirkin, G.R. 1992. Psychosocial predictors and outcomes of exercise in patients attending multidisciplinary obesity treatment. *International Journal of Obesity* 16 (suppl. 1): 84.

Fox, K.R., and Vehnekamp, T.J. 1992. Gender comparisons of self-perceptions, physical fitness, exercise and dietary habits of college students. *Journal of Sports Sciences* 10 (1): 282.

Giddens, A. 1991. *Modernity and self-identity*. Cambridge: Polity.

Gruber, J.J. 1986. Physical activity and self-esteem development and children: A meta analysis. *American Academy of Physical Education Papers* 19: 30-48.

Guidano, V.F. 1986. The self as mediator of cognitive change in psychotherapy. In *Perception of the self in emotional disorder and psychotherapy*, ed. L.M. Hartman and K.R. Blankstein, 305-30. New York: Plenum Press.

Hall, S. 1992. The question of cultural identity. In *Modernity and its futures*, ed. S. Hall, D. Hell, and T. McGrew, 374-425. Cambridge: Polity.

Hart, E.A., Leary, M.R., and Rejeski, W.A. 1989. The measurement of social physique anxiety. *Journal of Sport and Exercise Psychology* 11: 94-104.

Harter, S. 1985. *Manual for the Self-Perception Profile for Children*. Denver: University of Denver.

—. 1988. *Manual for the Self-Perception Profile for Adolescents*. Denver: University of Denver.

—. 1990. Causes, correlates, and the functional role of global self-worth: A life-span perspective. In *Competence considered*, ed. R.J. Sternberg and J. Kolligian, 67-97. New York: Vail-Ballou.

—. 1993. Causes and consequences of low self-esteem in children and adolescents. In *Self-esteem: The puzzle of low self-regard*, ed. R.F. Baumeister, 87-116. New York: Plenum Press.

—. 1996. Historical roots of contemporary issues involving the self-concept. In *Handbook of self-concept: Developmental, social, and clinical considerations*, ed. B.A. Bracken, 1-37. New York: Wiley.

Harter, S., Marold, D.B., and Whitesell, N.R. 1991. A model of psychosocial risk factors leading to suicidal ideation in young adolescents. *Development and Psychopathology* 4: 167-88.

Horn, T.S., and Weiss, M.R. 1991. A developmental analysis of children's self-ability judgments in the physical domain. *Pediatric Exercise Science* 3: 310-26.

James, W. 1892. *Psychology: The briefer course*. New York: Henry Holt.

Kelly, G.A. 1955. *The psychology of personal constructs*. New York: Norton.

Kendzierski, D. 1994. Schema theory: An information processing focus. In *Advances in exercise adherence*, ed. R.K. Dishman, 137-60. Champaign, IL: Human Kinetics.

La Ronde, C., and Swann Jr., W.B. 1993. Caught in the crossfire: Positivity and self-verification strivings among people with low self-esteem. In *Self-esteem: The puzzle of low self-regard*, ed. R.F. Baumeister, 147-66. New York: Plenum Press.

Leary, M.R. 1992. Self-presentation processes in exercise and sport. *Journal of Sport and Exercise Psychology* 14: 339-51.

—. 1995. *Self-presentation: Impression management and interpersonal behavior*. Dubuque, IA: Brown & Benchmark.

Leary, M.R., Tchividjian, L.R., and Kraxberger, B.E. 1994. Self-presentation can be hazardous to your health: Impression management and health risk. *Health Psychology* 13: 461-70.

Lecky, P. 1945. *Self-consistency: A theory of personality*. New York: Island Press.

Linville, P.W. 1985. Self-complexity and affective extremity: Don't put all of your eggs in one cognitive basket. *Social Cognition* 3 (1): 94-120.

Lockhart, B.D. 1989. Unconditional worth: A philosophical perspective. Paper presented at the Annual Conference of the American Alliance for Physical Education, Recreation and Dance, April, Boston.

Maehr, M.L., and Braskamp, L.A. 1986. *The motivation factor: A theory of personal investment.* Lexington, MA: Lexington Books.

Marcia, J. 1980. Identity in adolescence. In *Handbook of adolescent psychology*, ed. J. Adelson, 159-87. New York: Wiley.

Markus, H. 1977. Self-schemata and processing information about the self. *Journal of Personality and Social Psychology* 35: 118-33.

Markus, H., and Wurf, E. 1987. The dynamic self-concept: A social psychological perspective. *Annual Review of Psychology* 38: 299-337.

Marsh, H.W. 1986. Global self-esteem: Its relation to specific facets of self-concept and their importance. *Journal of Personality and Social Psychology* 51: 1224-336.

—. 1987. The hierarchical structure of self-concept and the application of hierarchical confirmatory factor analysis. *Journal of Educational Measurement* 24: 17-19.

—. 1992. *Self-Description Questionnaire II: Manual.* Sydney: Publication Unit, Faculty of Education, University of Western Sydney.

—. 1993. Relations between global and specific domains of self: The importance of individual importance, certainty and ideals. *Journal of Personality and Social Psychology* 65: 975-92.

—. 1994. The importance of being important: Theoretical models of relations between specific and global components of physical self-concept. *Journal of Sport and Exercise Psychology* 16: 306-25.

Marsh, H.W., Richards, G.E., Johnson, S., Roche, L., and Tremayne, P. 1994. Physical Self-Description Questionnaire: Psychometric properties and multitrait-multimethod analysis of relations to existing instruments. *Journal of Sport and Exercise Psychology* 16: 270-305.

Marsh, H.W., and Sonstroem, R.J. 1995. Importance ratings and specific components of physical self-concept: Relevance to predicting global components of self-concept and exercise. *Journal of Sport and Exercise Psychology* 17: 84-104.

Maslow, A. 1954. *Motivation and personality.* New York: Harper & Row.

Miller, W.R., and Rollnick, S. 1993. *Motivational interviewing: Preparing people to change addictive behaviour.* New York: Guilford.

Murphy, G. 1947. *Personality: A biosocial approach to origins and structure.* New York: Harper & Row.

Mutrie, N., and Davison, R. 1994. Physical self-perceptions in exercising older adults. *Journal of Sports Sciences* 12 (2): 203.

Page, A., Ashford, B., Fox, K.R., Biddle, S.J.H. 1993. Evidence of cross-cultural validity for the Physical Self-Perception Profile. *Personality and Individual Differences* 14 (4): 585-90.

Page, A., Fox, K.R., McManus, A., Armstrong, N. 1994. Profiles of self-perception change following an eight week aerobic training programme. *Journal of Sports Sciences* 12: 204.

Rogers, C.R. 1951. *Client-centered therapy.* Boston: Houghton Mifflin.

Rosenberg, M. 1965. *Society and the adolescent self-image.* Princeton, NJ: Princeton University Press.

Rotter, J.B. 1990. Internal versus external control of reinforcement: A case history of a variable. *American Psychologist* 45: 489-93.

Shepard, L.A. 1979. Self-acceptance: The evaluative component of the self-concept construct. *American Educational Research Journal* 16: 139-60.

Sonstroem, R.J. 1984. Exercise and self-esteem. In *Exercise and sport sciences reviews*, vol. 12, ed. R.L. Terjung, 123-55. Lexington, MA: Collamore Press.

Sonstroem, R.J., Harlow, L.L., and Josephs, L. 1994. Exercise and self-esteem. Validity of model expansion and exercise associations. *Journal of Sport and Exercise Psychology* 16: 29-42.

Sonstroem, R.J., and Morgan, W.P. 1989. Exercise and self-esteem: Rationale and model. *Medicine and Science in Sports and Exercise* 21 (3): 329-37.

Sonstroem, R.J., and Potts, S.A. 1996. Life adjustment correlates of physical self-concepts. *Medicine and Science in Sports and Exercise* 28: 619-25.

Sonstroem, R.J., Speliotis, E.D., and Fava, J.L. 1992. Perceived physical competence in adults: An examination of the Physical Self-Perception Profile. *Journal of Sport and Exercise Psychology* 14: 207-21.

Spencer, S.J., Josephs, R.A., and Steele, C.M. 1993. Low self-esteem: The uphill struggle for self-integrity. In *Self-esteem: The puzzle of low self-regard*, ed. R.F. Baumeister, 21-36. New York: Plenum Press.

Stryker, S. 1987. Identity theory: Developments and extensions. In *Self and identity*, ed. K. Yardley and T. Holness, 89-103. New York: Wiley.

Tesser, A. 1988. Towards a self-evaluation maintenance model of social behavior. In *Advances in experimental social psychology*, vol. 21, ed. L. Berkowitz, 181-227. New York: Academic Press.

Tice, D.M. 1993. The social motivations of people with low self-esteem. In *Self-esteem: The puzzle of low self-regard*, ed. R.F. Baumeister, 37-54. New York: Plenum Press.

Welk, G.J., Corbin, C.B., and Lewis, L. 1995. Physical self-perceptions of high school athletes. *Pediatric Exercise Science* 7: 152-61.

Werner, E.E. 1989. Vulnerability and resiliency: A longitudinal perspective. In *Children at risk: Assessment, longitudinal research, and intervention*, ed. M. Brambring, F. Losel, and H. Skowronek, 157-72. Berlin: Walter se Gruyter.

White, R.W. 1959. Motivation reconsidered: The concept of competence. *Psychological Review* 66: 297-333.

Whitehead, J.R. 1995. A study of children's physical self-perceptions using an adapted physical self-perception questionnaire. *Pediatric Exercise Science* 7: 132-51.

Wylie, R.C. 1974. *The self-concept: A review of methodological considerations and measuring instruments*. Vol. 1. Lincoln, NE: University of Nebraska.

—. 1979. *The self-concept*. Vol. 2, *Theory and research on selected topics*. Lincoln, NE: University of Nebraska.

Wilfley, D.E., and Brownell, K.D. 1994. Physical activity and diet in weight loss. In *Advances in exercise adherence*, ed. R.K. Dishman, 361-93. Champaign, IL: Human Kinetics.

PART II

POPULATIONS
AND
PRACTICE

CHAPTER 6

BODY IMAGE, EXERCISE, AND EATING BEHAVIORS

CAROLINE DAVIS

Considerable research has demonstrated a trend over the past 30 years toward the ideal of ultrathinness as the standard of female attractiveness (e.g., Garner et al. 1980; Mazur 1986; Silverstein, Perdue, Peterson, Vogel, and Fantini 1986). Furthermore, this trend has been gaining momentum (Morris, Cooper, and Cooper 1989; Wiseman et al. 1992). For example, Brenner and Cunningham (1992) reported that whereas the heights of a sample of New York fashion models were significantly greater than those of the average young woman (+9%), their weights were significantly lower than average (–16%). In fact, a disconcerting 73% of them were below the lower limits of recommended age-matched weight. Undoubtedly, comparisons made with such fashion icons have contributed to the estimated 90% of North American women who are dissatisfied with their body shape and size (Probast and Lieberman 1992).

Substantially less emphasis has been given to the study of men and body image. Recent reports suggest, however, that cultural attitudes toward the male body are in a state of change, that more than ever before men desire a muscular, mesomorphic body shape, and that men are moving further along a continuum of "bodily concern" (see Mishkind et al. 1986 for a review). Nevertheless, research is unclear about the impact this is having on the satisfaction or dissatisfaction men feel about their bodies. For example, some studies indicate relatively little body dissatisfaction or discrepancy between men's actual and ideal body size (e.g., Fallon and Rozin 1985; Rozin and Fallon 1988; Zellner, Harner, and Adler 1989), while other research (e.g., Davis and Cowles 1991; Drewnowski and Yee 1987; Mishkind et al. 1986) has demonstrated that males and females are equally dissatisfied with their shape and their size. It seems that measurement issues—in particular, differences in dissatisfaction indexes—may be at the heart of these problems. Whereas the vast majority of women would like to weigh less, some men wish to reduce their body size (i.e., reduce fatness) and others to increase it (i.e., increase muscularity). Both these responses, it must be acknowledged, are expressions of dissatisfaction.

In recent years, the mass media have been vilified for perpetuating images, among both sexes, of beauty and sexual attractiveness that are blatantly unrealistic and therefore unattainable for most. Although the media are not the only promoters of these images, nor perhaps the originators of such standards, their popularity in our image-oriented culture makes them at least the most powerful influence (see Silverstein, Perdue, Peterson, and Kelly 1986). While it is arguable that the media are more flagrant in the messages they present to women, men have certainly not been spared strong incentives to try to improve their physical appearance in conformation to an ideal standard. For example, a recent study reported that while the number of dieting articles in women's magazines was 10-fold that found in men's magazines, men were disproportionately subjected to articles promoting muscle tone and bodybuilding (Andersen and DiDomenico 1992).

Some contend that the moral climate of contemporary society reflects a profound self-absorption and that our culture has been characterized, over the past few decades, by a pervasive and increasing *narcissism* (also see Sparkes, chapter 4). Lasch (1979) argues that throughout this century there has been a growing sense that the world is moving inexorably toward destruction and annihilation. Individuals are losing their sense of historical continuity—the feeling of originating in the past and perpetuating into the future. As a consequence, we have spawned a generation who have retreated into the pursuit of purely personal aspirations, a generation whose concerns are not for spiritual salvation but for psychic well-being and good health that are often manifested as a rampant hedonism:

> The mass media, with their cult of celebrity and their attempt to surround it with glamour and excitement . . . give substance to, and thus intensify, narcissistic dreams of fame and glory, encourage the common [individual] to identify with the stars and to hate the "herd," and make it more and more difficult to accept the banality of everyday existence. (Lasch 1979, 21)

Perhaps there is no better testimony to this social and cultural phenomenon than the efforts of many of us to achieve bodily perfection at almost any cost.

Taking the point of view that body image is a psychobiological construct, it is my intention in this chapter to provide research evidence and theoretical considerations that show the dynamic influence of two inter-related behaviors—dieting and exercise—in how we come to view our physical selves.

BODY IMAGE AND ITS ASSESSMENT

In earlier research, self-esteem was viewed primarily as a unidimensional personality construct (e.g., Coopersmith 1967; Janis and Fields 1959). More recently, a hierarchical approach has been taken whereby global self-esteem is dependent on a number of lower-order dimensions that include, among other constructs, *body esteem* (Shavelson, Hubner, and Stanton 1976). Investigators have further refined the concept of body esteem by demonstrating empirically its multidimensional nature and differences in its structure that vary according to gender (Franzoi and Shields 1984). Clearly, *body image—* that is, the manner in which we view our body and the mental representation we have of it—forms an integral part of our body esteem and overall self-worth.

It is generally agreed that body image comprises both cognitive aspects, including perceptions about our bodies and our bodily experiences, and emotional aspects concerning the pleasure or displeasure, and satisfaction or dissatisfaction, we feel about its appearance and its function (see Pruzinsky and Cash 1990). Furthermore, these cognitions and emotions are purely *subjective* and therefore may bear close resemblance to reality or virtually none whatsoever. How we come to possess the myriad thoughts and feelings that compose our body experience is also complex. The validity of the multidimensional approach to the study of body image has been demonstrated in numerous studies, both with clinical samples and in the general population. In general, correlations between the perceptual and the attitudinal aspects of body image have been negligible (see Gardner and Tockerman 1992 for a review). By necessity, the two components of body image depend on different measurement procedures.

The perceptual aspect of body image relates to the congruence between subjective assessment of body size and shape and objective measurement. This index has usually been referred to as *body image distortion* or *size-estimation accuracy*. These techniques can be classified into two categories: *body-part* and *whole-body* procedures. Literally dozens of body-part procedures have been developed, but the general principle requires that respondents match the width of the distance between two points to their estimation of the width of some body site. Generally these images are presented on video monitors or photographically. In whole-body procedures, respondents are presented with a visual real-life image that is modified to appear progressively smaller or progressively larger than it really is, and they are asked to select the stimulus image that they believe bears the closest resemblance to their own image.

In general, assessment of the attitudinal component of body image has relied on self-report measures of body dissatisfaction whereby respondents rate the degree of satisfaction they experience about a number of specific body parts (e.g., Franzoi and Shields 1984; Garner and Olmsted 1984; Secord and Jourard 1959), or the extent of their feelings of fatness (Cooper et al. 1987). One difficulty is that many of these measures were designed for women and have not been validated for men. There also exist numerous sets of serial figure drawings (ranking sequentially from emaciated to obese) that are used to assess *ideal* and *perceived* body shape. From these two assessments a discrepancy measure can be calculated that serves as a measure of body dissatisfaction.

While there exists a very large body of literature concerning the convergence of assessments made, both within and between the perceptual and the subjective measurement techniques, it is not within the scope of this chapter to elaborate on these issues. Thompson, Penner, and Altabe (1990) have written a very comprehensive review of this complex topic.

ENDOGENOUS INFLUENCES ON BODY IMAGE

In addition to the far-reaching and diverse effects of social and environmental circumstances in the formation of body image concepts, a number of endogenous factors are influential, even pivotal, in the determination of body image perceptions. These can be characterized as either factors that are biological in origin, or factors that form part of the unique psychosocial *persona* of each individual.

BODY SIZE AND COMPOSITION

While body image may be influenced by a number of factors such as how energetic the body is, how well it performs the tasks required of it, and how frequently it breaks down, the preeminent factor in the formulation of the attitudes we hold about our physical self, at least during most of our lives, is the degree to which it conforms to the cultural ideals of beauty and sexual attractiveness. Although some may disagree on the reasons, there is no doubt that traditionally, and to a much greater degree than seen among men, women have slavishly followed the dictates of fashion in their pursuit of these ideals (see Mazur 1986). The history books are replete with examples of the time, money, and discomfort that women have invested in their quest for feminine beauty. In recent years, however, this activity has approached a frenzied obsession. Regrettably, *perfection* for women is now defined by an aesthetic yardstick that is so unrealistic, aberrant, and potentially unhealthy that for the majority, reasonable efforts to achieve this standard are destined to failure.

It is hardly surprising, therefore, that body weight (most frequently represented as Body Mass Index [BMI]: weight[kg]/height[m^2]) and body fat content have consistently been found, particularly among women, to correlate positively with measures of body dissatisfaction (Bailey et al. 1990; Brodie and Slade 1988; Davis, Durnin et al. 1994), of "feeling fat" (Strauman et al. 1991), and of dietary restraint—even among non-obese women (Davis, Shapiro et al. 1993; Davis, Durnin et al. 1993) and boys and girls (Fox, Page, Armstrong, and Kirby 1994; Fox, Page, Peters, Armstrong, and Kirby 1994). Estimates of the strength of these relationships vary considerably across studies as a result of differences in questionnaire assessments, choice of anthropometric indexes, and, in some cases, the characteristics of the samples tested. Surprisingly, however, the shared variance between body image and weight or fatness does not typically extend beyond about 30%.

Research has identified other anatomical features that influence the degree to which women report dissatisfaction with their bodies, a preoccupation with dieting, or both. One study found that waist-to-hip circumference ratio (WHR; lower values indicating greater femoral/buttocks, as opposed to abdominal, distribution of fat) was inversely related to weight preoccupation and disordered eating behavior, even though WHR was positively related to BMI (Radke-Sharpe, Whitney-Saltiel, and Rodin 1990). In other words, the larger a woman's hip circumference is, relative to her waist size, the more she is weight preoccupied. These findings are rather at odds with a recent series of studies demonstrating that for male judges the figure drawings rated most physically attractive were those showing women of normal weight and a low WHR (Singh 1993).

There is also evidence that certain regions of a woman's body are more salient determinants of body dissatisfaction than others. A recent study investigated relationships between the dissatisfaction ratings for various body parts and the girth of their respective anatomic referents among a group of college women. Only hips and buttocks retained a systematic association between ratings and measurements when corrected for the effects of body fatness (Bailey et al. 1990). Furthermore, Davies and Furnham (1986) found that slender and narrow hips were the body feature most sought after by adolescent girls (see Page and Fox, chapter 9, for further discussion).

While there was an inverse relationship between stature and body dissatisfaction among adult men, this association was not found among adult women (Gupta, Schork, and Dhaliwal 1993). However, other aspects of the fat-free mass have been implicated in body image perceptions and related behaviors. After controlling for body mass and percentage body fat, frame size (estimated from the sum of four bone diameter measurements: ulnar, bicondylar femur, biacromium, and bi-iliac) was found to be positively associated with body and weight dissatisfaction among women (Davis, Durnin et al. 1993; Davis, Durnin et al. 1994). In fact, in one of these studies

(Davis, Durnin et al. 1994), results indicated that the hip diameter measurement was a more salient factor in the determination of body dissatisfaction than the overall estimate of frame size. When women declare that they want to be "thinner," it seems that thin is precisely what they want to be since thin implies *narrow* as well as *lean*.

Evidence for this preference is highlighted by changes in the images of women who represent the ideal standard of beauty and perfection. For example, the body shape of English fashion models between 1967 and 1987 showed an increasing tendency toward smaller breasts and narrower hips (Morris, Cooper, and Cooper 1989). *Playboy* centerfold models have become increasingly lean and almost hipless in the last 20 years (Mazur 1986), and Miss America contestants from 1979 to 1985 showed a significant decrease in percentage of expected weight while the only girth measurement to change was hip size, which decreased (Wiseman et al. 1992).

PERSONALITY

There is ample evidence that North American and other Western societies encourage, even reward, our pursuit of the socially imposed standards of body aesthetics. Not only does this symbolize the attainment of a plethora of personal virtues and achievements, but it has also come to signify physical fitness and health. Not surprisingly, numerous studies have found a positive relationship between happiness and physical attractiveness (e.g., Mathes and Kahn 1975; Noles, Cash, and Winstead 1985). However, excessive body image concerns, weight preoccupation, and related behaviors do not occur simply because of social pressures on women to conform to a very slender standard of female beauty. Clearly, certain personality characteristics tend to amplify some individuals' responses to these pressures (Striegel-Moore, McAvay, and Rodin 1986). Since the body image standards to which women are expected to aspire are presently far beyond what most can achieve sensibly, if at all, a psychological conundrum may develop when personal vulnerabilities clash with unrealistic cultural expectations. As a consequence, some may fall victim to extreme and dysfunctional attitudes and behaviors concerning their body and how to care for it.

Negative attitudes about the body and disordered eating behaviors have been associated with low self-esteem among adult men and women (Brenner and Cunningham 1992; Mintz and Betz 1986) and among adolescent boys and girls (Fox, Page, Armstrong, and Kirby 1994; Fox, Page, Peters, Armstrong, and Kirby 1994). However, the relationship tends to be stronger for females of all ages. Williams et al. (1993) also found that eating-disordered patients reported significantly lower self-esteem than nonclinical dieters, and concluded that poor self-esteem is a trait of anorexia and bulimia nervosa. Other research indicates that depressed mood is associated with poor body image and with measures of disordered eating (Denniston, Roth, and Gilroy 1992; McCauley et al. 1988; Noles, Cash, and Winstead 1985).

Despite the fact that causal evidence is not entirely clear, or wholly justified, the inference in many of these studies is that low self-esteem is a precursor of poor body image and consequent weight and diet concerns. This issue relates to a recurrent theme in this book concerning the directionality of influence within the self-esteem complex. A sounder view is that body image derives not only from an individual's cognitive and emotional development, but that feelings about one's body can influence other psychological characteristics like affect and self-esteem (Lerner and Jovanovic 1990) and that actual attractiveness plays an integral role in the development of positive body image perceptions, particularly during early adolescence (see Keelan, Dion, and Dion 1992 for a review). In other words, body image has a dual role both as a consequence and as an antecedent of psychological functioning. In view of the social rewards that the attractive enjoy, an objectively beautiful body is likely to enhance one's general self-esteem and positive affect. On the other hand, those who have developed a diminished sense of self-worth through poor social and personal interactions are naturally more likely to view their bodies negatively (see Lerner and Jovanovic 1990).

The relationships between body image attitudes/dieting behaviors and other aspects of personality such as emotional reactivity (*neuroticism*) have also been investigated. Individuals who are characterized by high levels of neuroticism are described as anxious, easily aroused, and preoccupied with things that might go wrong (Eysenck and Eysenck 1975, 1991). In other words, they tend to respond emotionally to generalized psychological and environmental stressors. A number of studies have demonstrated that neuroticism is positively related to body dissatisfaction in both women (Davis and Cowles 1989; Dionne et al. 1995) and men (Davis et al. 1991) and, among both sexes, to dietary restraint and concerns about eating and weight even after the effects of body mass are partialled out (Davis, Durnin et al. 1993; Davis et al. 1990; Davis, Shapiro et al. 1993). In our current cultural climate, high emotional reactivity is likely, therefore, to foster a worrying preoccupation with weight and shape among women even, it seems, in the absence of objective reasons for such concern.

In a recent study, an interesting interaction was found in women between neuroticism and body focus. This construct is related to the concept of *centrality* discussed by Fox in chapter 5 and represents the degree to which psychological well-being is dependent upon satisfaction with one's appearance. A strong relationship between weight preoccupation and neuroticism was essentially present only at high levels of body focus (Davis and Fox 1993). That is, only at high levels of neuroticism *and* body focus do women report excessive weight preoccupation.

Some have claimed that weight preoccupation, particularly among normal or underweight women, reflects among other things a strong *narcissistic* dynamic (Sacks 1987), or self-admiring preoccupation with the body (Katz 1986). While research on the topic is limited, one study did find that more narcissistic individuals evaluated their physical appearance more favorably, considered appearance and fitness to be more important, and engaged in more appearance- and fitness-related activities, especially bodybuilding (Carroll 1989; Jackson, Ervin, and Hodge 1992). In a recent study, however, we found that high narcissism is only associated with good body esteem when neuroticism levels are low (Davis, Claridge, and Brewer 1996). As neuroticism increases, body esteem decreases at every level of narcissism, but most steeply among highly narcissistic individuals. Our results demonstrate clearly the adaptive as well as the maladaptive sides of narcissism. On the one hand, narcissism can enhance psychological well-being; however, in the setting of an emotionally unstable personality, it appears to have the opposite effect.

In summary, it seems that unduly low self-esteem, high neuroticism, and perfectionism are the most common psychological correlates of weight and diet concerns, at least among women. They are also among the most commonly reported premorbid personality characteristics of anorexic and bulimic women (Solyom, Freeman, and Miles 1982; Williamson et al. 1985).

AGE

There is little doubt that our present culture not only idealizes female slenderness but also glorifies the young and places considerable importance on youthful looks. It has consistently been reported that attitudes toward aging are remarkably similar across the life span and that these attitudes are primarily negative. For example, the later years of life are associated with loneliness, depression, poor health, intellectual decline, and resistance to change (e.g., Babladelis 1987; Doka 1985/1986; Peterson, Hall, and Peterson 1988). Few would argue that there exists, however, a double standard in the degree to which older adults experience the negative social consequences of aging. While in a general sense modern society deems it a misfortune to lose one's youth, this loss seems to be more poignant for women since the burden of physical beauty rests more squarely on their shoulders, and since a greater degree of power and prestige is often accorded the middle-aged man than the middle-aged woman (Berman, O'Nan, and Floyd 1981).

Because most of the research on body image has been conducted on adolescents and young adults, its nature and correlates across the full range of the adult life span are less well understood. Clearly, there are physical changes associated with aging that may have significant implications for the way in which older adults view their bodies and for how they deal, psychologically and behaviorally, with the inevitable ravages of time. Attempts to counteract the cutaneous signs of aging are evidenced, for example, by the dramatic increases in the numbers of women seeking cosmetic plastic surgery in the form of blepharoplasty (eyelid surgery), rhytidectomy (face-lift), and liposuction (Pruzinsky and Edgerton 1990).

Although weight and body fat tend to increase with age, large sample surveys indicate a surprising increase in frequency of health-related practices with increased age, except for weight control and physical activity participation (Bausell 1986; Prohaska et al. 1985). It has been suggested that many older adults fear injury, tend to underestimate their own physical abilities (Conrad 1976), and deem physical activity participation a less "appropriate" behavior as their age increases (Ostrow and Dzewaltowski 1986). Prohaska et al. (1985) also found that middle-aged and older adults were less likely than younger adults to view regular exercise as disease preventive. On the other hand, there are many examples of older men and women who clearly value fitness and activity, as they pursue it throughout later life.

Research is generally consistent in the finding that women of all ages report greater body dissatisfaction than men, and importantly, that these differences do not appear to diminish or increase much with age (Altabe and Thompson 1993; Davis and Cowles 1991; Pliner, Chaiken, and Flett 1990). In fact, high levels of body image dissatisfaction have been demonstrated in children as young as nine years old (Hill, Oliver, and Rogers 1991; Thelan et al. 1992). However, in one study that examined various aspects of body disparagement, it was found that although age was not related to a measure of *general* body dissatisfaction among women (after controlling for body weight, physical activity, and personality factors), it was inversely related to a measure of *specific* body dissatisfaction (Dionne et al. 1995). Younger women were more critical of their hips, thighs, and buttocks. Related research has also indicated that women, more than men, want to weigh less, and that these differences occur among young and older adults (Pliner, Chaiken, and Flett 1990; Rozin and Fallon 1988).

While some have found that the affective importance of appearance decreases with age (Pliner, Chaiken, and Flett 1990), others have observed no differences between men and women, regardless of age, in their degree of body focus (Davis and Cowles 1991; Davis, Shapiro et al. 1993). In one of these studies (Davis, Shapiro et al. 1993), body focus was also directly related to dietary restraint (after controlling for body fat content) in all age-by-sex groups except among men between the ages of 40 and 60. It appears that attitudes to aging also influence body image. Gupta, Schork, and Dhaliwal (1993) found that women and, to a lesser degree, men who were concerned about the effects of aging (independent of age or body size) tended to be more preoccupied with losing weight and more dissatisfied with their appearance.

In summary, body image disparagement, at least among women, does not seem to alter significantly across most of the adult life span. Although little research has investigated whether the nature of this dissatisfaction changes with age, we do have some indication that women become less critical of their hips and thighs and buttocks as they mature. One can only speculate that the body dissatisfaction of older women may reflect certain cutaneous (e.g., loss of elasticity) and subcutaneous (e.g., diminished muscle tone) effects of aging rather than the degree to which they perceive a discrepancy between their own body and that of the lean, slender, and youthful ideal. The mechanisms by which dissatisfaction translates into the behavioral choices of the individual remain unclear and underresearched. For example, no explanations have been provided for the differences in the way older people either accept aging as a natural and inevitable process or challenge it by using strategies such as cosmetic surgery, dieting, or exercise.

RACE, CULTURE, AND ETHNICITY

There is general agreement that an inverse relationship exists between socioeconomic status (SES) and fatness among women, but only in *developed* countries. Among men, the nature of this relationship is still unclear. On the other hand, in *developing* countries there is a strong positive relationship between SES and fatness both for men and for women, since plumpness or moderate fatness is actually valued and idealized in many of these societies (see Sobal and Stunkard 1989 for a review). Some have argued that this standard has evolutionary significance since natural selection has favored those who are efficient at storing fat during times of food shortages, which historically were frequent and unpredictable (Probast and Lieberman 1992). Therefore, the sanctity that Western societies now place on rakish female thinness is clearly a cultural anomaly, and one that has naturally evoked a number of social, ecological, and feminist theories of explanation (see Andersen et al. 1992 for a review).

No doubt as a direct consequence of our current preference for ultraslender women, there has been, over the past 30 years, a higher prevalence of eating disorders among women in Europe and North America than in the developing countries, including Japan (Ohzeki et al. 1990), and among black women in Western societies (Dolan 1991). However, recent reports suggest that these differences may be decreasing in magnitude (Ohzeki et al. 1993; Smith and Krejci 1991).

In the light of these findings, racial differences and ethnic affiliations have been credited as important predisposing factors in the development of women's subjective body image experiences. Attempts to understand and explain these associations have prompted a number of studies whose purpose has been to investigate cross-cultural perceptions of the ideal female body shape, and specifically to ascertain how these social standards influence women's body image attitudes and behaviors.

In general, studies comparing African-American and white American women have found significant body image differences, even after controlling for group differences in body mass. For example, in one investigation, black American female college students reported greater body satisfaction and fewer weight and diet concerns than their white peers (Rucker and Cash 1992), while other research has found less disparagement of obesity and greater body esteem among obese black women compared to obese white women (Harris, Walters, and Waschull 1991; Rand and Kuldau 1990). However, simple group comparisons are likely to overlook other subtleties in the nature of these differences. For example, a recent study (Allan, Mayo, and Michel 1993) produced evidence of an interaction between SES and race in the determination of body image attitudes. African-American women of lower SES were significantly different both from African-American women of higher SES and from white women, irrespective of SES. Both quantitative and qualitative data indicated that African-American women of lower SES were objectively heavier, viewed themselves as heavier, and perceived an attractive body size as larger. Furthermore, in the families of lower SES African-American women, there was little or no stigma associated with obesity and therefore no perceived pressure among the women to engage in weight loss activities. It seems, therefore, that the pursuit of an ultraslender body does not dominate the social and sexual identity of many African-American women, particularly those of lower SES, to the same degree as it does white women.

This finding meshes with other research in traditional African-Caribbean cultures where full-figured women are perceived to have higher status. For instance, Furnham and Baguma (1994) found that both male and female Ugandan university students tended to rate drawings of figures that were heavy to obese as much more attractive and healthier than did the equivalent group of British students. Furnham and Alibhai (1983) also found that Kenyan Asians tended to perceive thin female shapes more negatively and fat shapes more positively than either British or British Asian women even though they were significantly heavier than the British subjects.

More recent research is generally in accord with these findings. Wardle and her colleagues found that Asian women in the United Kingdom were more satisfied with their body size and less likely to want to lose weight than white women, and that they selected a slimmer female body ideal than did white women (Wardle et al. 1993). However, these results were confounded by the fact that the Asian women were also slimmer than their white counterparts. After this factor was statistically controlled for, group differences in body image were substantially reduced, and in some cases they disappeared. The authors suggest that the more positive body image attitudes found among Asian women may not necessarily reflect cultural differences in ideals of female body size. They may simply imply more tolerant attitudes to obesity, or the fact that body image perceptions are a less emotive issue among Asian women than among Western white women.

In summary, there is evidence that white women in Western societies prefer a thinner and leaner body shape than their Asian, African, or African-American counterparts. Nevertheless, in some cases, these differences appear to be diminishing, especially when comparisons are made with nonwhite women of higher SES or with those who have been raised in Western cultures.

GENDER-ROLE ORIENTATION AND SEXUAL PREFERENCE

Some believe that the rather polarized images that currently typify the body ideals of men and women reflect a backlash against the gender equality toward which society has been moving over the past 30 years or so. It has been suggested, for example, that the hypermesomorphic male physique may be one of the last remaining ways in which men can assert their masculinity in a world that they previously dominated and that is now threatened by the movement of women into positions of power and authority. Similarly, the ultraslender female ideal may be the "last bastion of femininity" at a time in which gender roles are blurred and status and wealth are no longer the exclusive domain of men (see Mishkind et al. 1986).

Others have proffered different explanations for our preference for the slender female body shape. On the basis of evidence that curvaceous and large-breasted women are typically perceived as less competent and less intelligent than nonvoluptuous women, Silverstein and his colleagues have proposed that these cultural associations have led women who are concerned about how others view their competence and intellect to aspire to a thin and nonvoluptuous appearance (Silverstein, Perdue, Peterson, Vogel, and Fantini 1986). The coincidence of the feminist revolution of the late 1960s and the advent of superslender female fashion images in the same period is an example that provides some support for this hypothesis. In addition, Silverstein and Perdue (1988) found that the drive-for-thinness as well as body dissatisfaction among bulimic women related more to a concern for professional success than to a concern about sexual attractiveness. Furthermore, during this century, a noncurvaceous female ideal has emerged at times when the proportion of women entering the workforce has been relatively high and rapidly increasing.

Several authors have drawn attention to the conflicting sociocultural messages with which women are currently bombarded (e.g., Brumberg

1989; Steiner-Adair 1986). On the one hand, they are inundated with media images of female beauty and the rewards consequent on achieving this standard. On the other, society is clear in the emphasis it places on the virtues of independence, intellectual freedom, individuality, and autonomy for women, both in the home and in the workplace. Indeed, the concept of *superwoman* arose precisely because of this conflict, and as a description of those women for whom the aspiration of success in many roles is paramount and integral to their sense of self-worth.

A small but compelling body of literature has investigated the influence of gender-role orientation and sexual preference on men's and women's attitudes toward their bodies and toward weight concerns. Among a sample of undergraduate women, it was found that the importance of appearance was positively related to both femininity (on a standard measure of masculinity and femininity) and to disordered eating (Timko et al. 1987). Women who were characterized by both feminine and masculine traits—in other words, those for whom many, rather than few, roles were important to their sense of self-worth—also reported a greater number of eating-disordered symptoms. Similarly, a recent study found that aspects of feminist ideology were related positively to body satisfaction among young and middle-aged women after controlling for other salient factors like body composition, physical activity, and personality factors (Dionne et al. 1995).

The observation that men are more attracted to and sexually aroused by physical characteristics than are women (see Mazur 1986), and the fact that homosexual women do not require validation from men, either sexually or emotionally, have led some to hypothesize that lesbian women may feel less pressure to conform to social standards of attractiveness and consequently to be more satisfied with their bodies and their appearance. Comparisons between lesbian and heterosexual women have tended to support this viewpoint. Three studies found that while lesbian women were significantly heavier than heterosexual women and preferred heavier physiques, they were more satisfied with their bodies and less concerned about their appearance in general (Brand, Rothblum, and Solomon 1992; Herzog et al. 1992; Siever 1994). Although one earlier study failed to find the expected differences between these groups, the authors themselves suggested that this may have been due to the small sample size and biased subject selection (Striegel-Moore, Tucker, and Hsu 1990).

Limited research has indicated that gay men report greater body dissatisfaction and weight preoccupation, and consider appearance more central to their sense of self-worth, than do heterosexual men (Brand, Rothblum, and Solomon 1992; Silberstein et al. 1989). These findings corroborate the viewpoint that appearance and physical attractiveness are more salient attributes in the gay male subculture than among straight men. They also offer some support to earlier evidence that homosexual men may have eating disorders more often than heterosexual men (e.g., Andersen and Mickalide 1983; Herzog et al. 1984). While the authors of a recent study claimed that there was no self-disclosure of homosexuality among any of the 12 male anorexics in their sample, they did acknowledge that effeminate features were more likely to be present (Touyz, Kopec-Schrader, and Beumont 1993).

While there is general agreement that body dissatisfaction is significantly less in lesbians and heterosexual men than in gay men and heterosexual women, there has been little attempt to explain these findings. One compelling explanation attributes the heightened emphasis on physical appearance found in gay men and heterosexual women to the fact that both these groups have a desire to attract and please men. The results of several studies over a number of years agree that men tend to be more concerned than women with the physical appearance of a potential mate (see Siever 1994 for a review).

BODY IMAGE STABILITY

On the face of it, we might reasonably assume that body image cognitions are as capricious and dynamic as many other attitudes and that they are influenced and altered by the vagaries of personal circumstance and mood. Nevertheless, the dominant paradigm in body image research has been predicated, almost entirely, on the notion that body image is a relatively stable construct, at least in the short term. Until quite recently, little attention had been given to the question of whether short-term situational factors can create fluctuations in body image perceptions. As a result, our understanding has been limited, and research is scant.

Within the context of the influence of media on standards of beauty and sexual attractiveness, two recent studies examined the changeability of body image. Myers and Biocca (1992) investigated how the mood and body satisfaction of young women were influenced by television programming and advertising that focused on the ideal, thin female body. The results were surprising and provocative. Although body shape perception was in fact changed by watching as little as 30 minutes of television, subjects reported *feeling thinner* than they normally did, and having enhanced affect, compared to a group of control subjects. Myers and Biocca speculated that for a brief period, their subjects may have imagined themselves *in* the attractive body presented by the advertising.

Exploring a different aspect of body image and its receptiveness to media influences, Hamilton and Waller (1993) found no differences in body size estimation when a group of women were exposed to a series of photographs featuring female fashion models or beautiful homes. On the other hand, a comparison group of anorexic and bulimic patients showed a 25% increase in body size estimation after exposure to the fashion photographs, but not to the neutral pictures. These results suggest that real-life stimuli may have differential effects in their contribution to body image perceptions that are dependent on the particular psychological characteristics of the individual. In a related study, and one that was rooted in the framework of social comparison theory, the investigators set out to assess how exposure to same-sexed peers of varying levels of attractiveness affected females' perceptions of their own physical attractiveness (Cash, Cash, and Butters 1983). As predicted, those exposed to attractive women reported lower levels of perceived physical attractiveness than those exposed to plainer women. However, this effect was found only when the attractive stimulus was believed to be a peer rather than a professional model. The authors conclude that in a practical sense, exposure to magazines filled with pictures of thin and beautiful models may have little immediate effect on women's body esteem although there may be long-term consequences on the manner in which society comes to view the female body.

The influence of a variety of other situational factors on body image has also been explored. For example, Wardle and Foley (1989) tested the sensitivity of body image to environmental conditions by taking assessments before and after subjects ate solid meals that differed with respect to how fattening they appeared to be. Only young women weighing within 10% of ideal body weight were included in the study. Results indicated that postmeal assessments of body dissatisfaction and feelings of fatness were greater than premeal assessments. However, the apparent (but not real) caloric differences between the two test meals did not produce differential effects.

Further research on the effects of food consumption on body image produced unexpected results (Thompson et al. 1993). Runners (a supposed high-risk group) were less negatively affected by a high-calorie milk shake than a group of sedentary controls. The authors concluded that perhaps body image-concerned individuals without the anticipation of a compensatory strategy such as exercise are likely to be more negatively affected. In a similar vein, the effect of negative versus positive body size feedback on body dissatisfaction was also assessed in female college students. Contrary to expectation, the negative feedback did not exacerbate body dissatisfaction or affect mood or self-esteem to a greater degree than did positive feedback. However, subjects who were compared to a more global group reported less dissatisfaction than those compared to a peer-matched group (Heinberg and Thompson 1992).

As a further test of the hypothesis that body image can be influenced by short-term situational factors, female subjects in another study were told, by means of a guided imagery technique, to imagine themselves in each of four different situations that invited varying degrees of body scrutiny (e.g., on the beach vs. getting dressed at home alone) (Haimovitz, Lansky, and O'Reilly 1993). Results indicated, not surprisingly, that women were more critical of their bodies in situations of greater exposure. Recently, Roth and Armstrong (1994) developed a feelings of fatness questionnaire and reported that female subjects demonstrated considerable cross-situational variability concerning their experience of bodily thinness and fatness. In particular, they found that body image is influenced by changes in affective state, public scrutiny, self-consciousness, and the nature of one's personal field. We are cautioned, however, that while feelings and thoughts about one's body may change as a result of a number of situational factors, we cannot conclude that a *global* level of body satisfaction is nonexistent (Haimovitz, Lansky, and O'Reilly 1993). Finally, biological factors have also been causally implicated in the fluctuation of body image. Altabe and Thompson (1990) examined the role of the menstrual cycle as a moderator of body image change and eating dysfunction, and found that body image and eating disturbances were greater during the perimenstrual than the intermenstrual phase.

In summary, although more evidence is required to state definitively the degree to which body image is fluid and changeable, there is good reason to believe that it comprises both relatively fixed and relatively dynamic components. That is, there is an indication that, under some circumstances, a woman's body image is an *elastic* construct that vacillates between her internalized ideal body and her external objective shape (Myers and Biocca 1992).

BODY IMAGE AND RELATED BEHAVIORS

As a result of the cultural value attached to appearance in Western societies, and in particular the prominence of body form, body image now plays an increasingly important role in the development and maintenance of the self. In an effort toward self-enhancement, both men and women make attempts to improve their bodies through a range of behaviors and activities, some of which have become extreme and counterproductive.

DIETARY RESTRAINT

Almost as many males as females report being dissatisfied with some aspect of their body shape or size (Cash 1990); however, *weight* (or perception of weight) is probably the predominant factor in the determination of body image, at least among women. Although health care professionals are actively promoting sensible eating in order to reduce the health risks of obesity, most experts agree that dieting is associated with body disparagement. In other words, dieting usually accompanies (and is probably motivated by) "feeling fat" even, it appears, in the absence of objective reasons for such concern (e.g., Striegel-Moore, McAvay, and Rodin 1986).

Estimates indicate that at any one time, nearly 50% of North American women are on a diet. Indeed, the money spent on diet books, calorie-reduced foods, and weight loss programs nearly doubled in the 1980s (Brownell

1991). There is also considerable evidence that even relatively slender adult women (e.g., Davis and Cowles 1991; Rodin, Silberstein, and Striegel-Moore 1985) and slim female adolescents (e.g., Maude et al. 1993; Page and Fox, chapter 9; Wardle and Beales 1986) want to lose weight and are actively dieting. Not surprisingly, the literature proliferates with numerous reports of exceedingly high levels of body dissatisfaction in patients suffering from anorexia and bulimia nervosa.

In the past decade, cultural attitudes toward the male body have undergone a change. It seems that more than ever before, men desire a muscular and hypermesomorphic body shape and that they are frequenting diet clinics at a greater rate than in the past (Mishkind et al. 1986). Furthermore, it is well known that the recreational use of anabolic steroids is widespread among men intent on maximizing their muscle mass.

In a recent study investigating the dieting behaviors of young adult and middle-aged men and women, we found that body dissatisfaction was strongly related to dietary restraint (after controlling statistically for body mass, physical activity levels, and certain salient personality characteristics) in all groups except middle-aged men (Davis, Shapiro et al. 1993). These findings led us to conclude that dieting is less likely to be an appearance-related behavior in this cohort and more likely to be a health-related activity, especially when one considers the well-publicized information on the association between obesity and cardiovascular disease. Earlier findings also support this contention (Davis and Cowles 1991). There was no relationship in older men between perceived weight relative to desired weight and a measure of body dissatisfaction, while there was a moderately strong relationship in women.

EXERCISE AND FITNESS

Two dominant subcultures, the fitness movement and competitive sport/athletics, provide a psychosocial backdrop and a framework within which to examine the relationship between body image perceptions and physical activity among men and women. It is no longer a moot point that regular physical activity participation confers a number of physiological and psychological benefits such as reduced risk of cardiovascular disease, osteoporosis, and hypertension (see Bouchard, Shephard, and Stephens 1993). Clearly, public attention is highly focused on matters of fitness and well-being; and government, health care professionals, and industry are now promoting a range of health-related behaviors in our communities. While this is to be applauded, what is problematic is the marketing of fitness and health, which in the past several years has systematically downplayed the importance of physical activity for physiological fitness and psychological well-being. Instead it has placed an overemphasis on the benefits of exercise in the pursuit of physical perfection as the preeminent manifestation of sexual attractiveness. Indeed, there is good evidence that women exercise more for the sake of appearance than for the health-related benefits of physical activity (Garner et al. 1985; Mishkind et al. 1986; Silberstein et al. 1988).

The nature of the relationship between body satisfaction and degree of exercise participation among the general population is likely to be complex, multifaceted, and perhaps not easily understood—a fact that may explain the inconsistencies found in the research literature. For example, Davis and Fox (1993) found that high-level female exercisers reported greater body satisfaction than low-level exercisers, while Imm and Pruitt (1991) found the reverse. In the Davis and Fox study, percentage body fat was significantly lower in the high-level group than in the low-level group, while the Imm and Pruitt study reported no body composition differences, a factor that may partially explain the discrepancy. In an earlier study, Davis and Cowles (1991) found no relationship between body satisfaction and frequency of exercising among young and middle-aged women, nor among middle-aged men. Similarly, there was no relationship between activity and body dissatisfaction among a group of young and middle-aged women after controlling for body fat content and personality factors known to influence body dissatisfaction (Dionne et al. 1995). Despite the contradictions found among women, there appears to be a moderately strong and positive association between exercise and body esteem among young men in the few studies reported (Davis and Cowles 1991; Davis et al. 1991).

Efforts to untangle what are contradictory research findings must recognize that the association between body satisfaction and physical activity is likely to be influenced by a number of factors including individual differences in personality characteristics and motivation. Most importantly, the relationship is surely a dynamic rather than a static one. For example, there is little doubt that for many women, involvement in a regular exercise program may, at the onset, produce a number of important biologic reinforcers like improved muscle tone, increased stamina, and perhaps even a reduction in weight and body fat content. Together these factors may, at least in the short term, enhance one's body esteem. However, assiduous involvement in an exercise regimen can also have certain negative consequences, particularly among the emotionally susceptible, the highly critical, or the fiercely competitive. Comparisons between one's own shape and that of the ultraslender, spandex-clad supermodels who are featured in exercise videos, *Shape* magazine, and the ubiquitous advertising of exercise clothing and equipment may foster a fault-finding view of one's physical appearance and an increasing sense of disenchantment. Furthermore, it may be that although exercise enhances a woman's perceived body image, her idealized body image begins to shift toward a thinner standard, with the resultant dissatisfaction remaining the same regardless of objective improvement. Finally, it may be that participation in some activities is more likely to promote body satisfaction than participation in others. For instance, there is some evidence of enhanced body image among both males and females engaging in weight training and bodybuilding activities (Tucker 1983; Tucker and Maxwell 1992). These are critical issues worthy of further attention, particularly given the increasing interest in the use of exercise as a medium for enhancing self-esteem and mental well-being (see Mutrie, chapter 11). However, cross-sectional data and simple correlational analyses such as those that proliferate in the current literature are unlikely to tease out the dynamic complexities of the relationship between exercise and body image.

WEIGHT PREOCCUPATION AND EXERCISE

The relationship between exercise and dieting has become the focus of increasing research attention since the mid- to late 1980s—an interest sparked by the popularity of the fitness movement and the concomitant high prevalence of eating pathologies among young women. Exercise has been variously touted as a robust buffer against disease, an opioid for psychological distress—even a key to the fountain of youth. Nevertheless, it has been found repeatedly that *weight control* is one of the principal reasons reported for exercising, especially among women (Markland and Hardy 1993; McDonald and Thompson 1992; Silberstein et al. 1988). This may reflect, in part, the increasing promotion of exercise in the media as a weight loss method. A survey of magazine articles from 1959 to 1988 found that the number of exercise articles from 1980 to 1988 actually surpassed the number of diet articles, indicating a trend toward exercise in place of, or at least together with, traditional calorie-reduced dieting for the purpose of slimming (Wiseman et al. 1992).

One of our studies indicated that chronic female dieters engaged in much more frequent and intense physical activity than nondieters even though the groups did not differ in percentage body fat (Davis et al. 1990). In a later study, investigating the relationship between exercise and dietary restraint among young and middle-aged men and women in the general population, we also found a positive relationship between these two factors among men of all ages, as well as among young women (Davis, Shapiro et al. 1993). However, research has not been entirely in agreement on the degree of the relationship between physical activity and weight preoccupation. This problem is clearly attributable to measurement and classification differences across studies (see Davis, Brewer, and Ratusny 1993). For example, those studies that have simply measured the *frequency* of physical activity have tended to find little or no relationship between it and weight preoccupation, at least among women (e.g., Davis and Fox 1993; Kiernan et al. 1992; Nudelman, Rosen, and Leitenberg 1988; Weight and Noakes 1987), while those that used interviews or questionnaires assessing the *commitment* aspects of exercising (e.g., the degree to which well-being is dependent on exercising, and the degree to which exercise is continued in the face of injury and fatigue) have found that exercise is positively related to weight and diet concerns (e.g., Davis, Brewer, and Ratusny 1993; Yates et al. 1992).

SPORT, ATHLETICISM, AND SLENDERNESS

There are a number of sports such as gymnastics, dance, and synchronized swimming in which success is determined not only by technical prowess but also by grace and physical appeal. For women in these sports, it is clear that an ultraslender form confers an important performance advantage. As a consequence, the typical female athlete confronts body image pressures at a number of levels, ranging from the performance-related pressures reinforced by coaches and trainers to those inherent in the judging criteria that give physically attractive athletes "the winning edge." In one study we found that female athletes in sports in which a slender body build is the idealized shape (e.g., gymnastics and long-distance running) reported a greater degree of body dissatisfaction than athletes in other sports, and than nonathlete controls, despite actually weighing significantly less than the other groups (Davis and Cowles 1989). A later study confirmed these results among a group of high-performance athletes competing at the national and international level in a variety of sports (Davis 1992). Similarly, Petrie (1993) found that 50% of a group of national-level gymnasts wanted to weigh less, though on average their BMI fell in the low normal range. While Taub and Blinde (1992) found no body dissatisfaction differences between groups they called "athletes" and "nonathletes," it is not clear how their groups were identified. In all probability, the subjects were students who simply participated in some recreational form of sport or exercise at the high school level. Therefore, it may be that a more negative body image is apparent only among the more proficient and competitive athletes.

Many have argued that these performance and appearance pressures render the female athlete at greater than normal risk of developing a serious clinical eating disorder (see Brownell and Rodin 1992; Sundgot-Borgen 1994 for reviews). For example, a number of studies have reported that female athletes frequently employ extraordinary, and often extreme, methods to reduce body fat. Estimates of the proportion of female athletes who have used at least one pathogenic weight loss technique have varied from 30% to over 60% depending on the sport or sports being examined (e.g., Black and Burckes-Miller 1988; Drummer et al. 1987; Petrie 1993).

Dancers—in particular ballet dancers—are also exposed to institutionalized pressures very similar to those experienced by many competitive athletes. In fact, it has been argued that the demand for thinness and dieting is greater in these women than in any other group in our society (Garner and

Garfinkel 1980). Indeed, evidence from a handful of studies over the past 15 years attests to the significantly higher prevalence of eating disorders (as much as a sevenfold increase) in ballet dancers than in the normal age-matched female population (Garner and Garfinkel 1980; le Grange, Tibbs, and Noakes 1994; Szmukler et al. 1985).

In a recent study of tertiary-care hospitalized eating-disordered women, we found that 60% of the patients we assessed had been involved in competitive athletics or dance before the onset of their disorder—a value far in excess of the percentage of competitive athletes in the general population (Davis, Kennedy et al. 1994). Although the specific causal associations are not entirely clear, it seems fair to conclude that institutionalized (albeit unrealistic) standards of body size in certain sports, and the interpersonal pressures attributable to coaches' performance-oriented expectations and demands, can have considerable etiological significance in the development of self-induced starvation among the female participants in these sports. There is little doubt that this environment fosters a heightened focus on physical appearance as well as an increased awareness of the relationship between weight and maximal performance.

EXCESSIVE EXERCISING

Terms such as *negative addiction* (Morgan 1979), *compulsive exercise* (Pasman and Thompson 1988; Yates 1991), and *exercise dependence* (De Coverley Veale 1987) have been used to describe activity that is extreme in frequency and duration, relatively resistant to change, and likely to be accompanied by an irresistible impulse to perform even in the face of injury, fatigue, or other personal demands. A flurry of debate followed the claim by Yates and her colleagues that obligatory running was an analogue of anorexia nervosa (Yates, Leehey, and Shisslak 1983), that dieting and exercise are *sister activities* with respect to etiology, and that a serious investment in one is likely to be accompanied by a preoccupation with the other (Yates 1991; Yates et al. 1992).

Although the concept of overexercising has been the subject of some discussion for the past decade, there exist no consistent classification criteria, nor is there any consensus concerning the psychological characteristics of this putative disorder. Many of the studies that have attempted to define excessive exercise have been based solely on behavioral measures that assess the frequency, duration, and intensity of leisure-time physical activity (e.g., Davis and Fox 1993; De Coverley Veale 1987; Nudelman, Rosen, and Leitenberg 1988). Although there have been some attempts to identify this behavior by means of a structured interview or self-report questionnaire (e.g., Blumenthal, O'Toole, and Chang 1984; Krejci et al. 1992), the approach has had a number of problems (see Hauck and Blumenthal

1992; Yates et al. 1992). For example, the studies have used samples composed exclusively of runners of varying abilities, ignoring the fact that overexercising can take many forms.

Measurement and classification issues seem to be at the heart of the problem. In general, those studies that have simply measured exercise frequency have found few psychological similarities between excessive exercisers and eating-disordered patients (e.g., Davis and Fox 1993; Nudelman et al. 1988; Weight and Noakes 1987). On the other hand, investigators who have assessed the psychological commitment to exercising by means of interview or questionnaire data have found strikingly similar effects (e.g., Davis, Brewer, and Ratusny 1993; Krejci et al. 1992; Yates et al. 1992). In particular, excessive exercisers have been found to have significantly greater weight and diet concerns than their nonexcessive counterparts, even in the absence of body composition differences. They were also found to be more perfectionistic and to have higher levels of anxiety, particularly when they were unable to exercise as a result of injury or illness (Coen and Ogles 1993; Kornbrust and MacKinnon 1994). The observations that obligatory exercisers feel anxious and guilty when they are unable to exercise, and that they exercise in the face of injury and fatigue, demonstrate remarkable similarity to the attitudes toward exercising found among a group of eating-disordered patients (Davis et al. 1995), suggesting that the two syndromes do share several psychological characteristics. Yates and her colleagues (Yates et al. 1994) believe that the relationship between the two syndromes is best described in terms of a risk-factor model. Perfectionistic and obsessive individuals with neurotic tendencies are more likely to get caught up in an exercise and dieting cycle that becomes self-perpetuating and gets out of control than those who have a relative absence of these characteristics (see Davis et al. 1995; Epling and Pierce 1992).

There is increasing evidence that excessive exercising, under certain circumstances, may place participants at higher risk of developing an eating disorder. The coexistence of excessive calorie restriction and hyperactivity among anorexia nervosa patients has been reported consistently by clinicians and researchers, both historically (Gull 1874; Inches 1895) and more recently (e.g., Bruch 1965; Touyz, Beumont, and Hoek 1987; Yates 1991). Perhaps the most provocative of the theories concerning the relationship between self-starvation and hyperactivity has been that proposed by Epling and Pierce (e.g., 1992). They claim that for many patients, anorexia is a physiologically mediated outcome likely to affect those who simultaneously subject themselves to a marked reduction in food intake and high levels of energy expenditure.

The impetus behind much of the thinking of Epling and Pierce about exercise and dieting was based on the food restriction-induced hyperactivity that has been studied in experimental animals for the past 30 years or more (e.g., Epling and Pierce 1984; Routtenberg and Kuznesof 1967; Russell et al. 1987). Until recently there has been little empirical evidence to support the notion of activity-induced anorexia in the human condition except for a handful of case reports drawn from a variety of sources (Beumont et al. 1994; Epling and Pierce 1992; Katz 1986; Kron et al. 1978). However, our recent study of eating-disordered patients, using both qualitative methods (based on patient interviews) and quantitative methods, has found strong support for the hypothesis that physical activity can play a central, even a causal, role in the development and maintenance of eating disorders (see Davis, Kennedy et al. 1994). There appears to be a powerful synergy that occurs when willful starvation is combined with strenuous physical activity whereby the behaviors potentiate one another. The driven, ritualized, and stereotyped nature of the eating and exercise behaviors of these patients strongly resembles the type of behaviors observed among patients with obsessive-compulsive disorder.

SUMMARY

Body image has been described as a loose mental representation of the body, and as such it may closely map onto the way the external world views us, or it may be quite disparate from this impression. Socially imposed standards of bodily perfection provide us with the template against which we come to form cognitions and emotions about our body. Clearly the extent to which body image matches the cultural ideal is a significant factor in determining the degree of body satisfaction we experience.

We have seen in this chapter that body image perceptions are derived from and maintained by a number of complex and interacting environmental and personal factors. There are, for example, enormous social pressures on women to emulate the ultraslender form that has come to represent the standard of female beauty and sexual attractiveness. In addition, factors such as body composition, age, personality characteristics, and gender-role orientation influence the way we perceive our bodies. We have also seen that body image functions both as a relatively stable psychological construct and as a state-dependent perception influenced by changing affect and circumstance.

The image we have of our body is clearly instrumental in fostering certain behaviors and attitudes. In turn, it may also be changed by certain behaviors. It has been noted that body image is the most extensively studied construct in the area of eating disorders research. Among women, body disparagement is strongly associated with perceived overweight and therefore with efforts to restrict food intake or to expend unwanted calories by increasing physical activity levels. On the one hand, weight loss (when successful) and moderate levels of exercise have been associated with enhanced body esteem. On the other hand, both these behaviors in excess, and in the presence of certain conditions, can increase substantially the risk of developing anorexia or bulimia nervosa.

REFERENCES

Allan, J.D., Mayo, K., and Michel, Y. 1993. Body size values of white and black women. *Research in Nursing and Health* 16: 323-33.

Altabe, M., and Thompson, J.K. 1990. Menstrual cycle, body image, and eating disturbance. *International Journal of Eating Disorders* 9: 395-401.

—. 1993. Body image changes during early adulthood. *International Journal of Eating Disorders* 13: 323-28.

Andersen, A.E., and DiDomenico, L. 1992. Diet vs. shape content of popular male and female magazines: A dose-response relationship to the incidence of eating disorders? *International Journal of Eating Disorders* 11: 283-87.

Andersen, A.E., and Mickalide, A.D. 1983. Anorexia nervosa in the male: An underdiagnosed disorder. *Psychosomatics* 24: 1066-75.

Anderson, J.L., Crawford, C.B., Nadeau, J., and Lindberg, T. 1992. Was the Duchess of Windsor right? A cross-cultural review of the socioecology of ideals of body shape. *Ethology and Sociobiology* 13: 197-227.

Babladelis, G. 1987. Young persons' attitudes toward aging. *Perceptual and Motor Skills* 65: 553-54.

Bailey, S.M., Goldberg, J.P., Swap, W.C., Chomitz, V.R., and Houser Jr., R.F. 1990. Relationships between body dissatisfaction and physical measurements. *International Journal of Eating Disorders* 9 (4): 457-61.

Bausell, R.B. 1986. Health-seeking behavior among the elderly. *The Gerontologist* 26: 556-59.

Berman, P.W., O'Nan, B.A., and Floyd, W. 1981. The double standard of aging and the social situation: Judgements of attractiveness of the middle-aged woman. *Sex Roles* 7: 87-96.

Beumont, P.J.V., Arthur, B., Russell, J.D., and Touyz, S.W. 1994. Excessive physical activity in dieting disorder patients: Proposals for a supervised exercise program. *International Journal of Eating Disorders* 15: 21-36.

Black, D.R., and Burckes-Miller, M.E. 1988. Male and female college athletes: Use of anorexia nervosa and bulimia nervosa weight loss methods. *Research Quarterly for Exercise and Sport* 59: 252-56.

Blumenthal, J.A., O'Toole, L.C., and Chang, J.L. 1984. Is running an analogue of anorexia nervosa? An empirical study of obligatory running and anorexia nervosa. *Journal of the American Medical Association* 252 (4): 520-23.

Bouchard, C., Shephard, R.J., and Stephens, T. eds. 1993. *Physical activity, fitness and health consensus statement*. Champaign, IL: Human Kinetics.

Brand, P., Rothblum, E., and Solomon, L. 1992. A comparison of lesbians, gay men and heterosexuals on weight and restrained eating. *International Journal of Eating Disorders* 11: 253-59.

Brenner, J.B., and Cunningham, J.G. 1992. Gender differences in eating attitudes, body concept, and self-esteem among models. *Sex Roles* 27 (7/8): 413-37.

Brodie, D.A., and Slade, P.D. 1988. The relationship between body-image and body-fat in adult women. *Psychological Medicine* 18: 623-31.

Brownell, K.D. 1991. Dieting and the search for the perfect body: Where physiology and culture collide. *Behavior Therapy* 22: 1-12.

Brownell, K.D., and Rodin, J. 1992. Prevalence of eating disorders in athletes. In *Eating, body weight and performance in athletes*, ed. K.D. Brownell, J. Rodin, and J. Wilmore, 128-45. Philadelphia: Lea & Febiger.

Bruch, H. 1965. Anorexia nervosa—its differential diagnosis. *Journal of Mental and Nervous Disorders* 141: 555-66.

Brumberg, J. 1989. *Fasting girls: A historical perspective on anorexia nervosa*. Boston: Princeton University Press.

Carroll, L. 1989. A comparative study of narcissism, gender, and sex-role orientation among bodybuilders, athletes, and psychology students. *Psychological Reports* 64: 999-1006.

Cash, T.F. 1990. The psychology of physical appearance: Aesthetics, attributes, and images. In *Body images: Development, deviance, and change*, ed. T.F. Cash and T. Pruzinsky, 51-79. New York: Guilford.

Cash, T.F., Cash, D.W., and Butters, J.W. 1983. "Mirror, mirror on the wall . . .?": Contrast effects and self-evaluations of physical attractiveness. *Personality and Social Psychology Bulletin* 9: 351-58.

Coen, S.P., and Ogles, B.M. 1993. Psychological characteristics of the obligatory runner: A critical examination of the anorexia analogue hypothesis. *Journal of Sport and Exercise Psychology* 15: 338-53.

Conrad, C.C. 1976. When you're young at heart. *Aging* 258: 11-13.

Cooper, P.J., Taylor, M.J., Cooper, Z., and Fairburn, C.G. 1987. The development and validation of the body shape questionnaire. *International Journal of Eating Disorders* 6: 485-94.

Coopersmith, S. 1967. *The antecedents of self-esteem*. San Francisco: Freeman.

Davies, E., and Furnham, A. 1986. Bodily satisfaction in adolescents. *British Journal of Medical Psychology* 59: 279-87.

Davis, C. 1992. Body image, dieting behaviors, and personality factors: A study of high-performance female athletes. *International Journal of Sport Psychology* 23: 179-92.

Davis, C., Brewer, H., and Ratusny, D. 1993. Behavioral frequency and psychological commitment: Necessary concepts in the study of excessive exercising. *Journal of Behavioral Medicine* 16: 611-28.

Davis, C., Claridge, G., and Brewer, H. 1996. The two faces of narcissism: Personality dynamics of body esteem. *Journal of Social and Clinical Psychology* 15: 153-66.

Davis, C., and Cowles, M. 1989. A comparison of weight and diet concerns and personality factors among female athletes and non-athletes. *Journal of Psychosomatic Research* 33 (5): 527-36.

—. 1991. Body image and exercise: A study of relationships and comparisons between physically active men and women. *Sex Roles* 25: 33-44.

Davis, C., Durnin, J.V.G.A., Dionne, M., and Gurevich, M. 1994. The influence of body fat content and bone diameter measurements on body dissatisfaction in adult women. *International Journal of Eating Disorders* 15: 257-63.

Davis, C., Durnin, J.V.G.A., Gurevich, M., LeMaire, A., and Dionne, M. 1993. Body composition correlates of weight dissatisfaction and dietary restraint in young women. *Appetite* 20: 197-207.

Davis, C., Elliott, S., Dionne, M., and Mitchell, I. 1991. The relationship of personality factors and physical activity to body satisfaction in men. *Personality and Individual Differences* 12: 689-94.

Davis, C., and Fox, J. 1993. Excessive exercise and weight preoccupation in women. *Addictive Behaviors* 18: 201-11.

Davis, C., Fox, J., Cowles, M.P., Hastings, P., and Schwass, K. 1990. The functional role of exercise in the development of weight and diet concerns in women. *Journal of Psychosomatic Research* 34 (5): 563-74.

Davis, C., Kennedy, S.H., Ralevski, E., and Dionne, M. 1994. The role of physical activity in the development and maintenance of eating disorders. *Psychological Medicine* 24: 957-67.

Davis, C., Kennedy, S.H., Ralevski, E., Dionne, M., Brewer, H., Neitzert, C., and Ratusny, D. 1995. Obsessive-compulsiveness and physical activity in anorexia nervosa and high-level exercising. *Journal of Psychosomatic Research* 39: 967-76.

Davis, C., Shapiro, C.M., Elliott, S., and Dionne, M. 1993. Personality and other correlates of dietary restraint. *Personality and Individual Differences* 14: 297-305.

De Coverley Veale, D. 1987. Exercise dependence. *British Journal of Addiction* 82: 735-40.

Denniston, C., Roth, D., and Gilroy, F. 1992. Dysphoria and body image among college women. *International Journal of Eating Disorders* 12: 449-52.

Dionne, M., Davis., C., Fox, J., and Gurevich, M. 1995. Feminist ideology as a predictor of body dissatisfaction in women. *Sex Roles* 33: 277-87.

Dolan, B. 1991. Cross-cultural aspects of anorexia nervosa and bulimia: A review. *International Journal of Eating Disorders* 10: 67-78.

Doka, K. J. 1985/1986. Adolescent attitudes and beliefs toward aging and the elderly. *International Journal of Aging and Human Development* 22: 173-87.

Drewnowski, A., and Yee, D.K. 1987. Men and body image: Are males satisfied with their body weight? *Psychosomatic Medicine* 49: 626-34.

Drummer, G.M., Rosen, L.W., Heuser, W.W., Roberts, P.J., and Councilman, J.E. 1987. Pathogenic weight control behaviors of young competitive swimmers. *The Physician and Sportsmedicine* 15: 75-87.

Epling, W.F., and Pierce, W.D. 1984. Activity-based anorexia in rats as a function of opportunity to run on an activity wheel. *Nutrition and Behavior* 2: 37-49.

—. 1992. *Solving the anorexia puzzle.* Toronto, ON: Hogrefe & Huber.

Eysenck, H.J., and Eysenck, S.B.G. 1975. *Manual for the Eysenck Personality Questionnaire.* San Diego: Educational and Industrial Testing Service.

—. 1991. *Manual of the Eysenck Personality Scales.* London: Hodder & Stoughton.

Fallon, A.E., and Rozin, P. 1985. Sex differences in perceptions of desirable body shape. *Journal of Abnormal Psychology* 94: 102-5.

Fox, K.R., Page, A., Armstrong, N., and Kirby, B. 1994. Dietary restraint and self-perceptions in early adolescence. *Personality and Individual Differences* 17: 87-96.

Fox, K.R., Page, A., Peters, D.M., Armstrong, N., and Kirby, B. 1994. Dietary restraint and fatness in early adolescent girls and boys. *Journal of Adolescence* 17: 149-61.

Franzoi, S.L., and Shields, S.A. 1984. The Body Esteem Scale: Multidimensional structure and sex differences in a college population. *Journal of Personality Assessment* 48: 173-78.

Furnham, A., and Alibhai, N. 1983. Cross-cultural differences in the perception of female body shapes. *Psychological Medicine* 13: 829-37.

Furnham, A., and Baguma, P. 1994. Cross-cultural differences in the evaluation of male and female body shapes. *International Journal of Eating Disorders* 15: 81-89.

Gardner, R.M., and Tockerman, Y.R. 1992. Body dissatisfaction as a predictor of body size distortion: A multidimensional analysis of body image. *Genetic, Social, and General Psychology Monographs*, 127-45. Washington, DC: Heldref.

Garner, D.M., and Garfinkel, P.E. 1980. Socio-cultural factors in the development of anorexia nervosa. *Psychological Medicine* 10: 647-56.

Garner, D.M., Garfinkel, P.E., Schwartz, D., and Thompson, M. 1980. Cultural expectations of thinness in women. *Psychological Reports* 47: 483-91.

Garner, D.M., and Olmsted, M.A. 1984. *Eating Disorder Inventory manual*. Lutz, FL: Psychological Assessment Resources.

Garner, D.M., Rockert, W., Olmsted, M.P., Johnson, C., and Coscina, D.V. 1985. Psychoeducational principles in the treatment of bulimia and anorexia nervosa. In *Handbook of psychotherapy for anorexia nervosa and bulimia*, ed. D.M. Garner and P. Garfinkel, 513-72. New York: Guilford.

Gull, W.W. 1874. Anorexia nervosa. *Transactions of the Clinical Society of London* 7: 22-28. Cited by A. Warah, 1993, Overactivity and boundary setting in anorexia-nervosa: An existential perspective, *Journal of Adolescence* 16: 93-100.

Gupta, M.A., Schork, N.J., and Dhaliwal, J.S. 1993. Stature, drive for thinness and body dissatisfaction: A study of males and females from a non clinical sample. *Canadian Journal of Psychiatry* 38: 59-61.

Haimovitz, D., Lansky, L.M., and O'Reilly, P. 1993. Fluctuations in body satisfaction across situations. *International Journal of Eating Disorders* 3: 77-84.

Hamilton, K., and Waller, G. 1993. Media influences on body size estimation in anorexia and bulimia: An experimental study. *British Journal of Psychiatry* 62: 837-40.

Harris, M.B., Walters, L.C., and Waschull, S. 1991. Gender and ethnic differences in obesity-related behaviors and attitudes in a college sample. *Journal of Applied Social Psychology* 21: 1545-66.

Hauck, E.R., and Blumenthal, J.A. 1992. Obsessive and compulsive traits in athletes. *Sports Medicine* 14: 215-27.

Heinberg, L.J., and Thompson, J.K. 1992. The effects of figure size feedback (positive vs. negative) and target comparison group (particularistic vs. universalistic) on body image disturbance. *International Journal of Eating Disorders* 12: 441-48.

Herzog, D.B., Norman, D.K., Gordon, C., and Pepose, M. 1984. Sexual conflict and eating disorders in 27 males. *American Journal of Psychiatry* 141: 989-90.

Herzog, D.B., Newman, K.L., Yeh, C.J., and Warshaw, M. 1992. Body image satisfaction in homosexual and heterosexual women. *International Journal of Eating Disorders* 11: 391-96.

Hill, A.J., Oliver, S., and Rogers, P.J. 1991. Eating in an adult world: The rise of dieting in childhood and adolescence. *British Journal of Clinical Psychology* 31: 95-105.

Imm, P.S., and Pruitt, J. 1991. Body shape satisfaction in female exercisers and nonexercisers. *Women & Health* 17: 87-96.

Inches, P. 1895. Anorexia nervosa. *The Maritime Medical News* 7: 73-75.

Jackson, L.A., Ervin, K.S., and Hodge, C.N. 1992. Narcissism and body image. *Journal of Research in Personality* 26: 357-70.

Janis, I.L., and Fields, P.B. 1959. A behavioral assessment of persuasibility: Consistency of individual differences. In *Personality and persuasibility*, ed. C.I. Hovland and I.L. Janis, 29-54. New Haven, CT: Yale University Press.

Katz, J.L. 1986. Long-distance running, anorexia nervosa, and bulimia: A report of two cases. *Comprehensive Psychiatry* 27 (1): 74-78.

Keelan, J.P.R., Dion, K.K., and Dion, K.L. 1992. Correlates of appearance anxiety in late adolescence and early adulthood among young women. *Journal of Adolescence* 15: 193-205.

Kiernan, M., Rodin, J., Brownell, K.D., Wilmore, J.H., and Crandall, C. 1992. Relation of level of exercise, age, and weight-cycling history to weight and eating concerns in male and female runners. *Health Psychology* 11: 418-21.

Kornbrust, A.M., and MacKinnon, J.R. 1994. *Psychological implications of obligatory exercise.* Presentation at the 15th annual meeting of the Society of Behavioral Medicine, April, Boston.

Krejci, R.C., Sargnet, R., Forand, K.J., Ureda, J.R., Saunders, R.P., and Durstine, J.L. 1992. Psychological and behavioral differences among females classified as bulimic, obligatory exerciser and normal control. *Psychiatry* 5: 185-93.

Kron, L., Katz, J.L., Gorzynski, G., and Weiner, W. 1978. Hyperactivity in anorexia nervosa: A fundamental clinical feature. *Comprehensive Psychiatry* 19: 433-39.

Lasch, C. 1979. *The culture of narcissism.* New York: Norton.

le Grange, D., Tibbs, J., and Noakes, T.D. 1994. Implications of a diagnosis of anorexia nervosa in a ballet school. *International Journal of Eating Disorders* 15: 369-76.

Lerner, R.M., and Jovanovic, J. 1990. The role of body image in psychosocial development across the life span: A developmental contextual perspective. In *Body images: Development, deviance, and change*, ed. T.F. Cash and T. Pruzinsky, 110-27. New York: Guilford.

Markland, D., and Hardy, L. 1993. The Exercise Motivations Inventory: Preliminary development and validity of a measure of individuals' reasons for participation in regular physical exercise. *Personality and Individual Differences* 15: 289-96.

Mathes, E.W., and Kahn, A. 1975. Physical attractiveness, happiness, neuroticism, and self-esteem. *The Journal of Psychology* 90: 27-30.

Maude, D., Wertheim, E.H., Paxton, S., Gibbons, K., and Szmukler, G. 1993. Body dissatisfaction, weight loss behaviors, and bulimic tendencies in Australian adolescents with an estimate of female data representativeness. *Australian Psychologist* 28: 128-32.

Mazur, A. 1986. U.S. trends in feminine beauty and overadaptation. *The Journal of Sex Research* 22 (3): 281-303.

McCauley, M.L., Mintz, L., and Glenn, A.A. 1988. Body image, self-esteem, and depression-proneness: Closing the gender gap. *Sex Roles* 18: 381-91.

McDonald, K., and Thompson, J.K. 1992. Eating disturbance, body image dissatisfaction, and reasons for exercising: Gender differences and correlational findings. *International Journal of Eating Disorders* 11: 289-92.

Mintz, L., and Betz, N. 1986. Sex differences in the nature, realism, and correlates of body image. *Sex Roles* 15: 185-95.

Mishkind, M.E., Rodin, J., Silberstein, L.R., and Striegel-Moore, R.H. 1986. The embodiment of masculinity. *American Behavioral Scientist* 29 (5): 545-62.

Morgan, W.P. 1979. Negative addiction in runners. *The Physician and Sportsmedicine* 7 (2): 57-68.

Morris, A., Cooper, T., and Cooper, P.J. 1989. The changing shape of female fashion models. *International Journal of Eating Disorders* 8 (5): 593-96.

Myers, P., and Biocca, F.A. 1992. The elastic body image: The effect of television advertising and programming on body image distortions in young women. *Journal of Communication* 42 (3): 108-33.

Noles, S.W., Cash, T.F., and Winstead, B.A. 1985. Body image, physical attractiveness, and depression. *Journal of Consulting and Clinical Psychology* 53: 88-94.

Nudelman, S., Rosen, J.C., and Leitenberg, H. 1988. Dissimilarities in eating attitudes, body image distortion, depression, and self-esteem between high-intensity male runners and women with bulimia nervosa. *International Journal of Eating Disorders* 7 (5): 625-34.

Ohzeki, T., Hanaki, K., Motozumi, H., Ishitani, N., Ohtahara, H., Sunaguchi, M., and Shiraki, K. 1990. Prevalence of obesity, leanness and anorexia nervosa in Japanese boys and girls aged 12-14 years. *Annals of Nutrition and Metabolism* 34: 208-12.

Ohzeki, T., Otahara, H., Hanaki, K., Motozumi, H., and Shiraki, K. 1993. Eating Attitudes Test in boys and girls aged 6-18 years: Decrease in concerns with eating in boys and the increase in girls with their ages. *Psychopathology* 26: 117-21.

Ostrow, A.C., and Dzewaltowski, D.A. 1986. Older adults' perceptions of physical activity participation based on age-role and sex-role appropriateness. *Research Quarterly* 57: 167-69.

Pasman, L., and Thompson, J.K. 1988. Body image and eating disturbance in obligatory runners, obligatory weightlifters, and sedentary individuals. *International Journal of Eating Disorders* 7 (6): 759-69.

Peterson, C.C., Hall, L.C., and Peterson, J.L. 1988. Age, sex, and contact with elderly adults as predictors of knowledge about psychological aging. *International Journal of Aging and Human Development* 26: 129-37.

Petrie, T.A. 1993. Disordered eating in female collegiate gymnasts: Prevalence and personality/attitudinal correlates. *Journal of Sport and Exercise Psychology* 15: 424-36.

Pliner, P., Chaiken, S., and Flett, G.L. 1990. Gender differences in concern with body weight and physical appearance over the lifespan. *Personality and Social Psychology Bulletin* 16: 263-73.

Probast, C.K., and Lieberman, L.S. 1992. Cultural influences on normal and idealized female body size. *Collegium Antropologium* 16: 151-56.

Prohaska, T.R., Leventhal, E.A., Leventhal, H., and Keller, M.L. 1985. Health practices and illness cognition in young, middle aged, and elderly adults. *Journal of Gerontology* 40: 569-78.

Pruzinsky, T., and Cash, T.F. 1990. Integrative themes in body-image development, deviance, and change. In *Body images: Development, deviance, and change*, ed. T.F. Cash and T. Pruzinsky, 337-49. New York: Guilford.

Pruzinsky, T., and Edgerton, M.T. 1990. Body-image change in cosmetic plastic surgery. In *Body images: Development, deviance, and change*, ed. T.F. Cash and T. Pruzinsky, 217-36. New York: Guilford.

Radke-Sharpe, N., Whitney-Saltiel, D., and Rodin, J. 1990. Fat distribution as a risk factor for weight and eating concerns. *International Journal of Eating Disorders* 9 (1): 27-36.

Rand, C.S.W., and Kuldau, J.M. 1990. The epidemiology of obesity and self-defined weight problems in the general population: Gender, race, age and social class. *International Journal of Eating Disorders* 9: 329-43.

Rodin, J., Silberstein, L.R., and Striegel-Moore, R.H. 1985. Women and weight: A normative discontent. In *Nebraska Symposium on Motivation*. Vol. 32, *Psychology and gender*, ed. T.B. Sonderegger. Lincoln, NE: University of Nebraska.

Roth, D., and Armstrong, J. 1994. Feelings of Fatness Questionnaire: A measure of the cross-situational variability of body experience. *International Journal of Eating Disorders* 14: 349-58.

Routtenberg, A., and Kuznesof, A.W. 1967. Self-starvation of rats living in activity wheels on a restricted feeding schedule. *Journal of Comparative and Physiological Psychology* 64: 414-21.

Rozin, P., and Fallon, A. 1988. Body image, attitudes to weight, and misperceptions of figure preferences of the opposite sex: A comparison of men and women in two generations. *Journal of Abnormal Psychology* 97: 342-45.

Rucker, C.E., and Cash, T.F. 1992. Body images, body-size perceptions, and eating behaviors among African-American and white college women. *International Journal of Eating Disorders* 12: 291-99.

Russell, J.C., Epling, W.F., Pierce, W.D., Amy, R.M., and Boer, D.P. 1987. Induction of voluntary prolonged running in rats. *Journal of Applied Physiology* 63: 2549-53.

Sacks, M.H. 1987. Eating disorders and long-distance running. *Integrative Psychiatry* 5: 201-11.

Secord, P.F., and Jourard, S.M. 1959. The appraisal of body cathexis: Body cathexis and the self. *Journal of Consulting Psychology* 17: 343-47.

Shavelson, R.J., Hubner, J.J., and Stanton, G.C. 1976. Self-concept: Validation of construct interpretations. *Review of Educational Research* 46: 407-11.

Siever, M.D. 1994. Sexual orientation and gender as factors in socioculturally acquired vulnerability to body dissatisfaction and eating disorders. *Journal of Consulting and Clinical Psychology* 62: 252-60.

Silberstein, L.R., Mishkind, M.E., Striegel-Moore, R.H., Timko, C., and Rodin, J. 1989. Men and their bodies: A comparison of homosexual and heterosexual men. *Psychosomatic Medicine* 51: 337-46.

Silberstein, L.R., Striegel-Moore, R.H., Timko, C., and Rodin, J. 1988. Behavioral and psychological implications of body dissatisfaction: Do men and women differ? *Sex Roles* 19 (3/4): 219-32.

Silverstein, B., and Perdue, L. 1988. The relationship between role concerns, preferences for slimness, and symptoms of eating problems among college women. *Sex Roles* 18: 101-6.

Silverstein, B., Perdue, L., Peterson, B., and Kelly, E. 1986. The role of the mass media in promoting a thin standard of bodily attractiveness for women. *Sex Roles* 14: 519-32.

Silverstein, B., Perdue, L., Peterson, B., Vogel, L., and Fantini, D.A. 1986. Possible causes of the thin standard of bodily attractiveness for women. *International Journal of Eating Disorders* 5: 907-16.

Singh, D. 1993. Adaptive significance of female physical attractiveness: Role of waist-to-hip ratio. *Journal of Personality and Social Psychology* 65: 293-307.

Smith, J.E., and Krejci, J. 1991. Minorities join the majority: Eating disturbances among Hispanic and Native American youth. *International Journal of Eating Disorders* 10: 179-86.

Sobal, J., and Stunkard, A.J. 1989. Socioeconomic status and obesity: A review of the literature. *Psychological Bulletin* 105 (2): 260-75.

Solyom, L., Freeman, R.J., and Miles, J.E. 1982. A comparative psychometric study of anorexia nervosa and obsessive neurosis. *Canadian Journal of Psychiatry* 27: 282-86.

Steiner-Adair, C. 1986. The body politic: Normal female adolescent development and the development of eating disorders. *Journal of the American Academy of Psychoanalysis* 14: 95-114.

Strauman, T.J., Vookles, J., Berenstein, V., Chaiken, S., and Higgins, E.T. 1991. Self-discrepancies and vulnerability to body dissatisfaction and disordered eating. *Journal of Personality and Social Psychology* 61: 946-56.

Striegel-Moore, R.H., McAvay, G., and Rodin, J. 1986. Psychological and behavioral correlates of feeling fat in women. *International Journal of Eating Disorders* 5 (5): 935-47.

Striegel-Moore, R.H., Tucker, N., and Hsu, J. 1990. Body image dissatisfaction and disordered eating in lesbian college students. *International Journal of Eating Disorders* 9: 493-500.

Sundgot-Borgen, J. 1994. Eating disorders in female athletes. *Sports Medicine* 17: 176-88.

Szmukler, G.I., Eisler, I., Gillies, C., and Hayward, M. 1985. The implications of anorexia nervosa in a ballet school. *Journal of Psychiatric Research* 19: 177-81.

Taub, D.E., and Blinde, E.M. 1992. Eating disorders among adolescent female athletes: Influence of athletic participation and sport team membership. *Adolescence* 27: 833-48.

Thelan, M., Powell, A., Lawrence, C., and Kuhnert, M. 1992. Eating and body image concerns among children. *Journal of Clinical Child Psychology* 21: 41-46.

Thompson, J.K., Coovert, D.L., Pasman, L.N., and Robb, J. 1993. Body image and food consumption: Three laboratory studies of perceived calorie content. *International Journal of Eating Disorders* 14: 445-57.

Thompson, J.K., Penner, L.A., and Altabe, M.N. 1990. Procedures, problems, and progress in the assessment of body images. In *Body images: Development, deviance, and change*, ed. T.F. Cash and T. Pruzinsky, 21-48. New York: Guilford.

Timko, C., Striegel-Moore, R.H., Silberstein, L.R., and Rodin, J. 1987. Femininity/masculinity and disordered eating in women: How are they related? *International Journal of Eating Disorders* 6: 701-12.

Touyz, S.W., Beumont, P.J.V., and Hoek, S. 1987. Exercise anorexia: A new dimension in anorexia nervosa? In *Handbook of eating disorders. Part 1: Anorexia and bulimia nervosa*, ed. P.J.V. Beumont, G.D. Burrows, and R.C. Casper, 143-57. Amsterdam: Elsevier.

Touyz, S.W., Kopec-Schrader, E.M., and Beumont, P.J.V. 1993. Anorexia nervosa in males: A report of 12 cases. *Australian and New Zealand Journal of Psychiatry* 27: 512-17.

Tucker, L.A. 1983. Effect of weight training on self-concept: A profile of those influenced most. *Research Quarterly* 54: 389-97.

Tucker, L.A., and Maxwell, K. 1992. Effects of weight training on the emotional well-being and body image of females: Predictors of greatest benefit. *American Journal of Health Promotion* 6: 338-44, 371.

Wardle, J., and Beales, S. 1986. Restraint, body image and food intake in children from 12 to 18 years. *Appetite* 7: 209-17.

Wardle, J., Bindra, R., Fairclough, B., and Westcombe, A. 1993. Culture and body image: Body perception and weight concern in young Asian and Caucasian British women. *Journal of Community and Applied Social Psychology* 3: 173-81.

Wardle, J., and Foley, E. 1989. Body image: Stability and sensitivity of body satisfaction and body size estimation. *International Journal of Eating Disorders* 8: 55-62.

Weight, L.M., and Noakes, T.D. 1987. Is running an analog of anorexia?: A survey of the incidence of eating disorders in female distance runners. *Medicine and Science in Sports and Exercise* 19 (3): 213-17.

Williams, G.-J., Power, K.G., Millar, H.R., Freeman, C.P., Yellowlees, A., Dowds, T., Walker, M., Campsie, L., MacPherson, F., and Jackson, M.A. 1993. Comparison of eating disorders and other dietary/weight groups on measures of perceived control, assertiveness, self-esteem, and self-directed hostility. *International Journal of Eating Disorders* 14: 27-32.

Williamson, D.A., Kelley, M.L., Davis, C., Ruggerio, L., and Blouin, D.C. 1985. Psychopathology of eating disorders: A controlled comparison of bulimic, obese, and normal subjects. *Journal of Consulting and Clinical Psychology* 53 (2): 161-66.

Wiseman, C.V., Gray, J.J., Mosimann, J.E., and Ahrens, A.H. 1992. Cultural expectations of thinness in women: An update. *International Journal of Eating Disorders* 11 (1): 85-89.

Yates, A. 1991. *Compulsive exercise and the eating disorders.* New York: Brunner/Mazel.

Yates, A., Leehey, K., and Shisslak, C. 1983. Running—an analogue of anorexia? *New England Journal of Medicine* 308 (5): 251-55.

Yates, A., Shisslak, C.M., Allender, J., Crago, M., and Leehey, K. 1992. Comparing obligatory and nonobligatory runners. *Psychosomatics* 33: 180-89.

Yates, A., Shisslak, C., Crago, M., and Allender, J. 1994. Overcommitment to sport: Is there a relationship to the eating disorders? *Clinical Journal of Sport Medicine* 4: 1-7.

Zellner, D.A., Harner, D.E., and Adler, R.L. 1989. Effects of eating abnormalities and gender on perceptions of desirable body shape. *Journal of Abnormal Psychology* 98: 93-96.

CHAPTER 7

SELF-ESTEEM IN CHILDREN AND YOUTH: THE ROLE OF SPORT AND PHYSICAL EDUCATION

JAMES R. WHITEHEAD AND CHARLES B. CORBIN

Whether or not we believe (as did Wellington) that the battle of Waterloo was won on the playing fields of Eton, there is little doubt that sport and physical activity are important and socially significant phenomena. Take our language: The bases of our idiomatic vocabularies are loaded with sporting metaphors. Look at our role models: We are often prepared to ignore major character flaws in our sport heroes so we can keep them on their lofty pedestals. In addition, not only do we worship physical performance, but we also revere fit physiques and figures as symbols of power and sex. We also respect our bodies as the vehicles that take us on our trips through life, although we often begrudge the fact that they have to be maintained lest they slow us down or fail to complete the journey. No wonder that perceptions of the physical self have become such a hot topic of academic study. Maybe the real wonder is that we have neglected the topic for so long.

Although physical educators (and others) have for decades extolled the values of physical education classes in the development of self-concept, self-esteem, and self-realization (e.g., Brown and Cassidy 1963; Pangrazi and Corbin 1995; Pangrazi and Darst 1985, 1991, 1997; Siedentop 1976; Williams 1927, 1959), they may have been a little vague in terms of definitions and a little short on empirical support. As Weiss (1987) pointed out, the lack of guiding theoretical perspectives has been a barrier to progress and understanding. In an effort to avoid the same criticism, this chapter will begin by introducing theory that will set the stage for a review of current knowledge of children's self-esteem development in the context of physical activity and sport involvement. The review will be followed by suggestions to practitioners. Throughout, a stance is taken that motivation and self-esteem are inextricably interlinked.

CHILDREN'S MOTIVATION AND SELF-ESTEEM: COMMON CONCEPTS?

Following a period of domination by mechanistic and drive theories of motivation, in 1959 Robert White, in an important monograph, provided a new theoretical proposition that was particularly pertinent to children's motivation. He proposed that children are born intrinsically motivated to be effective in their environments. According to White, intrinsic or *effectance* motivation persists as a desire to master the tasks of life, and the payoff for successful mastery is a feeling of competence, or *efficacy*, that is pleasurably satisfying.

Perhaps a preliminary validation of White's essay was demonstrated de facto by the intrinsic interest of the many psychological researchers who rushed to test his proposals. There have been some notable developments. One major field of advancement is represented by the work of Deci and his colleagues (e.g., Deci 1975; Deci and Ryan 1985), whose investigations of how extrinsic motivation affects intrinsic motivation led to the formal statement of *cognitive evaluation theory*, a major contemporary theory of psychology.

DECI AND RYAN'S DEVELOPMENT OF MOTIVATIONAL THEORY

In a nutshell, cognitive evaluation theory postulates that intrinsic motivation depends on perceptions of competence and (locus of) causality. Like White (1959), Deci and Ryan (1985) saw the intrinsic need for competence as a foundation stone of intrinsic motivation. However, on the basis of the work of deCharms (1968) and others, they also proposed another intrinsic need—the need to be self-determining or autonomous—as a second foundation stone. According to cognitive evaluation theory, events that promote perceptions of competence will increase a child's intrinsic motivation, and conversely, events that diminish perceptions of competence will reduce intrinsic motivation. Worse still, if events lead a youngster to perceptions of incompetence, amotivation (a state akin to learned helplessness) may be the result. However, according to the theory, intrinsic motivation can flourish only in an atmosphere of self-determination or autonomy. If a young person feels that an activity is being done to earn pay or a reward, or is being forced by coercion, then his or her perception shifts from a sense of autonomy to one of external control. Intrinsic motivation would then be undermined, leaving the individual likely to quit once the extrinsic inducement or coercion is removed. Put simply, perceptions of external control are pressuring—and the feelings of pressure and tension are not compatible with a pleasurable sense of efficacy. At best, the pressure might turn play into work, or at worst, lead to resentment and defiance.

More recently, cognitive evaluation theory has evolved and has been renamed *self-determination theory* (Deci 1992; Deci and Ryan 1991, 1995; Rigby et al. 1992). In this evolved model, the primary psychological needs of *autonomy, competence,* and *relatedness* lead individuals to seek and meet the optimal challenges that result in healthy development of the self (Deci and Ryan 1991). In the model, the need for autonomy is given more emphasis, and the need for relatedness has been added. Relatedness is described as the need "to relate to and care for others, to feel that those others are relating authentically to one's self, and to feel a satisfying and coherent involvement with the social world more generally" (243).

Self-determination theory has also moved well beyond a simplistic dichotomous notion of extrinsic versus intrinsic motivation. Current thinking posits that there is a motivational continuum (see fig. 7.1) ranging from amotivations through four types of extrinsically motivated behaviors to true intrinsically motivated behaviors, which are defined as behaviors done for their inherent pleasure of knowledge, accomplishment, and stimulation (Vallerand et al. 1992). What characterizes the four types of extrinsic motivation is the degree of autonomy inherent in the regulation of behavior. Within these differences in autonomy can be found important implications for a youngster's sense of self.

The first of the four types of extrinsic motivation, *external regulation,* is characterized by behaviors that are externally controlled in the sense that they are done for payment or reward or because of coercion or threat of punishment. Obviously, although externally regulated behaviors are "motivated," they are not self-determined. Extensive research has shown that external regulation tends to undermine intrinsic motivation, may be pressuring, and can lead to resentment and defiance (see Deci and Ryan 1985 for a review). Such motivation is thus not conducive to a sense of relatedness to the social environment, nor is it likely to bring a sense of autonomy into an individual's self-concept.

In the second type of extrinsic motivation, *introjected regulation,* behaviors are motivated by internalized controlling factors that lead young people to feel that they "ought to" or "should" perform a behavior because of an impending internal pressure such as guilt or shame. As before, this type of

Motivation continuum categories   **Reasons for behaviors**

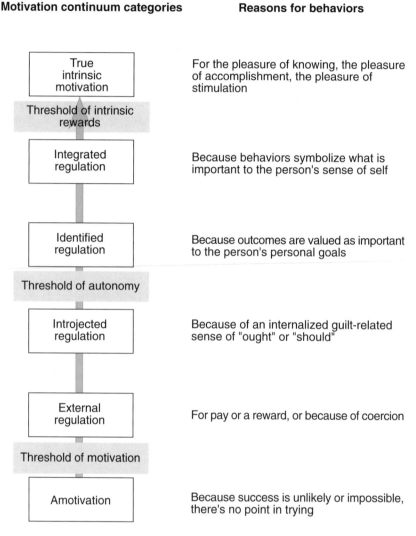

Motivation continuum categories	Reasons for behaviors
True intrinsic motivation	For the pleasure of knowing, the pleasure of accomplishment, the pleasure of stimulation
Threshold of intrinsic rewards	
Integrated regulation	Because behaviors symbolize what is important to the person's sense of self
Identified regulation	Because outcomes are valued as important to the person's personal goals
Threshold of autonomy	
Introjected regulation	Because of an internalized guilt-related sense of "ought" or "should"
External regulation	For pay or a reward, or because of coercion
Threshold of motivation	
Amotivation	Because success is unlikely or impossible, there's no point in trying

Figure 7.1   A continuum of motivation categories.

Note. The continuum is based on self-determination theory writings. The thresholds have been added by the authors of this chapter.

motivation is unlikely to build a sense of autonomy, and worse, when the pressure is to behave as a "good person should," the individual's self-esteem may be on the line.

While the first two types on the continuum are the antithesis of self-determined motivation because of the control by factors external to the person (or external to the person's psychological self), the second two are types of autonomous regulation of behavior. In the first of these, *identified regulation*, behaviors are freely chosen because the individual instrumentally values the consequences or outcomes of the behaviors for the reason that they are desired aspects of that person's sense of self. In other words, the outcomes are important personal goals.

In the second type (and thus the fourth on the continuum), the motivation is described as *integrated regulation* because behaviors thus motivated are symbolic of, or valued as integral parts of, the individual's sense of self. In other words, they symbolize what it is about the person's identity that he or she deems important.

Although identified and integrated regulation are fully self-determined forms of motivation, they differ from true intrinsic motivation in that they are instrumental; the behaviors they lead to are not done for their own sake as are truly intrinsically motivated behaviors. However, as Rigby et al. (1992) have pointed out, because behaviors motivated by identified or integrated regulation are self-determined, "they are fully endorsed by and congruent with one's sense of self" (168). Thus, in simple theoretical terms, identified regulation, integrated regulation, and intrinsic motivation form the basis of a person's self-determined quest to develop and maintain a positive and healthy sense of self. In plainer language, those are the motivations that enable individuals to feel independent, confident, and "effective" in life.

COMPETENCE MOTIVATION: HARTER'S REFINEMENTS

Another major field of advancement that has particular significance for understanding children's self-perceptions and motivation has also followed White's work. Under the general rubric of self-worth development, Susan Harter and her colleagues (e.g., Harter 1978, 1981a, 1985a, 1985b, 1990, 1993; Harter and Connell 1984; Harter and Jackson 1993) set out to identify the components of children's motive systems and to explore how these components develop. Her early work necessarily required considerable development of instrumentation (e.g., Harter 1981b, 1985b) for use in theory building and testing. Harter's prolific publication of her findings in subsequent research has enabled a wider understanding of the development and role of self-worth (e.g., Harter 1990). Notable features of her work have been a focus on the development of the specific competence/adequacy perceptions that predict global self-esteem and the study of the antecedents of specific and global perceptions. In terms of the ways in which children develop their sense of self-esteem, Harter's work (e.g., 1990) has painted a picture of children showing increasingly sophisticated abilities to describe and understand various components of self-esteem as they move from childhood to youth. Four- to seven-year-olds, for example, appear to be able to make judgments about cognitive competence, physical competence, social acceptance, and behavioral conduct. However, an interesting finding from factor analysis techniques is that children of this age group cannot clearly differentiate cognitive from physical competence, or social acceptance from behavioral conduct. Despite their relative inability to fully differentiate aspects of self, young children do have a sense of self-worth, which, not surprisingly perhaps, is based upon rather concrete and descriptive characteristics. Perhaps the most noticeable characteristic is the highly positive slant that children give to their descriptions of their behaviors, their preferences, and their characteristics. As Harter (1988) expressed it, these children have "a rather disjointed account of 'all things bright and beautiful' about the self" (48). Alternatively, as Hannah Whitehead (aged four) characterized Harter's expression, "Daddy, I'm the best, and you're the best— we're *both* the best!"

In middle childhood, more components of self-esteem can be identified, and they can be differentiated from one another. Harter (1985b) found scholastic competence, social acceptance, athletic competence, physical appearance, and behavioral conduct to be specific content areas related to the global self-worth of children in this age range. The somewhat fantasy-based confusion of actual with ideal self displayed by the younger children is now replaced with the use of social comparison to evaluate the self. A focus on personal abilities and characteristics now develops— including self-conceptualizations of emotional and affective attributes. Negative as well as positive self-evaluations are now present in what is a more accurate self-judgment (Harter 1988).

Anyone who remembers his or her own adolescence, or is currently in regular contact with adolescents, will be well aware of the intense preoccupation with the self that characterizes this age group. Perhaps because of their ability for abstract thought in addition to their heightened awareness of the social environment and their place in it, adolescents begin to integrate self-evaluations such as those related to morality, romantic relationships, and close friendships into their overall self-esteem. A tendency to feel the critical evaluation of significant others and the social world at large often leads to self-criticism and to instability of self-perceptions as the quest to form a coherent identity progresses (Harter 1988, 1990). The gist of the psychological task being attempted by these young people is an effort to form a coherent and consistent self-theory. As Erikson (1977) described it in his characterization of the "eight ages of man," the critical task for adolescents is to form an identity, and the danger they face is role confusion. While being at the threshold of adult life may hold much promise and excitement, it is also a time when self-esteem can plunge to distressingly low levels where depression and anxiety may even spawn suicidal thoughts (Harter 1993). Clearly it is a critical stage, and Harter's recent work has given particular attention to its pitfalls and problems (see Brettschneider and Heim, chapter 8, for a more complete discussion on development tasks in adolescence).

Important foundation stones of Harter's work have been the influence of two early psychologists. One of these, James (1892), theorized that global self-esteem resulted when individuals were successful in areas where they had "pretensions" (in other words, when people did well at things that were important to them personally). The other early psychologist, Cooley (1902), theorized that self-esteem was formed by looking at one's reflection in the metaphorical mirror of social appraisal. Thus, to Cooley, self-esteem was a "looking glass self" formed from interpretations of the reactions of other people to one's characteristics and behaviors. Following those two influences, Harter has been particularly interested in the effect on an individual's overall (global) self-esteem or competence perceptions in subdomains that are either important or unimportant, and in the effect of social support on global self-esteem.

From the first perspective, Harter found that the James-type model was not relevant to young children since they could not clearly conceptualize self-evaluations and importance perceptions simultaneously. However, she has noted considerable support for the model with older children, who appear to be particularly vulnerable to lowered self-esteem when they cannot psychologically discount the importance of perceptions of incompetence in subareas of their self-esteem structures. Harter also found that the Cooley perspective is valid, with social support showing considerable effects on self-esteem from middle childhood onward. The interrelationships of those aspects are perhaps best seen in visual form (see fig. 7.2).

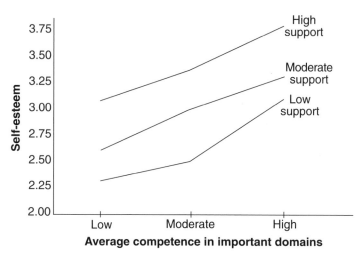

Figure 7.2 Additive effects of competence in domains of importance and social support on self-esteem.

Adapted, by permission, from S. Harter, 1993, Causes and Consequences of Low Self-Esteem in Children and Adolescents. In *Self-Esteem: The Puzzle of Low Self-Regard*, edited by R.F. Baumeister (New York: Vail-Ballou), 100.

As is often the case, it appears that the notion of more-is-better is too simplistic, and this caveat applies to the effects of social support on self-esteem. Harter (1993) has cautioned that recent work indicates the particular importance of *unconditional* support for building self-esteem in young people. In other words, children and youth should have the security of knowing that their worth is valued whatever their abilities and performance. In contrast, *conditional* support from socially significant others that is contingent upon certain behaviors, achievements, attitudes, etc., may have negative effects on self-esteem. Harter (1993) has speculated that this is the case because conditional support tends to be perceived as controlling rather than enhancing. Harter also observed, it should be noted, that this does not mean that teachers, parents, and others should not use behavioral contingencies—but that the contingencies should have consequences other than withdrawal of support for, or denigration of, the child's sense of worth. This point has obvious practical application, and relevant suggestions will be given later in this chapter. What is of interest at this point is whether the two research "camps," Harter's and Deci's, are dealing with similar constructs. Thus the next task is to attempt a comparison.

SELF-ESTEEM AND SELF-DETERMINED MOTIVATION: DIFFERENT NAMES—SAME GAMES?

Arguably, there are more conceptual similarities than differences between the theoretical perspectives just presented. Indeed, much of the support for this observation comes from a recent paper by Deci and Ryan (1995) arguing that autonomy is the basis for true self-esteem. Deci and Ryan's rationale is clearly conceptually congruent with Harter's (1993) point about conditional versus unconditional support. In fact, the similarities appear most obvious when the social contexts that allow people to satisfy their basic psychological needs are examined (Deci 1992).

The gist of Deci and Ryan's (1995) position is that the concept of self-esteem should be reconsidered with a clear distinction made between *contingent* and *true* self-esteem. Deci and Ryan define contingent self-esteem as dependent on living up to some external or internalized controlling standard. Such controlling standards could be, for example, feeling pressured to achieve the athletic success deemed important by one's peers or having to live up to internalized parental expectations. In contrast, true self-esteem is described as being more solidly based in a stable sense of self that does not depend on meeting external standards. Thus, a person with a true self-esteem would be able to act autonomously without constantly feeling that his or her self-esteem was in jeopardy or, to use the psychological terminology, the individual would not be ego involved.

Under the concept of the controlled-to-autonomous continuum of motivated behaviors postulated by self-determination theory, the lack of autonomy inherent in external regulation and introjected regulation of behavior implies that ego involvement is present. In contrast, identified or integrated regulation, or true intrinsic motivation, implies that motivated behaviors are consistent with a sense of self (thus self-determined)—rather than being driven by a pressure to maintain the self.

Perhaps another way to evaluate the theoretical constructs for similarities is to go back to the roots of both. White's (1959) monograph was about the intrinsic urge for competence or mastery. There is obvious logic to the notion that achieving competence or mastery within one's phenomenological environment through self-determined efforts would lead to a positive self-evaluation—or high self-esteem. Thus, in those terms, self-determined motivation and true self-esteem are one and the same.

For Deci and his fellow researchers, identified and integrated regulation and pure intrinsic motivation thrive in social contexts that support autonomy and relatedness. For Harter and her colleagues, self-esteem flourishes when social support from important others is unconditional. In fact, Deci suspects that autonomy support, relatedness, and social support are complementary, "at least to a considerable degree" (E.L. Deci, personal communication, 7 February 1995). Thus, for both groups, the bottom line would appear to be that contexts that unconditionally support mastery and minimize external control and ego involvement are likely to lead to the development of a healthy sense of self and to encourage the most desirable types of motivation. Both groups have cited many studies that support the premises reviewed here, but the next questions for this chapter relate to whether the theories apply to the physical domain. Specifically, what do we know about the content, structure, and development of physical self-esteem in children and youth, and equally important, do the theoretical perspectives outlined hold up when children and youth are involved in sport, physical activity, and physical education settings?

RESEARCH IN PHYSICAL DOMAINS

Following the general theoretical introduction, the aim of the section below is to outline more specifically what we do know about the content, structure, and development of physical self-esteem in children and youth. Of equal importance, it attempts to examine whether the theoretical perspectives discussed earlier hold up when children and youth are involved in sport, physical activity, and physical education settings.

CONTENT AND STRUCTURE OF CHILDREN'S PHYSICAL SELF-ESTEEM

The original work of Fox in researching the content and structure of physical self-esteem and the subsequent work by Marsh have been dealt with extensively elsewhere in this book. To summarize briefly in order to set the context for further discussion, Fox and Corbin (1989) and Fox (1990), working with U.S. college students, identified four physical self-esteem subdomains (body attractiveness adequacy, sport competence, strength competence, and physical condition adequacy) that are subordinate to global perceptions of physical self-esteem and overall self-esteem in a hierarchical structure. While Fox used extensive qualitative open-ended procedures to initially identify the four subdomains, Marsh et al. (1994), in contrast, named nine subdomains based on an earlier factor analysis of physical fitness test scores of Australian school students aged 9, 12, and 15 years (Marsh 1993). Using confirmatory factor analysis, and other statistical analyses of data from high school students, Marsh et al. (1994) supported the validity of those nine fitness-related self-esteem subdomains.

Attempting to replicate Fox's (1990) data with seventh- and eighth-grade students, Whitehead and Corbin (1988) found support for an adapted Physical Self-Perception Profile (PSPP) questionnaire except for some factor cross loadings between the subscales measuring attractive body and physical condition. With some minor rewriting of items in this children and youth version of the PSPP (CY-PSPP), Whitehead (1995) and also Welk, Corbin, and Lewis (1995) were able to demonstrate evidence of self-esteem content and structure, as well as construct validity similar to that obtained in Fox's earlier work with college students. Findings were further supported by confirmatory factor analysis of data from a large sample from this age group (Eklund, Whitehead, and Welk in press).

The available data obtained from these instruments paint an interesting picture. When the data are graphed, the most obvious phenomena are the clear gender differences and the similarities between profiles across ages and data sets. When one looks at available data from Marsh et al. (1994) and Whitehead (1995) that cover early-to-late adolescence (and samples from both the United States and Australia), the consistency is striking (see figs. 7.3 and 7.4). Similar patterns are also described independently with German adolescents by Brettschneider and Heim (see chapter 8). First, males rate themselves by one-half point to a whole point higher than females in almost every subscale on all three instruments. Second, on the profiles, most noteworthy are the relatively low scores for appearance-related perceptions, particularly in females, and the high importance of attractiveness relative to importance of competence in other areas, especially in older adolescent females. Also interesting are the relatively low importance ratings given to sport and strength by U.S. females. In the terminology of Harter, it appears that U.S. females have a hard time discounting the importance of appearance compared to the importance of sport and strength competencies. More will be said about perceptions of attractiveness later in this chapter (discussed also in Davis, chapter 6, and Page and Fox, chapter 9).

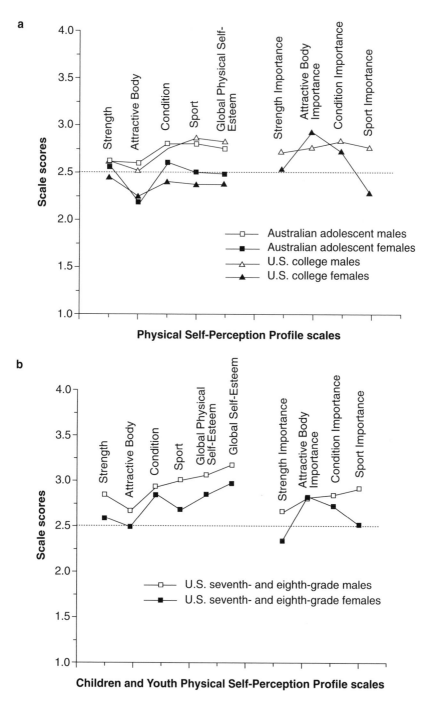

Figure 7.3   (a) Physical Self-Perception Profile scores of US college students and Australian adolescents. (b) Children and Youth Physical Self-Perception scores (US children). Dashed line indicates the midpoint between positive and negative responses.

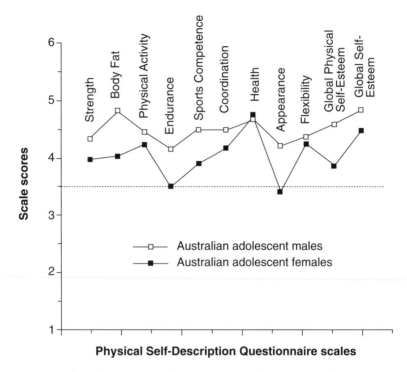

Figure 7.4   Profile of Australian adolescent scores on the Physical Self-Description Questionnaire.

THEORY AND REALITY: DO THEY CORRELATE?

If the theories of self-esteem and motivation described in this chapter are valid, then support for their principles should be found in practice. Thus, for example, we should find that young people are attracted to (and stick with) sports and physical activities that promote a positive sense of self and match the description of self-determined types of motivation. Specifically, we should find that children are attracted to activities that promote their competence through mastery and optimal challenge, that allow them a sense of autonomy or choice, have valued benefits, and promote positive affect. Such attraction should particularly occur when significant others (parents, teachers, coaches, peers, etc.) support involvement unconditionally. In contrast, if the sports or physical activities do not have those attributes, or undermine them, or if significant others are pressuring, are coercive, or use only contingent support, we should find a high dropout rate from involvement in these activities.

Perhaps more persuasively, if the theories really do have utility of application, then when conditions are experimentally manipulated to produce conditions that theoretically promote positive self-esteem and/or self-determined and intrinsic motivation, such outcomes should actually occur. Thus, the next task of this chapter is to review the appropriate literature.

Participation Versus Attrition

Perhaps a good place to start is to look at the reasons young athletes give for participating in sports—and their primary reason is simply expressed as "fun" (Gill, Gross, and Huddleston 1983; Scanlan and Lewthwaite 1986). When investigators delved further they found that the feeling of fun depended primarily on a sense of skill mastery, personal accomplishment, and excitement, all experienced in an atmosphere of optimal challenge. Less important were extrinsic factors such as getting rewards, winning, or pleasing others (Wankel and Kreisel 1985; Wankel and Sefton 1989). These findings were corroborated in a review by Gould (1987). His focus was on attrition from sport, and the good news was that many "dropouts" cited interest in other activities as their reason for quitting and that many returned to sports later. However, in line with the theoretical expectations, major reasons for withdrawal from sports were no fun, or boredom, and more specifically, lack of success and skill improvement, overemphasis on competition, and dislike of the coach. Clearly, theory and reality do correspond according to these types of studies, because the needs for competence, autonomy, and relatedness are obviously salient. However, an interesting question at this stage is whether there are any differences between age groups, particularly in light of the age-related differences in competence development, noted earlier, that Harter described.

Age and Feedback Factors

Horn and Weiss (1991) have provided some useful answers via their developmental analysis of children's self-ability judgments in physical activities. Their study supported the view that children depend more and more on peer comparison in competence judgments as they grow older, with younger children relying more heavily on adult feedback. The study also showed that children who focused on self-comparison factors such as personal skill improvement rated their self-competence higher than those who compared themselves to peers. This led to overestimation of ability for the self-comparers (in relation to teachers' ratings of their ability) and underestimation for the peer-oriented children.

These findings have obvious relevance to motivation and self-esteem, and given the earlier findings from Gould's (1987) study, they raise further questions about the nature of ability-relevant feedback and the way in which it affects competence perceptions and motivation in the physical domain. This is a particularly interesting topic given an apparent anomaly found by Horn (1985) in a study of junior high school female softball players. In that study Horn found that criticism from coaches was associated with higher perceived competence in children while positive reinforcement was associated with lower perceived competence.

Horn suggested that the apparent contradiction between her findings and theoretical expectation occurred because positive feedback was used randomly as encouragement, whereas criticism was contingent on performance errors and was often combined with information on how to improve. The validity of this speculation was supported in a study by Black and Weiss (1992). According to the results, when children felt that coaches gave information after desired performances, and gave information plus encouragement after undesirable performances, the children perceived more success, competence, enjoyment, and preference for optimal challenge. Clearly, in line with the psychological theories, when coaches give information on how to personally improve and when they use encouragement judiciously, they promote positive competence perceptions and facilitate motivation in children's sport and physical activity. In theoretical terminology, it seems that an emphasis on personal improvement or task mastery by coaches is one of the major factors that promote positive motivation and self-perception outcomes.

Motivational Orientations

The finding just reviewed is replicated in literature on children's achievement goal orientations. Task mastery as opposed to ego involvement was discussed earlier in this chapter (also see Biddle, chapter 3 for a more general overview). Briefly, the term ego involvement implies that perceived success is being judged against some external or internalized pressuring standard. Comparison with the ability and successes of one's peers is a typical example. Several studies have examined these contrasting competence-assessment scenarios in children.

Duda et al. (1992) found that task orientation was associated with a focus on cooperation and effort. In contrast, children who were ego oriented believed in ability plus work avoidance and deceptive tactics as a route to success. In terms of motivational affect, task orientation was linked to enjoyment of sport and was negatively related to boredom, while children with high ego orientation tended to find sport more boring. In a subsequent study, Fox et al. (1994) investigated the effects of task and ego orientation in combination rather than in terms of one versus the other. Since the two orientations have been shown to be independent of each other, it is possible to be high or low in both or to have various high-low combinations. With 11-year-old children, the researchers found that the addition of ego involvement to high task involvement might even enhance enjoyment and that it was not detrimental to motivation; in light of the previous findings, this suggests that a high task orientation functions as a "safety net" against potential negative effects of ego orientation.

In the physical education context, Goudas, Biddle, and Fox (1994b) examined how perceived autonomy, competence, and goal orientations influence intrinsic interest in 12- to 14-year-old school children. They found that children who were high on task mastery orientation and perceived autonomy were higher in intrinsic interest. Interestingly, the authors noted that as predicted by self-determination theory, competence was associated with intrinsic interest only in the context of perceived autonomy.

Most recently, a study from Greece indicated that the theory generalizes across cultures. Papaioannou (1995) studied the effects of the motivational climate of the physical education lesson on the intrinsic motivation and anxiety of high- and low-competence early adolescents (aged 13 ±0.5 years). The results showed that a high task focus sustained motivation in children at all levels of perceived competence. Moreover, low-competence children were less anxious about participating in sport and physical activity with high-ability peers when a task-oriented atmosphere was emphasized.

Goudas and Biddle (1994) further developed the work of Papaioannou on physical education class climate with 13- to 15-year-old British children. In support of the goal profile approach, they found that the degree of mastery climate perceived by the children predicted their intrinsic motivation beyond that accounted for by perceived competence. This was not the case for performance climate scores. Children who perceived their class to be high in both mastery and performance climate reported greater intrinsic motivation and perceived competence.

Collectively, this evidence clearly indicates that children who adopt a mastery orientation, and perceive that they operate in a teaching/coaching climate that encourages mastery, have a sounder motivational base.

Experimental Studies

The studies that we have reviewed show consistency in supporting the theoretical predictions outlined in the first part of this chapter. However, they have been mostly correlational in design, and studies capable of addressing cause and effect would enable more confidence in application of theory. Unfortunately, while many such studies have been conducted in settings other than those of sport/physical education (for a review see Deci and Ryan 1985), only a few relevant to the context of this chapter could be found.

To begin, it is appropriate to mention a meta-analysis by Gruber (1985) of interventions exploring the relationship of physical activity to self-esteem in children. Of a total of 84 such studies, Gruber found that 27 had sufficient data to be used in the meta-analysis. The general conclusion was that "participation in directed play and/or physical education programs contributes to the development of self-esteem in elementary age children" (42). Furthermore, children low in global self-esteem benefited most from physical activity programs, especially children who were emotionally disturbed and/or from other special populations. Also there was evidence that the type of program made a difference in self-esteem gains, with aerobic fitness activities being most effective. Individualized teaching methods were found to be more effective than group methods and teacher-dominated methods.

Gruber noted a wide variety of measurement techniques used in the study of self-esteem of children. Virtually all studies used global self-esteem scales. As noted earlier in this book, it was not until the 1980s, after the time when most of the studies reviewed by Gruber were conducted, that the measurement of subcomponents of self-concept was popularized. Since Gruber reported his findings, Anshel, Muller, and Owens (1986) reported a sports-related self-esteem benefit resulting from involvement in a sports day camp. In this study no general self-esteem benefit was reported. Likewise, Blackman et al. (1988) and Brown et al. (1992) noted improvements in subcomponents of self-esteem after involvement in dance and aerobic fitness activities, respectively. No global self-esteem benefits were reported by Blackman et al. (1988). Together, these recent results suggest that activity programs are more likely to have an effect on specific subcomponents of self-esteem (especially physical self-esteem) than on more global measures.

While the studies just reviewed show evidence of cause and effect in that improved self-esteem was consequent to children's involvement in physical activity programs, very few investigations have manipulated conditions to directly test hypotheses related to the relevant theories. Marsh and Peart (1988) examined the effects of putting the focus on peer comparison (competitive) versus group cooperation (cooperative) in a fitness program experiment using high school girls as subjects. They found that both groups gained in fitness in comparison to a control group, but physical ability and physical appearance self-concept were enhanced in the cooperative condition and were lowered in the competitive condition.

In a similar type of experiment, Lloyd and Fox (1992) structured a six-week aerobic fitness program for adolescent girls so that for one group the instructional and informational focus was on self-referencing and task mastery while for another group the focus was on external referencing and ego orientation. They found that motivation and enjoyment were higher in the task mastery-focused condition. Equal numbers of girls with high and low ego orientation had been assigned to each group, and the researchers found that level of ego involvement changed in line with the class climate girls were placed in. The girls with low ego orientation increased in ego involvement in the ego focused group and the girls with high ego orientation decreased in ego involvement in the mastery-focused group. The authors concluded that these results have important implications for physical education curricular design and its potential to impact on motivation.

Cuddihy (1995) compared teenage students who completed a special "Fitness for Life" class with students who had completed a more traditional physical education program. The Fitness for Life program was designed to teach fitness concepts and self-assessment skills and to provide students with the information necessary to make autonomous decisions concerning physical activity participation. Results indicated that students involved in the Fitness for Life approach more frequently classified themselves as "high in competence." In turn, those who were high in feelings of physical activity competence were more likely to give effort in physical activity and to perceive activity to be important.

The motivational outcomes of traditional school fitness testing have been a controversial issue, particularly when peer comparison is forced via percentile-based interpretation of results for the purpose of giving fitness awards. On the basis of application of cognitive evaluation and related theories, the practice has been criticized in review and opinion papers (e.g., Corbin, Whitehead, and Lovejoy 1988). Criticisms were based on the notion that holding all students to high physical fitness standards that many could not hope to achieve, even with considerable effort, would lead to lower feelings of competence and control. Some national groups (American Alliance for Health, Physical Education, Recreation and Dance [AAHPERD] and Cooper Institute for Aerobics Research) began to study alternative methods of motivating children. The Canada Fitness Award scheme (based on high percentile standards similar to the U.S. President's Award scheme) was also undergoing review because of the same concerns.

The team reviewing the Canada Fitness Award scheme engaged an independent research group to conduct a nationwide qualitative study. The results revealed that disappointment and reduced self-esteem were experienced by those children who attained only the lower awards offered by the program (Butler Research Associates, Inc. 1990). On the basis of that study the Canada Fitness Award was discontinued and a new program, focused on promoting healthful activity (The Canadian Active Living Challenge), was designed and has recently been instituted in Canada. (It is worth noting that recently AAHPERD and Fitnessgram jointly implemented a similar program called "You Stay Active" in the United States.)

In a direct experimental test of the effects of percentile-based fitness test score interpretation on intrinsic motivation, Whitehead and Corbin (1991) randomly gave either high or low percentile-based bogus feedback, or no feedback, to young adolescents after a novel shuttle run-type fitness test. They found that receiving a high percentile score boosted perceived competence and intrinsic motivation compared to control (no feedback), while receiving a low percentile score reduced perceived competence and intrinsic motivation. Thus, again the motivation theory was supported, and the problems of forcing the competence-judging focus on peer comparison were emphasized.

These findings are supported by a further study that investigated the motivation of children after a shuttle run fitness test (Goudas, Biddle, and Fox 1994a). As evidenced by the goal perspective profiles discussed earlier, children who were less successful were more likely to have found the event motivational if they were a member of the high mastery/low ego orientation group.

Section Summary

The thrust of this chapter so far has been to argue that for all intents and purposes, the development and maintenance of a healthy self-esteem, and the development and maintenance of the most desirable forms of motivation, are one and the same. As Deci and Ryan (1995) have pointed out, intrinsic motivation and self-determined types of extrinsic motivation are characterized by total involvement of the self—and thus would be accompanied by the experience of true self-esteem.

Throughout the development of school physical education and youth sport, there has been a universal and intuitive belief by professionals that such programs hold tremendous potential for developing self-esteem in children. In the opinion of the authors of this chapter, there is now a wealth of general research that supports that view, and enough in the physical domain to give us sufficient confidence to make authoritative recommendations for effective practice. Indeed, excellent theory-based recommendations have already been made by others (e.g., see Fox 1992; Weiss 1987). Thus the subsequent sections of this chapter attempt to strengthen and update such practical recommendations taking account of the recent and important developments in theory and research that have been described and summarized so far.

FROM THEORY TO PRACTICE

Before moving to specifics, several more comments are warranted. First, while the focus has quite appropriately been on developing and maintaining positive motivation and self-esteem, both common sense and the research cited so far make it obvious that the opposite is possible. As the media regularly point out, negative outcomes are unfortunately also commonplace. Thus, because involvement in sport and physical education has the potential—like a double-edged sword—to cut both ways and produce what Martens (1978) termed "joy and sadness," many of our recommendations will be given in the form of Do's and Don'ts. These will suggest ways of promoting positive outcomes and avoiding negative results.

Second, positive outcomes that can come from these recommendations extend beyond the realm of self-esteem enhancement. Evidence indicates that those who feel good about themselves physically are more likely to participate in regular physical activity, an outcome that is essential to optimal health and well-being of people of all ages. The recommendations presented in this chapter are designed to promote self-esteem but are also intended to motivate healthfully active lifestyles.

Finally, a distinction needs to be made between sport (and sports skills) and physical activity (and skills necessary to be a lifetime exerciser). We have argued that self-esteem, particularly physical self-esteem, is something that results from successful experiences that are at least somewhat autonomous. Thus, we believe that learning sports skills and success in sports can lead to self-esteem and that self-esteem can lead to a desire to persist in sports. However, sports are not necessarily something that all people choose to become involved with, even if they possess high self-esteem. National surveys clearly show that American adults often choose alternatives to sports (running, swimming, bicycling, hiking, walking, etc.) in pursuit of health and fitness benefits. Accordingly, participation in these activities is also associated with high self-esteem, and reciprocally this is an important reason people choose to be involved in these activities. Learning sports skills is important to success in sport. Learning lifetime activity skills that promote independence and autonomy, such as self-assessment and program planning skills, can be equally important to active living.

The first section of recommendations will be generally applicable to the whole children-to-youth age range. Age-specific suggestions will follow.

• **DO emphasize task mastery.** Arguably, the most important goal of sport and physical educators should be the promotion of physical activity involvement for life—and at the same time the building of motivation and a healthy sense of self. The research heavily supports the practice of building physical competence perceptions through a focus on individual improvement. Teachers and coaches can really make a difference by facilitating and reinforcing skill development and personal progress and accomplishment. However, note that this doesn't mean that children have to be isolated. Their sense of making a valuable contribution to a group in an atmosphere of team mastery or cooperation is important too, and it also satisfies what self-determination theory has termed the need for relatedness.

• **DON'T overemphasize peer comparison and competition.** Peer comparison of physical abilities is inevitable as kids grow and develop. However, sensitive teachers and coaches can keep comparison in perspective if they remain mindful of the goal of lifetime involvement in physical activity. The research has suggested that when kids have the security of a strong sense of task mastery, the addition of competition may increase enjoyment; but the problem arises when children with low fitness or low skill levels are inappropriately forced into peer comparison or competition. In that situation, for every winner there will be a loser whose physical self-esteem and motivation will be impaired.

• **DO promote self-determination.** Fortunately, to promote perceptions of autonomy or choice, teachers and coaches do not have to let children and youth do whatever they want! Allowing choice (say of sport skill drills) from a limited range would help foster the perception of choice, particularly if good reasons could be explained for constraints. Care should be taken not to give such explanations in an overly directive, extrinsic motivation-laden manner. The aim should be to help children and youth feel that they have some responsibility for, and a sense of ownership toward, what they are doing rather than feeling that something is being done *to* them. Within physical education, efforts to teach students to test their own fitness and set personal improvement standards, and efforts to teach students skills in program planning that they can use to make personal program plans, are appropriate.

• **DON'T make support contingent on performance.** If kids feel that the only way they can earn approval from parents, teachers, coaches, and peers is to achieve a certain standard of performance, then the motivational focus will be on what self-determination theory has termed external or introjected regulation. This will mean that self-esteem is on the line and contingent on the performance, and the formation of true (noncontingent) self-esteem will be obstructed. If kids feel that important others have regard for their worth irrespective of their performance, then they will want to do their best and will enjoy doing so unencumbered by pressure.

• **DO give appropriate encouragement and technical feedback.** The research cited earlier shows that encouragement is important but that it can backfire if not used judiciously. When the focus is on mastery, kids appreciate honest feedback especially when it is followed by technical information that shows them how to improve. Reinforcing mastery efforts with praise is certainly appropriate, but care should be taken to avoid random praise that may be interpreted as a sign that "coach is being nice to us because we aren't doing well." A sport example that combines encouragement with good technical feedback might be something like "You are working well at that jump shot. Now, you can really make it great if you concentrate on getting your elbow. . . ."

• **DON'T become reliant on extrinsic rewards or pressures.** In addition to the cautions already expressed about making support contingent on performance, consider the motivational implications of creating the impression that the only reason for participating in sport or physical activity is awards, medals, grades, and the like. Remember that the long-term goal is lifetime participation in physical activity. That goal is unlikely to be fulfilled if ego orientation is salient and if self-determined motivation is undermined by extrinsic motivators and pressures.

• **DO promote intrinsic fun and excitement.** As teachers and coaches we start out ahead on this one. Physical activity and sport are inherently pleasurable sources of accomplishment and stimulation. All we have to do is remember what "fun" is for kids—and maintain it!

• **DON'T turn "playout" into workout.** Some adults feel that "play" sounds frivolous and does not connote serious attention to task. Close attention to the effort many kids expend in physical games at recess would help dispel that view, as would seeing the persistence of many children at difficult physical skills when they sense continued task mastery. In some cases coaches may be tempted to expect children to comply with training programs involving continuous vigorous exercise with the intent of "getting them fit" for success. Too often, these programs are based on adult models that are inappropriate and not "fun" for the child athlete. In general, for young children a large volume of activity at a range of intensities typical of free play is recommended as opposed to continuous high-intensity training (Corbin, Pangrazi, and Welk 1994). In adolescence, some youths will choose more vigorous training programs, but high-intensity exercise is *not* necessary in order for health benefits to result, and high-intensity sustained activity is not perceived to be fun by many children and adolescents.

• **DO promote a sense of purpose by teaching the value of physical activity to health and wellness.** The work of Harter, Fox, and others, as reviewed earlier, has shown that importance or value perceptions are key links in the self-esteem and motivation puzzle. Thus knowledge of the benefits of physical activity will help to promote motivation for future involvement (Cuddihy 1995; Slava, Laurie, and Corbin 1984). Knowledge will obviously also facilitate autonomy perceptions, and additionally, according to Vallerand et al. (1992), the pleasure of acquiring knowledge is itself a component of intrinsic motivation. However, there are two points to remember on this topic. First, keep a positive focus on physical activity as a fun way of helping people to look good, feel good, stay healthy, and experience life-in-the-years as opposed to mere years of life. Second, remember the double-edged sword phenomena. If importance is stressed at the same time that perceptions of physical incompetence are created, then self-esteem and motivation will be compromised. Knowledge of the benefits of physical activity should always be accompanied by advice about how to improve.

• **DON'T create amotivation by using poor practice or spreading misinformation.** It is obvious to most that mastery would not be facilitated by teaching bad technique or giving misleading feedback. Thus we should take care to jealously guard good standards of practice among coaches and teachers. The most common of the poor practices are probably dangerous or ineffective methods of weight loss such as fad diets, spot-reducing exercise, passive exercise, the use of sauna suits, and use of dubious "dietary supplements" (Jarvis 1992; Lightsey and Attaway 1992). When people make continued attempts that are doomed to failure because the methods are futile, a learned-helplessness state of amotivation is a likely outcome. As professionals, we should make efforts to keep up to date with science and combat misinformation and quackery.

SPECIFIC RECOMMENDATIONS: CHILDREN

As noted early in the chapter, self-esteem is more generalized in children than in adults, or at least children are less capable of differentiating among subdomains of self-esteem. This is probably so because children are concrete thinkers who are less capable of abstract interpersonal communication and comparisons for self-assessment than are older youth or adults. Children rely more on direct consultation with adults. Also, there is evidence to indicate that the relationship of fitness to physical activity is quite low (r = approximately .15) in children (Morrow and Freedson 1994; Pate, Dowda, and Ross 1990). Thus, children who expect to see concrete evidence (fitness score improvements) of their efforts (exercise) may be disappointed if they give effort in activity and do not see immediate concrete gains. In view of this information, some specific recommendations for children follow.

• **DO help children establish positive effort-benefit ratio perceptions.** Design activities that are perceived to be high in benefit (fun and excitement) and perceived to be low in effort (not based on adult abstract standards). As Fox (1992) put it, children "should be allowed to dream a little longer, so that when a youngster declares he is much stronger than his father, then so be it. This phase of innocent mastery involvement should be allowed to continue. What is important is the doing of the activity and the associated improvement and fun" (48). Furthermore, the limited attention span of youngsters suggests that careful planning is required to produce experiences that yield small but noticeable short-term benefit and thus keep motivation high.

• **DO help children learn fundamental skills.** Done properly, skill learning can provide optimal challenge and at the same time help establish a firm foundation for real physical competence. Important improvements in skill can be experienced quite quickly with good guidance.

• **DO help children set goals that are attainable.** If a goal is too high, the chance of attaining it, even with effort, is low. Unrealistic goals lead to poor effort-benefit ratio perceptions.

• **DON'T use physical activity as a form of punishment.** Using exercise as punishment makes it less fun, gives children the message that it must be a bad experience, and devalues the person administering the punishment.

SPECIFIC RECOMMENDATIONS: ADOLESCENTS

By adolescence, concrete thinking has usually given way to more abstract thinking. Teens are building identity and self-esteem by using social comparison and feedback from significant others as means of making self-assessments. Adult consultation is used less than is the case with children, and peer consultation is valued. The body is changing rapidly, as are the standards against which the self is judged. Many who were successful in sport as children have already dropped out when they have had the opportunity (Martens 1978), for reasons already noted. Those who display special physical abilities are more likely to be persistent in their involvement, while those with lower abilities are more likely to have dropped out. Body attractiveness is a valued subdimension of physical self-esteem especially among girls for whom perceived attractiveness and global self-esteem correlate so highly as to be almost synonymous (Harter 1993). However, in contrast, girls at this age are often able to discount skill, fitness, and strength as unimportant to their physical self-esteem. Boys are less able to discount the skill, fitness, and strength dimensions and may judge themselves too harshly on those factors, just as girls may set unrealistic goals for body attractiveness. The following are some specific recommendations for adolescents:

• **DO help teens set personal rather than comparative standards for fitness and fatness.** There are many factors that determine fitness and fatness over which we have little control. Understanding those factors helps prevent perceived incompetence and amotivation (see the next two recommendations).

• **DO help teens understand the importance of heredity to physical fitness and body fatness.** Research evidence suggests that inherited physical characteristics and potential for physical "trainability" greatly affect an individual's fitness and fatness levels (Bouchard 1994). Knowing the influence of heredity may help teens to be able to personalize fitness and fatness goals. At the same time youngsters should be encouraged to recognize, celebrate, and appreciate individual differences among themselves.

• **DO help teens understand that many society and media standards are unrealistic.** For example, many girls may have to adopt an unhealthy lifestyle to become as lean as the models and actresses they see in magazines and on television. Thus, do use fitness and fatness standards that are attainable and that are based on healthful information rather than standards that are comparative and exclusive.

• **DO help teens to identify alternative physical activities.** If an adolescent has dropped out of organized sport programs (or any other type of physical activity program), there are many alternative activities that are fun and also have health and wellness benefits.

• **DON'T base physical education class grades on personal physical fitness scores.** Grading on physical fitness scores puts the emphasis on uncontrollable factors and extrinsic motivation.

• **DO create Fitness for Life-type personal fitness courses.** Courses like Fitness for Life allow choice and reward students for learning autonomous skills such as personal program planning. That in turn facilitates feelings of competence and involvement in lifetime activity. The Department of Defense Dependent Schools worldwide have successfully implemented such a program for all its high school students (Watson, Sherrill, and Weigand 1994), as have five different states in the United States and several provinces in Canada.

• **DO create a fitness center approach to physical education.** Adults who exercise are more likely to do so if the facilities are close to home and allow them to take part in the kinds of activities they personally enjoy (Sallis 1994). Some schools have recently started fitness/wellness centers that allow students to be active in much the same way as adults who join a fitness club or who have fitness facilities at work.

• **DON'T perpetuate the negative trappings sometimes associated with school-based physical activity.** Examples are insufficient time to dress, no hair dryers, bullies in the shower room, lack of privacy that emphasizes physical appearance concerns, and compulsory uniforms or other clothing that detracts from individuality, autonomy, and feelings of worth.

• **DO make physical activity attractive.** A recent survey (Burkhart 1994) indicated that the foremost participation activity among 9- to 18-year-olds was "hanging out." Hanging out competes with physical and other activities for time, and in fact hanging out may have more positive consequences to self-esteem than physical activity. If physical activity is to be valued by teens we must find ways to make it attractive enough to be regarded as part of the developing identities of young people.

SPECIFIC RECOMMENDATIONS: GIRLS AND YOUNG WOMEN

Girls and women often lack confidence under certain conditions in physical activity settings. This is the case when physical activity is perceived as "male" in orientation, when it is competitive or evaluative, and when feedback concerning performance is lacking (Corbin 1984). To be sure, values and standards are changing, and in the last two decades more girls have become involved in sport programs of all types. However, there continue to be more boys than girls who are active in sports, and in general, girls are less physically active than boys. As noted earlier, they have lower scores on self-esteem and physical self-esteem subscales, and this warrants some special recommendations:

- **DO help to change stereotypes of what are "girl" and "boy" activities.** This can be achieved by providing appropriate models of girls in activity and by helping parents understand the capabilities of girls in sport and activity. Data indicate that team sports, collision or contact sports, and sports that involve strength and speed are less likely to be viewed as "girl" activities. Individual sports, net and racquet sports, and activities with an artistic component such as gymnastics or skating are more likely to be judged as "girl" activities. As perceptions change, confidence among girls and women may likewise change.

- **DO help girls understand that competition is OK.** Girls need to understand that competition is not unfeminine, but at the same time it is important for those who don't like competition to realize that there are many fun and beneficial noncompetitive activities.

- **DO help girls (and boys for that matter) develop a sound self-reward system.** Individuals with low self-esteem and low self-confidence, including many girls in sport and physical activity, need external feedback in order to learn when their performance is "good." Unfortunately, providing them with feedback may produce a temporary feeling of competence but at the same time build dependence on extrinsic support. Care should be taken to encourage the development of self-praise so that a self-reward system can become internalized.

SUMMARY

For years physical education, organized sport, and recreation agencies have promoted a variety of forms of physical activity with a view to enhancing the self-esteem of children and youth. The best evidence suggests that when properly used, physical activity can indeed provide positive benefits to physical self-esteem and at the same time facilitate the most desirable forms of motivation. However, it is also apparent that physical activity and physical education programs can be double-edged swords. Used inappropriately they can have negative effects on self-esteem and motivation.

While more research is needed, especially on the application of psychological theory to physical settings, it is clear that sport and physical education do have great potential to benefit the self-esteem and motivation of children and youth. Based on the information presented in this chapter, guidelines for teachers, coaches, and activity leaders have been suggested to help enhance both a positive physical sense of self and the physical activity levels of children and youth in the years ahead.

REFERENCES

Anshel, M.H., Muller, D., and Owens, V.L. 1986. Effects of a sports camp experience on the multidimensional self-concepts of boys. *Perceptual and Motor Skills* 61: 1275-79.

Black, S.J., and Weiss, M.R. 1992. The relationship among perceived coaching behaviors, perceptions of ability, and motivation in competitive age-group swimmers. *Journal of Sport and Exercise Psychology* 14: 309-25.

Blackman, L., Hunet, G., Hilyer, J., and Harrison, P. 1988. The effects of dance team participation on female adolescent physical fitness and self-concept. *Adolescence* 23: 437-48.

Bouchard, C. 1994. Heredity and health-related fitness. *Physical Activity and Fitness Research Digest*, vol. 1, no. 4, 1-8. Washington, DC: President's Council on Physical Fitness and Sports.

Brown, C., and Cassidy, R. 1963. *The theory of physical education*. Philadelphia, PA: Lea & Febiger.

Brown, S.W., Welsh, M.C., Labbe, E.E., Vitulli, W.F., and Kulkarni, P. 1992. Aerobic exercise in the psychological treatment of adolescents. *Perceptual and Motor Skills* 45: 252-54.

Burkhart, B. 1994. Hanging out: Kids say it's the "in thing." *Arizona Republic*, 16 April, D1.

Butler Research Associates, Inc. 1990. *An evaluation of Canada Fitness Awards: A qualitative study*. Report to Fitness Canada. Ottawa, ON: Butler Research Associates, Inc.

Cooley, C.H. 1902. *Human nature and the social order*. New York: Scribner.

Corbin, C.B. 1984. Self-confidence of females in sports and physical activity. *Clinics in Sports Medicine* 3 (4): 895-908.

Corbin, C.B., Pangrazi, R.P., and Welk, G.J. 1994. Toward an understanding of appropriate physical activity levels for youth. *Physical Activity and Fitness Research Digest*, vol. 1, no. 8, 1-8. Washington, DC: President's Council on Physical Fitness and Sports.

Corbin, C.B., Whitehead, J.R., and Lovejoy, P.Y. 1988. Youth physical fitness awards. *Quest* 40: 200-18.

Cuddihy, T.F. 1995. Intrinsic motivation and physical activity in the high school: Traditional vs. conceptually based physical education. Ph.D. diss., Arizona State University.

deCharms, R. 1968. *Personal causation: The internal affective determinants of behavior*. New York: Academic Press.

Deci, E.L. 1975. *Intrinsic motivation*. New York: Plenum Press.

—. 1992. On the nature and function of motivation theories. *Psychological Science* 3: 167-71.

Deci, E.L., and Ryan, R.M. 1985. *Intrinsic motivation and self-determination in human behavior*. New York: Plenum Press.

—. 1991. A motivational approach to self: Integration in personality. In *Nebraska Symposium on Motivation*. Vol. 38, *Perspectives on motivation*, ed. R. Dienstbier, 237-88. Lincoln, NE: University of Nebraska.

—. 1995. Human autonomy: The basis for true self-esteem. In *Agency, efficacy, and self-esteem*, ed. M. Kernis. New York: Plenum Press.

Duda, J.L., Fox, K.R., Biddle, S.J.H., and Armstrong, N. 1992. Children's achievement goals and beliefs about success in sport. *British Journal of Educational Psychology* 62: 313-23.

Eklund, R.C., Whitehead, J.R., and Welk, G.J. In press. Validity of the Children & Youth Physical Self-Perception Profile: A confirmatory factor analysis. *Research Quarterly for Exercise and Sport*.

Erikson, E.H. 1977. *Childhood and society*. St. Albans, U.K.: Triad/Paladin.

Fox, K.R. 1990. *The Physical Self-Perception Profile manual*. DeKalb, IL: Office for Health Promotion, Northern Illinois University.

—. 1992. Physical education and self-esteem. In *New directions in physical education: Toward a national curriculum*, vol. 2, ed. N. Armstrong, 33-54. Champaign, IL: Human Kinetics.

Fox, K.R., and Corbin, C.B. 1989. The Physical Self-Perception Profile: Development and preliminary validation. *Journal of Sport and Exercise Psychology* 11: 408-30.

Fox, K.R., Goudas, M., Biddle, S.J.H., Duda, J.L., and Armstrong, N. 1994. Children's task and ego goal profiles in sport. *British Journal of Educational Psychology* 64: 253-61.

Gill, D.L., Gross, J.B., and Huddleston, S. 1983. Participation motivation in youth sports. *International Journal of Sport Psychology* 14: 1-14.

Goudas, M., and Biddle, S.J.H. 1994. Perceived motivational climate and intrinsic motivation in school physical education classes. *European Journal of Psychology of Education* 9 (3): 241-50.

Goudas, M., Biddle, S.J.H., and Fox, K.R. 1994a. Achievement goal orientations and intrinsic motivation in physical fitness testing with children. *Pediatric Exercise Science* 6: 159-67.

—. 1994b. Perceived locus of causality, goal orientations, and perceived competence in school physical education classes. *British Journal of Educational Psychology* 64: 453-63.

Gould, D. 1987. Understanding attrition in children's sport. In *Advances in pediatric sports sciences*, vol. 2, ed. D. Gould and M.R. Weiss, 61-85. Champaign, IL: Human Kinetics.

Gruber, J.J. 1985. Physical activity and self-esteem development in children: A meta-analysis. *The Academy Papers* 19: 330-48.

Harter, S. 1978. Effectance motivation reconsidered: Toward a developmental model. *Human Development* 21: 34-64.

—. 1981a. A model of mastery motivation in children: Individual differences and developmental change. In *Aspects of the development of competence: The Minnesota Symposia on Child Psychology*, vol. 14, ed. W.A. Collins, 215-55. Hillsdale, NJ: Erlbaum.

—. 1981b. A new self-report scale of intrinsic versus extrinsic orientation in the classroom: Motivational and informational components. *Developmental Psychology* 17: 300-12.

—. 1985a. Competence as a dimension of self-evaluation: Toward a comprehensive model of self-worth. In *The development of the self*, ed. R. Leahy, 55-121. New York: Academic Press.

—. 1985b. *Manual for the self-perception profile for children*. Denver: University of Denver.

—. 1988. Developmental processes in the construction of the self. In *Integrative processes and early socialization: Early to middle childhood*, ed. T.D. Yawkey and J.E. Johnson, 45-78. Hillsdale, NJ: Erlbaum.

—. 1990. Causes, correlates, and the functional role of global self-worth: A life-span perspective. In *Competence considered*, ed. R.J. Sternberg and J. Kolligian, 67-97. New York: Vail-Ballou.

—. 1993. Causes and consequences of low self-esteem in children and adolescents. In *Self-esteem: The puzzle of low self-regard*, ed. R.F. Baumeister, 87-116. New York: Plenum Press.

Harter, S., and Connell, J.P. 1984. A model of children's achievement and related self-perceptions of competence, control, and motivational orientation. In *The development of achievement-related cognitions and behaviors*, ed. J. Nicholls, 219-50. Greenwich, CT: JAI Press.

Harter, S., and Jackson, B.K. 1993. Young adolescents' perceptions of the link between low self-worth and depressed affect. *Journal of Early Adolescence* 14: 383-407.

Horn, T.S. 1985. Coaches' feedback and changes in children's perceptions of their physical competence. *Journal of Educational Psychology* 77: 174-86.

Horn, T.S., and Weiss, M.R. 1991. A developmental analysis of children's self-ability judgments in the physical domain. *Pediatric Exercise Science* 3: 310-26.

James, W. 1892. *Psychology: The briefer course.* New York: Henry Holt.

Jarvis, W.T. 1992. Quackery: A national scandal. *Clinical Chemistry* 38: 1574-86.

Lightsey, D.M., and Attaway, J.R. 1992. Deceptive tactics used in marketing purported ergogenic aids. *National Strength and Conditioning Association Journal* 14 (2): 26-31.

Lloyd, J., and Fox, K.R. 1992. Achievement goals and motivation to exercise in adolescent girls: A preliminary intervention study. *British Journal of Physical Education Research Supplement* 11: 12-16.

Marsh, H.W. 1993. The multidimensional structure of physical fitness: Invariance over gender and age. *Research Quarterly for Exercise and Sport* 64: 256-73.

Marsh, H.W., and Peart, N.D. 1988. Cooperative and competitive physical fitness training programs for girls: Effects on physical fitness and multidimensional self-concepts. *Journal of Sport and Exercise Psychology* 10: 390-407.

Marsh, H.W., Richards, G.E., Johnson, S., Roche, L., and Tremayne, P. 1994. Physical Self-Description Questionnaire: Psychometric properties and multitrait-multimethod analysis of relations to existing instruments. *Journal of Sport and Exercise Psychology* 16: 270-305.

Martens, R. 1978. *Joy and sadness in children's sports.* Champaign, IL: Human Kinetics.

Morrow, J.R., and Freedson, P.S. 1994. Relationship between habitual physical activity and aerobic fitness in adolescents. *Pediatric Exercise Science* 6: 315-29.

Pangrazi, R.P., and Corbin, C.B. 1995. Physical education curriculum. In *Content of the curriculum*, 2nd ed., ed. A.A. Glatthorn, 174-201. Alexandria, VA: Association for Supervision and Curriculum.

Pangrazi, R.P., and Darst, P.W. 1985. *Dynamic physical education for secondary school students.* Minneapolis: Burgess.

—. 1991. *Dynamic physical education for secondary school students.* 2nd ed. New York: Macmillan.

—. 1997. *Dynamic physical education for secondary school students.* 3rd ed. Boston: Allyn and Bacon.

Papaioannou, A. 1995. Differential perceptual and motivational patterns when different goals are adopted. *Journal of Sport and Exercise Psychology* 17: 18-34.

Pate, R.P., Dowda, M., and Ross, J.G. 1990. Association between physical activity and fitness in American children. *American Journal of Diseases of Children* 144: 1123-29.

Rigby, C.S., Deci, E.L., Patrick, B.C., and Ryan, R.M. 1992. Beyond the intrinsic-extrinsic dichotomy: Self-determination in motivation and learning. *Motivation and Emotion* 16: 165-85.

Sallis, J.F. 1994. Influences on physical activity of children, adolescents, and adults OR determinants of active living. *Physical Activity and Fitness Research Digest*, vol. 1, no. 7, 1-8. Washington, DC: President's Council on Physical Fitness and Sports.

Scanlan, T.K., and Lewthwaite, R. 1986. Social psychological aspects of competition for male youth sport participants: IV. Predictors of enjoyment. *Journal of Sport Psychology* 8: 25-35.

Siedentop, D. 1976. *Physical education: Introductory analysis.* Dubuque, IA: W.C. Brown.

Slava, S., Laurie, D.R., and Corbin, C.B. 1984. Long-term effects of a conceptual physical education program. *Research Quarterly for Exercise and Sport* 55: 161-68.

Vallerand, R.J., Pellétier, L.G., Blais, M.R., Brière, N.M., Sénécal, C., and Vallieres, E.F. 1992. The

Academic Motivation Scale: A measure of intrinsic, extrinsic, and amotivation in education. *Educational and Psychological Measurement* 52: 1003-17.

Wankel, L.M., and Kreisel, P.S.J. 1985. Factors underlying enjoyment of youth sports: Sport and age group comparisons. *Journal of Sport Psychology* 7: 51-64.

Wankel, L.M., and Sefton, J.M. 1989. A season-long investigation of fun in youth sports. *Journal of Sport and Exercise Psychology* 11: 355-66.

Watson, E.R., Sherrill, A., and Weigand, B. 1994. Curriculum development in a worldwide system. *Journal of Physical Education, Recreation and Dance* 65 (1): 17-20.

Weiss, M.R. 1987. Self-esteem and achievement in children's sport and physical activity. In *Advances in pediatric sport sciences*, vol. 2, ed. D. Gould and M.R. Weiss, 87-119. Champaign, IL: Human Kinetics.

Welk, G.J., Corbin, C.B., and Lewis, L. 1995. Physical self-perceptions of high school athletes. *Pediatric Exercise Science* 7: 152-61.

White, R.W. 1959. Motivation reconsidered: The concept of competence. *Psychological Review* 66: 297-333.

Whitehead, J.R. 1995. A study of children's physical self-perceptions using an adapted physical self-perception questionnaire. *Pediatric Exercise Science* 7: 133-52.

Whitehead, J.R., and Corbin, C.B. 1988. Physical competency/adequacy subdomains and their relationship to global physical self-worth, and global general self-worth. Paper presented at the Annual Conference of the Association for Applied Sport Psychology, October, Nashua, NH.

—. 1991. Youth fitness testing: The effect of percentile-based evaluative feedback on intrinsic motivation. *Research Quarterly for Exercise and Sport* 62: 225-31.

Williams, J.F. 1927. *The principles of physical education*. Philadelphia, PA: W.B. Saunders.

—. 1959. *The principles of physical education*. 7th ed. Philadelphia, PA: W.B. Saunders.

CHAPTER 8

IDENTITY, SPORT, AND YOUTH DEVELOPMENT

WOLF-DIETRICH BRETTSCHNEIDER AND RÜDIGER HEIM

One of the major tasks of adolescence is the establishment of a coherent identity. This provides a stable and consistent basis on which to function in adult life. This chapter attempts to link the physical self and involvement in sport with identity formation during the turmoil of the adolescent years.

IDENTITY AND SELF-CONCEPT

There have been a variety of prominent theories on youth identity, some of which were developed decades ago and are at present experiencing a remarkable renaissance (e.g., Cooley 1902; Erikson 1971; Havighurst 1972; James 1890; Marcia 1980; Mead 1934). The discussion about *identity formation* has been particularly strongly influenced by the work of Erikson and Marcia. On the other hand, as described in several chapters throughout this book, programs of research on *self-concept* have mostly drawn from the theoretical legacies of James, Cooley, and Mead. There have been few attempts to integrate theories of identity with self-concept, and none have focused on the sport and exercise domain.

Erikson (1971) described critical life arenas that are the major focus of identity formation in adolescence. These include such domains as preparing for a future career, reevaluating ethical standards, and adopting a set of social roles. Erikson maintained that within each of these areas, the adolescent should first experience identity diffusion and exploration. A major challenge then follows that requires the creation of a sense of personal continuity across settings while the individual establishes both distinctiveness and uniqueness. Studies examining identity development have been stimulated to a large degree by Marcia's (1980) research and his model of identity status, which sought to capture both the process involved in identity formation and individual differences in coping with identity issues. Investigators who have followed a more sociological approach have emphasized that the timing of identity processes may differ depending on the particular domain and on the social and cultural context in which identity formation takes place.

Historically, the term identity has been used differently in the various approaches and has remained ambiguous. A central meaning, however, is emerging that has commonalities in the psychological and sociological literature. The term *identity* can be used (a) when a person describes himself or herself as unique and distinctive and (b) when this definition is shared with the social environment. It follows from this definition that identity has at least two definable components, which are termed *personal identity* and *social identity*. Personal identity develops on the basis of continuity of self-experience in the course of the life span. Social identity derives from the image that others help create for the self and is often called the *looking glass self*. The development of identity in adolescence can be viewed in terms of the process through which an individual establishes a balance between personal and social identity.

Despite hypotheses and deliberations such as these, psychological and sociological studies of identity development have failed to provide a clear and cohesive picture. Attempts to operationalize assumptions about identity development and to provide an empirically verifiable foundation have been rare and have usually produced, at best, modest support for the theoretical tenets. Marcia (1980) sums up the situation: "Studying identity in adolescence is not a task for the methodologically hypersensitive" (159).

It is interesting to note that the wealth of theoretical conjecture along with lack of empirical confirmation evident in the study of identity is reversed in the traditional self-concept literature. Before the 1980s, hundreds of self-concept studies were undertaken; however, the vast majority were atheoretical and lacked consistency and clarity of terminology. In particular, theoretical models undertaking to describe the genesis of self-concept and its change in the course of the life span were absent. However, the last decade has seen considerable progress (see Marsh, chapter 2). Domains of self-evaluation such as the academic, social, emotional, and physical self have now been clearly identified and supported empirically for adolescents (Marsh 1988, 1989). Within these domains, the self appears to become increasingly complex and differentiated throughout childhood and adolescence (Harter 1990).

The self-concept originates from self-gathered information that changes on the basis of experiences in the individual environment and represents the complete knowledge of a person about self. Each person develops perceptions and ideas of his/her abilities, characteristics, and personal ways of acting, eventually providing a sense of meaning and a self-rating of quality (self-esteem). In this sense, the self-concept is the result of a *naive theory* or an internal model of a person, which directs behavior and which is either confirmed or modified on the basis of behavior and experiences (see Shavelson, Hubner, and Stanton 1976, 411). The self-concept is therefore the result of perceptions and actions of a person in the environment through a reflexive process, a theme that has emerged repeatedly throughout this book.

In the absence of sound theoretical guidance or empirical support, it is assumed for the purposes of this discussion that self-concept and identity are closely linked. Individuals can only regard themselves as unmistakable, distinct, or unique (identity) when they are able to sufficiently describe themselves (self-concept). So Waterman (1985) states in his definition: "identity refers to having a clearly delineated self-definition, a self-definition comprised of those goals, values, and beliefs which the person finds personally expressive, and to which he or she is unequivocally committed" (6). Waterman calls for area-specific identity concepts, similar to the multi-dimensionality of self-concept, that incorporate the areas of profession, gender role, political ideology, philosophy of life, and spare-time culture. The connection between such self-concept and identity models can, at least for our purposes, be expressed pragmatically. Self-concept is composed of the differentiated knowledge of a person about different relevant areas of his/her everyday life and aspects of personality. Identity, on the other hand, represents the complete integration of different self-perceptions and values and their reflexive processing. This self-knowledge is required for bio-graphical continuity and allows the formation, within the social context, of a structured totality of cognitions.

According to Blustein and Palladino (1991), the integration of self-knowledge and values produces a coherent ego identity. It is character-ized by a clear and stable self-definition that has an internalized set of personal standards and a continuity in values and attitudes. Harter has suggested that adolescents who are unsuccessful at integrating their mul-tiple attributes into a coherent and unified theory of self are at risk of incomplete identity development (Harter 1990).

The role of the body concept appears to be crucial in this process. Almost all books on developmental psychology include a chapter on the physical aspects of the development of young people. There is remarkable agree-ment across this literature about the importance of the body and of the physical self-concept for identity development in adolescence. Undoubt-edly the nature of the rapidly changing body through sexual maturation provides an additional challenge to the formation of a coherent identity for youngsters. In addition, socialization theorists and sociologists in the course of recent decades have emphasized the emerging status of the youthful body as a social power resource (Bourdieu 1982; Shilling 1994; Zinnecker 1990). In this context, they are increasingly documenting the role of the body in the social positioning of young people in modern industrial societies and the status that sport has attained as a vehicle for dealing with one's own body. But empirical findings that can verify these assumptions have not yet come forth. Similarly, studies of sport have failed to utilize theories and models to explain the complex relationships among sport involvement, body concept, and identity development in young people.

To a large extent, this is not surprising. The solution to unraveling the Gordian knot that holds together the different theoretical approaches and research methods of the various disciplines is elusive. The systematic integration of principles from socialization theory and developmental psychology in the study of the body and its relationship with sport involvement has yet to be attempted. Conversely, sport has rarely been used as an arena through which to extend the development of theory in these two scientific disciplines.

THE CONCEPT OF DEVELOPMENT TASKS

The state of theory and research concerning identity development and aspects of the physical self described so far provides a sobering picture. As there appears to be no single comprehensive theory available at present for advancing this area of work, reference is now made to aspects of theories and models concerning youth identity formation that seem plausible as ways of addressing sport and youth development relationships.

The concept of development tasks seems particularly pertinent. Identity development and self-concept development have been considered central themes of youth since Erikson (1971). Gaining identity and the construction of a self-concept are at the same time closely linked to coping with development tasks typical of that age (Havighurst 1972). The notion of development tasks combines relevant concepts from several theoretical perspectives on human development. These include the following views:

1. Development continues over the whole life span, within which adolescence, as a determinant of adult development, is particularly significant. This is the time, as childhood is completed, for searching processes and new orientations (Lerner and Spanier 1980).

2. Development takes place in the framework of a dialectic individual-environment relationship. Changes in the person accompany changes in the environment and vice versa (Bronfenbrenner 1980).

3. The model of the individual-environment interaction requires the subject to actively arrange the social and ecological context, which will reciprocally have an influence on the individual (Hurrelmann 1983; Oerter and Montada 1987).

ADOLESCENT DEVELOPMENT TASKS

Development tasks, which according to Havighurst (1972) are influenced to varying degrees by biological and personality factors as well as cultural and social factors, can be considered as definable connecting links between social requirements and individual needs, interests, and aims (Dreher and Dreher 1985). Havighurst (1972) defines a development task as "a task which arises at or about a certain period in the life of the individual, successful achievement of which leads to his happiness and to success with later tasks, while failure leads to unhappiness in the individual, disapproval by society and difficulty with later tasks" (2). Development tasks by definition, therefore, vary in nature across the life span. An analysis of the literature reveals several development tasks that are likely to have salience to young people in Western industrial countries (Havighurst 1972; Oerter 1987). These include

1. acceptance of one's own physical appearance and the physical changes involved with growth and sexual maturation,

2. development of a circle of friends, with the establishment of deeper relationships with peers of both genders,

3. detachment from the parental home and the gaining of independence,

4. assumption of male or female roles and related social behaviors,

5. the beginning of intimate relationships and preparation for partnership,

6. preparation for career, involving the development of aspirations and an awareness of what is required to achieve them,

7. development of socially acceptable behaviors and the acceptance of political and community responsibility, and

8. development of one's own view of life and a value system as a guide for personal behaviors.

In accord with and in continuation of the work of Havighurst (1972), these development tasks are characterized by several formal features:

1. Development tasks are partly universal and partly dependent on the sociocultural context. For example, the physical changes experienced by boys and girls throughout puberty are primarily a result of biological programming that in normal healthy youngsters is an anthropological

constant. The acceptance of these maturational changes, however, is subject to sociocultural influences (see Sparkes, chapter 4, for a more complete discussion). In this way, for example, Turkish girls who have been taught by their families to follow the rules of the Koran, which strictly forbids females to expose their bodies, attach a different value to their body shape than perhaps young females in California. The latter have been brought up to see that attractive bodies are in frequent use as a marketable commodity.

2. The prominence of tasks is determined to some extent by the period in the life span. For example, taking on a permanent partner and starting a family would not be tasks typical of adolescence. Other development tasks arise in varying form in different phases in the course of life. This is true, for example, for the construction of a value system as an ethical guide for one's own behavior.

3. A further feature is the interdependence of development tasks. For example, there are connections between the development of peer relationships and detachment from the parental home. Similarly, the development of same- and opposite-gender peer relationships and the confidence achieved through acceptance of physical appearance may be critically linked for some adolescents.

4. Development tasks also show a historical dimension. Social demands as well as individual value orientation and aims are part and parcel of the transformation process and are subject to the relevant spirit of the times. In this way, the current ubiquitous "body boom" and the importance that our society attaches to physical appearance and attractiveness significantly influence how young people perceive and deal with their bodies.

IMPORTANCE OF DEVELOPMENT TASKS

An interesting question relates to the sense of importance and priority that adolescents attach to each development task. Table 8.1 (from Dreher and Dreher 1985) shows how adolescents evaluate the importance of the main developmental tasks they face. In open-ended interviews, tasks that emerge as most important are preparation for career, the search for the self, and the establishment of peer relations. Gender differences are apparent and reveal the gender-specific stereotypes found in other studies (e.g., Marsh 1989). Girls tend to consider the body more important than do boys, although the data do not allow us to determine which elements of the body are salient. Boys appear to be more interested in intimate relations than are girls, a result that is surprising at first sight. However, it may suggest that intimate relations are tied to the importance of sexual relations for adolescent boys. Further qualitative and quantitative research is needed to provide more detail and insight into constructs underlying these importance ratings.

Table 8.1 Evaluation of the Importance of Developmental Tasks by 15- to 18-Year-Old Male and Female Adolescents (N = 440)

Rank	Male		Female	
1	School/job	94%	School/job	94%
2	Self	93%	Self	94%
3	Peer relations	91%	Values	92%
4	Future	80%	Peer relations	91%
5	Values	78%	Body	88%
6	Body	78%	Future	86%
7	Intimate relations	74%	Detachment	64%
8	Role	58%	Partnership/family	50%
9	Detachment	55%	Intimate relations	49%
10	Partnership/family	46%	Role	42%

Note: Percentage refers to the categories of agreement *very important* and *important*.

Data from E. Dreher and M. Dreher, 1985, Entwicklungsaufgaben im Jugendalter: Bedeutsamkeit und Bewältigungskonzepte. In *Entwicklungsaufgaben und Bewältigungsprobleme in der Adoleszenz*, edited by D. Liepmann and A. Strikgrud (Göttingen, Germany: Hogrefe), 63.

Development tasks allow some insight into the relationship between self-concept and identity in youth. For development tasks to be successfully accomplished, a cognitive and perceptual base is required that controls and directs behavior. This foundation represents the self-concept of a person. The establishment of identity is to a large extent dependent on the ability of the adolescent to complete development tasks successfully. In this sense, therefore, it could be argued that identity represents the integration of the different areas of the self-concept through the achievement of development tasks. The dependence of development tasks on social and cultural influences has already been pointed out, and is equally valid for identity and self-concept.

THE TREND TOWARD INDIVIDUALIZATION

Social transformation processes have a significant influence on the structure and content of youth development tasks and therefore the development of identity. Thus central cultural changes observable in modern industrial societies also affect adolescence. *Pluralization* and *individualization* are terms sociologists have used to describe the main processes of change in modern differentiated societies. Modern life is characterized by a growing particularization of areas of life such as family time, leisure, education, and career. In a society that is no longer relatively uniform for all people and is increasingly pluralized, it becomes more difficult for the individual to integrate these different experiences. The standardized biography of former times has been replaced by a patchwork biography (Beck 1986; Schulze 1993).

This trend in Western societies is reflected in the phase of adolescence. In the course of the last few decades, adolescents have not been able to rely on given standards, values, and life patterns to the same extent as in the past. The opportunity for adolescents to describe and define themselves on the basis of sound, traditionally valid models has become increasingly limited. Society no longer dictates to adolescents who they are, yet it insists that they create their own identity. Today, teenagers' roles are so unclear that not only do they not know who they are, but also they have little raw material with which they can begin to develop an identity (Koteskey, Walter, and Johnson 1990, 55). As they can no longer rely on secure traditional ties such as age-specific social norms, modern adolescents are, unlike the generations of their parents and grandparents, called upon to be the producers of their own biographies and to draw upon their own decisions.

This has produced a double-edged sword for adolescents. On the brighter side, the changes have allowed a growing spectrum of biographical options for adolescents—a freedom to create a new youth identity. Conversely, the search for the *real me* during this dynamic and intense period of transition has proven to be a much more complex challenge. Adolescents have had to develop productive strategies for coping with identity issues and developmental tasks, and there has been a greater susceptibility to disturbed identity development.

As the secure traditional ties provided by family or religious value systems have declined in our societies and remained unreplaced by strong new alternatives, for many *the body* has become the last bastion on which to build a reliable sense of identity. In recent years the relationship between the body and identity has become stronger. People are increasingly concerned with the management and appearance of the body, both as constituent of the self and as a social symbol (Beck 1986; Shilling 1994).

According to a thesis presented by Zinnecker (1990) in an expansion of the Bourdieu concept of capital resources (Bourdieu 1982), the new emphasis on the body has allowed it to take on the quality of a social power resource. Similar to our money (economic capital), our relationships (social capital), our qualifications (educational capital), or our experience of life (cultural capital), the body has a social currency value that can be converted into economic, cultural, and social profit. In short, a sporting, fit, and aesthetic body has become a source of power and status in society.

SELF-CONCEPT AND SPORT INVOLVEMENT

The improved status of body capital for adolescents seems directly linked to the increase in importance within society that sport has acquired in the course of recent decades. It is important to note here that in Germany and many other European countries, sport carries a fairly broad definition that includes health-related exercise and recreational as well as competitive sport. Under these conditions the appearance and the performing aspects of the body have gained in salience and in the opportunity they provide for identity formation and youth development. The central question that arises in the context of youth development tasks concerns how young people profit in terms of self-concept and identity development by emphasis on the body and involvement in sport (see Kurz and Brinkhoff 1989).

Our knowledge about the physical self-concept of adolescents and its importance for the development of identity is limited. However, in recent years, the development of multidimensional models and instruments (see Marsh, chapter 2) has provided considerable impetus in this area. Physical self-concept is now firmly established as a measurable and integral part of the overall self-concept (Fox 1992; Fox and Corbin 1989; Marsh and Redmayne 1994). In the following sections, results from large-scale empirical studies conducted with German adolescents will be summarized in order to shed some light on the nature of the physical self and its relationship with sport involvement, health, and lifestyles.

ADOLESCENT PHYSICAL SELF-CONCEPT

A recent study by Brettschneider and Bräutigam (1990) surveyed 4118 German adolescents between the ages of 12 and 21. Age distribution, gender (51.5% male), and social strata were adequately represented in this stratified random sample from Northrhine-Westphalia, the largest state in Germany. One focus of this youth study was on the structure of the physical self-concept, and in particular, the impact that variables such as age, gender, and education have on the way adolescents view their own bodies and their health. An instrument developed and validated by Mrazek (1987) was used. Questions concerned descriptive and evaluative cognitions referring to attributes such as sport competence and fitness (e.g., "I take care to keep fit" and "I think it is important to be sporty"), physical self-acceptance (e.g., "My body is beautiful" and "I am comparatively good looking"), tidy appearance ("I believe it is important to look good" and "I take care my clothes are clean"), figure ("I sometimes worry about my figure" and "I really ought to lose a few pounds"), health (e.g., "My body is prone to all sorts of illnesses" and "My state of health varies"), and weight and diet (e.g., "I check my weight" and "I try to live on a healthy diet").

The data provided preliminary evidence across a large sample of German youngsters about the nature of their physical self-perceptions. In particular, the size of the sample allowed some unique insights into the impact of a range of categorical variables. The following is a summary of the main findings:

1. Factor analyses offered a six-factor solution for the physical self-concept. The first factor to emerge involved sport competence and fitness. The second was an appearance factor consisting of being well groomed, and the third emphasized the cleanliness aspects of self and consisted of items concerned with showering and washing hair regularly. The next three factors also concerned appearance but centered on figure, weight control, and regulation of eating habits. This factor structure confirmed Mrazek's (1987) original findings with 12- to 16-year-old adolescents as well as reflecting the existence of subcomponents of the physical self that have been confirmed in research using other instruments with adolescent groups (Marsh 1988; Page et al. 1993).

2. Analyses of variance indicated that there was greater variance across gender than across age. These findings would seem to suggest that the gender-specific elements of the physical self-concept are already largely developed before the 12th year of life and do not undergo substantial changes during puberty or adolescence. The contours of classical sexual stereotypes were surprisingly apparent. Girls and young women placed greater emphasis on a well-groomed appearance and personal hygiene, awareness of figure problems, weight control, and controlled eating habits. Boys and young men emphasized sportiness and physical fitness. Whereas girls and young women pay particular attention to the care and control of their body appearance, boys and young men emphasize the active, physical, and generally more athletic side of the self-concept. This gendered emphasis has also been revealed in studies with young British adolescents (Fox et al. 1994).

3. Minor age effects are noticeable. The emphasis that 13- to 15-year-olds place on sport competence and physical fitness is less pronounced in older age groups. Likewise, youths tend to pay greater attention to the care and control of their body as they grow older. These results seem to suggest that the great physical changes that the developing adolescent body undergoes do not cause a major identity crisis (perhaps with the exception of figure problems in some girls).

4. Pupils of higher social strata emphasize sport competence and physical fitness and perceive fewer health problems than pupils of lower social strata. No clear further differences in physical self-concept patterns emerged between socioeconomic status groups.

ADOLESCENT EVALUATIONS AND PERCEPTIONS OF HEALTH

In the light of the increasing importance placed by society on an individual's health and fitness, adolescents from the same sample were asked to evaluate their health-related status. Currently the issue of lifestyle-related health is complex. In the eyes of some adolescents, the pursuit of individual *healthiness*, in much the same way as the body itself, may have been elevated to the status of *social supercategory*. On the other, there is perhaps a belief on the part of some youth of today that health is not an issue. Though both these statements may find some empirical support, the rapid increase in body-related disorders such as anorexia nervosa and bulimia among females, overweight and obesity, and the growing number of adolescents suffering from psychological stress symptoms indicate the importance of investigating health perceptions among young people. No formalized definition of health was used in this study in order to allow subjects the freedom to express the nature of health in their own terms. Specifically, questions were posed to elicit the perceived status of general health, stability of health status, and anxieties related to health. The following is a summary of the main findings:

1. The majority of adolescents studied (62%) believed themselves to be in a generally stable state of good health, especially when asked to compare themselves to others. They had few anxieties about health and did not regard it as a particularly pressing or important subject. Good health tended to be taken for granted.

2. Approximately 15% of adolescents were uncertain about their health status and believed themselves to be generally less healthy and more prone to illness than others. Hence, it would appear that for approximately one in every seventh adolescent, health is an important concern that occupies some degree of mental energy.

3. Pupils from lower social strata schools (upper division of elementary school in Germany) expressed considerably more health problems than pupils from higher social strata schools (grammar school in Germany). Elementary school pupils also seemed to be more prone to illness and had greater health anxieties than grammar school pupils.

4. Girls and young women perceived more health problems than boys and young men. Although these gender differences were statistically significant, they were overridden by greater differences among adolescents from different social strata.

5. There was no evidence of an age effect when health perceptions of the 13- to 15-year-old and the 18- to 21-year-old groups of adolescents were compared.

In summary, German adolescents are clearly concerned about their bodies. These findings are consistent with research documenting the importance that modern society attaches to the performing and appearance aspects of the body. Boys consider physical fitness and sport competence to be more important than do girls, whereas girls place more value on aspects of physical appearance. Currently, health and illness concerns do not seem to pose a major problem for adolescents, but in comparison to boys, girls report that they have more concerns and anxieties about their health. Furthermore, the perceptions of adolescents of lower social status support national health reports indicating that poorer health status and greater incidence of health problems occur in the lower social classes.

These data are in accordance with the consensus in self-concept research, which indicates that the physical self-concept represents a potential problem area, in particular for many female adolescents. Although the data do not provide direct evidence, it is plausible that the susceptibility of adolescent girls to lower perceptions of attractiveness and health, accompanied by high levels of concern, may have a negative impact on their overall levels of global self-esteem. Many boys, on the other hand, may benefit from their emphasis on physical abilities.

SPORT INVOLVEMENT AND PHYSICAL SELF-CONCEPT

The research just described, which provides insight into the physical self-concepts of a large sample of German adolescents, leads to further questions regarding the relationships between perceptions of the body, self-concept, and sport involvement. The hypothesis that differences in physical self-concepts might be found upon comparison of groups of young people involved in sport with those less involved deserves particular attention. Baur and Brettschneider (1994) reanalyzed the data obtained in their earlier study on more than 4000 young people between the ages of 12 and 21. A comparison was made between those who reported having memberships to sport clubs and those who did not. In view of the sport culture in Germany, it can be assumed that the group of club members would be much more actively involved in sports. For example, club members would usually enter a sport club at the age of six to eight years. They would be dedicated to a specific kind of sport, would train once or twice a week regularly, and also would take part in competitions. The result of the analyses were as follows:

1. All the young people in the sample, regardless of level of sport involvement, valued an attractive figure/physique. The physical self-concepts of young sport club members were dominated by sport competence and fitness. The young non-club members, on the other

hand, tended to focus more on body stylization, represented by smart appearance and grooming.

2. Young sport club members tended to judge their health more positively than non-club members of the same age.

The physical self-perception profile typical of youth who are involved in higher-level sport differs in orientation from that of young people not involved and tends in many ways to be more positive. The extent to which engaging in sports and attending sport clubs socialize youngsters to feel better about themselves cannot be established from these data. It is possible, however, that the sport club is a highly social place that fosters positive attitudes toward the body and health at a critical time in identity development. Possible mechanisms for more positive physical self-concepts might be through sporting achievements or successful social interaction and group membership. Of course, an alternative explanation is that group selection has taken place, with differences in competence and self-perceptions having been in existence before entry to the club. It is likely that both mechanisms are operating. Boys and girls who are members of a sport club tend to be attracted or selected because of their emerging abilities. However, the club offers adolescents the opportunity to express and improve physical competence and also provides experiences through which some development tasks can be tackled. In this sense sport allows self-affirmation through physical performance, security in dealing with the body, and opportunity for the development of social and emotional relationships with peers.

ELITE SPORT INVOLVEMENT AND SELF-CONCEPT

It is now clear that self-concept consists of several elements, and not only of physical abilities and attractiveness. These other facets may have greater influence on the development of youth identity than sport involvement. Empirical findings comparing the relative salience of the various elements of self-concept to identity formation are still rare, and the data available are contradictory (Mrazek and Hartmann 1989). Of interest in the context of elite sport involvement is the relative impact of high-level sport performance on these factors. Research so far has been typified by theoretical and methodological limitations, with few investigations having used multidimensional scales. Furthermore, studies have lacked clear operational definitions of participation in sport in terms of frequency, intensity of involvement, and degree of commitment, so comparisons across results cannot effectively be made. Most studies have been cross-sectional so that causality has not been determined. Given the potentially high investment made by many youngsters in terms of time and effort dedicated to sport, as well as the financial input by community organizations, studies are needed that can begin to produce a realistic appraisal of the impact that high-level sport involvement has on youngsters and their identity development.

In response to this need, we are currently conducting a large-scale longitudinal study in Germany in an effort to estimate the impact of elite sport involvement (among other issues) on multiple elements of self-concept. Self-concept is being measured at various time points. However, only the first wave of results are currently available for discussion. The study was initiated in 1992 using two samples of youngsters. Sample I involved 700 male and female student athletes from elite sport schools, aged between 12 and 17 years, who were competitive in various sports. Most of the respondents from these schools in Berlin had passed the talent selection system of the former German Democratic Republic; consequently, they had been identified as highly gifted children and youth and had been involved in a well-elaborated scheme for developing excellence in sport. A considerable number of these students are Olympic medalists and/or international and national champions. This outstanding group of highly talented athletes was compared to the subjects of Sample II, who composed an appropriately matched control group from regular schools in Berlin.

As part of the study, elements of self-concept were measured through use of a modified and translated version of the Self-Description Questionnaire (SDQII) (Marsh 1988). In order to produce a more complete picture of the physical self-concept, the physical scales of the SDQII were replaced with the item battery previously and successfully used by Brettschneider and Bräutigam (1990).

Physical Self-Concept

Comparisons were made between the responses of the young elite athletes and those of the control group (see table 8.2). Gender groups were added as a second independent variable, and age was used as a covariate. Table 8.2 summarizes the mean scores and the F values for the gender and sport involvement groups. The majority of elements of the body concept of the student athletes, regardless of gender, emerged as significantly more positive than those of the control group. Differences were particularly noticeable in the areas of sport competence and fitness, well-groomed appearance, awareness of figure problems, and weight control. These results are not surprising for males, among whom sporting prowess has always been particularly highly valued. However, for females, the results show a similar effect and indicate that athletic involvement and athleticism are not necessarily in conflict with an acceptable female or feminine adolescent identity.

The results of a correlation analysis between the factors of the body concept and the general self-concept provide further insight into the links between body and general self-concept. For both samples, a clear negative relationship can be identified between perceptions of figure and health problems and general self-concept. Young people who testified to fewer

Table 8.2   Physical Self-Concept Scores of Elite Adolescent Athletes and Controls

Scales of physical self-concept	Means					F values		
		Gender		Sport involvement		Gender	Sport involvement	Inter-action
	Total $N=1688$	Male $n=822$	Female $n=864$	Control group $n=977$	Top athletes $n=711$			
Appearance	2.30	2.23	2.37	2.11	2.57	0.92	39.14***	0.00
Figure	3.09	2.70	3.47	2.90	3.37	179.06***	35.31***	1.01
Fitness	3.78	3.56	3.98	3.18	4.60	15.26***	708.81***	5.15*
Health	3.57	3.45	3.69	3.50	3.66	24.59***	5.20*	1.09
Weight control	2.58	2.85	2.32	2.41	2.81	124.06***	78.74***	0.01
Hygiene	3.89	4.12	3.67	3.81	4.00	189.12***	9.31**	8.89**

*Significant at $p < 0.05$; **significant at $p < 0.1$; ***significant at $p < .001$.

problems in these areas scored more positively regarding their general self-concept. As might be expected, sport competence and fitness is also closely tied to general self-concept in the young elite athletes. The general self-concept of young people in the control group, in contrast, appears to depend to a greater extent on their evaluation of their physical appearance.

General Self-Concept

Factor analyses of the items in the SDQII produced a clear nine-factor solution, explaining about 68% of variance for both groups of young people. These results confirm the findings of Marsh (1988) and provide evidence of the differentiation of German youth self-concept into the following factors: general self, emotional stability, honesty and trustworthiness, mathematical skills, verbal skills, general school abilities, relations with parents, relations with same-sex peers, and relations with opposite-sex peers. These factors reflect the appropriate scales of the SDQII and the four facets of the self-concept they are meant to represent: general self-concept, emotional self-concept, academic self-concept, and social self-concept.

It is immediately clear that student athletes on average have a more positive general self-concept than nonathletes and that this is particularly reflected in higher self-ratings of social relationships (peers of opposite sex and parents) and general school abilities (see table 8.3). The athletes did not

Table 8.3	Self-Concept Scores of Elite Adolescent Athletes and Controls							
	Means				**F values**			
		Gender		Sport involvement				
Scales of self-concept	Total N=1688	Male n=822	Female n=864	Control group n=977	Top athletes n=711	Gender	Sport involvement	G X Sp
General	4.74	4.84	4.64	4.64	4.88	23.86***	25.21***	5.51*
Opposite sex	4.10	4.13	4.08	3.94	4.33	0.63	31.46***	0.32
Same sex	4.73	4.62	4.84	4.71	4.75	43.46***	6.28*	0.07
Parents	5.08	5.11	5.05	4.98	5.22	0.04	32.50***	0.01
Honesty	4.24	4.20	4.29	4.22	4.28	11.13***	4.77*	4.16*
Emotional	3.89	4.06	3.71	3.84	3.96	83.75***	2.01	0.03
Mathematical	3.82	4.07	3.56	3.73	3.95	72.93***	4.84*	12.42***
Verbal	4.07	3.91	4.25	4.08	4.07	69.49***	0.83	6.64**
School	4.16	4.16	4.16	4.06	4.29	0.79	33.10***	8.62*

*Significant at $p < 0.05$; **significant at $p < 0.01$; ***significant at $p < 0.001$.

score significantly lower than the control group in any of the subscales. Gender differences also were found, with females scoring lower on general self, mathematical abilities, and emotional stability. These data confirm findings of other studies, revealing gender-specific stereotypes (Marsh 1989). There was also evidence of an interaction effect between gender and athletic involvement. Although male student athletes scored higher than their control group counterparts on 3 of 9 subscales (general self, relations with peers of opposite sex, and parent relationships), differences between the female student athletes and controls were evident for 5 of 9 subscales (general self, mathematical abilities, general school abilities, relations with peers of the opposite sex, and parent relationships). Mean differences also tended to be greater between the female groups. Of further interest is the finding that gender differences that are extremely apparent in the general population do not exist within athletic groups to the same degree.

In summary, both young male and female elite athletes demonstrate more positive self-concepts than other young people. For females, the contrast between those involved in elite sports and those not involved appears to be greater than for males. Two possible mechanisms may be in operation to produce these differences. First, sporting talent is more common in those with higher self-concept, and these youngsters have been selected into the sport clubs. Second, success in sport has generalized to other elements of the self-concept, producing a more positive profile. Elite sport clubs might speed up this process as they provide opportunities for extending sport skills and for sport success, elevated social status, and social interaction. It is likely that both these mechanisms are influential in explaining the observed self-concept differences, and that this effect is more substantial for females.

With only the first wave of data available in the current project, it is not yet possible to estimate the contribution of involvement in elite sport to self-concept and identity development. Continued work with this longitudinal project will provide time-dependent data points that should allow more incisive conclusions about causality to be drawn. However, the hypothesis that sport involvement at an elite level is *detrimental* to the self-concepts and mental adjustment of the adolescent is certainly not supported by these data. Returning to the concept of development task, the results suggest that high commitment and involvement in elite sport during adolescence does not lead to emotional poverty and a loss of social interaction. Rather, the assumption is supported that sport makes it easier to establish deeper relationships with people of the same age and of both genders. Since relationships with parents are rated higher among the sport group, the development task of detachment from the parental home seems to be resolved with fewer and less traumatic conflicts. Furthermore, there is no evidence that sporting commitments prevent young people from developing their intellectual abilities. The high scores in the area of academic self-concepts of athletes suggest that they feel very confident academically. The findings with female elite athletes indicate that girls are more likely to benefit than to suffer from their sport involvement in terms of overcoming the traditional gender stereotype.

LIFESTYLE AND THE PHYSICAL SELF

Of course, not all young people are involved in competitive sport, but even those who are not regularly involved in sport have developed their perceptions about sport and its immediate social significance and value. The same applies to the body and its appearance. We have already seen that there are differences in the physical self-perception profiles of two different adolescent groups. This raises important questions about how individual adolescents and groups of adolescents link the sporting and body aspect of their physical self-concepts with their lifestyles.

Lifestyle is a short and precise descriptor of a person's attempt as a member of a society to organize his/her life in a specific and therefore distinctive way. It is an essentially Western phenomenon that provides a means of establishing and portraying one's individuality. It often involves attempts to gain access to valued social and cultural groups or subgroups. The main function of lifestyle, through the adoption of values, roles, memberships, and behavior patterns, can be seen to be the expression, development, and preservation of one's personal and social identity. In the context of this book, the notions of identity and lifestyle might offer a broader sweep of the brush in the explanation of adolescent behavior than has been recently offered by the traditional self-perception approach. Identity and lifestyle tend to direct attention to coherence and consistency among behaviors. On the other hand, self-perception research through its focus on multidimensionality has directed attention to the fragmentation of self and the prediction of specific behaviors.

Everyday routines provide stability for the self, but behavioral choices help display private identity agendas to significant others. This is often most openly manifested in situations in which there is maximum freedom of expression, as in the ways adolescents choose to use their leisure time. Sport, fitness activities, and other behaviors related to body concept can all be seen as important elements and symbols of lifestyles.

Several questions arise from these considerations. For example, do adolescents who choose to be involved in sports have different lifestyles in general than those who do not engage in sport? Do they have different political and social orientations? Is sport involvement an adequate parameter for the differentiation of adolescents' lifestyles?

Although the concept of lifestyle remains somewhat cloudy and thus makes comparisons between studies difficult, researchers in Germany have begun to address some of these issues. Although two early studies failed to indicate significant differences in lifestyles of those who did and did not take part in sport (Fuchs 1985; Sack 1986), a third study by Fuchs and Fischer (1987) provided more convincing results. Body, sport, and games as well as other elements of lifestyles were observed in a more differentiated way than previously. Cluster analyses identified four groups who were distinguishable on dimensions representing culturally relevant areas of activity in which young people of today can develop their lifestyles and express their views of life. These groups were (a) those who sympathize with protest movements; (b) those who regard writing diaries, letters, and poems as essential activities; (c) those who enjoy activities that take them away from everyday routines; and (d) those who emphasize body stylization and strive to improve their bodies through activities such as aerobics, jogging, or bodybuilding. The research question was concerned with the existence of a common focus on the body for *all* young people, regardless of their differing political, social, and cultural orientations.

Distinctive profiles were apparent. The resulting configurations suggested a close link between specific activity choices and lifestyles. Those who tended to try to escape from everyday routines and those who were interested in writing (groups b and c) shared a dislike for politics. Both groups also shared a tendency to be characterized by traditional "adult" orientations and an absence of the nonconventional or rebellious approaches to life that are typical of adolescents. With regard to the body and sport involvement, the two groups were similar insofar as they regarded these as important elements of their lifestyles. The remaining two groups (groups a and d) were opposite to each other. This was valid for their global outlook on life as well as for their attitudes toward politics. Those young people who participated in sports and cared about their physical appearance tended to be apolitical, whereas the group of politically involved adolescents appeared not to be interested in body maintenance and sport. These two groups were, in effect, worlds apart from each other as far as the relation between body, sport, and lifestyle is concerned. This latter study indicates that the study of lifestyle and its links with identity and self-concept appears to offer a means of understanding the broader behavioral patterns of adolescents that may not be revealed by self-perception measurement alone. In particular it locates adolescents more completely in the social and cultural context in which they develop.

Some further insight into emergent lifestyles of adolescents was provided by the study with several thousand German adolescents by Brettschneider and Bräutigam (1990) that has already been described. Within this study, which focused on links between body, sport, and lifestyle, attitudes toward aspects of life such as family, friends, training, job, leisure, politics, sport, and body as well as health and nutrition were assessed. Gender, age, and educational strata provided independent variables on which lifestyles could be compared and differentiated. Factor and cluster analyses of the different attitudes have provided a basis for drawing up a lifestyle typology for these adolescents. Types of subjects have been formed that maximize within-group similarity/homogeneity while at the same time producing maximum between-group separation.

The resulting configurations suggest close links between adolescents' general orientation toward life and their attitude toward parents, adults, and peers on the one hand and their sport concepts, body image, and health evaluations on the other. Space allows only a brief description (for further detail see Brettschneider 1992; Brettschneider and Bräutigam 1990) of the types that emerged from the analyses:

Type 1. This represents a small group (5%) of adolescents whose appreciation of sport is limited. They are interested in computers, in music, or in leisure-time activities that do not involve sport. Their often overweight or undermuscled body does not epitomize the cultural body ideal, but they seem not to be unduly concerned with their appearance. Their social network is intact, and relations with friends and parents are equally harmonious.

Type 2. A further small group of adolescents (4%) are involved in sport and see the instrumental value of sport in terms of body image promotion. They are highly interested in body maintenance activities that are considered to be a means of enhancing and displaying masculine virility. Their views on life do not indicate clear plans for the future. They meet adults in a very reserved manner, and same-sex peer groups rather than parents or other adults provide the major reference points of everyday life. We may say that *action* and *motion* are the elements that characterize the lifestyle of this group.

Type 3. Almost one-fifth (17%) of the sample belong to a group whose lifestyle is influenced by a negative body concept. Their well-being is impaired by delicate health and a general feeling of physical discomfort. There is a strong longing for a slim and athletic figure, which is thought to enhance personal attractiveness. There is a complex interaction between the sport concept, body image, and self-concept and attitudes toward social and political affairs.

Type 4. The next group (13%) consists of young people who are absorbed in a constant search for individuality and self-expression. Their energy is spent promoting stylization of life in fashion, leisure, and music as well as in sport, the latter being based more on fun and a recreational atmosphere than on training and performance. These adolescents are hoping to maintain or produce a fit and slim body and are characterized by a health-oriented hedonism. They do not seem concerned about their future or their relationship to adults and their parents. Style and individualism are the priorities.

Type 5. Approximately 61% of the population have a profile that by majority membership represents the *normal adolescent biography* of today. In this large group of inconspicuous adolescents we find boys and girls in whose biography the sport concept as well as the other facets of lifestyle is well balanced. Achievement versus fun and competition versus spontaneous activity are not seen as alternatives, but as two sides of the same coin. In such an interpretation, sport in all its variety is a commonly accepted element in adolescents' mainstream lifestyles. These adolescents are relatively satisfied with their body image and their physical and facial attractiveness. They do not pay much attention to weight control and do not express health problems. They live on good terms with their parents and their peers and have a positive outlook on life.

Surprisingly, neither age effects nor gender and social strata effects could be identified in this typology. Contrary to expectations, there were not significantly more females in the nonsport groups or more males from lower social strata in the action group. This proposed five-cluster solution presents a typology that clearly shows the connection between body, sport, and lifestyle. Typologies such as these provide a means of roughly categorizing subjects on a range of psychosocial variables and can be tested by comparison of behavioral patterns across groups. Stability of membership can be addressed over time. However, typologies have limitations, as classification error is likely to be high. They are probably best used to provide an initial heuristic classification as a basis on which to build and test more complex sets of hypotheses.

SUMMARY

This chapter has outlined the main features of the physical self-concepts of young German people. The details of some of the specific components have been presented, and the extent to which they vary according to gender, age, and sport involvement in a large sample has been detailed. Furthermore, the physical self-concepts of adolescents have been set alongside other aspects of the self-concept such as academic and social relationships. There is good empirical evidence that sport involvement, even at the highest levels, does not have a negative impact on the self-concept and that it may have considerable benefit in this regard. Sport appears to provide an arena for achievement, and the development of a positive physical self-concept may contribute to other aspects of self-concept and self-esteem.

Comparative analysis between youths with high commitment to sport and those with limited sporting involvement shows clear differences regarding information sources for body image. For example, the youngster enrolled in a sport club is likely to rely on perceptions of sport competence, physical achievement, and fitness. The adolescent not involved in sport will accentuate aesthetic body stylization.

The role of sport and the physical self-concept have also been discussed in the context of identity formation and development tasks. Sport and exercise involvement appear to have considerable potential to contribute to the development of youth identity, particularly in our current social situation, in which sport prowess and physical appearance are valid as personal resources and provide valuable social capital. Evidence has been presented to support the notion that sporting commitment helps in the process of coping with developmental tasks such as the acceptance of the body and establishment of social networks.

The meaning of sport and body concept and youth identity was also examined in relation to adoption of specific lifestyles, defined as a package of values, attitudes, and behaviors. Research was described that indicates the existence of a close relationship between the general life orientations of young people, their social relations, their leisure-time choices, and their physical self-concepts. Sport and body concepts proved to be a surprisingly useful vehicle for developing a typology of lifestyles that appear to be on offer to young people.

In conclusion, physical self-concept, general self-concept, and lifestyles are closely interrelated in the adolescent. These factors appear to be critical in the accomplishment of development tasks and identity formation. Youth sport involvement, because of its social valence and its relationship to the body, offers a fruitful vehicle for the study of these important issues in the emerging young adult. As yet, it has not been possible to fully address the impact of sport on self-concept and identity development, as data have been primarily correlational in nature. We await results from the longitudinal study currently underway to provide more critical insight.

REFERENCES

Baur, J., and Brettschneider, W.-D. 1994. *Der Sportverein und seine Jugendlichen*. Aachen, Germany: Meyer und Meyer.

Beck, U. 1986. *Risikogesellschaft. Auf dem Weg in eine andere Moderne*. Frankfurt, Germany: Suhrkamp.

Blustein, D.L., and Palladino, D.E. 1991. Self and identity in late adolescence: A theoretical and empirical integration. *Journal of Adolescent Research* 4 (4): 437-53.

Bourdieu, P. 1982. *Die feinen Unterschiede*. Frankfurt, Germany: Suhrkamp.

Brettschneider, W.-D. 1992. Adolescents, leisure, sport and lifestyle. In *Sport and physical activity: Moving towards excellence*, ed. T. Williams, L. Almond, and A. Sparkes, 536-50. London: Spon.

Brettschneider, W.-D., and Bräutigam, M. 1990. *Sport in der Alltagswelt von Jugendlichen*. Frechen, Germany: Rittersbach.

Bronfenbrenner, U. 1980. *Die Ökologie der menschlichen Entwicklung*. Stuttgart, Germany: Klett.

Cooley, C.H. 1902. *Human nature and the social order*. New York: Scribner.

Dreher, E., and Dreher, M. 1985. Entwicklungsaufgaben im Jugendalter: Bedeutsamkeit und Bewältigungskonzepte. In *Entwicklungsaufgaben und Bewältigungsprobleme in der Adoleszenz*, ed. D. Liepmann and A. Stiksrud, 56-70. Göttingen, Germany: Hogrefe.

Erikson, E.H. 1971. *Identität und Lebenszyklus*. Frankfurt, Germany: Suhrkamp.

Fox, K.R. 1992. The complexities of self-esteem promotion in physical education and sport. In *Sport and physical activity: Moving towards excellence*, ed. T. Williams, L. Almond, and A. Sparkes, 383-89. London: Spon.

Fox, K.R., and Corbin, C.B. 1989. The Physical Self-Perception Profile: Development and preliminary validation. *Journal of Sport and Exercise Psychology* 11: 408-30.

Fox, K.R., Page, A., Armstrong, N., and Kirby, B. 1994. Dietary restraint and self-perceptions in early adolescence. *Personality and Individual Differences* 17: 87-96.

Fuchs, W. 1985. Sport und Sportverein. In *Jugendliche und Erwachsene '85. Generationen im Vergleich. Band 2*, ed. A. Fischer, W. Fuchs, and J. Zinnecker. Opladen, Germany: Leske and Budrich.

Fuchs, W., and Fischer, C. 1987. Körperstilisierung im Kontext prägnanter Sinnmuster. Hagen, Germany: Fernuniversität Hagen.

Harter, S. 1990. Self and identity development. In *At the threshold: The developing adolescent*, ed. S.S. Feldman and G.L. Elliot, 352-87. Cambridge, MA: Harvard University Press.

Havighurst, R.J. 1972. *Developmental tasks and education.* New York: McKay.

Hurrelmann, K. 1983. Das Modell des produktiv realitätsverarbeitenden Subjekts in der Sozialisationsforschung. *Zeitschrift für Sozialisationsforschung und Erziehungssoziologie* 3 (1): 91-103.

James, W. 1890. *Principles of psychology.* New York: Henry Holt.

Koteskey, R.L., Walter, J.S., and Johnson, A.W. 1990. Measurement of identity from adolescence to adulthood: Cultural, community, religious, and family factors. *Journal of Psychology and Theology* 18 (1): 54-65.

Kurz, D., and Brinkhoff, K.-P. 1989. Sportliches Engagement und jugendliche Identität. In *Sport im Alltag von Jugendlichen*, ed. W.-D. Brettschneider, J. Baur, and M. Bräutigam, 95-113. Schorndorf, Germany: Hofmann.

Lerner, R.M., and Spanier, G. 1980. *Adolescent development. A life span perspective.* New York: Columbia University Press.

Marcia, J. 1980. Identity in adolescence. In *Handbook of adolescent psychology*, ed. J. Adelson, 159-87. New York: Wiley.

Marsh, H.W. 1988. *Self-Description Questionnaire II: Manual.* Sydney: Publication Unit, Faculty of Education, University of Western Sydney.

—. 1989. Age and sex effects in multiple dimensions of self-concept: Preadolescence to early adulthood. *Journal of Educational Psychology* 81 (3): 417-30.

Marsh, H.W., and Redmayne, R.S. 1994. A multidimensional physical self-concept and its relation to multiple components of physical fitness. *Journal of Sport and Exercise Psychology* 16: 45-55.

Mead, G.H. 1934. *Mind, self and society.* Chicago: University of Chicago.

Mrazek, J. 1987. Struktur und Entwicklung des Körperkonzepts im Jugendalter. *Zeitschrift für Entwicklungspsychologie und Pädagogische Psychologie* 19: 1-13.

Mrazek, J., and Hartmann, I. 1989. Selbstkonzept und Körperkonzept. In *Bewegungswelt von Kindern und Jugendlichen*, ed. W.-D. Brettschneider, J. Baur, and M. Bräutigam, 219-30. Schorndorf, Germany: Hofmann.

Oerter, R. 1987. Jugendalter. In *Entwicklungspsychologie*, ed. R. Oerter and L. Montada, 265-338. München, Germany: Psychologie Verlags Union.

Oerter, R., and Montada, L. 1987. *Entwicklungspsychologie.* München, Germany: Psychologie Verlags Union.

Page, A., Ashford, B., Fox, K.R., and Biddle, S.J.H. 1993. Evidence of cross-cultural validity of the Physical Self-Perception Profile. *Personality and Individual Differences* 16: 585-90.

Sack, H.-G. 1986. Zur Bedeutung des Sports in der Jugendkultur. In *Sport und Verein*, ed. G.A. Pilz, 114-31. Reinbek, Germany: Rowohlt.

Schulze, G. 1993. *Die Erlebnisgesellschaft. Kultursoziologie der Gegenwart.* Frankfurt, Germany: Campus.

Shavelson, R.J., Hubner, J.J., and Stanton, G.C. 1976. Self-concept: Validation of construct interpretations. *Review of Educational Research* 46 (3): 407-41.

Shilling, C. 1994. *The body and social theory.* London: Sage.

Waterman, A.S., ed. 1985. *Identity in adolescence: Process and contents.* San Francisco: Jossey-Bass.

Zinnecker, J. 1990. Sportives Kind und jugendliches Körperkapital. *Neue Sammlung* 30 (4): 645-53.

CHAPTER 9

ADOLESCENT WEIGHT MANAGEMENT AND THE PHYSICAL SELF

ANGELA PAGE AND KENNETH R. FOX

The primary task of adolescence is to build a coherent and consistent identity that will provide a solid platform for the responsibilities of adult life. Brettschneider and Heim (see chapter 8) describe several identity tasks of adolescence. One of the potentially more challenging tasks is the acceptance and integration of the body and the physical self into the emerging identity. Sparkes (see chapter 4) has already discussed in detail how the body is ascribed the power to label, project messages, and determine memberships in modern society. Thus the body, the way it looks and performs, is unavoidably implicated in identity formation as it provides the public display of the self in its interactions with the social world.

Davis (see chapter 6) has described the pressures to adopt cultural views of the body—the slim female form or the strong, muscular physique for males. For the adolescent, this pressure comes at a time of vulnerability and identity inexperience. While seeking comfort with a drastically changing and maturing body, and at a particularly malleable and impressionable age, the adolescent has to establish himself or herself *through* the body with friendship groups and to satisfy the demands of the wider cultural standards.

At the same time, health policy makers and practitioners see adolescence as a key phase in the development of health behaviors. They are anxious that health decisions are made and healthy lifestyle patterns adopted. This chapter focuses on a critical issue for adolescents that brings several forces together: the issue of managing and molding the body, particularly in terms of weight management, against a backdrop of pressure to conform to peer, social, and political demands and standards.

DO YOUNG PEOPLE NEED TO MANAGE THEIR WEIGHT?

The focus on weight management as a desirable health promotion strategy has recently intensified. This greater emphasis is attributable to dramatic increases in levels of overweight and obesity and associated metabolic complications, such as increased risk of cardiovascular disease, certain cancers, diabetes, hypertension, and a range of bone, joint, and skin disorders (Department for Health 1993; Royal College of Physicians 1983). For example, in the United Kingdom a marked increase in levels of obesity (defined as body mass index [BMI] > 30), from 6% to 13% in males and 8% to 15% in females, was reported in the period 1980 to 1991. Similar trends for overweight (BMI 25-29.9) have been identified. In the United States, the direct and indirect cost of obesity has been estimated at $39.3 billion (Colditz 1992), while the direct cost alone of obesity in Britain has been conservatively assessed at £29.35 million (West 1994). Furthermore, this cost will be considerably multiplied if trends are projected to the year 2005, when one in five males and one in four females in Britain will be classed as clinically obese. These patterns are not limited to the United Kingdom and the United States; many other countries are identifying obesity as a major public health problem (Wilfley and Brownell 1994).

Similar trends are evident in young people, and Britain shares with other countries an appreciable proportion of overweight children and adolescents (Chinn and Rona 1994; Gortmaker et al. 1987; Shear et al. 1988). The most complete data for adolescents are found in the United States, where specific body fatness measures have been used to chart the upward trend in overweight and obesity in recent decades. Using data from the National Children's Youth Fitness Survey in 1985 and National Health Examination Survey in the 1960s, Lohman (1992) found that the prevalence of unhealthy levels of fatness in both early and late adolescence in the United States had increased markedly from 1963 to 1980. The incidence of overfatness rose rapidly from 13% to 19% in 12-year-old boys and from 20% to 25% in girls. For males, prevalence then decreased with age, but continued to rise to a peak of 40% for 14- to 16-year-old girls.

The young person is therefore seen as an important target for the treatment and prevention of overweight and obesity (Garrow 1991; James 1995). This focus is timely, as the fatness trends are accompanied by evidence of low levels of activity (Armstrong et al. 1990; Riddoch et al. 1991). The research of Armstrong and colleagues (1990), for example, has demonstrated that a group of British adolescents (250 boys and girls, 11-16 years old) experienced few sustained bouts of aerobic activity (10 to 20 minutes, assessed by 24-hour heart rate monitoring) when measured for three consecutive days in a week. Girls were found to be less active than boys, with over half the girls not experiencing a single 10-minute episode of at least moderate activity in a three-day period (compared to approximately one-third of boys). Additionally, this gender gap appeared to widen with age from about 12 years. Story et al. (1991) also suggested that the "caloric excesses which lead to weight gain in obese adolescent girls appears to arise from their low activity levels rather than high caloric consumption" (997). This awareness of relatively low activity levels in adolescents has led to specific guidelines both for increasing daily lifestyle physical activity and for taking part in at least three bouts of sustained activity (20 minutes) per week that require moderate to vigorous levels of exertion (Sallis and Patrick 1994).

Furthermore, the increasing prevalence of inactive leisure pursuits such as watching television and playing computer games is a concern as evidence is emerging that links these activities directly to obesity (Walker and Gerhardt 1990). Indeed, Dietz and Gortmaker (1985) went so far as to quantify the relationship, indicating that in a group of 12- to 17-year-olds, the incidence of obesity rose by 2% for each additional hour of television watched daily. Additionally, foods often consumed while watching were energy dense and of limited nutritional value (e.g., sugared breakfast cereals, sweets, cakes, biscuits, and sweetened carbonated beverages). While research in this area is in its infancy, the contemporary pressures for and consequences of sedentary living for the health of the adolescent appear to be considerable.

Change in eating styles is also an important contributory factor to increasing levels of overweight and obesity. Although gradual reduction in energy consumption has taken place since 1960 (as a result of decreased number and size of meals), the percentage of energy intake as fat in the diet remains high and is positively correlated with obesity (Gibney 1995). Consumption of many low-fat, low-energy-dense foods has also fallen (potatoes, fresh vegetables, and most types of bread). These trends are important, as a reduction in fat consumption can have rapid health profile improvements. For example, a reduction in consumption of saturated fats has been associated with reductions in total serum cholesterol in both obese and normal-weight populations (Miller et al. 1990; Royal College of Physicians 1983). There have also been recent changes in eating patterns in Britain, with more meals eaten out of the home (Ministry of Agriculture, Food, and Fisheries 1993) and an increase in the popularity of convenience foods. However, the full effects of these changes are not yet known.

The argument is often presented that the adolescent phase is the time when most individuals acquire and consolidate attitudes and behavioral patterns that they carry through life (Becque et al. 1988; Koff and Rierdan 1991). The observation that fat children and adolescents are more likely to become fat adults has further focused attention on youth as a critical intervention period (Garrow 1986, 1992). By the age of seven years there is a high probability that obese children will remain obese into adult life (Fowler 1989; Walker and Gerhardt 1990). For example, Kemper et al. (1990) report a moderate to high stability of percentage body fat ($r = 0.59$-0.72) and blood lipid profiles ($r = 0.35$-0.76) from the early teens to young adult age (13 to 21 years). Similarly, Lefevre et al. (1990) report comparable correlations between four skinfold thicknesses from 12 to 17 years. Interestingly, there may be gender differences in the extent to which adolescents maintain high levels of adiposity into the adult years. For example, Dietz (1994) suggests that approximately 30% of all obese adult women were obese adolescents, whereas only 10% of obese adult males had onset of their obesity as teenagers. Furthermore, approximately 70% of obese males, but only 20% of obese females, returned to normal weight over a 10-year period. These findings indicate that girls may be at particular risk for adult obesity if their disease is present or develops during adolescence, and that "adolescent-onset obesity in females that persists into adulthood may herald a lifelong problem" (957). Data from the Harvard Growth Study also indicated that morbidity and mortality were increased for those men who were overweight (BMI > 75th percentile) during adolescence compared to their lean counterparts (Must et al. 1992). However, because of the necessarily long time scale inherent in tracking levels of overweight from youth to adult years, few well-designed studies are available. That some tracking occurs is evident, but the proportion of adolescents likely to stay fat as adults remains open to debate.

The worst scenario would suggest that should these trends continue, more youngsters will continue to have increasingly limited activity, particularly adolescent girls, and there will be increased access to and perhaps consumption of high-fat convenience foods. The result is likely to be an increased incidence of adolescent overweight and obesity. Should this be the case, the already burgeoning adult statistics will be swollen by a new generation of overweight youngsters who will reach obesity levels at a younger adult age, increasing the length of time and probably the consequences of their condition. This would seriously reduce quality of life and increase health care costs. Therefore, the answer to the question "Do young people need to manage their weight?" is certainly yes, at least for a substantial majority.

However, this secular trend toward overfatness is paralleled by a cultural increase in body focus. Several discussions presented throughout this book have indicated the importance of the body as a medium through which people portray identities, enact roles, and acquire status. It is not surprising that adolescents are becoming increasingly concerned about maintaining an attractive body and a culturally acceptable body shape. Girls in particular appear very sensitive and in many cases oversensitive to the issue of fatness (Striegel-Moore, Silberstein, and Rodin 1986). It is clear that this concern is not a result of an awareness of the health risks attached to getting too fat, but a reaction to a pervasive cult of slenderness (Tinning 1985) that is largely perpetuated through the media. For adolescent females (and to a lesser extent males) it appears that fatness is bad simply because it looks bad and does not conform to the image of the day. As a result of the intensity of such influences on the impressionable adolescent, many take up unhealthy dietary practices and many more feel decidedly unhappy with their bodies. The maladaptive practices associated with such a profile (self-starvation, self-induced vomiting, laxative use, and binge eating) may lead to deterioration in physical as well as psychological health status (Cooper, Anastasiades, and Fairburn 1992).

Examples of the potential physical consequences of these behaviors include severe dental decay, swollen salivary glands, low levels of potassium, deterioration of skin and hair, and prolonged amenorrhea (Button 1993; Russell 1979). In the most extreme cases (characteristic of individuals with bulimia and anorexia nervosa), renal failure, cardiac abnormalities, and severe endocrine dysfunction may ultimately prove fatal (Button 1993). Concern is fueled by the documented rise in the incidence of eating disorders, ironically in parallel with the rises reported for overweight and obesity. For example, in their research Szmuckler et al. (1986) report an increase in the total number of cases of anorexia from an annual incidence of 1.6 per 100,000 in 1969 to 4.06 per 100,000 in 1978 to 1982. Although the incidence is still relatively low it is of concern, as the prognosis for treatment is poor (Button 1993).

This situation poses a serious problem for health promoters and educators. On the one hand, we are facing increasing levels of fatness that require immediate intervention in order to reverse trends. On the other hand, we are seeing new generations of youngsters showing often unwarranted and misdirected overconcerns to be slim. Clearly, there is a case here for investigating adolescence and the phenomenon of fatness and weight management in more depth.

WHAT FACTORS CONTRIBUTE TO ADOLESCENT WEIGHT MANAGEMENT DECISIONS?

Of particular interest are those factors that might distinguish between health-building as opposed to health-destructive weight management. From a minimalist physical health perspective, attempts by adolescents to control their weight might be considered appropriate if they are *warranted* (in terms of the need for fat reduction/increase), *appropriate* (in terms of the methods used), and *effective* (in terms of both adoption and maintenance of weight change). Alternatively, if weight management appears *unwarranted* (i.e., is not accompanied by underfatness/overfatness), *excessive* (uses practices that are maladaptive), and/or *futile* (permanent weight change is unlikely), then it may be considered inappropriate. However, this represents a narrow perspective of the adolescent weight management system that does not take full account of psychological issues. For example, Leary, Tchividijian, and Kraxberger (1994) have identified several self-presentation strategies that can be hazardous to physical health but also offer mental benefits, such as sunbathing, cosmetic surgery, various dietary behaviors, and steroid abuse. In the eyes of the adolescent, these could be considered quite logical behaviors as they promote a culturally acceptable body image and stimulate positive social reinforcement. Analysis of adolescent weight management decision-making should be conducted through consideration of both physical and psychosocial determinants and consequences.

To date, although several theoretical perspectives have been applied to elements of the weight management problem, no theoretical model has been produced to guide research in this area. Consequently it is difficult to compare and contrast studies, as they usually address different elements and relationships, and no studies have managed to address all of the dominant aspects of the process at any single time. The framework shown in figure 9.1 is presented as a vehicle for locating or anchoring various aspects of inquiry. It is based firmly in an expectancy-value paradigm. It assumes that weight-related behavior is a result of attempts by adolescents to utilize whatever information is available to them to rationally weigh alternatives and outcomes through a decision-making process. It recognizes that the information display is often unreliable and invalid and that adolescents by nature are experimenting and changing people. This points to a weakness in the framework in that it does not adequately encapsulate the dynamics of weight status and perceptions that are necessary for a more complete picture. For example, a youngster of average fatness may have lost weight and be restraining eating in order to maintain weight loss, but have a positive image as a result of a sense of personal control and achievement. Another may similarly be of unremarkable fatness and never have had a fatness problem, but still be restraining eating because of a fear of getting fat. Nevertheless, we have used the framework to direct our own research and hope it will encourage more systematic, comprehensive, and integrated research in the future.

More specifically, the framework demonstrates that several possible components may influence adolescent weight management decisions. The physical status components are those identified in the literature as potential predictors of adolescent weight management decisions. The psychological factors appear consistently as potential intermediary factors between weight

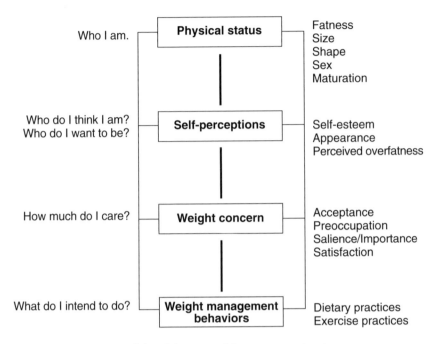

Figure 9.1   Components of the adolescent weight management system.

status and behaviors. The element of weight concern is likely to represent the extent to which weight is of central concern to the adolescent; this element is hypothesized to be a function of specific factors such as salience/importance, satisfaction, and acceptance, which determine the degree of weight preoccupation. All these factors will impact on weight management decisions and behaviors. Exercise, eating behaviors, and drastic dietary aids all represent forms of behavioral outcome. Finally, feedback loops represent modifications to physical and psychological status as a result of these behaviors.

To maintain an open discussion, it is emphasized that decisions may be concerned with weight gain—through increasing body fat and/or muscle—as well as with weight loss and weight maintenance. Also it is important to remember that a substantial group of people may not feel the need to be concerned about their weight at all. However, because of the pervasiveness of concerns to change the body by losing fat or weight, together with the current increase in actual levels of fatness, this topic will dominate the remainder of the chapter.

FATNESS, SIZE AND SHAPE

Some form of weight management strategy may be warranted if a youngster is already fat or likely to become fat to the extent that health is threatened. From the data already presented in this chapter, it is clear that this is the case for a substantial percentage of young people. Several studies have included a range of anthropometric variables alongside other factors to directly address the role of physique or body shape in determining weight concerns. For example, Dwyer, Feldman, and Mayer (1967), in an early example, looked at a range of physical and psychological factors to investigate which attributes were characteristically used by adolescent girls in deciding to try to lose weight. Although the measure of fatness was restricted to a single skinfold thickness (triceps), this represented one of the first and surprisingly few studies to take a comprehensive approach to measurement of body size and shape. The authors found for these 446 females (mean age 17.4 years) that dieters tended to be significantly larger than nondieters with respect to all measurements that contributed to or reflected general bulkiness. However, the heavier weights of dieters as opposed to nondieters appeared to be attributable largely to higher bone and muscle components (such as greater arm circumferences [24.3. vs. 23.3 cm] and bi-iliac [27.7 vs. 26.8] and biacromial [34.1 vs. 33.3 cm] diameters, respectively [all significant at $p < .001$]), rather than excess fat. The authors acknowledge difficulties with separating out relative effects of build as opposed to fatness in their study. However, similar results have been shown with young adult females in a more comprehensive study by Davis, Durnin et al. (1993). This research reinforced findings from their earlier study of older women with whom BMI was more predictive of dietary restraint than fatness (sum of four skinfolds). They extended the investigation to include parameters of frame size (standardized score for wrist, knee, shoulder, and hip girths) in a sample of 100 females (mean age 21.2). They found that this index of frame size was significantly and independently related to restraint to a greater extent than either fatness or BMI.

Our own research has further developed these issues by investigating males as well as females across adolescence, from 11 to 18 years of age. This range is important, as the high rate of growth and sexual maturation of early to mid-adolescence is likely to reveal a complex interaction between the body, its change, and weight management decisions. Work with 11- and 12-year-old boys and girls (Fox, Page, Armstrong, and Kirby 1994; Fox, Page, Peters, Armstrong, and Kirby 1994) revealed a diversity of anthropometric profiles in high and low dietary restraint groups. High dietary restraint boys were bigger (waist and hip circumference), heavier (weight), and fatter (sum of seven skinfolds) than their low dietary restraint counterparts. Among the girls the differences between the high and low restraint groups were less marked, and there was a broad range of fatness levels among the high restraint group. Also, a significant difference was found in bitrochanteric (hip) skeletal width between high and low dietary restraint girls. High dietary restraint girls were also more sexually mature as assessed by Tanner's indexes. It seems that for more boys than girls, intention to lose weight by dieting is founded in actual fatness levels.

Our work with a group of older male and female adolescents ($N = 629$) aged 14 to 18 years (Page and Fox 1994a, 1994b) reinforced these findings (see table 9.1) with results less confounded by maturational differences.

Discriminant analyses indicated that for males, BMI, waist-to-hip ratio, and percentage fatness (estimated from skinfolds) were the best discriminators between those who desired weight loss compared to those who desired no change. For females, however, only BMI and bi-iliac bone width entered into the significant discriminant function. Classification of cases was more accurate for males than for females, indicating that physical measures were more important distinguishing variables in the males' weight management decisions. The failure of percentage body fat to enter follow-up analyses for females indicates once again that actual fatness per se may not be as

Table 9.1   Body Dimensions for Reported Weight Change Groups

	Males				Females			
	No change (n = 68)		Weight loss (n = 20)		No change (n = 47)		Weight loss (n = 65)	
	Mean	SD	Mean	SD	Mean	SD	Mean	SD
Height (m)	1.77	0.06	1.78	0.04	1.64	0.06	1.64	0.06
Weight (kg)	67.26	10.63	82.41	10.43	55.06	9.82	62.06	7.67
BMI	21.41	2.43	26.09	2.93	20.57	3.35	23.01	2.67
Circumferences (mm)								
Waist	741.65	53.78	837.47	78.42	645.98	64.40	686.77	61.94
Hip	968.68	56.31	1043.60	54.07	921.69	75.54	974.27	61.05
Waist/hip ratio	0.76	0.03	0.81	0.06	0.70	0.04	0.70	0.04
Skinfolds (mm)								
Triceps	10.98	4.56	16.88	6.77	16.75	6.41	19.70	5.51
Calf	9.15	3.34	13.63	7.09	15.78	7.08	19.27	6.02
Subscapular	8.99	2.84	15.43	7.66	11.62	3.81	14.48	4.59
Fat %	14.97	5.42	23.27	9.03	24.77	6.26	28.57	5.90
Bone widths (mm)								
Biacromial	390.68	25.64	405.17	17.65	351.47	18.03	361.47	14.39
Bi-iliac	277.53	14.45	284.75	15.80	248.21	25.97	264.94	22.03

important a variable in female weight management decisions as in those of males. The entering of bone breadths into the analyses would support previous research indicating that skeletal frame size (particularly in the hips) is a more critical indicator. However, as will be discussed later, it is possible that body width, particularly through maturation, may be *perceived* as fatness by adolescent girls.

ONSET OF SEXUAL MATURATION

The profound physical and psychological shifts that characterize maturation have strong implications for individual weight management decisions. Harter (1993) highlighted the systematic decline in perceptions of appearance with age from childhood in females as compared to males. It is no surprise that this trend parallels the process of maturation. The physical changes that accompany maturation in females are especially salient because aspects of the body that are subject to the greatest change may form the basis for both their own and opposite-sex judgments of overall attractiveness. For example, Lerner, Karabenick, and Stuart (1973) found that males considered the shape of legs, hips and thighs more important in determining opposite-sex attractiveness than in determining their own attractiveness. Females tended to concur. For males, similar relationships were observed for height and width of shoulders. Maturation represents a critical stage for how males and females view their body and its salience in defining the physical self. Cohn et al. (1987) suggest that "as boys mature and increase in body mass, their ideal figure increases in size. For girls, however, perceived body size and preferred body size do not develop in tandem and this appears to result in increased body dissatisfaction" (277). This appears to be particularly the case for early-maturing females, in whom these distinctions are magnified. Early maturation for males commands a social advantage, with associated positive body image and general self-worth (Lintunen et al. 1988) that according to some authors produces a benefit that is maintained during and after adolescence. For girls the reverse is true, with a less positive body image evident in early-maturing females (who are likely to be taller, wider, and fatter) than in less mature girls.

Considerable evidence links this early maturational status directly to eating and weight concerns, with early-maturing girls having a greater current-ideal discrepancy (Cohn et al. 1987) and increased risk for meeting criteria for eating disorders (Killen et al. 1991). An increase in BMI is also positively related to the likely manifestation of an eating disorder, but the relationship is smaller in magnitude (1.03) compared to the 1.8-fold increase related to sexual maturity index. Also in line with current theory, *perceptions* of pubertal timing may be more critical than actual timing (Dubas, Graber, and Peterson 1990). It appears therefore that early-maturing males fare much better in terms of psychological well-being than early-maturing females.

However, it would be interesting to examine late-maturing groups more specifically, as they too may also exhibit particular body image and weight-related characteristics. For example, late-maturing males may experience high levels of body dissatisfaction and wish to gain size and muscle bulk. Late-maturing females may, however, have relatively positive body image profiles owing to the likelihood that their current image (prepubertal) more closely matches the cultural ideal. However, one important caveat to these speculations is the observation that independent of maturational stage, the focus on appearance has been found to be less marked for males than for females. Further research would benefit from clearly identifying both early and late maturational stages for both males and females to extend these views beyond the intuitive phase.

Maturational gender differences are also expressed with respect to perceptions of specific body parts. For females, the very body parts considered most salient in terms of weight management (hips, thighs, buttocks), as well as appearance, tend to be the major fat storage locations and are labeled as providing the most dissatisfaction (Damhorst, Littrell, and Littrell 1988). Davies and Furnham (1986) found the source of body dissatisfaction in females to be even more precise, indicating that the "slimness of hips appears to be the feature most sought after and is manifest in tremendous dissatisfaction with hip measurement" (285).

The maturation/body image/weight management behavior relationship appears to oscillate as the adolescent continues to develop physically. Attie and Brooks-Gunn (1989) reported that body shape becomes the primary focus, and that efforts to control weight intensify during the middle and early high school years (when most girls are completing their pubertal development) and may function as a triggering event for the first of many attempted weight loss regimes. Attie and Brooks-Gunn conclude:

> the process of integrating changes in physical appearance and bodily feelings requires a reorganization of the adolescent's body image and other self-representations. Female body image is intimately bound up with subjective perceptions of weight; prepubescent girls who perceive themselves to be underweight are most satisfied, followed by those who think they are simply average. Taken together, the findings suggest that dieting emerges as the body develops and is in part a function of body image transformations occurring at puberty. (19)

The potential confusion between the changing form of the body during sexual maturation and a desire to conform to cultural standards has direct implications for self-worth (Brooks-Gunn and Warren 1988). The developmental challenge of accepting a new emerging body is set face to face with narrow and inflexible definitions of good looks and beauty, particularly for girls. This is at a time when the self is particularly unconsolidated and unstable (Harter 1993). Furthermore, girls tend to lack self-confidence more than boys, particularly in the physical domain (Corbin 1984). When we add to this the evidence that parents and peers tend to respond differently to youngsters of different pubertal status (Steinberg 1987), we might expect many young people to take some time to come to terms with the realities of their bodies and feel a sense of worth.

In support of this, Attie and Brooks-Gunn concluded that it was not until middle to late adolescence that self-perception variables explained more of the variance in compulsive eating than physical factors. They suggested that the absence of longitudinal effects for physical maturation, psychopathology, and family factors on eating behavior implied that the variables associated with eating problems in later adolescence are independent of those implicated in early adolescence. It is also possible that by late adolescence those who have emerged as successful in the task of body acceptance can be distinguished by their self-perceptions and self-esteem from those who have not, and that this difference is reflected in their weight-related behaviors. Overall, therefore, we might expect that intermediary self-perception variables such as self-acceptance and centrality confound the relationship between physical factors such as early maturation and global self-esteem and subsequent behaviors. Certainly this seems to be reflected in the literature, with some authors suggesting that early maturation may have limited impact or even prove favorable at a later stage (Lintunen et al. 1988).

Sexual maturation cannot be solely responsible for the origin of body dissatisfaction. For example, the trend begins before puberty (Hill and Robinson 1991), and excessive weight concerns, even anorexia (see DiNicola, Roberts, and Oke 1989), have been identified in young children. Other factors may interact with or work independently of the maturation process to promote weight concerns in the adolescent.

SELF-PERCEPTIONS OF THE BODY

Figure 9.1 implies that self-perceptions and weight concerns act as filters or mediators between physical status and weight management behaviors. As Dwyer, Feldman, and Mayer (1967) suggest, "Apparently the prospective dieter must come to perceive herself as too heavy or too fat before she will undergo the inconvenience of dieting" (1055). For example, Davies and Furnham (1986) report that 46% of 12-year-old British schoolgirls wished to lose weight even though very few could be classified as overweight. However, it is important that although weight concerns are evident in males, these concerns are often directly opposite in nature to those usually expressed by females. For example, Moore (1990) reported that 42% of males were dissatisfied with their body weight and that 68% of the dissatisfied males viewed themselves as underweight. This is in stark contrast to the situation for the females, among whom 67% were dissatisfied with their weight but 63% of these believed that they were overweight. These differences existed even though the same proportion (40%) of boys and girls were actually overweight. So although the nature and precursors of weight concerns may differ from those of females, they can be identified in males. Further research studies need to include both males and females to compare and contrast groups more consistently than has been done in the past. This expanded research focus is especially pertinent in the light of increasing evidence that males appear to be catching up in terms of the cultural pressures to maintain a stereotypical body form.

The ways in which these self-perceptions have been measured and interpreted are diverse and inconsistent (see Davis, chapter 6), making it difficult to establish the true level of concern for overfatness in the normative adolescent population as well as among adolescents in more clinically defined extremes. Furthermore, few studies have measured or interpreted findings in the light of the wealth of contemporary self-esteem theory that has been discussed throughout this book.

SALIENCE AND CENTRALITY OF WEIGHT CONCERNS

Self-perceptions of the body do not provide the complete picture. For example, it is possible to feel small or even fat but remain relatively unperturbed, even in a culture that emphasizes height or leanness. Taking a broader stance, it may be that some adolescents simply do not worry about their bodies in comparison to other aspects of their lives. The issue of *centrality* is a potentially important confounder that has been omitted from a large section of the literature (discussed by Fox, chapter 5). Clifford (1971) suggests that "attempts to measure body satisfaction assume that attitudes one has toward one's body are important personality variables, particularly relevant to body images or schemata" (119).

Indirect evidence of the centrality of appearance issues is provided by Harter (1993), who discusses the degree to which appearance dominates self-esteem. She concludes:

In study after study, at any developmental level my colleagues and I have examined, including older children, adolescents, college students and adults, we have repeatedly discovered that self-evaluations in the domain of physical appearance are inextricably linked to global self-esteem. The correlations between perceived appearance and self-esteem are staggeringly high and robust across the life span, typically between 0.70 and 0.80. . . . The evaluation of one's looks takes precedence over every other domain as the number one predictor of self-esteem, causing us to question whether self-esteem is only skin-deep. (96-97)

Harter and colleagues (Harter and Waters 1989, cited in Harter 1993; Zumpf and Harter 1991, cited in Harter 1993) have shed further light on the centrality of appearance to self-esteem. The authors investigated the direction of the link between appearance and self-esteem, specifically whether perceptions of appearance were more likely to determine self-esteem or vice versa. They found almost equal numbers of adolescents endorsing both these views. However, those individuals who endorsed the view that appearance preceded or determined self-esteem had more negative psychological profiles. They reported feeling worse about their appearance, being more preoccupied with their looks, having lower self-esteem, and being more affectively depressed than the group who considered self-esteem to precede judgments of appearance. This pattern was particularly pronounced for adolescent females. Unfortunately, the social and interpersonal value attached to physical appearance and weight promotes the view that appearance determines self-esteem rather than vice versa. As Harter (1993) notes, this represents a "psychological liability for females in particular, undermining their evaluation of both outer and inner self" (99).

Harter (1993) further points to the excessive pressures bound up in media images, suggesting that "the standards are paradoxical and punishing for women. All of these magazines relentlessly insist that women (a) attend fiercely to their appearance (hair, face and particularly weight) at the same time as they (b) cook a vast array of fattening foods for themselves and their family!" (96). More specific for the physical self, implicit in these portrayals is the view that seeking to change appearance, even by cosmetic surgery, is likely to enhance one's self-esteem.

Although the media are also placing greater emphasis on the importance of appearance and body tone for men, there does not appear to be the singular focus on weight and looks as the source of self-acceptance and self-esteem that seems to exist for women. For men, intelligence, job competence, athletic ability, wealth, and power are all routes to positive evaluation in the eyes of others as well as self. Furthermore, the physical stereotype promoted for males, while exaggerated with respect to muscularity and body tone, is at least in line with the natural maturational process for males.

Dealing more specifically with issues of weight, Wadden et al. (1991) state, "Despite the substantial literature on this topic, it is difficult to judge the significance of reports of weight dissatisfaction in the absence of comparative data. Studies generally have not assessed girls' weight concerns relative to concerns about family, grades, friendships, health and related matters" (408). In response, the authors investigated the extent to which 453 female and 355 male adolescents (aged 15 years) rated, on a 10-point scale from 1 (none at all) to 10 (extreme amount), their degree of daily worries associated with 15 factors. They found that females worried more about looks than any other issue. Females scored higher than males on degree of worry about weight, figure, looks, nuclear war, popularity with the opposite sex, and the family. Males, on the other hand, scored higher than girls on reported time spent worrying about money and sport. The authors concluded that weight not only was a normative discontent in these females but was ranked among the two most salient worries (weight and figure). In contrast, for males, weight ranked as one of the least salient, and worry about physique was moderately important. Financial success, therefore, holds the same prominent position for males that weight and figure hold for females. Furthermore, levels of concern were generally greater for females, and 10 of the 15 worries correlated with trait anxiety in females but only 1 (grades) did for males, indicating that there were physical and mental consequences of this concern for females. Looks ranked first for girls and second for boys. The authors were unable to specify the elements of appearance on which this was anchored; however, the high ranking of weight and figure would suggest that these are substantial contributors for females.

Throughout our work with the Physical Self-Perception Profile (Fox 1990; Fox and Dirkin 1992; Fox and Vehnekamp 1991; Page et al. 1993) with adolescents and college students, we have found that the physical self-worth of females of all ages is narrowly based on their score on the subscale measuring body attractiveness, to the exclusion of other aspects of the physical self. For males, other components such as sport competence, physical conditioning, and strength also contribute. This results in a higher degree of discrepancy between ideal and actual physical self for females that almost totally originates in dissatisfaction with appearance of the body. Males, on the other hand, have lower discrepancy scores in the physical domain, and several components of the physical self are implicated.

In our research with young adolescents (Fox, Page, Armstrong, and Kirby 1994) using Harter's Self-Perception Profile for Adolescents (Harter 1988) and several additional specific items, we explored the relationship between several components of looks and general self-worth. Confirming previous research, table 9.2 indicates that perception of appearance is the strongest correlate of self-esteem for both boys and girls compared to other life domains.

However, analysis of specific components of appearance highlights gender differences, with perceptions of overfatness, face and hair dissatisfaction, and subsequently looks preoccupation being more strongly associated with self-esteem for females. It is interesting to note that facial features and hair are also salient in their relationship with self-esteem. This reminds us that overfatness is just one aspect of the body image of youngsters and that they are sensitive about several elements of their physical appearance. Perceiving that one's nose is too large or one's complexion is spotty may be more dominant for some than issues concerning fat or physique. Equally,

Table 9.2 Correlates of Global Self-Esteem in 12-Year-Old Boys and Girls

	Boys (n = 113)	Girls (n = 130)
Appearance	0.61**	0.69**
Athletic	0.44**	0.28*
Close friends	0.59**	0.43**
Social	0.52**	0.38**
Scholastic	0.25*	0.43**
Clothes concern	0.01	0.19
Face dissatisfaction	0.39**	0.50**
Hair dissatisfaction	0.28*	0.38**
Looks preoccupation	0.08	0.33**
Weight dissatisfaction	-0.23	-0.49**

$*p < .05, ** p < .01.$

appearance is not the only aspect of self that young adolescents are concerned about. Table 9.2 also shows that athletic abilities are related to self-esteem for boys and that scholastic competence is more prominent for girls. For both, social competence is tied to self-esteem, although of course appearance may be implicated in this relationship.

Centrality should be explicitly assessed as an independent variable within research designs. It is critical to explaining why individuals with very similar physical and self-perception profiles react in very different ways. For this purpose, perceived importance scales have been developed to accompany the self-perception profiles of Harter and Fox, and these have been useful for identifying sources of discrepancy between actual and desired aspects of self. However, we believe centrality to be a much more complex matter than importance. Our own work (Page and Fox 1994b) with older adolescents attempted to explore the concept of centrality of weight concerns more directly through a range of indexes. These included the importance of weight to self in general, weight dissatisfaction, weight acceptance, weight preoccupation, and weight salience. Findings indicated that these constructs could be independently measured and were low to moderately related to each other ($r = 0.19$-$0.47, p < .05$). With the exception of acceptance for males, they were also independently able to differentiate between adolescents seeking weight loss and those who expressed no desire for change. The indexes were able to correctly classify 63.2% of males and 67.6% of females in discriminant analyses (33% = chance). Furthermore, for females, including these centrality variables in multivariate analyses as covariants extinguished almost all previously significant relationships between intended weight change and both body dimensions (size, shape, and weight) and physical self-perceptions (overfatness, appearance, self-esteem). These preliminary analyses indicate that the factors of important salience—acceptance, dissatisfaction, and preoccupation—represent the cognitive and behavioral manifestations of centrality. These are clearly only preliminary analyses of a complex construct. Measurement tools need to be refined so that researchers can move toward defining a cohesive scale. However, the greater ability of these relatively crude indexes to distinguish between weight management groups and either physical status or self-perceptions merits further research attention.

HOW ARE YOUNG PEOPLE MANAGING THEIR WEIGHT?

Considerable evidence now exists that many adolescents carry out a wide range of weight management practices. Specifically, research has provided data to support an increase in the prevalence of restrained eating and dietary practices in the female adolescent population (Dwyer, Feldman, and Mayer 1967; Heunemann et al. 1966; Koff and Rierdan 1991) that parallels the increase observed in adult women (Dacey et al. 1991; Striegel-Moore, Silberstein, and Rodin 1986). An increase in the use of more drastic weight control strategies such as fasting, vomiting, and the consumption of diet pills, laxatives, and diuretic pills in non-obese adolescent girls has also been documented (Koff and Rierdan 1991; Szmuckler et al. 1986).

It appears not only that dieting is manifest in increasingly more extreme practices but also that it is prevalent in younger age groups. Wardle and Beales (1986) indicate that the intention to restrict food intake in 12-year-olds is comparable to that in older adolescents and adult women. Furthermore, research by Hill and Robinson (1991) indicates that dietary intentions are reflected in actual food restriction in children as young as 9 years old. In the United States, dieting has been reported at even younger ages. For example, Maloney, McGuire, Daniels, and Specker (1989) identified children as young as 7 who were carrying out a range of weight management practices. Weight loss was claimed by 28.2% of the 7- to 8-year-old girls with 37.5% reporting increased exercise, 17.5% admitting caloric restriction, and 5% reporting maladaptive eating behaviors such as bingeing and vomiting to achieve weight change.

There is also considerable evidence that in some individuals there is a progression from less extreme weight management practices to more pathological behaviors such as anorexia or bulimia nervosa. This merits particular concern, as the adolescent phase is the one in which the development of serious eating disorders is most prevalent (Borgen and Corbin 1987; Cooper and Taylor 1985; Cooper, Anastasiades, and Fairburn 1992; Wadden et al. 1989), with increases in disordered eating largely found in females in their midteens to mid-20s (Lucas et al. 1988; Szmuckler et al. 1986).

Research suggests that a continuum may exist linking normative dieting behavior to clinical eating disorders with differences evident only in terms of severity (Attie and Brooks-Gunn 1989; King 1989; Patton 1988). This has important implications for health promotion. If, for example, milder forms of dieting (such as restriction of food intake) are causally linked to the development of eating disorders, then it could be argued that any form of weight management may represent cause for concern. However, evidence for a close and inevitable link between mild weight management practices and the extreme behaviors characteristic of eating-disordered individuals is equivocal. As Wertheim and colleagues (1992) suggest, "In order to confirm the continuum hypothesis, adolescents who use extreme dieting techniques or binge eating should show similar psychosocial features as those with disordered eating but of lesser intensity" (152). However, empirical examples supporting the continuum hypothesis, both behaviorally and psychologically, are rare (Mintz and Betz 1988); and many researchers argue that a range of distinct and unique personality factors place only certain individuals at risk of developing eating disorders (Striegel-Moore, Silberstein, and Rodin 1986).

If serious eating disorders are a result of a profile of high-risk psychosocial characteristics, then the degree of attention paid to the problem has not necessarily facilitated our understanding of the complexities of the adolescent weight management system. It could be argued that the focus on pathological eating disorders and their strict diagnostic criteria has detracted from the prevalence of less severe but more common characteristics and practices evident in a much larger proportion of adolescents. The incidence of eating disorders has increased but still only affects a small minority of individuals. While the upward trend is of obvious concern, especially given the seriousness of the diseases and poor prognosis for treatment (Button 1993), the extent of the milder but more widespread occurrence of low body dissatisfaction and unhealthy dietary habits may also carry serious health consequences.

There is now growing evidence that extreme weight management practices and indeed concern with weight in general are not restricted to females. For example, Moore (1990) as well as Story et al. (1991) identified subgroups of adolescent males who desired excessive weight loss and showed disturbed eating and weight loss patterns yet did not consider themselves to have an eating problem. Story and colleagues (1991) also reported that although males represented a much smaller proportion of chronic dieters (> 10 diets in the last year or always dieting), they were more than nine times more likely to report vomiting on a weekly basis than their nondieting male counterparts. Also, male adolescents are now consistently represented (albeit to a much lesser extent than females) in clinical diagnoses for both anorexia (male:female ratio 1:12) and bulimia (1:10). However, our own data (see table 9.3) on the weight management strategies adopted by male and female adolescents (Page and Fox 1994a, 1994b) indicated that males rarely report extreme weight management practices, whereas for girls these are quite prevalent.

One important distinction in the approach of males to weight management is that they generally appear to favor exercise as a means for achieving weight/shape management in comparison to females. This is evident in our own data and elsewhere in the literature (e.g., Heunemann et al. 1966; Wardle and Marsland 1990). For example, Heunemann et al. (1966) report that by age 17, males have a 1:1 diet-to-exercise ratio, whereas females favor dieting with a 2.5:1 diet-to-exercise ratio. The greater use of exercise for weight management in males could be attributable to several factors. First, it has been consistently found that males score higher than females on perceived competencies in the physical domain and so are more attracted to exercise and sport (Whitehead and Corbin, chapter 7; Fox 1990). It is also clear that females tend to see desirable body shape as something to be achieved through fat reduction, which is perceived to be most easily accomplished through dietary restriction. For boys, however, the "look" is

Table 9.3	Reported Weight Management Practices for Males and Females				
	Males			Females	
	n	%		n	%
Avoiding fatty foods	12	26.08		71	51.40
Eating smaller amounts	9	19.56		51	36.96
Increasing amount of exercise	27	58.69		63	45.65
Skipping meals usually eaten	5	10.87		43	31.16
Going on an advertised diet	-	-		10	7.25
More than one crash diet/year	1	2.17		18	13.04
Fasting for 24 hours or more	-	-		17	12.30
Using diet pills	2	4.35		6	4.50
Binge eating	-	-		9	6.52
Making oneself vomit	-	-		20	14.50

a combination of leanness and muscularity. They see that exercise, mainly through weight training, can build and tone muscle. There is an argument that it is this recently increased emphasis on the muscular body for males that has fueled the current explosion in use of steroids in high school males in the United States (Leary, Tchividjian, and Kraxberger 1994).

The increased use of exercise for weight management in both males and females has fueled debate about whether the health and empowerment messages attributed by some to exercise may have been superseded by culturally driven body narcissism (Kirk 1993; Tinning 1985). The role of exercise with respect to adolescent weight management is therefore poten- tially conflicting. "On the one hand, research examining self-esteem vari- ables suggests that athletic involvement enhances self-image, sociability and feelings of self-worth. . . . On the other hand, studies examining weight and dieting behavior suggest that athletic activity is associated with dissat- isfaction with body weight and body image, and repeated dieting attempts" (Striegel-Moore, Silberstein, and Rodin 1986, 248). Although many studies have not included exercise alongside dietary practices in the context of weight management, research is growing in this area. Some find greater support for the negative role of exercise through increased body focus and subsequent weight preoccupation, and criticize the promoted link between fitness and thinness (see Davis, chapter 6). However, evidence for this view is sporadic and must be balanced by findings that indicate a positive role for exercise in preserving and indeed enhancing physical self-perceptions (see Mutrie, chapter 11).

A strong research tradition has contended that the intrinsic nature and benefits of exercise can militate against the potentially negative role of exercise for weight management. Apart from the well-documented positive physiological and psychological factors associated with increased exercise (see Biddle and Mutrie 1991; Bouchard et al. 1990) in comparison to dieting, exercise for weight management may be uniquely beneficial as a strategy (Adame et al. 1990). As Cannon and Einzig (1983) suggest, "Exercising the body is a positive discipline in contrast with the negative discipline of dieting . . . once the body has become accustomed to exercise, a run, a dance session, a yoga class is something to look forward to: a freedom, not a restriction" (216-17).

Weight Management Strategies: To Promote or Not?

We return to the dilemma facing the health promoter and educator. We have a situation in which the incidence of overfatness and obesity is rapidly increasing to the extent that health is threatened. At the same time we are experiencing an escalation in concern for appearance as the Western world places more emphasis on the body as a site for projecting identity and status.

At first sight, it appears that these parallel trends could be causally related. To take one stance, perceptions of overfatness are a result of actual levels of fatness, and as we pass through a period of adjustment the increased awareness will result in self-regulation, weight loss, and eventual reductions in incidence of overweight. To take the alternative stance, often put forward by the anti-diet lobbyists, cultural trends have resulted in an obsession with unrealistic and unattainable levels of slenderness. Attempts at self-regulation of fatness are doomed to failure, lowered self-efficacy, and a loss of self-esteem, resulting in overeating and increases in levels of overweight.

Throughout this chapter we have tried to present the complexity of interacting variables that contribute to the formula of the adolescent fatness problem and have pointed out that any single and extreme explanation can be no more than naive and overly simplistic. We have made the case that reduced levels of physical activity and increased intake of high-energy-dense food are the probable causes of the secular increase in fat levels. At the same time, we have acknowledged that many young girls are overconcerned about fatness, mainly because of cultural expectations, and are unnecessarily attempting to lose weight through a range of futile and unhealthy dietary practices. This may lead some to more serious eating disorders. We also see increasing pressures on young males to look lean and muscular, leading some to steroid abuse. We recognize that these behaviors place the physical and mental well-being of adolescents at great risk.

There is a need for research to recognize that adolescents are not a homogenous group with respect to their relationships with their bodies. An approach must be taken that identifies different profile clusters based on physical, psychological, and behavioral variables. Until this happens, research findings will always be confounded by a range of interacting variables. Furthermore, at minimum, an individual's profile must be crudely determined before professional judgments can be made about a youngster's weight management needs. Indicators might be, for instance, actual fatness levels, recent history of fatness, levels of concern and satisfaction, global measures of self-worth, weight management behaviors, and degree of risk of sustained or increased fatness into adulthood as determined by factors such as family history.

Our preliminary work indicates that different types of individuals with respect to physical and psychological weight profiles may be identifiable (Fox, Page, Armstrong, and Kirby 1994; Fox, Page, Peters, Armstrong, and Kirby 1994; Page and Fox 1994a, 1994b). The following are variable combinations that characterize different groups of adolescents:

1. Those who are not overfat and are not concerned about fatness

2. Those who are not overfat, who have recently lost weight, are still concerned, and are successfully maintaining weight loss

3. Those who are not overfat but believe themselves to be fat, are concerned, and are restraining their eating

4. Those who are overfat, are concerned, perceive themselves to be fat, and are restraining eating but increasing their weight

5. Those who are overfat, who are not concerned, and are not using weight management strategies

6. Those who feel underweight or too small

We need more research to help us identify such groups so that the antecedents and consequences can be more fully documented. Clearly the groups hold different implications for intervention design. For example, a member of group 3 would require quite different treatment from a member of group 5. This diversity calls for a customized element to programs and would tend to suggest that a blanket approach to health promotion is untenable. However, critical issues across large sectors of the spectrum of profiles do exist to suggest that there is a place for some comprehensive messages.

The issue of the cultural milieu has attracted debate. Sweeting (1994) presents a pessimistic view: "So all we need is a root-and-branch educational overhaul and a complete rewriting of our cultural expectations about size, shape and appearance. The return of the woolly mammoth looks more likely" (3). However, Kirk (1993) reminds us, "There are spaces, cracks in the apparently seamless surface of media images, which leave room for skepticism, doubt and criticism" (19). It is possible that health promotion could identify these weaknesses, promote discussion among adolescents, and provide alternative visions that are healthier and more realistic.

There is some evidence to suggest that girls are already well aware of cultural pressures but feel ill equipped to withstand them. As Sieghart (1994) suggests, "It is too easy to blame women for having too little confidence. . . . But it is not surprising that their esteem is low, that they feel fat even when they are not. In a society that is based so much on looks, you have to be superhumanly confident to buck the trend" (3). Evidence clearly shows that with respect to their physical selves females generally lack self-confidence that would help them become more accepting. One approach at the global level would be to encourage a more balanced and multidimensional self-worth in females, more similar to that often evident in males. Opportunities to increase the importance and competence in other life domains such as the academic would help to balance the dominant influence often exerted by appearance on females' sense of self. Also, increasing opportunities for greater competence with respect to their physical selves would help to improve physical self-worth generally. One potential is physical activity. The right approach to exercise may have a dual benefit. On the one hand, if approached sensitively, exercise can provide a sense of personal control and empowerment for female adolescents. On the other hand, adopting exercise in the weight management context could militate against use of more extreme practices and perhaps avoid "dieting" altogether. This also seems particularly pertinent given the evidence suggesting that a contributor to the higher incidence of fatness in girls is inactivity.

Perhaps we tend to underestimate the capabilities of the adolescent to make decisions. There seems to be support for the idea that adolescents are able to make rational decisions but that often the information on which decisions are based is flawed or unreliable. If this is the case, then an educational approach to weight management using convincing arguments and evidence holds great value. We believe that adequate knowledge levels remain a problem. Interviews with adolescent girls (Page 1994) have indicated that girls see weight loss as worth seeking simply because the potential social rewards are high. They experiment with dietary practices such as laxatives, appetite suppressants, and vomiting in attempts to find easy solutions to weight loss. The use of such practices is ephemeral for the majority, as through trial and error people eventually learn of their lack of effectiveness or side effects. In short, they decide through experience what is valuable, and the majority "graduate" to more sensible practices and realistic views of their bodies. This would suggest that there is scope through education to facilitate the graduation process. Information presented in an engaging format about topics such as body composition, healthy ranges of body fatness, the fallacies underlying the range of dietary aids and gimmicks, and the basis of effective weight loss can only be helpful and allow more informed decision-making. For those who genuinely need to be aware of weight increases, information, guidance, and assistance will help produce more effective results from weight regulation.

Social norms have had powerful influences on health behaviors as seen, for example, in the stigma surrounding smoking and the consequent reduction in this behavior (although interestingly there has not been the same effect on adolescent females in the United Kingdom [Department for Health 1993]). There is, however, potential to make extreme dietary practices socially unacceptable. A recent focus on eating disorders and associated practices in the media may have even increased awareness and use of these practices in vulnerable adolescents. However, if the practices were attacked more aggressively and targeted with detailed information fed through the media and health educators directly to the adolescent, it is possible that the stigma attached to such behaviors might actually overcome the temptation to use them for weight management. Small peer groups are important targets for this kind of strategy, as success with small but influential groups might have more impact from the ground up than public and less focused campaigns. However, national government initiatives, particularly with respect to control over advertising and marketing of slimming aids, also has strong potential to change attitudes on a more global scale. The same applies to physical activity, in that it can be made more appealing to adolescent girls. For instance, many schools now include activities such as aerobics dance and swimming for fitness in their physical education programs.

SUMMARY

Young people, who traditionally have been considered fairly immune to preventive health messages (Jansson 1993), are investing considerable interest and energy in behaviors that affect the looks and health of their bodies. This drive is largely initiated by a need to shape and control appearance rather than to stay healthy. In many cases, this strong motive leads the adolescent to investment in and experimentation with unhealthy behaviors, as the potential payoffs are perceived to be high. The health educator therefore is faced with the challenge of directing such energy into healthy strategies and pursuits.

Some would argue that we should not promote weight management in adolescence because of the risk of developing excessive body concerns and eating disorders. Others would maintain that trends in overweight are such that the problem cannot be ignored and that adolescence is a critical time for intervention. Each of these viewpoints has merit and therefore needs consideration in any health promotion policy. However the argument is to some extent irrelevant. Adolescents will respond, come what may, to the demands that society places upon them in their struggle for their identity. A major problem is caused by the poor quality of information on which adolescents base their decision-making with regard to their bodies. What they require is comprehensive assistance through education and media campaigns that bring credit to healthy strategies, followed by support systems that help them set realistic expectations and successful programs for themselves.

REFERENCES

Adame, D.D., Johnson, T.C., Cole, S.P., Mathiasson, H., and Abbas, M.A. 1990. Physical fitness in relation to amount of physical exercise, body image and locus of control among college men and women. *Perceptual and Motor Skills* 70: 1347-50.

Armstrong, N., Balding, J., Gentle, P., Williams, J., and Kirby, B. 1990. Peak oxygen uptake and physical activity in 11-16 year olds. *Pediatric Exercise Science* 2: 349-58.

Attie, I., and Brooks-Gunn, J. 1989. Development of eating problems in adolescent girls: A longitudinal study. *Developmental Psychology* 25 (1): 70-79.

Becque, M.D., Katch, V.L., Rocchini, A.P., Marks, C.R., and Moorehead, C. 1988. Coronary risk incidence of obese adolescents: Reduction by exercise plus diet intervention. *Pediatrics* 81 (5): 605-12.

Biddle, S.J.H., and Mutrie, N. 1991. *The psychology of physical activity and exercise: A health-related perspective*. London: Springer-Verlag.

Borgen, J.S., and Corbin, C.B. 1987. Eating disorders among female athletes. *The Physician and Sportsmedicine* 15 (2): 89-95.

Bouchard, C., Shephard, R.J., Stephens, T., Sutton, J.R., and McPherson, B.D., eds. 1990. *Exercise, fitness and health*. Champaign, IL: Human Kinetics.

Brooks-Gunn, J., and Warren, M.P. 1988. The psychological significance of secondary sexual characteristics in 9-11 year old girls. *Child Development* 59: 161-69.

Button, E.J. 1993. *Eating disorders: Personal construct therapy and change*. Chichester: Wiley.

Cannon, G., and Einzig, H. 1983. *Dieting makes you fat*. London: Century.

Chinn, S., and Rona, R.J. 1994. Trends in weight-for-height and triceps skinfold thicknesses for English and Scottish children, 1972-1982 and 1982-1990. *Paediatric and Perinatal Epidemiology* 8: 90-106.

Clifford, E. 1971. Body satisfaction in adolescence. *Perceptual and Motor Skills* 33: 119-25.

Cohn, L.D., Adler, N.E., Irwin, C.E., Millstein, S.G., Kegeles, S.M., and Stone, G. 1987. Body figure preferences in male and female adolescents. *Journal of Abnormal Psychology* 96 (3): 276-79.

Colditz, G.A. 1992. Economic cost of obesity. *American Journal of Clinical Nutrition* 55: 503S-507S.

Cooper, M.J., Anastasiades, P., and Fairburn, C.G. 1992. Selective processing of eating—shape- and weight-related words in persons with bulimia nervosa. *Journal of Abnormal Psychology* 101 (2): 352-55.

Cooper, P.J., and Taylor, M.J. 1985. Body image disturbance in bulimia nervosa. *British Journal of Psychiatry* 153 (suppl. 2): 32-36.

Corbin, C.B. 1984. Self-confidence of females in sports and physical activity. *Clinics in Sports Medicine* 3 (4): 895-908.

Dacey, C.M., Nelson III, W.M., Clark, V.F., and Aikman, K.G. 1991. Bulimia and body image dissatisfaction in adolescence. *Child Psychiatry and Human Development* 21 (3): 179-84.

Damhorst, M.L., Littrell, J.M., and Littrell, M.A. 1988. Age differences in adolescent body satisfaction. *The Journal of Psychology* 121 (6): 553-62.

Davies, E., and Furnham, A. 1986. Body satisfaction in adolescent girls. *British Journal of Medical Psychology* 59: 279-87.

Davis, C., Durnin, J.V.G.A., Gurevich, M., Le Maire, A., and Dionne, M. 1993. Body composition correlates of weight dissatisfaction and dietary restraint in young women. *Appetite* 20: 197-207.

Davis, C., Shapiro, C.M., Elliot, S., and Dionne, M. 1993. Personality and other correlates of dietary restraint: An age by sex comparison. *Personality and Individual Differences* 14 (2): 297-305.

Department for Health. 1993. *The Health of the Nation: One year on*. London: Department for Health.

Dietz, W.H. 1994. Critical periods for obesity development. *American Journal of Clinical Nutrition* 59: 995-99.

Dietz, W.H., and Gortmaker, S.L. 1985. Do we fatten our children at the television set? Obesity and T.V. watching in children and adolescents. *Pediatrics* 75: 807-12.

DiNicola, V.F., Roberts, N., and Oke, L. 1989. Eating and mood disorders in young children. *Psychiatric Clinics of North America* 12 (4): 873-93.

Dubas, J.S., Graber, J.A., and Peterson, A.C. 1990. A longitudinal investigation of adolescents' changing perceptions of pubertal timing. *Developmental Psychology* 27 (4): 580-86.

Dwyer, J.T., Feldman, J.J., and Mayer, J. 1967. Adolescent dieters: Who are they? *American Journal of Clinical Nutrition* 20: 1045-56.

Fowler, B.A. 1989. The relationship of body image perception and weight status to recent change in weight status of the adolescent female. *Adolescence* 95: 557-68.

Fox, K.R. 1990. *Physical Self-Perception Profile manual.* DeKalb, IL: Office for Health Promotion, Northern Illinois University.

—. 1994. Understanding young people and their decisions about physical activity. *British Journal of Physical Education* 25 (1): 15-19.

Fox, K.R., and Dirkin, G.R. 1992. Psychosocial predictors and outcomes of exercise in patients attending multidisciplinary obesity treatment. *International Journal of Obesity* 16 (suppl. 1): 84.

Fox, K.R., Page, A., Armstrong, N., and Kirby, B.J. 1994. Dietary restraint and self-perceptions in early adolescence. *Personality and Individual Differences* 17 (1): 87-96.

Fox, K.R., Page, A., Peters, D.M., Armstrong, N., and Kirby, B.J. 1994. Dietary restraint and fatness in early adolescent girls and boys. *Journal of Adolescence* 14: 149-61.

Fox, K.R., and Vehnekamp, T.J. 1991. Gender comparisons of self-perceptions, physical fitness, exercise and dietary habits in college students. *Journal of Sports Sciences* 10 (1): 282.

Garrow, J. 1986. Obesity—public health enemy No 2? *Health Education Journal* 45 (1): 57-78.

—. 1991. Importance of obesity. *British Medical Journal* 303: 704-6.

—. 1992. The management of obesity: Another view. *International Journal of Obesity* 16 (suppl. 2): 559-63.

Gibney, M. 1995. Epidemiology of obesity in relation to nutrient intake. Symposium abstract. *International Journal of Obesity* 19 (suppl. 5): S1.

Gortmaker, S.L., Dietz, W.H., Sobol, A.M., and Wehler, C.A. 1987. Increasing paediatric obesity in the United States. *American Journal of Diseases of Children* 141: 535-40.

Harter, S. 1988. *The Self-Perception Profile for Adolescents.* Denver: University of Denver.

—. 1993. Causes and consequences of low self-esteem in children and adolescents. In *Self-esteem: The puzzle of low self-regard,* ed. R.F. Baumeister, 87-116. New York: Plenum Press.

Heunemann, R.L., Shapiro, L.R., Hampton, M.C., and Mitchell, B.W. 1966. A longitudinal study of gross body composition and body conformation and their association with food and activity. *American Journal of Clinical Nutrition* 18: 325-38.

Hill, A.J., and Robinson, A. 1991. Dieting concerns have a functional effect on the behaviour of nine-year-old girls. *British Journal of Clinical Psychology* 30: 265-67.

James, W.P.T. 1995. Reversing the increasing problem of obesity in England. A report from the nutrition and physical activity task forces. Unpublished summary document. London: Department of Health.

Jansson, S. 1993. Food and health: Experience from Sweden. *Health Education Journal* 52 (4): 253-55.

Kemper, H.C., Snel, J., Verschuur, R., and Storm-van-Essen, L. 1990. Tracking of health and risk indicators of cardiovascular diseases from teenager to adult: Amsterdam Growth and Health Study. *Preventive Medicine* 19: 642-55.

Killen, J.D., Hayward, C., Litt, I., Hammer, L.D., Wilson, D.M., Miner, B., Barr-Taylor, C.,

Varady, A., and Shisslak, C. 1991. Is puberty a risk factor for eating disorders? *American Journal of Diseases of Children* 146: 323-25.

King, M.M. 1989. Eating disorders in a general practice population: Prevalence, characteristics and follow up at 12-18 months. *Psychological Medicine* (suppl. 14): 1-34.

Kirk, D. 1993. *The body, schooling and culture*. Victoria, Australia: Deakin University.

Koff, E., and Rierdan, J. 1991. Perceptions of weight and attitudes towards eating in early adolescence. *Journal of Adolescent Health* 12: 307-12.

Leary, M.R., Tchividjian, L.R., and Kraxberger, B.E. 1994. Self-presentation can be hazardous to your health: Impression management and health risk. *Health Psychology* 13 (6): 461-70.

Lefevre, J., Beunen, G., Claessens, A.L., Lysens, R., Maes, H., Renson, R., Simons, J., Steens, G., Vanden-Eynde, B., and Vanreusel, B. 1990. Stability in the level of subcutaneous fat between adolescence and adulthood. In *Sports, medicine and health*, ed. G.P.H. Hermans. London: Elsevier Science.

Lerner, R.M., Karabenick, S.A., and Stuart, J.L. 1973. Relations among physical attractiveness, body attitudes, and self-concept in male and female college students. *Journal of Psychology* 85: 119-29.

Lintunen, T., Rahkila, P., Silvennoinen, M., and Osterback, L. 1988. Psychological and physical correlates of early and late biological maturation in 9- to 11-year-old girls and boys. In *Young athletes: Biological, psychological and educational perspectives*, ed. R.M. Malina, 85-91. Champaign, IL: Human Kinetics.

Lohman, T.G. 1992. *Advances in body composition assessment*. Champaign, IL: Human Kinetics.

Lucas, A.R., Beard, C.M., O'Fallon, W.M., and Kurland, L.T. 1988. Anorexia nervosa in Rochester, Minnesota: A 45-year study. *Mayo Clinic Proceedings* 63: 433-42.

Maloney, M.J., McGuire, J., Daniels, S.R., and Specker, B. 1989. Dieting behaviour and eating attitudes in children. *Pediatrics* 84: 482-87.

Miller, W.C., Linderman, A.K., Wallace, J., and Niederpruem, M. 1990. Diet composition, energy intake and exercise in relation to body fat in men and women. *American Journal of Clinical Nutrition* 52: 426-30.

Ministry of Agriculture, Food, and Fisheries. 1993. *National Food Survey*. London: Her Majesty's Stationery Office.

Mintz, L.B., and Betz, N.E. 1988. Prevalence and correlates of eating disordered behaviours among undergraduate women. *Journal of Counselling Psychology* 35 (4): 463-71.

Moore, D.C. 1990. Body image and eating behaviour in adolescent boys. *American Journal of Diseases of Children* 144: 475-79.

Must, A., Jacques, P.F., Dallal, G.E., Bajema, C.J., and Dietz, W.H. 1992. Long-term morbidity and mortality of overweight adolescents: A follow-up of the Harvard Growth Study of 1922 to 1935. *New England Journal of Medicine* 327: 1350-55.

Page, A. 1994. The psychology of adolescent weight management. Ph.D. diss., University of Exeter.

Page, A., Ashford, B., Biddle, S.J.H., and Fox, K.R. 1993. Evidence of cross cultural validity for the Physical Self-Perception Profile. *Personality and Individual Differences* 14 (4): 585-90.

Page, A., and Fox, K.R. 1994a. Adolescent weight management: To what extent are weight concerns founded in fatness? *International Journal of Obesity* 18 (suppl. 2): 162.

—. 1994b. Psychological and physical factors associated with adolescent weight management. *International Journal of Obesity* 18 (12): 838.

Patton, G.C. 1988. The spectrum of eating disorders in adolescence. *Journal of Psychosomatic Research* 32: 579-84.

Riddoch, C., Mahoney, C., Murphy, N., Boreham, C., and Cran, G. 1991. The physical activity patterns of Northern Irish schoolchildren ages 11 to 16 years. *Pediatric Exercise Science* 3: 300-309.

Rosenberg, M. 1979. *Conceiving the self.* New York: Basic Books.

Royal College of Physicians. 1983. Obesity: A report of the Royal College of Physicians. *Journal of the Royal College of Physicians* 17 (1): 51-58.

Russell, G.F. 1979. Bulimia nervosa: An ominous variant of anorexia nervosa. *Psychological Medicine* 9: 429-48.

Sallis, J.F., and Patrick, K. 1994. Physical activity guidelines for adolescents: Concensus statement. *Pediatric Exercise Science* 6: 302-14.

Shear, C.L., Freedman, D.S., Burke, G.L., Harsha, D.W., Webber, L.S., and Berenson, G.S. 1988. Secular trends of obesity in early life: The Bogalusa Heart Study. *American Journal of Public Health* 78: 75-77.

Sieghart, M.A. 1994. Rebels against the female body. *Times* (London), 9 April, 1-3.

Steinberg, L. 1987. Impact of puberty on family relations: Effects of pubertal status and maturational timing. *Developmental Psychology* 27: 451-60.

Story, M., Rosenwinkel, K., Himes, J.H., Resnick, M., Harris, L.J., and Blum, R.W. 1991. Demographic and risk factors associated with chronic dieting in adolescents. *American Journal of Diseases of Children* 415: 994-98.

Striegel-Moore, R.H., Silberstein, L.R., and Rodin, J. 1986. Toward an understanding of risk factors for bulimia. *American Psychologist* 41 (3): 246-63.

Sweeting, A. 1994. What's eating you? *Guardian* (Manchester), 23 March, 2-3.

Szmuckler, G., McCance, C., McCrone, L., and Hunter, D. 1986. A psychiatric case register study from Aberdeen. *Psychological Medicine* 16: 49-58.

Tinning, R. 1985. Physical education and the cult of slenderness: A critique. *Australian Council for Health, Physical Education and Recreation National Journal* 107: 10-13.

Wadden, T.A., Brown, G., Foster, G.D., and Linowitz, J.R. 1991. Salience of weight-related worries in adolescent males and females. *International Journal of Eating Disorders* 10 (4): 407-14.

Wadden, T.A., Foster, G.D., Stunkard, A.J., and Linowitz, J.R. 1989. Dissatisfaction with weight and figure in obese girls: Discontent but not depression. *International Journal of Obesity* 13: 89-97.

Walker, A.R.P., and Gerhardt, C. 1990. Why are girls so dissatisfied with their shape? *SAMT* 77: 2-4.

Wardle, J., and Beales, S. 1986. Restraint, body image and food attitudes in children from 12 to 18 years. *Appetite* 7: 209-17.

Wardle, J., and Marsland, L. 1990. Adolescent concerns about weight and eating: A social-developmental perspective. *Journal of Psychosomatic Research* 34 (4): 377-91.

West, R. 1994. *Obesity.* London: Office of Health Economics.

Wertheim, E.H., Paxton, S.J., Maude, D., Szmuckler, G.I., Gibbons, K., and Hiller, L. 1992. Psychosocial predictors of weight loss behaviours and binge eating in adolescent girls and boys. *International Journal of Eating Disorders* 12 (2): 151-60.

Wilfley, D.E., and Brownell, K.D. 1994. Physical activity and diet in weight loss. In *Advances in exercise adherence,* ed. R.K. Dishman, 361-93. Champaign, IL: Human Kinetics.

CHAPTER 10

DISABILITY, IDENTITY, AND INVOLVEMENT IN SPORT AND EXERCISE

CLAUDINE SHERRILL

Disability is a multidimensional identity that is specific to culture and history, is socially constructed, and is mediated by time of onset, nature of impairment, socioeconomic status, gender, ethnicity, and the multitude of roles, expectancies, aspirations, and perceptions that each individual incorporates into the self. *Socially constructed*, in this definition, refers to reciprocal interactions between self and others that, throughout the life span, contribute to the dynamics of self-perception and self-actualization.

Of the many identities assumed by the human species, disability is the least understood and the most feared. Yet one of six individuals in peaceful, industrial nations copes with personal disability at some time in his or her life (Shapiro 1993). The ratio is greater, of course, in third world countries and geographical regions torn by war or famine. The incidence of disability also increases drastically after the age of 65, when over half of the population incorporate some form of disability into their self-concepts.

The purposes of this chapter are to enhance awareness of people with disability as the world's largest minority (Gliedman and Roth 1980; Shapiro 1993), to explore the different meanings of disability, to review research linking disability and self-concept, and to share ideas pertaining to disability and the physical self in relation to sport and exercise. The physical world of sport and exercise is seen as a particularly revealing arena for examining critical relationships between disability and the self. I write from the perspectives of (a) participant-observer in the disability sport movement; (b) adapted physical activity teacher-trainer, researcher, and theorist; and (c) life span coping with asthma (my own) and various impairments and disabilities of my family and significant others. There has been a noticeable absence of theoretical application to the study of disability and self-concept, and the published empirical work is limited and often outdated. However, observational and interview data are abundant, and the content of this chapter thus is based on both quantitative and qualitative sources. The latter include, but are not limited to, interviews with more than 400 international-level athletes with physical, sensory, or mental disabilities.

DISABILITY TERMINOLOGY AND DEFINITIONS

Of the many variables that might affect the self-esteem of individuals with disabilities, terminology is among the most powerful. Words convey the reflected appraisals of others and shape the interactions through which individuals perceive and experience the world. Consider how it feels to be called *Champ, Cripple, Special Olympian, Retard, Star,* and *Moron.* Names, nicknames, and personalized descriptors of perceived strengths and weaknesses affect feelings about the self and others as do categorical labels for race, ethnicity, religion, sex, gender, appearance, and performance abilities (Horne 1985; McDavid and Harari 1966; Walton 1937). Politically and humanistically correct terms exist for each disability category but vary by country, culture, and time period in history. The World Health Organization (1980) recommended standardization of the terms in most frequent use, which include *impairment, handicap,* and *disability.* Today, *disability* has become the preferred term, the first word to emerge by consensus from within the disability community itself (Shapiro 1993). Despite the negative etymology of its prefix, disability is increasingly accepted as a neutral phrase that is applicable in all contexts requiring categorization labels. Impairment is regarded as a synonym, but handicap is perceived as offensive in most countries.

PERSON- OR NOUN-FIRST PROTOCOL

Political and humanistic correctness now also requires person-first terminology (American Psychological Association 1994). This means that the adjective *disabled* is no longer a correct way to modify nouns. Instead, we should place the noun first, so that the appropriate phrase becomes *individuals with disabilities, individuals with cerebral palsy,* or *individuals in wheelchairs.* Likewise, it is offensive to refer to categories like *the disabled* or *the paraplegics* rather than recognizing that individuals have many identities, of which only one is disability.

Person-first terminology is advocated by virtually every disability organization except those representing the Deaf community and Deaf sport (Stewart 1991). The philosophy underlying this difference is that deafness is a cultural and linguistic separateness from the hearing-speaking world, not a disability.

Disability sport, not *disabled sport*, is the correct term for sports adapted, developed, or conducted specifically for athletes with disabilities (Williams 1994a). Also appropriate are *wheelchair sports, cerebral palsy (CP) sports, blind sports*, and the like.

DISABILITY: A CONTEMPORARY DEFINITION

Disability, for the purposes of this chapter, refers to individual differences in appearance, structure, function, and performance that are perceived as *undesirable* by self and/or others. This definition departs from the traditional constructs of disability as a limitation, loss, or defect and strives to capture new directions in thought and action that are emerging from the civil rights disability movement of the 1990s (Barton 1993; Shapiro 1993; Sherrill 1993a; Williams 1994a). Many individuals regarded as disabled do not feel negative about the difference often perceived by others as sad, disfiguring, or untenable (Safilios-Rothschild 1976; Sherrill, Hinson, Gench, Kennedy, and Low 1990; Weinberg 1988). Today we recognize that disability varies in salience and personal meaning for each individual. This definition of disability, and therefore the whole discussion on terminology, are inextricably tied to the evolution of the self, how the self is defined, and in particular how the disability is integrated and accepted as part of the self.

The challenge is to define disability in ways that empower individuality and individualization rather than perpetuating the negative bias historically associated with certain categorical differences (Barton 1993; Wright 1983). It is no longer humanistically or politically correct to conceptualize disability as a global construct or category. Disability is a multidimensional personal descriptor that is unique to each individual and constitutes only a part of his or her being. The trend is toward viewing disability as neither bad nor good but rather as invested with personal meaning acquired through reciprocal interactions with the total ecology (i.e., both internal and external environments). The internal environment, or body sensations, can provide input that is assessed as undesirable (pain, strain, awkwardness), while the external environment (human and nonhuman) bombards the brain with perceptual data that can be interpreted in many ways. Life for individuals with disabilities consists of continuously adapting, acting and reacting, and thereby modifying what is perceived as undesirable or desirable. Disability is thus a dynamic process heavily influenced and challenged by cultural norms in attitudes to disability, political expediencies, and other aspects of the ever-changing environment.

THE SOCIAL CONSTRUCTION OF DISABILITY

Societies influence the way individuals construct their disability identities and thus their self-esteem through normative attitudes, beliefs, practices, and policies. The early Greeks and Romans, for example, killed or abandoned infants born with defects. Today in most countries, every effort is made to sustain life and to maximize independence, productivity, and societal integration. Medical and surgical advances continue to change the ways that disease, accidents, war wounds, developmental disabilities, and old age are viewed. Diagnosis and subsequent treatment, however, are mediated by economics and politics. Few families can afford to pay the high costs of surgery, treatment, and rehabilitation without insurance or government assistance. Likewise the expense of special education, adapted physical activity, and therapy that many individuals need can exceed school, community, and national resources.

Politics therefore ultimately influence priorities and decisions regarding which disabilities most require medical, surgical, educational, and rehabilitative services. Laws that provide money for services typically include categories and definitions of disabilities that qualify for these services. These definitions, in turn, are accepted by professionals who establish precise diagnostic criteria and procedures for selecting the individuals who shall receive services. The stringency of the diagnostic criteria varies according to money available so that when the economy is buoyant, more persons qualify for services than when the economy is recessive. The type of government (e.g., democracy, autocracy) and the dominant political party obviously affect enactment and operationalization of laws pertaining to disability. Social construction of the disability identity thus occurs at macro (governmental, societal, cultural) and micro (individual interaction) levels. Ultimately, both influence the processing of disability within the individual.

PREJUDICE AND DISCRIMINATION

Despite the efforts of legislation, litigation, government-funded education, and other "top-down" processes to maximize the independence, productivity, and societal integration of individuals with disability, prejudice (beliefs and attitudes) and discrimination (actions and practices) continue to negatively influence opportunities, lifestyles, and therefore self-perceptions.

Individuals with disabilities are typically undereducated. Approximately 9% have college degrees, compared with 23% of able-bodied peers in the same age range (Bowe 1990). About 40% of adults with disabilities lack high school diplomas, a fact that partially explains underemployment and low salaries. The laws that a society passes and enforces with regard to education of individuals with disabilities reflect the extent to which such individuals are valued as potential members of the workforce and contributors to society at large. Overall, the mean earnings of individuals with disabilities are 35% less than those of nondisabled peers. Males and females with disabilities in the United States who hold year-round, full-time jobs have average salaries of $24,000 and $16,000 a year, respectively (Bowe 1990). Only about one-third of the working-age population with disabilities, however, hold full-time jobs as opposed to 79% of able-bodied peers. Employment in today's society is an important determinant of self-esteem (Rosenberg and Pearlin 1982). The higher the income, the more opportunity the individual has to experience high self-esteem, assuming that the goods and experiences that can be acquired with money are valued and desired. Most individuals with disabilities want to work and need incomes commensurate with those of able peers in order to achieve desired lifestyles and feel good about themselves (Eisenberg, Griggins, and Duval 1982; Yuker 1988).

This financial inadequacy is reflected in difficulties involved in high-level sport participation. The more successful the athlete with disability becomes, the greater the challenge to raise entry fees, travel expenses, and other funds. For example, U.S. Paralympic athletes each contributed $1000 to $2500 toward their Summer 1992 competition in Barcelona (Sherrill et al. 1993). The opportunities for commercial sponsors vary also, with able-bodied athletes eagerly sought after, a few wheelchair athletes funded, and almost no attention given athletes with other disabilities.

Fewer individuals with disabilities participate in physical activity in general than the able population (Brown and Gordon 1987; Schmidt-Gotz, Doll-Tepper, and Lienert 1994; Williams 1994b). Possible reasons for this discrepancy include difficulties in availability of and access to facilities and programs, and poor or ambivalent attitudes toward integrating individuals with disabilities into regular sport and exercise settings.

STIGMATIZATION

Stigma theory is frequently cited as the body of knowledge that best explains dimensions of the disability identity that limit self-actualization (Crocker and Major 1989; Goffman 1963; Katz 1981; Katz, Haas, and Bailey 1988; Shapiro 1993; Sherrill 1986). Stigmatization refers to discriminatory or unjust treatment directed toward persons perceived as different. First conceptualized by Erving Goffman (1963), *stigma* is an undesired differentness, an attribute perceived as discrediting, a failing, a shortcoming, or a handicap. Three factors particularly contribute to stigmatization: (a) fear of individuals different from oneself, (b) association of differentness with inferiority and/or danger, and (c) belief that persons with stigmata (plural of stigma) are not quite human and thus need not be accorded the same acceptance, respect, and regard given others. According to Goffman, the major barrier is outsider status (i.e., perceptions and feelings about nonacceptance or partial acceptance by insiders).

Commonly reported incidents of teasing, hurtful comments, staring, and other behaviors that cause discomfort are the overt result of stigmatization (Shapiro 1993; West 1984; Wright 1983).

Virtually all athletes with blindness and cerebral palsy who were interviewed in the early 1980s described incidents of discrimination that match Goffman's examples of stigmatization (Sherrill 1986). Among the themes most often illustrated was "different treatment," the most notable form of which was being ignored and/or subjected to lower expectations than able-bodied siblings and peers. Athletes typically used a global they/me or they/us reference system that revealed deep-seated hurt and concern about outsider status.

Uniqueness Versus Categorization

Individuals with disabilities are so diverse that in reality, each identity is entirely unique. Individuals born with mental retardation, cerebral palsy, and spina bifida, for instance, have little in common with adults who acquire disability through accidents, disease, famine, war, or the degeneration of old age. An individual recovering from a stroke feels little affinity for someone with cerebral palsy, even though their speech and movement patterns may be similar. In a sense, each individual with a disability is a social minority of one, aware of the personal distinctiveness of his/her difference and how it affects interactions with others. The social construction of disability, however, is often flawed by insensitivity to uniqueness. People tend to categorize others as "like me" or "not like me." Individuals with disabilities tend automatically to be placed in the "not like me" category on the basis of the single attribute perceived as most salient (disability) rather than evaluated as a whole person. This tendency to categorize all individuals with disabilities, or stereotyping, is a particularly hurtful type of prejudice. Unfortunately, many of society's institutions support dichotomies (e.g., special education vs. regular education; disability sport vs. mainstream sport) that reinforce this type of prejudice and further contribute to the depersonalization of individuals with disabilities.

Categorization or stereotyping underlies the evolution of social minority theory, which is a prominent psychosocial paradigm (Bickenbach 1993; Sherrill 1993a). Pioneer works by Wright (1960, 1983) and Gliedman and Roth (1980) advanced this theory positing that people with disabilities are minority or marginal groups in the same sense as are racial, ethnic, and sexual minorities. The shared experiences that unite minorities are stigmatization, stereotyping, and various forms of oppression that violate individual rights and devalue uniqueness. Central to contemporary psychosocial theorizing is the following definition of *minority*:

> The concept "minority" refers to any social category within a society (1) that is set apart and defined by the majority as incompetent/inferior or abnormal/dangerous on the basis of presumed physical, cultural, and/or behavioral differences from majority norms; (2) that is categorically and systematically discriminated against by majority authorities and is thereby subject to some degree of oppression (denial of political rights), neglect (denial of economic rights), and/or diminution (denial of social rights/human dignity); and (3) that, as a consequence of the self-fulfilling prophecy of systematic or structural discrimination, comes to occupy a socially subordinate, disadvantaged, and stigmatized position within the society. (Kallen 1989, 50)

Using this definition, many theorists argue that the self-concept of individuals with disabilities is shaped more by their minority status than by other social forces (Bickenbach 1993; Wright 1988).

Just as ethnic groups and racial minority groups are distinct from each other, so also are disability subgroups. Essential to understanding the social construction of disability is differentiation between the major subgroups (e.g., blindness, cerebral palsy, deafness, amputations, spinal cord injuries, mental retardation). Individuals within disability subgroups seldom feel much comradeship or common cause with others who have different disabilities (Bickenbach 1993; Fichten 1988) despite their subjection to similar forms of discrimination or oppression.

ATTITUDINAL HIERARCHIES

Research on attitudinal or preference hierarchies indicates that some disabilities are consistently ranked more favorably than others (Yuker 1988). Knowledge about such hierarchies helps us better understand interactions that differentially affect self-esteem development. Much research has been conducted on the specific disabilities that generate the most discomfort and/or poorest attitudes. Invariably persons with mental retardation and cerebral palsy (congenital conditions) are at the bottom (poorest attitudes) of the preference hierarchy; people with hearing problems are near the middle; and persons with physical disabilities are near the top (Yuker 1988). Preference for some disabilities, such as blindness, seems to depend on context. Persons who are blind rank high in social situations, in the middle in teaching or rehabilitation service delivery, and very low on employment (Yuker 1988). The hierarchy of preference expressed by individuals with disabilities mirrors that of able-bodied persons (Fichten 1988; Mastro et al.

1996). For example, elite athletes with physical disabilities do not like to be linked with elite athletes with mental retardation and thus prefer that competition sites be separate (Atha 1994; Sherrill 1986).

The generalization of prejudice against mental retardation to other disabilities by the general public is an example of the *spread phenomenon* (Wright 1983) and constitutes one of the greatest barriers to the development of self-esteem. Many athletes with cerebral palsy, for example, recall school placement in classes where everyone was mentally retarded. Until adolescence or adulthood, these athletes believed they were mentally retarded. Often disability sport has provided a medium through which they have discovered others like themselves, initiating a group identity that for the first time "felt good." The insensitive and inappropriate categorization of people with disabilities, either through ignorance or through poor policies, often undermines the development of positive identities and causes frustration for many (Wyeth 1989).

Research on preservice physical educators (i.e., undergraduate students) also reveals cultural differences in attitudes toward particular disability labels when the context is anticipated integration into regular physical education. In the United States, preservice teachers favor learning disabilities, defined by researchers as including mental retardation (DePauw and Goc Karp 1990; Rizzo 1984), whereas the reverse is true in Europe (Downs and Williams 1994; Schmidt-Gotz, Doll-Tepper, and Lienert 1994). These findings may reflect different patterns of media coverage (e.g., Special Olympics), direct contact, and formal training on the two continents.

AMBIVALENCE

Ambivalence is a major force that confounds the social construction of disability. Social psychologists such as Katz (1981) report research indicating that the able population is not prejudiced per se by disability but vastly uncomfortable in the presence of large differences. This *mere difference hypothesis* also applies to discrepancies between expected and perceived attributes of objects like taste, color, sound, and temperature.

From childhood on, able-bodied people learn to embrace the security of similarity, to become as others are, to make friends with and choose as spouses individuals who are similar to self. A little difference may be tolerated, even considered interesting, but large differences (especially for long durations) cause discomfort. When people are exposed to someone perceived as very different, the common response is ambivalence (Albrecht 1976; Katz 1981; Katz, Hass, and Bailey 1988; Safilios-Rothschild 1976). There is perhaps curiosity, but also fear, generalized discomfort, or both. When individuals are perceived as both different *and* disadvantaged, feelings of aversion and hostility often accompany contradictory feelings such as sympathy and compassion. This results in ambivalent behaviors that are not easily interpreted by individuals with disabilities. Also complicating this phenomenon is the overprotectiveness of some families, which limits the social contacts and interactions that ordinarily lead to better understanding of selves and others.

In summary, it is clear that perceptions of the different disabilities vary considerably at the individual, institutional, and cultural level. Beliefs, attitudes, intentions, and behaviors mediate interactions with individuals with disabilities, which in turn can influence their self-concepts. Generalizations about self-concepts of global disability groups should not be made because such statements mask important differences and subsequently the mechanisms that produce them.

FACTORS AFFECTING SELF-ESTEEM DEVELOPMENT

The discussion to this point has illustrated the processes underlying the social construction of disability. Societal and political sources of tensions, pressures, and constraints face the individual with disability when developing a coherent and positive identity. However, factors at the individual level also have potential to make a significant impact on self-esteem development.

AGE AT ONSET OF DISABILITY

Age at onset of disability is one of the most important variables affecting subsequent life experiences and potentially physical self-perceptions and self-esteem. Onset of disability may be specified by life stages or simplified into a bipolar *congenital* (born with) versus *acquired* categorization system. According to Shapiro (1993, 7), fewer than 15% of individuals with disabilities are born with disability conditions. Most acquire disability through poor health and fitness practices, disease, vehicle and other accidents, violence, or famine.

The 15% of all individuals with congenital disabilities, however, are the most visible because of legislation pertaining to schooling and social services. Of these, individuals with mental retardation compose the largest majority, excluding the category of specific learning disabilities, which appears to be largely a North American designation. The size of the population with mental retardation is approximately 7.5 million in the United States and 250 million worldwide. Almost all school-age children with mental retardation in the United States are socialized into one of the Special Olympics programs, several of which have been integrated and inclusive since the early 1990s (e.g., Unified Sports, Partners Clubs). Local Special Olympics chapters, using community facilities when possible, supplement school programming and also provide sports for individuals no longer in school. In general, research on Special Olympics participation and self-esteem has indicated a positive relationship (Gibbons and Bushakra 1989; Klein, Gilman, and Zigler 1993; Riggen and Ulrich 1993; Wright and Cowden 1986). The operation of Special Olympics varies, however, country by country, so no cross-cultural generalizations can be drawn.

In contrast to the life experiences of individuals with mental retardation in relation to sport, individuals with congenital *physical* and *sensory* disabilities have sterile sport biographies. Cerebral palsy and spina bifida are the most common causes of congenital physical disability, with incidence of about 3 occurrences in every 1000 births, whereas the incidence for mental retardation is about 30 in 1000 births. The small number of individuals with congenital physical disabilities limits the availability of sport adapted to specific abilities, especially for those in wheelchairs. Although some individuals are included in neighborhood or school able-body sport, most report no real participatory sport experience until about age 18 (Sherrill and Rainbolt 1986). This phenomenon also limits the ways in which the general public, including professionals, see and perceive individuals with congenital physical disabilities as opposed to those with mental retardation.

Wheelchair athletes visible in newspaper, media, and spectator contexts typically acquire their condition as adolescents or young adults after the benefit of many years of sport socialization. Most injuries that result in spinal cord paralysis, for instance, are sustained after age 16 (Trieschmann 1988). Historically, athletes with spinal cord injuries have dominated sport, partly because they were the first of the Paralympic family to form national and international sport organizations (Guttmann 1976) and partly because they consistently are the largest percentage of first-place winners in track, field, and swimming (Weiss and Curtis 1986). Individuals with spinal cord paralysis also compose the largest percentage of athletes at the quadrennial Summer Paralympics (Sherrill et al. 1993). The second-largest group of international competitors are those with amputations and *les autres conditions*, most of which are not congenital.

Research indicates that age at which spinal cord injury or amputation occurs is significantly related to self-esteem and attitudes toward physical activity in wheelchair athletes (Hopper 1986; Kennedy 1980). Specifically, individuals injured after their 17th birthday have higher self-esteem and more positive attitudes than those injured earlier.

PARENTS AND SIGNIFICANT OTHERS

Virtually all aspects of parenting and family relations are affected by the birth of a visibly different child (Blacher 1984; Fewell and Vadasy 1986; Seligman 1983). Although roles are changing, most fathers of children with disability are minimally involved in child rearing (Lillie 1993). Multiple regression research indicates that active sport involvement of boys with learning disabilities is influenced more by mothers than by other family members (Brame 1994; Podosek 1994). The reverse is true of the able population.

Children with congenital disabilities are also affected by attitudes and behaviors of peers and teachers. Unless planned intervention promotes acceptance, children at age four who are different begin to experience social rejection and avoidance by peers (Siller 1984; Weinberg 1978). Research indicates that children without disabilities do not automatically include slow and/or different children in their activities (Jenkins, Speltz, and Odom 1985). Numerous research studies also indicate that physical educators and university students preparing to teach physical education have poor, neutral, or ambiguous attitudes toward integrating students with disabilities in regular sport and exercise classes (DePauw and Goc Karp 1990; Downs and Williams 1994; Rizzo 1984; Rizzo and Vispoel 1991; Schmidt-Gotz, Doll-Tepper, and Lienert 1994). These attitudes undoubtedly influence teacher behaviors, although little experimental research has addressed relationships between these variables in a physical education setting.

Research also shows that disability labels affect teacher expectations for achievement as well as recommendations for program placement (Combs and Harper 1967; Dunn 1968; Hobbs 1975). Low expectations lead teachers to treat students with disabilities differently from others, and this subsequently affects the way peers treat them. Through the reflected appraisal or looking glass phenomenon, students with disabilities begin to perceive themselves as others do and self-esteem is diminished. Participation motivation then suffers and teacher expectations are further confirmed.

GENDER

Females with disabilities tend to experience more prejudice and discrimination than males, especially within the context of sport, where the 1:3 or 1:4 ratio makes females a subculture minority (Sherrill 1993b; 1993c). Gender seems to interact differentially with disability in comparisons of self-esteem. For example, no significant gender differences in self-regard are found among wheelchair athletes (Sherrill, Silliman, Gench, and Hinson 1990) and blind athletes (Sherrill, Gench, Hinson, Gilstrap, Richir, and Mastro 1990). However, female athletes with CP score lower on self-regard than able-bodied peers, whereas male counterparts score higher (Sherrill 1990). Magill and Hurlbut (1986) also reported lower self-esteem for adolescent females with CP than for males. It has been reported that females with MR and/or learning handicaps also have lower self-esteem than males (Piers 1984).

TYPE OF DISABILITY

In spite of the many variables and mechanisms discussed so far in this chapter that have potential to cause or contribute to poor self-esteem, both the rehabilitation and the special education literature caution against generalization. For the sake of addressing the question of whether individuals with disability have different levels of self-esteem from their able-bodied equivalents, physical disability will be considered separately from mental retardation and learning disabilities.

Physical Disability

Comprehensive reviews of literature since the 1940s indicate that (a) no particular personality characteristic, attribute, or limitation can be associated with physical or sensory disability and (b) severity of disability is not significantly correlated with level of psychological adjustment (Shontz 1970; Wright 1983; Yuker 1988). Shontz (1970) cited 59 sources that support these conclusions. Of the many books that summarize research on the psychology and/or sociology of physical disability, the classic monograph by Beatrice Wright (1960, 1983) provides the most extensive coverage of self-concept. Wright (1983) emphasizes that

> people with disabilities do not, in general, feel more inferior than their able-bodied counterparts in spite of common beliefs to the contrary . . . the self-concept cannot reflect all views encountered, only some. The two-way integration process guarantees and assures that the individual plays an important part in fashioning his or her own self-concept. Most persons do not take belittling views of others without struggling to protect their egos and affirm their own worth. They give differential weight to the opinion of others in order to support a more adequate self-concept. They modify their own values. They learn to sort out the views of others from their own, and are selective in their associates. Undoubtedly there are other reasons. . . . (229)

Wright's beliefs dominate disability psychology and have been particularly influential in shaping definitions and theories, as discussed earlier in this chapter. Wright posits that it is the personal meaning of a disability that is important in self-concept formation rather than the disability itself. Personal meaning is derived from multiple psychosocial factors "that underlie the way disability as a value loss is perceived and reacted to by other people, as well as the self" (Wright 1983, 6). Wright credits Kurt Lewin, Carl Rogers, and various ecological psychologists as the primary sources of ideas that have helped her develop personal meaning theory.

The concept that individuals with disabilities do not necessarily perceive their conditions and identities as bad, tragic, or negative is supported by recent research. Studies have focused on the wish question: "If you were given one wish, would you wish that you are no longer disabled?" Results generally indicate that only about 50% of respondents say yes (Weinberg 1988). This would suggest that for many, the disablement is not necessarily the major determinant of self-esteem for people with disabilities.

Much quantitative research supports this notion, as no global self-esteem differences between individuals with physical disability and the equivalent able population are generally reported (e.g., Arnold and Chapman 1992; Hutzler and Bar-Eli 1993; Nelson and Gruver 1978; Sherrill 1990; Sherrill, Hinson, Gench, Kennedy, and Low 1990; Super and Block 1992). However, consensus has not been fully reached, as several studies have reported opposite findings. The confounding effect of different ages of onset and etiologies may explain some inconsistencies. For example, research and literature reviews on congenital physical disability tend to indicate lower self-esteem than in the able population and/or self-esteem problems (Anderson and Clarke 1982; Campbell 1977; Hutzler and Bar-Eli 1993; King et al. 1993). Also, self-rating differences may be evident only at the domain-specific level. King et al. (1993), for example, reported that subjects with disabilities were lower than able-bodied peers on only three of nine scales (both genders on perceived athletic competence and perceived romantic appeal, males only on perceived scholastic competence, and females only on perceived social competence).

Furthermore, the difficulties of working in this area have often led to poor research designs with mediator variables not adequately controlled. In summary, problems that compromise the validity of findings have included (a) combining congenital and acquired etiologies, (b) combining recently injured with long-term-injured individuals, and (c) combining genders, ethnic groups, and individuals of different socioeconomic status. Green, Pratt, and Grigsby (1984), for example, emphasize that about four years are needed after a spinal cord injury for self-concept to stabilize. Physical disability is so complex and variable that no generalizations can be safely made about self-esteem.

Mental Retardation

In contrast to the large body of literature on the psychology of physical disability, little is known about individuals with mental retardation (MR). This is partly because of measurement difficulties. The first attempts to describe the self-esteem of individuals with MR occurred in the 1960s (Edgerton 1967; Gorlow, Butler, and Guthrie 1963; Guthrie, Butler, and Gorlow 1961). George Guthrie and colleagues published several studies based on the Laurelton Self-Concept Scale developed specifically for individuals with MR. This 100-item scale required yes or no responses and separate scoring to indicate acceptance of positive items and rejection of negative items about self. In spite of indications of acceptable reliability and validity, the instrument did not become well known, and subsequent researchers used investigator-generated scales or the yes/no scale of Piers and Harris (1964), which was normed for the able population.

The revised manual for the Piers-Harris Children's Self-Concept Scale (Piers 1984) provides a review of research with individuals with MR. More positive self-esteem is likely in males, in those living at home versus those living in institutions, and in those in classes with others of similar rather than higher ability. Type of school placement is not consistently related to self-esteem and experimental treatments seldom result in statistically significant improvements in self-esteem in individuals with MR. Finally, comparisons of self-esteem of individuals with and without MR yield inconsistent results.

Given the reservations already outlined in this book (see Marsh, chapter 2) concerning the limitations of unidimensional scales, and earlier comments in this chapter regarding the shaping of self by the individual, these general findings need to be interpreted carefully. Other reviews of the self-concept literature have also emphasized measurement problems (Lawrence and Winschel 1973; Zigler and Hodapp 1986). In particular, instruments that require yes or no responses are believed to be weak because individuals with MR, when in doubt, tend to say yes (Alvarez and Adelman 1986; Sigelman et al. 1981). This overstatement phenomenon is believed to be founded in a self-protection tendency rather than an inability to make accurate self-evaluative judgments.

Another concern is research that combines heterogeneous individuals into groups such as those with familial and nonfamilial MR (Zigler and Hodapp 1986). Approximately 75% of individuals with MR have familial etiology, meaning that the cause is a combination of family genes and environment. Children with familial MR are likely to have self-concepts confounded by lower socioeconomic status and different biographies in relation to those reared in traditional middle-class, two-parent homes.

Researchers in the 1990s have begun to use the multidimensional instruments of Harter (1982), Harter and Pike (1984), and Marsh and Barnes (1982), although users of the Harter instruments express concern about their validity for individuals with MR (Gibbons and Bushakra 1989; Riggen and Ulrich 1993). Researchers, for example, have cautioned that the factor structure of multidimensional scales may be different for individuals with MR (Silon and Harter 1985; Ulrich and Collier 1990). In contrast, Widaman et al. (1992) highly recommend the Self-Description Questionnaire II (Marsh and Barnes 1982) for eighth graders with *learning handicaps*. This is a term used in California that subsumes children who might in other places be labeled as having mild MR, learning disabilities, behavior disorders, or neurological impairments. Factor analysis revealed that the factor structure for the 240 children with learning handicaps was similar to factor structures for children in regular classes and educationally marginal children.

The Widaman et al. (1992) study of differences in adolescents' self-concepts as a function of academic level, ethnicity, and gender may therefore gain recognition as the first large-scale multidimensional self-concept study to include children with MR. On five of the seven nonacademic scales (Physical, Appearance, Honesty, Emotions, and Opposite Sex Relations), there were no significant differences between children with learning handicaps and children with educational marginality. These groups, however, both scored significantly lower than students in regular classes. Findings also indicated ethnicity and gender main effects for most of the nonacademic scales, with black students and males scoring best on most scales.

The Widaman et al. (1992) approach of grouping together children with various types of mental disabilities is controversial in the United States, where most states make substantial distinctions between the diagnostic categories of MR and learning disabilities (SLD or LD). In Europe and Australia, however, grouping such children together into a "Special Needs" category seems relatively common. For example, athletes who represent the International Sports Federation for Persons with Mental Handicaps in sport events governed by the International Paralympic Committee (IPC) are called athletes with learning difficulties.

Learning Disabilities

Whereas research on self-esteem of individuals with MR in the United States seems unsystematic, inconclusive, and perhaps until recently largely invalid, research on individuals with LD has been synthesized into an excellent meta-analysis (Prout, Marcal, and Marcal 1992) and two review articles (Bryan 1986; Chapman 1988). These three sources concur on the generalized tendency for children and adolescents with LD to score in a negative direction. Furthermore, academic self-concepts are more negative than global measures of self-esteem. Most of the research reviewed, however, used unidimensional scales and did not specifically address the physical self.

Renick and Harter (1988), in particular, have spearheaded a movement to use multidimensional perceived competence scales specifically developed and validated for adolescents with LD. Analyses indicate, however, that the perceived athletic competence items on their LD instrument are the same as those on the scale for the able population (Harter 1988). Presumably the items work similarly. Podosek (1994) appears to be the first to have specifically examined perceived athletic competence and physical appearance scores of boys with LD. She reported that perceived athletic competence explained a substantial part of the variance in sport participation, whereas perceived physical appearance, perceived global worth, and actual sport skills did not. Clearly, much further research is required in this area if we are to identify important group differences along with the mechanisms that produced any differences.

Interactions of Disability Type With Gender

Findings on gender thus seem related to the attitudinal hierarchy of disability preference held by society, discussed earlier in this chapter. For disability groups held in higher esteem by society (physical disabilities and blindness), gender differences in self-esteem are not apparent. The reverse is true for disability groups held in lower esteem by society (CP and MR). Research indicates that women attach greater importance to reflected appraisal as a source of self-esteem than men do (Schwalbe and Staples 1991). Thus, for the disability groups that experience the most discrimination and prejudice, women are differentially affected. This is especially true in elite Paralympic sports, where women with severe disabilities are more underrepresented than male peers and where gender inequalities rank low in priority among the many problems that the predominantly male power structure is addressing (Sherrill 1993c).

SELF-ESTEEM PROCESSES AND DISABILITY

Traditionally, four principles have been recognized as guiding self-esteem formation: (a) reflected appraisal, (b) social comparison, (c) self-attribution, which is closely associated with self-efficacy, and (d) psychological centrality (Rosenberg and Kaplan 1982). Self-esteem principles may function in different ways for individuals with and without disabilities. Additionally, new principles may be needed.

FOUR BASIC PRINCIPLES OF SELF-ESTEEM FORMATION

Reflected appraisal, for example, is experienced within the context of ambiguous social attitudes and behaviors that are confounded by prejudice and discrimination, stigmatization, stereotyping, marginalization, and over-protection. Social comparison is more complex than for able-bodied peers in that self-judgments may be based on comparison with peers with or without disabilities and vary according to environment (segregated, partially integrated, fully integrated). The ecosystems of individuals with disabilities are characterized by much ambiguity that heightens confusion about appropriate role models, motivational orientations, and internal/external controls. Self-attribution, the cognitive appraisal of self on the basis of past successes and failures, may suffer from imbalance when failures exceed successes and/or effort expended is not commensurate with outcomes. Psychological centrality, which refers to the hierarchical ordering of the many self-concept domains (e.g., athletic, social, academic), may be blocked by defense mechanisms. Little is known about how hierarchical personal meaning systems are affected by specific physical, sensory, or mental limitations. Does athletic competence, for instance, become *more* or *less* salient when significant others assume that one cannot become an athlete?

MASTERY CHALLENGE: A FIFTH PRINCIPLE

To date, most adapted physical activity professionals have primarily stressed the principle of self-attribution and/or self-efficacy in their discussion of self-esteem formation (Craft and Hogan 1985; Greenwood, Dzewaltowski, and French 1990; Hedrick 1984; Hopper 1986). Working from the skill development perspective described by Sonstroem (see chapter 1), they may be relying too heavily on the assumption that motor skill improvement is the best approach to increasing self-esteem and enjoyment of physical activity. Little attention has been focused on individuals whose personal bests are considerably lower than those of peers and/or whose severe conditions functionally negate any hope of success in some activities. When adversity, barriers, and challenges characterize life, individuals require additional support. Sherrill (1993a) therefore put forward a fifth self-concept development principle, *mastery challenge*, to give added visibility to humanistic theory (Harter 1978; Maslow 1954; Rogers 1951). This principle emphasizes the importance of strategies that (a) empower individuals to master challenges they perceive as hard, unpleasant, dangerous, or likely to result in failure and (b) provide added support and empathy for persons who fail a lot and/or face unusual barriers or constraints.

Mastery challenge relates equally to "I can do" (perceived competencies) and "I am" (social identity descriptors) components of self-concept. Sherrill (1993a) agrees with Rosenberg and Kaplan (1982), who stress that "I am" and "I can do" components are equally important. Perceptions and beliefs about self (e.g., "I am female"; "My family is poor"; "I am African-American"; "I am different"; "I am clumsy"; "I am an only child") affect attitudes, intentions, and behaviors, which in turn dynamically influence the self-esteem of different components, dependent on context. Global *I am* feelings may be more salient for individuals with disabilities because of life experiences in which they are repeatedly judged on the single attribute of disability or undesired difference. Unconsciously, they may model and thereby reinforce the centrality of disability. The notion of mastery challenge therefore may be of considerable importance as a process to encourage through interventions designed to develop self-esteem and well-being.

GROWTH THROUGH ADVERSITY

Closely associated with the mastery challenge principle is the *growth through adversity* hypothesis that appears frequently in rehabilitation and disability sport literature (Green, Pratt, and Grigsby 1984; Lazarus and Folkman 1984; Sherrill 1990). Adversity seems to promote growth in some persons who draw on internal adaptive resources and coping mechanisms to develop strong integrated identities. Some authors suggest that strength gained through coping with disability generalizes to other areas of life, increases internal locus of control and confidence, and helps explain why individuals with disabilities sometimes score higher on self-esteem domains than test manual norms and able-bodied comparison groups (Green, Pratt, and Grigsby 1984; Sherrill 1990). Sport participation and competition can provide the ideal type of mastery challenge to help individuals stretch themselves far beyond the limitations that their disability may initially offer. However, little is known about the circumstances that allow or encourage such positive growth under what might be considered challenging conditions.

DEFENSIVENESS AND DENIAL

In sharp contrast with positive growth through adversity, individuals with disability may attempt to preserve their self-esteem through mechanisms such as defensiveness, denial, or rationalization (Edgerton 1967; Fitts 1972; Goffman 1963; Wright 1983; Yuker 1988). Of course, this can also be true of the able-bodied population (see Fox, chapter 5; Rosenberg and Kaplan 1982). Denial has been addressed most in the disability psychology literature, and the approach is typically different for individuals with physical and mental disabilities. Pioneer researchers believed that denial was a first response to spinal cord injury and/or one of the initial stages of adjustment, but today the existence of stages is considered a myth (Trieschmann 1988). Each individual's coping strategies are unique, with different amounts of time required to work through the mixed feelings evoked by loss (Crocker 1993). According to Trieschmann (1988), "Denial seems to occur in a very small proportion of persons who become suddenly disabled" (85). Hope of recovery feelings like "I will walk again" should not be confused with denial, which is typically manifested by refusal to participate in rehabilitation because such activities are perceived as unnecessary.

Adjusting to a sudden loss evokes all kinds of defense mechanisms and coping strategies for the first few months, a time during which the self-concept is extremely unstable. Within four years, however, most individuals exhibit personality strengths and weaknesses (including self-concept dimensions) similar to those of their preinjury selves (Green, Pratt, and Grigsby 1984; Trieschmann 1988). Psychologists describing physical disability thus tend to minimize the role of defense mechanisms in acquired disability after the first few months.

Unlike the situation of acquired disability, in which an individual has to actively involve himself or herself in *reconstituting* the self, congenital physical disability is unavoidably implicated in the formation and development of the self. The issue is therefore confounded by childhood socialization processes, demography, and ecology. The degree to which denial and defensiveness are operative has not been resolved.

In contrast to studies regarding physical disability, research on individuals with mental retardation frequently describes denial of inadequacies, blame, and attempts at "passing" as nonretarded. The qualitative research by Edgerton (1967) is classic in this regard. Entitled *The Cloak of Competence: Stigma in the Lives of the Mentally Retarded*, the book describes in great detail the lives of 48 adults with MR who are living in the community on their own after discharge from a state institution. Much of their energy is devoted to denying their inadequacies and convincing others that they are like everyone else. Edgerton states, "For the mildly retarded, acceptance of their affliction is intolerable. The stigma is too great, too global, and too self-destructive. Acceptance of this affliction is incompatible with self-esteem" (212).

CAUSES AND CORRELATES OF INDIVIDUAL DIFFERENCES

The causes and correlates of individual differences in the formation and/or preservation of self-esteem remain intriguing questions that have yet to be answered. The overgeneralizations, preconceived notions, and flawed assumptions about disability that are still taught in many universities need to be replaced by a moral and ethical concern for individuality and careful, stringent training in domain-specific assessment. Detailed qualitative investigative techniques such as that offered by the life history approach should be emphasized. Assessment protocols should include multidimensional self-concept measures. Responses should be examined to determine their congruence with observations of significant others as well as trained professionals. A combination of approaches may then help us understand substantial issues such as the ways congenital and acquired disabilities are processed in the emergence and maintenance of the self.

SELF-ESTEEM IN ATHLETES WITH DISABILITY

Most of us believe that sport, properly conducted, provides opportunities for experiencing success and achievement and positive feelings about many aspects of self. Given the growth through adversity hypothesis described earlier, sport may have even greater potential for those with disabilities. However, only limited evidence exists to support these views.

Reviews of research on disability sport have focused on social and psychological dimensions (Sherrill 1986, 1990), psychological implications of physical activity (Benson and Jones 1992), psychological benefits (Hutzler and Bar-Eli 1993), cognitively oriented theories in sport and exercise psychology (Crocker 1993), and disability sport socialization (Sherrill and Rainbolt 1986; Williams 1994a, 1994b; Zoerink 1992) rather than self-esteem per se. Hutzler and Bar-Eli (1993) offer the most extensive review of self-concept and self-esteem research, concluding that (a) general improvements in self-esteem result from sport participation and (b) sport participants with disabilities have significantly higher self-esteem than inactive individuals with disabilities. However, this review included only 13 studies, most of which had weak sampling and/or research designs by today's standards. Brief summaries of the four strongest studies follow.

Szyman (1980) and Hopper (1986), who administered the Tennessee Self Concept Scale and the Rosenberg Self-Esteem Scale, respectively, both reported a significant relationship between sport participation and global self-esteem for adult wheelchair athletes. Additionally, Hopper (1986) reported that four variables were significant contributors to self-esteem: (a) greater amount of time spent participating in wheelchair sports, (b) older age at onset of injury, (c) less severe injuries, and (d) less personal commitment to sport. Hopper speculated that athletes not so heavily committed to sport may have a broader foundation of perceived competence (e.g., employment, relations with spouse). Age, amount of money spent on sports, and score on a sport role socialization instrument were not associated with self-esteem.

Valliant et al. (1985), in the first of three studies to examine self-esteem differences between individuals with disabilities who are active and nonactive in sports, reported significantly higher self-esteem in active individuals. Subsequent research indicated negligible differences in self-esteem (Martino et al. 1987; Super and Block 1992). All three investigations focused on wheelchair athletes but used different measures of self-esteem. None of the research designs adequately controlled for the many categorical or mediating variables that might influence findings, or provided evidence of causal relationships.

Patrick (1986) reported that over a five-month period of sport competition, 10 novice wheelchair athletes increased in self-esteem significantly more than 12 veteran athletes who each had three or more years of experience. Again, moderating variables were not adequately described, but these findings seem to support the conclusion of Green, Pratt, and Grigsby (1984) that self-esteem stabilizes about four years after injury. Additionally, as with findings across most populations, research with athletes with disabilities generally shows that those initially low in self-esteem usually make the most gains, given the right circumstances. Presumably the novices in Patrick's study were introduced to wheelchair sport within a few months of injury.

The review of literature by Crocker (1993), unlike others, does not directly address self-esteem. By examining theories of stress and emotion, attribution, and planned behavior, Crocker promotes critical thinking about variables that should be studied in conjunction with self-concept. Future research on self-esteem and domain-specific components needs to build on theory. Thus far, existing research on wheelchair athletes tends to be atheoretical and simplistic. Studies continue to show that positive self-esteem is related to wheelchair sport participation and elite or international athletic status (Campbell and Jones 1994), but contributing variables and underlying mechanisms are not posited or analyzed. Perhaps one way forward, given difficulties of access and measurement with some disability groups, is qualitative research. For example, no literature review has recognized the excellent qualitative study of Patrick and Bignall (1984), who describe how marathon wheelchair racers reconstruct their identities by developing competence in a sport that can be shared with able-bodied runners. One of the greatest rewards, they posit, is increased sense of control, which in turn provides the impetus for the process of becoming. The recent work of Wuerch and Sherrill (1996) on empowerment of women wheelchair road racers offers insight into relationships between self-efficacy, self-esteem, and self-determination.

SELF-REGARD/SELF-ACCEPTANCE DILEMMA

The extensive work of Sherrill and colleagues on self-regard and self-acceptance as dimensions of self-actualization has been largely overlooked because reviewers, presumably for the sake of brevity, report only total self-actualization scores rather than subscale and profile data. Self-actualization, as measured by the Personal Orientation Inventory (POI) of Shostrom (1966), is defined as "becoming the best one can be." It is a multidimensional construct that requires two major scales (time competence and inner directedness) and 10 subscales for full description. Subscales like self-regard and self-acceptance can, however, be examined separately; these provide valuable data, and both are relevant to self-esteem. Validity and reliability studies that have been conducted on the POI are reviewed by Sherrill (1990).

Over a five-year period Sherrill and colleagues administered the POI to 155 male and 101 female elite athletes with disabilities (CP, n = 133; visual impairments, n = 52; spinal paralysis/amputation wheelchair conditions, n = 71). Studies of six different samples of elite athletes with disabilities (males and females with CP, visual impairments, and non-CP wheelchair conditions) indicated that all groups except females with CP and males with visual impairments scored significantly higher than profile manual norms on self-regard (Sherrill 1990; Sherrill, Gench, Hinson, Gilstrap, Richir, and Mastro 1990; Sherrill and Rainbolt 1988; Sherrill, Silliman, Gench, and Hinson 1990). Self-regard, measured by 16 items, was defined as affirmation of self because of worth or strength.

In contrast, all groups of athletes except females in wheelchairs scored significantly lower than profile manual norms on self-acceptance, measured by 26 items and defined as affirmation of self in spite of weaknesses or deficiencies. Moreover, visual inspection of self-actualization profiles, based on 12 subscales, revealed that self-acceptance was weaker than any other dimension. This split in feelings toward self is also manifested by some able-bodied male athletes and may be an essential difference between athletes and the general population on which able-body norms are based.

Data for these studies were collected during international sports competitions, and it seems likely that athletic selves were more salient than other dimensions when inventories were completed. Follow-up interviews supported the ambiguity revealed in the hard data. Elite athletes with disabilities felt good about their accomplishments. They seemed unforgiving toward selves (as well as others), however, as they described goals that were not achieved (e.g., a personal best or a first-place medal).

The importance of examining separate dimensions of self-actualization, as for self-esteem, was reinforced by the fact that when all athletes (regardless of disability) were compared with profile manual able-body norms on total self-actualization scores, there were no significant differences. Neither were there gender differences. This once again indicates a need for methods and instrumentation capable of illustrating different elements of change. These early data suggest that differential and temporal effects of self-regard and self-acceptance may provide important insight into the way athletes with disabilities process critical events in their lives. Other researchers have emphasized the importance of exploring sources of self-deprecation as well as self-enhancement (Schwalbe and Staples 1991).

PERCEIVED COMPETENCE THEORY AND SPORT

Researchers have recently applied Harter's perceived competence theory (1978, 1982, 1988) to children in Special Olympics (Gibbons and Bushakra 1989), adult Special Olympians in segregated and unified sport settings (Riggen and Ulrich 1993), physically awkward children (Cantell, Ahonen, and Smyth 1994; Dunn and Watkinson 1994), boys with LD (Podosek 1994), and adolescents with physical disabilities (King et al. 1993; Sherrill, Hinson, Gench, Kennedy, and Low 1990). An age-appropriate multidimensional self-perception profile served as the data collection instrument in each of these studies (Harter 1982, 1988; Harter and Pike 1984; Renick and Harter 1988). Research purposes have varied widely and have produced mixed results that include evidence of benefits for perceived social acceptance and physical competence in sport competition, but also lower profile scores than for able-bodied equivalents.

Research guided by perceived competence theory thus far seems to be similar to studies of global self-esteem, although it provides additional information as domain-specific as well as global measures are being used. However, little new information has been generated about underlying mechanisms. What is needed is attention to Harter's overall competence motivation theory (Harter 1978), which included such components as (a) domain-specific mastery attempts, (b) success and failure outcomes of mastery attempts, (c) the construct of optimal challenge, (d) influence by significant others, (e) intrinsic/extrinsic motivation orientation, (f) perceived competence, (g) perceived control, and (h) affective outcomes such as enjoyment and anxiety. Perceived competence remains a very small part of disability, identity, and involvement in sport and exercise. Alternative models or theories are needed also that explore disability differences in principles of self-esteem formation (i.e., reflected appraisal, social comparison, self-attribution, psychological centrality, and mastery challenge). Certainly, recent developments such as achievement goal and intrinsic motivation and self-determination theories described in earlier chapters in this book (see Biddle, chapter 3; Corbin and Whitehead, chapter 7) hold promise and await application with populations with disabilities.

In addition to further validation of the Harter scales when used specifically for individuals with disabilities, other instruments merit attention. Flintoff (1994), for instance, administered the Physical Self-Perception Profile of Fox and Corbin (1989) to young athletes with CP. Like many coaches of international teams, Flintoff noted that the athlete identity is one of competence and responsiveness to challenge. Lintunen's (1987) Perceived Physical Competence Scale has been validated for use with adolescents with physical disabilities (Lintunen, Heikinaro-Johansson, and Sherrill 1995). Ulrich and Collier (1990) have developed a pictorial scale specifically for measuring perceived physical competence of young children with MR. Further use and development of scales such as these focusing on the physical self, through more precise documentation, offer a key to understanding some of the critical mechanisms underpinning self-esteem development in individuals with disabilities.

SUMMARY

The social construction of the disability identity occurs at macro (governmental, societal, cultural) and micro (individual interaction) levels and is strongly influenced by prejudice, discrimination, stigmatization, categorization, stereotyping, and ambivalence. Self-identity of individuals with disabilities may be shaped more by their minority status than by other social forces. Self-esteem is affected by age at onset of disability, the nature of the disability, gender, beliefs and practices of parents and significant others, and stable attitudinal hierarchies of disability preferences that characterize all segments of society.

Group data suggest that individuals with congenital and early childhood disabilities tend to have lower self-esteem than individuals with acquired disabilities. Clearly, individuals have a capacity to neutralize their disability or even turn it to advantage in terms of their overall self-regard. However, research design has to be more sensitive to the negative effect of grouping individuals with diverse disability etiologies. Furthermore, multidimensional assessments are required to provide a richer profile of the self-concept and to locate specific areas that characterize change.

In general, sport seems to offer positive opportunities for self-esteem development. However, the mechanisms for this remain unclear. The sport environment could be a particularly useful vehicle for examining the processes that constitute the social construction of disability identity. However, inquiry must extend beyond description and comparison and address causal relationships that have practical value for teachers and coaches. Theories and models such as self-actualization theory are required to guide research goals and the careful validation of data collection instruments and protocols for special groups. Of particular importance may be closer examination of the growth through adversity hypothesis and the relative meaning and salience of various self-esteem sources to individuals with disabilities in various sport contexts and life stages.

REFERENCES

Albrecht, G.L. 1976. Socialization and the disability process. In *The sociology of physical disability and rehabilitation*, ed. G.L. Albrecht, 3-38. Pittsburgh: University of Pittsburgh.

Alvarez, V., and Adelman, H.S. 1986. Overstatements of self-evaluations by students with psychoeducational problems. *Journal of Learning Disabilities* 19 (9): 567-71.

American Psychological Association. 1994. *Publication manual of the American Psychological Association*. 4th ed. Washington, DC: American Psychological Association.

Anderson, E.M., and Clarke, L. 1982. *Disability in adolescence*. London: Methuen.

Arnold, P., and Chapman, M. 1992. Self-esteem, aspirations, and expectations of adolescents with physical disability. *Developmental Medicine and Child Neurology* 34 (2): 97-102.

Atha, B. 1994. Issues in classification in sport for the mentally handicapped. In *Vista '93—the outlook*, ed. R.D. Steadman, E.R. Nelson, and G.D. Wheeler, 304-9. Alberta, AB: Rick Hausen Center.

Barton, L. 1993. Disability, empowerment, and physical education. In *Equality, education, and physical education*, ed. J. Evans, 43-54. Lewes, England: Falmer.

Benson, E., and Jones, G. 1992. Psychological implications of physical activity in individuals with physical disabilities. In *Sport and physical activity: Moving towards excellence*, ed. T. Williams, L. Almond, and A. Sparkes, 278-83. London: Spon.

Bickenbach, J.E. 1993. *Physical disability and social policy*. Toronto, ON: University of Toronto.

Blacher, J., ed. 1984. *Severely handicapped young children and their families*. New York: Academic Press.

Bowe, F. 1990. Employment and people with disabilities: Challenges for the nineties. *Office of Special Education and Rehabilitation Services News in Print* 3 (3): 2-6.

Brame, D.L. 1994. *Organized sport involvement of boys with learning disabilities*. Master's thesis, Texas Woman's University, Denton.

Brown, M., and Gordon, W.A. 1987. Impact of impairment on activity patterns of children. *Archives of Physical Medicine and Rehabilitation* 68: 828-32.

Bryan, T.H. 1986. Self-concept and attributions of the learning disabled. *Learning Disabilities Focus* 1 (2): 82-89.

Campbell, E., and Jones, G. 1994. Psychological well-being in wheelchair sport participants and nonparticipants. *Adapted Physical Activity Quarterly* 11: 404-15.

Campbell, M. 1977. Psychological adjustment of adolescents with myelodysplasia. *Journal of Youth and Adolescence* 6 (4): 397-407.

Cantell, M.H., Ahonen, T.P., and Smyth, M.M. 1994. Clumsiness in adolescence: Educational, motor, and social outcomes of motor delay detected at 5 years. *Adapted Physical Activity Quarterly* 11: 115-29.

Chapman, J.W. 1988. Learning disabled children's self-concept. *Review of Educational Research* 58 (3): 347-71.

Combs, R.H., and Harper, J.L. 1967. Effects of labels on attitudes of educators toward handicapped children. *Exceptional Children* 33: 399-403.

Craft, D.H., and Hogan, P.I. 1985. Development of self-concept and self-efficacy: Considerations for mainstreaming. *Adapted Physical Activity Quarterly* 2: 320-27.

Crocker, J., and Major, B. 1989. Social stigma and self-esteem: The self-protective properties of stigma. *Psychological Review* 96: 608-30.

Crocker, P.R.E. 1993. Sport and exercise psychology and research with individuals with physical disabilities: Using theory to advance knowledge. *Adapted Physical Activity Quarterly* 10: 324-35.

DePauw, K.P., and Goc Karp, G. 1990. Attitudes of selected college students toward including disabled individuals in integrated settings. In *Adapted physical activity: An interdisciplinary approach*, ed. G. Doll-Tepper, C. Dahms, B. Doll, and H. von Selzam, 149-57. Berlin: Springer-Verlag.

Downs, P., and Williams, T. 1994. Student attitudes toward integration of people with disabilities in activity settings: A European comparison. *Adapted Physical Activity Quarterly* 11 (1): 32-43.

Dunn, J.L., and Watkinson, J. 1994. A study of the relationship between physical awkwardness and children's perceptions of physical competence. *Adapted Physical Activity Quarterly* 11: 275-83.

Dunn, L.M. 1968. Special education for the mildly retarded—is much of it justifiable? *Exceptional Children* 35: 5-22.

Edgerton, R.B. 1967. *The cloak of competence: Stigma in the lives of the mentally retarded*. Berkeley: University of California.

Eisenberg, M.G., Griggins, C., and Duval, R.J., eds. 1982. *Disabled people as second-class citizens*. New York: Springer.

Fewell, R.R., and Vadasy, P.F., eds. 1986. *Families of handicapped children*. Austin, TX: Pro-Ed.

Fichten, C.S. 1988. Students with physical disabilities in higher education: Attitudes and beliefs that affect integration. In *Attitudes toward persons with disabilities*, ed. H.E. Yuker, 171-86. New York: Springer.

Fitts, W.H. 1972. *The self-concept and psychopathology*. Nashville: Counselor Recordings and Tests.

Flintoff, M. 1994. *An investigation into the relationship between the self-esteem and sport of persons with cerebral palsy.* Master's thesis, University College, Dublin, Ireland.

Fox, K.R., and Corbin, C.B. 1989. The Physical Self-Perception Profile: Development and preliminary validation. *Journal of Sport and Exercise Psychology* 11: 408-30.

Gibbons, S.L., and Bushakra, F.B. 1989. Effects of Special Olympics participation on the perceived competence and social acceptance of mentally retarded children. *Adapted Physical Activity Quarterly* 6: 40-51.

Gliedman, J., and Roth, W. 1980. *The unexpected minority: Handicapped children in America.* New York: Harcourt Brace Jovanovich.

Goffman, E. 1963. *Stigma: Notes on the management of a spoiled identity.* Englewood Cliffs, NJ: Prentice Hall.

Gorlow, G., Butler, A., and Guthrie, L. 1963. Correlates of self-attitudes of retardates. *American Journal of Mental Deficiency* 67: 549-55.

Green, B.C., Pratt, C.C., and Grigsby, T.E. 1984. Self-concept among persons with long-term spinal cord injury. *Archives of Physical Medicine and Rehabilitation* 65: 751-54.

Greenwood, C.M., Dzewaltowski, D.A., and French, R. 1990. Self-efficacy and psychological well-being of wheelchair tennis participants and wheelchair nontennis participants. *Adapted Physical Activity Quarterly* 7: 12-21.

Guthrie, G., Butler, A., and Gorlow, L. 1961. Patterns of self-attitudes of retardates. *American Journal of Mental Deficiency* 66: 222-29.

Guttmann, L. 1976. *Textbook of sport for the disabled.* Aylesbury, Bucks, England: HM & M.

Harter, S. 1978. Effectance motivation reconsidered. *Human Development* 21: 34-64.

—. 1982. The Perceived Competence Scale for Children. *Child Development* 53: 87-97.

—. 1988. *Manual for the Self-Perception Profile for Adolescents.* Denver: University of Denver.

Harter, S., and Pike, R. 1984. The Pictorial Perceived Competence Scale for Young Children. *Child Development* 55: 1969-82.

Hedrick, B. 1984. The effect of wheelchair tennis participation and mainstreaming upon the perceptions of competence of physically disabled adolescents. PhD diss. University of Illinois, Urbana-Champaign. Abstract in *Dissertation Abstracts International* 45: 299A (University Microfilms no. 8409778).

Hobbs, N. 1975. *The future of children: Categories, labels, and their consequences.* San Francisco: Jossey-Bass.

Hopper, C. 1986. Socialization of wheelchair athletes. In *Sport and disabled athletes,* ed. C. Sherrill, 197-202. Champaign, IL: Human Kinetics.

Horne, M. 1985. *Attitudes toward handicapped students: Professional, peer, and parent reactions.* Hillsdale, NJ: Erlbaum.

Hutzler, Y., and Bar-Eli, M. 1993. Psychological benefits of sports for disabled people: A review. *Scandinavian Journal of Medical Science and Sports* 3: 217-28.

Jenkins, J., Speltz, M., and Odom, S. 1985. Integrating normal and handicapped preschoolers: Effects on child development and social interaction. *Exceptional Children* 52 (1): 7-17.

Kallen, E. 1989. *Label me human: Minority rights of stigmatized Canadians.* Toronto, ON: University of Toronto.

Katz, I. 1981. *Stigma: A social psychological analysis.* Hillsdale, NJ: Erlbaum.

Katz, I., Haas, R.G., and Bailey, J. 1988. Attitudinal ambivalence and behavior toward people with disabilities. In *Attitudes toward persons with disabilities*, ed. H.E. Yuker, 47-57. New York: Springer.

Kennedy, M.J. 1980. *Sport role socialization and attitudes toward physical activity of wheelchair athletes*. Master's thesis, University of Oregon, Eugene.

King, G.A., Shultz, I.Z., Steel, K., and Gilpin, M. 1993. Self-evaluation and self-concept of adolescents with physical disabilities. *American Journal of Occupational Therapy* 47 (2): 132-40.

Klein, T., Gilman, E., and Zigler, E. 1993. Special Olympics: An evaluation by professionals and parents. *Mental Retardation* 31 (1): 15-23.

Lawrence, E.A., and Winschel, J.F. 1973. Self-concept and the retarded: Research and issues. *Exceptional Children* 39: 310-18.

Lazarus, R.S., and Folkman, S. 1984. *Stress, appraisal, and coping*. New York: Springer.

Lillie, T. 1993. A harder thing than triumph: Roles of fathers of children with disabilities. *Mental Retardation* 31 (6): 438-43.

Lintunen, T. 1987. Perceived physical competence scale for children. *Scandinavian Journal of Sports Sciences* 9: 57-64.

Lintunen, T., Heikinaro-Johansson, P., and Sherrill, C. 1995. Use of the perceived physical competence scale for adolescents with disabilities. *Perceptual and Motor Skills* 80: 571-77.

Magill, J., and Hurlbut, N. 1986. The self-esteem of adolescents with cerebral palsy. *American Journal of Occupational Therapy* 40 (6): 402-7.

Marsh, H.W., and Barnes, J. 1982. *Self-Description Questionnaire II*. Sydney: University of Western Sydney.

Martino, S., deGuili, C., Paciucci, P., and Crupi, L. 1987. Reazione alla frustrazione ed autostima in soggetti portatori di handicap practicanti sport. *Movimento* 3 (1): 5-8.

Maslow, A. 1954. *Motivation and personality*. New York: Harper & Row.

Mastro, J.V., Burton, A.W., Rosendahl, M., and Sherrill, C. 1996. Attitudes of elite athletes with impairments toward one another: A hierarchy of preference. *Adapted Physical Activity Quarterly* 13 (2): 197-210.

McDavid, J.W., and Harari, H. 1966. Stereotyping of names and popularity in grade-school children. *Child Development* 37: 453-59.

Nelson, M., and Gruver, G.G. 1978. Self-esteem and body image concept in paraplegics. *Rehabilitation Counseling Bulletin* 22 (2): 108-13.

Patrick, D.R., and Bignall, J.E. 1984. Creating the competent self: The case of the wheelchair runner. In *The existential self in society*, ed. J.A. Kotarba and A. Fontana, 207-21. Chicago: University of Chicago Press.

Patrick, G.D. 1986. The effects of wheelchair competition and acceptance of disability in novice athletes. *Therapeutic Recreation Journal* 20: 61-71.

Piers, E.V. 1984. *Piers-Harris Children's Self-Concept Scale test manual*. Rev. ed. Los Angeles: Western Psychological Services.

Piers, E.V., and Harris, D.B. 1964. Age and other correlates of self-concept in children. *Journal of Educational Psychology* 55 (2): 91-95.

Podosek, H.A. 1994. *Predictors of active sport interest in boys with learning disabilities*. Master's thesis, Texas Woman's University, Denton.

Prout, H., Marcal, S.D., and Marcal, D.C. 1992. A meta-analysis of self-reported personality characteristics of children and adolescents with learning disabilities. *Journal of Psychoeducational Assessment* 10 (1): 59-64.

Renick, M.J., and Harter, S. 1988. *Manual for the Self-Perception Profile for Learning Disabled Students.* Denver: University of Denver.

Riggen, K., and Ulrich, D. 1993. The effects of sport participation on individuals with mental retardation. *Adapted Physical Activity Quarterly* 10: 42-51.

Rizzo, T.L. 1984. Attitudes of physical educators toward teaching handicapped pupils. *Adapted Physical Activity Quarterly* 1: 267-74.

Rizzo, T.L., and Vispoel, W.P. 1991. Physical educators' attributes and attitudes toward teaching students with handicaps. *Adapted Physical Activity Quarterly* 8 (1): 4-11.

Rogers, C.R. 1951. *Client-centered therapy.* Boston: Houghton Mifflin.

Rosenberg, M., and Kaplan, H.B., eds. 1982. *Social psychology of the self-concept.* Arlington Heights, IL: Harlan Davidson.

Rosenberg, M., and Pearlin, L.I. 1982. Social class and self-esteem among children and adults. In *Social psychology of the self-concept,* ed. M. Rosenberg and H.B. Kaplan, 268-88. Arlington Heights, IL: Harlan Davidson.

Safilios-Rothschild, C. 1976. Disabled persons' self-definitions and their implications for rehabilitation. In *The sociology of physical disability and rehabilitation,* ed. G.L. Albrecht, 39-56. Pittsburgh: University of Pittsburgh.

Schmidt-Gotz, E., Doll-Tepper, G., and Lienert, C. 1994. Attitudes of university students and teachers towards integrating students with disabilities in regular physical education classes. *Physical Education Review* 17 (1): 45-57.

Schwalbe, M.L., and Staples, C.L. 1991. Gender differences in sources of self-esteem. *Social Psychology Quarterly* 54 (2): 158-68.

Seligman, M., ed. 1983. *The family with a handicapped child.* New York: Grune & Stratton.

Shapiro, J.P. 1993. *No pity: People with disabilities forging a new civil rights movement.* New York: Times Books/Random House.

Sherrill, C. 1986. Social and psychological dimensions of sports for disabled athletes. In *Sports and disabled athletes,* ed. C. Sherrill, 21-33. Champaign, IL: Human Kinetics.

—. 1990. Psychosocial status of disabled athletes. In *Problems in movement control,* ed. G. Reid, 339-64. New York: Elsevier.

—. 1993a. *Adapted physical activity, recreation, and sport: Crossdisciplinary and lifespan.* 4th ed. Dubuque, IA: Brown & Benchmark.

—. 1993b. Women with disabilities. In *Women in sport,* ed. G.L. Cohen, 238-48. Newbury Park, CA: Sage.

—. 1993c. Women with disability, Paralympics, and reasoned action contact theory. *Women in Sport and Physical Activity Journal* 2 (2): 51-60.

Sherrill, C., Gench, B., Hinson, M., Gilstrap, T., Richir, K., and Mastro, J. 1990. Self-actualization of elite blind athletes. *Journal of Visual Impairment and Blindness* 84 (2): 55-60.

Sherrill, C., Hinson, M., Gench, B., Kennedy, S.O., and Low, L. 1990. Self-concepts of disabled youth athletes. *Perceptual and Motor Skills* 70: 1093-98.

Sherrill, C., Paciorek, M., Davis, R., and Rich, S. 1993. Paralympics 1992: Excellence and challenge. *Palaestra* 9 (2): 25-42.

Sherrill, C., and Rainbolt, W. 1986. Sociological perspectives of cerebral palsy sports. *Palaestra* 2 (4): 20-26.

—. 1988. Self-actualization profiles of male able-bodied and cerebral palsied athletes. *Adapted Physical Activity Quarterly* 5 (2): 108-19.

Sherrill, C., Silliman, L., Gench, B., and Hinson, M. 1990. Self-actualization of elite wheelchair athletes. *Paraplegia* 28: 252-60.

Shontz, F.C. 1970. Physical disability and personality: Theory and recent research. *Psychological Aspects of Disability* 17 (2): 51-69.

Shostrom, E. 1966. *Manual for Personal Orientation Inventory*. San Diego: Educational and Industrial Testing Service.

Sigelman, C.I., Budd, E.C., Spanhel, C.L., and Schoenrock, C.J. 1981. When in doubt, say yes: Acquiescence in interviews with mentally retarded persons. *Mental Retardation* 19: 53-58.

Siller, J. 1984. Attitudes toward the physically disabled. In *Attitudes and attitude change in special education: Theory and practice*, ed. R.L. Jones, 184-205. Reston, VA: Council for Exceptional Children.

Silon, E., and Harter, S. 1985. Perceived competence, motivational orientation and anxiety in mainstreamed and self-contained educable mentally retarded children. *Journal of Educational Psychology* 77: 217-30.

Stewart, D.A. 1991. *Deaf sport: The impact of sports within the deaf community*. Washington, DC: Gallaudet University.

Super, J.T., and Block, J.R. 1992. Self-concept and need for achievement of men with physical disabilities. *Journal of General Psychology* 119 (1): 73-80.

Szyman, R.J. 1980. The effect of participation in wheelchair sports. PhD diss. University of Illinois, Urbana-Champaign. Abstract in *Dissertation Abstracts International* 41: 804A-805A (University Microfilms no. 8018209).

Trieschmann, R.B. 1988. *Spinal cord injuries: Psychological, social, and vocational rehabilitation*. 2nd ed. New York: Demos.

Ulrich, D.A., and Collier, D.H. 1990. Perceived physical competence in children with mental retardation: Modification of a pictorial scale. *Adapted Physical Activity Quarterly* 7: 338-54.

Valliant, P.M., Bezzubyk, I., Daley, L., and Asu, M.E. 1985. Psychological impact of sport on disabled athletes. *Psychological Reports* 56: 923-29.

Walton, W.E. 1937. The affective value of first names. *Journal of Applied Psychology* 21: 396-409.

Weinberg, N. 1978. Preschool children's perceptions of orthopedic disability. *Rehabilitation Counseling Bulletin* 21: 183-89.

—. 1988. Another perspective: Attitudes of people with disabilities. In *Attitudes toward persons with disabilities*, ed. H.E. Yuker, 141-53. New York: Springer.

Weiss, M., and Curtis, K.A. 1986. Controversies in medical classification of wheelchair athletes. In *Sport and disabled athletes*, ed. C. Sherrill, 93-100. Champaign, IL: Human Kinetics.

West, P.C. 1984. Social stigma and community recreation participation by the mentally and physically handicapped. *Therapeutic Recreation Journal* 18 (1): 40-49.

Widaman, K.F., MacMillan, D.L., Hemsley, R.E., Little, T.D., and Balow, I.H. 1992. Differences in adolescents' self-concept as a function of academic level, ethnicity, and gender. *American Journal on Mental Retardation* 96 (4): 387-404.

Williams, T. 1994a. Disability sport socialization and identity construction. *Adapted Physical Activity Quarterly* 11: 14-31.

—. 1994b. Sociological perspectives on sport and disability: Structural functionalism. *Physical Education Review* 17 (1): 14-24.

World Health Organization. 1980. *International classification of impairments, disabilities, and handicaps: A manual of classification relating to the consequences of disease.* Geneva: World Health Organization.

Wright, B.A. 1960. *Physical disability—A psychological approach.* New York: Harper & Row.

—. 1983. *Physical disability—A psychosocial approach.* 2d ed. Philadelphia: Harper & Row.

—. 1988. Attitudes and the fundamental negative bias: Conditions and corrections. In *Attitudes toward persons with disabilities,* ed. H.E. Yuker, 3-21. New York: Springer.

Wright, J., and Cowden, J. 1986. Changes in self-concept and cardiovascular endurance of mentally retarded youth in a Special Olympics swimming program. *Adapted Physical Activity Quarterly* 3: 177-83.

Wuerch, G., and Sherrill, C. 1996. Sport as empowerment: Perspectives of women wheelchair road racers. Unpublished thesis, Texas Woman's University, Denton.

Wyeth, D.O. 1989. Breaking barriers and changing attitudes. *Journal of Osteopathic Sports Medicine* 3: 5-10.

Yuker, H., ed. 1988. *Attitudes toward persons with disabilities.* New York: Springer.

Zigler, E., and Hodapp, R. 1986. *Understanding mental retardation.* Cambridge: Cambridge University Press.

Zoerink, D.A. 1992. Exploring sport socialization environments of persons with orthopedic disabilities. *Palaestra* 8 (3): 38-44.

THE THERAPEUTIC EFFECTS OF EXERCISE ON THE SELF

NANETTE MUTRIE

Exercise (that is, planned and structured physical activity, often supervised) has been promoted in several forms of medical treatment for some time (Bouchard et al. 1990). Researchers have focused mostly on the physiological impact of exercise, and less attention has been paid to the psychological outcomes of exercise or the factors that determine the initiation and adherence of people to programs of exercise. These latter two issues define the major areas of exercise psychology. Rejeski and Thompson (1993) have recently provided an excellent historical review of the discipline. They suggest that the lack of attention to psychological in comparison to physiological issues has in part been due to the dominance of the biomedical model and the reluctance of the medical community to discard the philosophy that mind and body are separate. However, in the view of Rejeski and Thompson, the situation is changing. They state, "The mind-body distinction has slowly, but noticeably yielded to the concept of biopsychosocial interactions—the position that the body, the mind, and the social context of human existence are reciprocally interdependent on one another" (7). This change in philosophy should open the door for exercise psychologists to become more involved in treatments, since an important theme in all settings is increasing feelings of physical and global self-worth. Rejeski and Thompson suggest, "There is ample evidence that physical abilities and physical conception of the self play an integral role in mental health" (7).

While evidence establishing the connection between exercise and mental health is increasing, there is still no clear consensus about the mechanisms for these positive effects. Biologically based explanations such as the endorphin hypothesis, the relaxation effect on muscle tension, or increased body temperature compete with psychological explanations such as improved physical self-perceptions, distraction from stressful stimuli, or positive social experiences (Biddle and Mutrie 1991; chapter 8; Plante 1993).

What is particularly interesting is the apparent independence of physiological and psychological changes caused by exercise (Martinsen, Hoffart, and Solberg 1989a, 1989b; Mutrie and Choi 1993; Plante 1993). It could well be that exercisers are sensitive to small biological changes that are not identified through standard assessments such as maximum oxygen uptake. This would make psychological and physiological change appear independent when in reality the relationship is hidden by the inadequacy of the measurement techniques. In addition, given the extent of physiological change brought about by exercise, it is probably wrong to assume that one and only one mechanism (e.g., endorphin production) will explain psychological change (e.g., improved mood). Cacioppo and Tassinary (1990) discuss the limitations of inferring psychological significance from physiological signals and offer a conceptual framework that could be used by researchers seeking to explain the relationship between physiological and psychological change with exercise. A further complicating factor in determining the mechanisms underlying psychological benefits from exercise is the potential effect of confounding by expectations of improved function. For example, arthritic patients who exercise may develop sufficient physical confidence to attempt tasks that normally they would not consider. The result is better exercise performance and greater participation even though there has been little if any physiological change in the standard measures of fitness.

A realistic perspective would suggest that biological and psychological explanations combine to explain how exercise involvement is linked to mental health. It is likely that in some situations, psychological mechanisms are directly responsible for generating a sense of mental well-being. At other times, psychological variables are likely to act as critical mediating filters through which physiological change is mentally processed.

A further aspect of exercise psychology relevant to therapeutic settings is the identification of psychosocial factors responsible for the initiation and maintenance of an exercise program that might be prescribed as part of a treatment. Much of the knowledge regarding adherence to exercise therapy has stemmed from the work carried out in cardiac rehabilitation (Rejeski and Thompson 1993). However, in many other treatment settings, such as for diabetes or osteoporosis, where exercise has been suggested as beneficial, there has been little or no research on the motivations for and barriers to exercise. The physical self-perceptions and confidence of patients with limited physical capacity may provide critical insight into levels of initial motivation and continued adherence to the exercise program.

Exercise has been shown to produce positive and significant short- and long-term functional changes in the body that can be highly beneficial in a range of treatments. However, it is clear that dealing with an illness, coping with rehabilitation from a life-threatening condition or an addiction, or managing life events such as aging or reproduction can pose a formidable motivational and emotional challenge. Recently, greater interest has been paid to the issue of quality of life as the primary outcome of any treatment (see Kaplan 1994). Although life quality is partly determined by functional status, it is ultimately experienced as feelings of self-worth and mental well-being. This chapter will deal with research findings concerning the role of exercise as a means of improving life quality in individuals in a range of treatment settings. Specific attention will be paid to the relationship between exercise-related self-perceptions as a motivational influence, as a means of coping with psychological stress, as treatment outcome, and as a mediating variable in the quality of life equation.

MENTAL ILLNESS

Over a decade ago, the U.S. National Institute of Mental Health sponsored a workshop that involved 15 of the best-known researchers in the field of exercise psychology. The aim of the two-day workshop was to reach agreement on what was then known about the relationship between exercise and mental health. After full discussion, this group provided consensus statements aimed at psychologists, physical educators, physicians, and exercise leaders concerned about how exercise might prevent the onset of mental health problems and also about how it might help restore mental health once problems had emerged. The consensus statements were published in 1987 (Morgan and Goldston) and endorsed by the International Society of Sport Psychology (1992).

More recently, meta-analytic studies of the use of exercise as a treatment for anxiety and depression have provided further substantial evidence for the positive effects of exercise (McDonald and Hodgdon 1991; North, McCullagh, and Vu Tran 1990; Petruzzello et al. 1991). The consensus statements of Morgan and Goldston (1987) were based on the findings of no more than 15 research projects, whereas these meta-analytic studies have often involved more than 100 separate studies. Thus, the confirmation of the consensus statements by meta-analysis provides compelling evidence of the role of exercise in reducing anxiety and depression. For example, in a review of the effect sizes established by the various meta-analyses, Mutrie and Biddle (1995) noted that studies examining the use of exercise as a treatment for depression resulted in an effect size of 0.53 to 0.55.

It would therefore appear that there is considerable acceptance of the view that exercise can positively influence mental illness. There is also agreement that the underlying mechanisms relating to the positive effects of exercise on mental illness are not yet known (Biddle and Mutrie 1991; Morgan and Goldston 1987; Plante 1993). It is not the aim of this chapter to provide an overview of the causes and symptoms of mental illness, but it is clear that how people feel about themselves is a critical dimension of prevention of mental illness and the restoration of mental health. For example, one theory of depression suggests that the illness is a result of a feeling of helplessness that is learned over a period of time and from a variety of situations and that causes the person to have an external locus of control (Abramson, Seligman, and Teasdale 1978; Seligman 1975). It has been suggested that exercise can play a role in helping the person who is suffering in this way to gain control in one area of life, namely, the physical self. In addition, if exercise is programmed correctly, the sense of achievement and progression from week to week builds on this sense of control and may provide a sense of mastery (Greist et al. 1981). Self-esteem has therefore featured as a potential explanation of how exercise can alleviate depression (Ossip-Klein et al. 1989).

There is a potential role for exercise in the treatment of other mental illness such as schizophrenia (Chamove 1988) and agoraphobia (Orwin 1981), but the reports tend to be preexperimental. In reviewing the very limited evidence for the use of exercise in the treatment of psychoses such as schizophrenia, Plante (1993) concluded, "The current research results suggest that exercise may assist these patients with mood and self-esteem factors much more than with thought disturbances associated with psychotic symptomatology" (367). Again, the critical importance of self-perceptions and the potential for exercise to positively influence elements of the self is highlighted for this patient group.

Other theories of mental illness are more biologically based, such as that of insufficient levels of certain neurotransmitters (e.g., endorphins, serotonin, or noradrenaline). Exercise is known to increase the circulating levels of these neurotransmitters, and it has therefore been hypothesized as a mechanism for improving mental health (Morgan 1985). The technology for accurately measuring these neurotransmitters is now more accessible, and a causal rather than speculative link may soon be demonstrated. However, as far as the person is concerned, the critical issue is how he or she feels. Whether the mechanisms underlying the effect are biological, psychological, or both, the way they are manifested through the self-system is important. I would therefore speculate that the way forward in this area is to use hierarchical models of self-concept to explore how exercise may influence the self and thus impact upon life adjustment and quality. The flourishing research described throughout this book, such as that incorporating the EXSEM model of Sonstroem (see chapter 1) and the improvements in instrumentation to assess psychological change (see chapter 2), can only work to enhance our understanding of these relationships and mechanisms.

In conclusion, it appears that the link between exercise and mental health has been well established, although whether this relationship is associative or causative is still not known. For practitioners in the field, this should provide support for including exercise programs as part of treatment packages, especially in institutional settings where activity levels tend to be very low. The evidence should also add further strength to the arguments presented by health promoters for the prevention of diseases (including mental illness) through increasing the percentage of the general population engaged in regular physical activity. However, further randomized controlled trials are necessary, and estimates of cost-effectiveness of exercise interventions are also required before the case for exercise as a treatment is fully established.

REHABILITATION

In this section, the role of exercise in the process of rehabilitation from acute medical conditions or health-threatening behavior will be reviewed. Particular attention will be paid to the psychological outcomes associated with exercise programs and to strategies related to enhanced initiation and maintenance of exercise patterns.

CARDIAC REHABILITATION

Exercise-based cardiac rehabilitation programs are in widespread use in the United States (Naughton 1985), but their introduction has been relatively slow in the United Kingdom (Gloag 1985). This is in spite of the greater percentage of the U.K. population who will suffer a myocardial infarction (MI) (Tunstall-Pedoe, Smith, and Crombie 1986). The reasons for this caution in the United Kingdom are unclear. The primary factor may be as simple as difficulty in finding the extra cost of mounting these programs within an already stretched National Health Service budget. Also, the early evidence regarding the effect of exercise in reducing subsequent mortality in MI patients was equivocal (Kallio and Hamalainen 1979; Naughton 1985), and this may have subdued the enthusiasm of medical consultants. More recently, Oldridge et al. (1988) conducted a meta-analysis and concluded that MI patients participating in a cardiac rehabilitation program that included exercise had a 25% reduction in mortality compared to controls.

Given the need to improve the efficiency of the cardiovascular system, it is not surprising to note that most research on the effect of exercise during cardiac rehabilitation has focused on physiological and cardiovascular parameters (Dugmore 1992). However, largely anecdotal observations of psychological gain (Carson et al. 1982; Johnstone 1985) have triggered more rigorous study of the psychosocial benefits, although Langosch (1988) has questioned the reliability of the few studies in this area. Three examples will be given.

1. Roviaro, Holmes, and Holmsten (1984) randomly assigned cardiac patients to either a supervised exercise program that was conducted three times per week ($n = 27$) or a routine care program that included exercise advice but no supervised sessions ($n = 19$). After three months of supervised training and at a follow-up four months later, the patients in the exercise-based rehabilitation had improved more than those in routine care on measures of cardiovascular functioning. They also reported more positive self-perceptions and psychosocial functioning, including reduced employment-related stress, more frequent sexual activity, and increased household activities. However, when these patients were followed up six years later (Holmes 1993), the initial advantages experienced by the exercise-based groups had disappeared. The authors suggested that the explanation lay in the increased level of activity in the routine care group and the decreased level in the group who initially had engaged in supervised exercise. This raises the question of how exercise classes within a hospital setting might achieve the long-term goal of creating independent exercisers capable of sustaining their exercise patterns after the initial supervision.

2. In one of the few U.K. studies to evaluate the psychological effects of an exercise-based cardiac rehabilitation program, Newton, Mutrie, and McArthur (1991) randomly assigned 22 post-MI patients to either routine care or exercise-based rehabilitation. After 10 weeks of the programs, statistical tests revealed consistent interactions between groups and time on the Profile of Mood States and the Beck Depression Inventory (BDI). The exercise group improved in four of the six subscales of the Profile of Mood States, in total mood disturbance, and in BDI scores, while the routine care group remained the same or deteriorated. Although these changes were small and the BDI scores were not out of the normal range, the consistent pattern is suggestive of a beneficial effect of exercise. Surprisingly, there were no differences between the two groups on performance of a standard treadmill test. It was suggested that the social interaction experienced by the exercise group and the sense of being in control of their own recovery could be potential explanations for the results. However, this was not objectively measured.

3. A much more extensive U.K. study involved 176 patients randomly assigned to either a home-based rehabilitation program or a placebo information-only condition (Lewin et al. 1992). Psychological adjustment

was assessed at six weeks, six months, and one year post-MI. The home-based program in this study included exercise but was multifactorial and covered stress management as well as management of distressing thought patterns deemed to be common in MI patients. The authors reported that the patients assigned to the home-based program showed better psychological adjustment after one year and had less contact with their general practitioner and fewer admissions to the hospital in the first six months than the placebo group. It was also suggested that the home-based program, costing between £30 and £50 per patient, was very cost effective. Unfortunately, from the point of view of the exercise psychologist, no details of exercise adherence were provided and there was no attempt to determine which elements of the home-based program were effective. While the design of this study was elegant, it did not allow the individual effect of exercise to be assessed. Potentially, exercise alone could be even more cost effective. It is therefore suggested that future studies isolate the elements of multifactorial packages in order to determine the efficacy of each element. Alternatively, exercise could be added to a standard package to test for any extra effect. The latter design is perhaps easier to put in place both ethically (no patients are denied treatment help) and practically (exercise is added to existing programs). Clearly this is another fertile area of research for exercise psychologists interested in how self-perceptions are implicated in recovery from illness.

ALCOHOL REHABILITATION

The topic of appropriate treatment for alcohol abuse has received much discussion, with no one method showing distinct advantages (Heather, Robertson, and Davies 1985). Rehabilitation from an addictive behavior involves establishing self-control strategies and finding coping strategies for the emotions involved with withdrawal and continued abstinence (Marlatt and Gordon 1985). Self-esteem is often at a very low level as the problem drinker faces the need for treatment and realizes the physical and mental damage that alcohol may have caused (Beck, Weissman, and Kovacs 1976). It is intriguing to note that one of the earliest documented pieces of research in exercise psychology was in the area of alcohol rehabilitation (Cowles 1898). Cowles' conclusion offers a challenge to current researchers to provide experimental evidence of the declared benefits of exercise:

> The benefits accruing to the patients from the well-directed use of exercise and baths is indicated by the following observed symptoms: increase in weight, greater firmness of muscles, better colour of skin, larger lung capacity, more regular and stronger action of the heart, clearer action of the mind, brighter and more expressive eye, improved carriage, quicker responses of nerves, and through them of muscle and

limb to stimuli. All this has become so evident to them that only a very few are unwilling to attend the classes and many speak freely of the great benefits derived. (108)

Problem drinkers often have low levels of cardiorespiratory fitness and muscle strength, and appropriate programs of exercise have been shown to be effective in improving these physical parameters (Donaghy, Ralston, and Mutrie 1991; Tsukue and Shohoji 1981). Since regular exercise has been associated with decreased levels of depression and anxiety (as discussed earlier in this chapter) and with increased self-esteem (see chapters 1 and 2), which are commonly reported problems in alcohol rehabilitation, the use of exercise as part of the treatment for alcohol rehabilitation has been piloted in several locations (Donaghy, Ralston, and Mutrie 1991; Frankel and Murphy 1974; Gary and Guthrie 1972; Murphy, Pagano, and Marlatt 1986; Palmer, Vacc, and Epstein 1988; Sinyor et al. 1982). In these studies the exercise programs can be considered lifestyle interventions that provide the problem drinker with the skills to undertake a positive health-promoting behavior (exercise). Simultaneously this may provide self-control strategies, coping strategies, and a healthier behavior alternative to drinking (Marlatt and Gordon 1985; Murphy, Pagano, and Marlatt 1986). The limited available evidence supports the association of exercise, when undertaken as part of a treatment package, with lowered depression and anxiety, reduced alcohol consumption, and increased abstinence. These pilot studies suffer from small subject numbers, limited follow-up, and nonrandomized treatment groups (apart from those of Murphy, Pagano, and Marlatt [1986] and Donaghy, Ralston, and Mutrie [1991], in which randomized designs were used). However, there is enough evidence to warrant further research with larger numbers of subjects and better design to establish whether a cause-effect relationship exists between regular exercise (both during and after treatment), abstinence, and improved well-being. Such a study, with a target of 100 patients randomly assigned to an exercise or a placebo (stretching) program and follow-up six months after treatment, is currently in progress in Scotland (Donaghy, Mutrie, and Smith 1993).

DRUG REHABILITATION

Evidence of the effect of exercise in drug rehabilitation programs is even harder to find than for alcohol rehabilitation. Indeed, the only research in this area comes in the form of unpublished dissertations (Adamson 1991; Hyman 1987; Murdoch 1988). The problems facing the patient in drug rehabilitation are similar to those in alcohol rehabilitation, with high levels of anxiety and depression as well as low self-esteem often reported (Banks and Waller 1988). Thus it might be assumed that exercise could have similar potential for a therapeutic effect. One unique problem for drug rehabilitation is the variety of drugs used and their effects during both addiction and withdrawal. For example, Murdoch (1988) carried out an experimental study on 14 people who were attempting to withdraw from tranquilizers (benzodiazepines). Patients were randomly assigned to an eight-week program involving either group therapy or exercise combined with group therapy. The chaotic nature of the subjects' lives during withdrawal meant that very few actually completed the program. The problems subjects faced included agoraphobia brought on by the withdrawal and difficulty in keeping appointments for fitness testing and supervised exercise; the researchers had problems contacting subjects to help maintain adherence to appointments (some subjects not having a telephone, some changing residence frequently). Thus statistical tests were not viable.

In addition, drug misuse often involves the use of many drugs by the same person (Arif and Westermeyer 1988). It may be that this heterogeneity among patients makes the standard clinical trial untenable. Treatment programs by nature are often residential, subject numbers will be small, and there is likely to be a large variation in the dependent variables. This makes the achievement of statistically significant changes improbable. Qualitative methods may therefore provide the best way to gather information.

Adamson (1991) used qualitative methods to evaluate the feasibility of exercise as part of a treatment for drug misuse in four residential settings. Using extensive interviews with residents who were offered exercise programs over an eight-week period, it was established that 10 of the 13 residents who participated in the exercise program felt that the exercise had given them psychological benefits. These included improved mood, having a clearer mind, sleeping better, and filling gaps created by withdrawal. All 13 subjects thought that exercise could help them continue to abstain from drugs. In explaining this, one said, "It [exercise] makes you feel as if you have achieved something . . . done something for yourself." The residential staff were also interviewed and had very positive feedback about the exercise programs. One of them said, "It [exercise] affected them where they were at physically and mentally and helped to build up and increase their self-esteem." Adamson (1991) concluded that an exercise program was feasible in a residential setting but that well-controlled research studies would be difficult to conduct because of the circumstances created by withdrawal from drugs.

In conclusion, this area of research is ready to be explored further by exercise psychologists. The effect of exercise on the self-esteem of addicts is particularly worthy of attention since the literature suggests low self-esteem as a central issue in substance abuse (Banks and Waller 1988). However, it is also suggested that qualitative research methods be employed, as the subject population and the effects of withdrawal make experimental design, which relies on subject compliance over time, very difficult. In addition, further research on the use of exercise in overcoming an addiction to nicotine might assist in understanding how exercise can play a role in other addictions. Smoking cessation programs at least are dealing with the same drug, and the withdrawal effects are more standard, thus allowing experimental designs to establish cause-effect relationships. Marcus et al. (1991) have reported promising pilot work suggesting that exercise as part of a smoking cessation program can help maintain abstinence from nicotine. It could be speculated that smokers are aware that they damage their health with nicotine and therefore do not hold their physical selves in high esteem. Exercise may operate to show that they can take positive steps for their health and may subsequently provide a means of experiencing an increased sense of worth about their bodies and themselves. However, such hypotheses will remain speculative until well-designed studies are conducted.

CHRONIC MEDICAL CONDITIONS

For several chronic medical conditions, evidence of the physiological benefits of exercise has indicated that exercise could provide positive treatment effects (see Bouchard et al. 1990). It is not the purpose of this chapter to review the evidence for the efficacy of physical exercise in reducing morbidity and mortality resulting from these conditions. The focus is the issue perhaps more central to the patient, which is the ability to function effectively in everyday life. What will therefore be reviewed is the evidence for the role of exercise in increasing quality of life. In addition, attention will be paid to difficulties experienced by intending exercisers that may be associated with lack of confidence in their physical abilities or difficulties with the medical condition. Evidence to be discussed concerns how patients view exercise and how exercise may help them cope with the psychological stress of four common chronic conditions, namely, diabetes, arthritis, osteoporosis, and asthma. It should be noted that this is not an exhaustive list of conditions in which exercise could have a beneficial role; the four chosen can serve as exemplars for the psychological issues.

DIABETES

Individuals with either Type 1 (insulin-dependent diabetes mellitus) or Type 2 (non-insulin-dependent diabetes mellitus) diabetes are usually advised to exercise as part of the treatment along with modification of diet and monitoring of glucose levels (Gordon 1993c; Wing et al. 1986). However, there is an ongoing debate in the literature regarding the efficacy of exercise for these persons (Berger and Kemmer 1990; Vranic and Wasserman 1990).

The psychological effects of facing a lifetime of dealing with diabetes and the consequent emotional and social adjustments are very well documented by health psychologists, as is the need for patient education (Dunn 1993).

Given the wealth of literature on these psychological issues in diabetes and the standard recommendation that exercise should be part of treatment, it is astonishing to note that neither the psychological benefits of exercise for diabetics nor patient exercise education has been researched. Two articles based on anecdotal evidence discuss the psychological effects of exercise for diabetics and make suggestions about appropriate exercise prescriptions (Norstrom 1988; Vasterling, Sementilli, and Burish 1988), but literature searches suggest that no experimental work has been carried out in this area. However, the anecdotal reports suggest that exercise provides the diabetic with a sense of control and a reduction in stress, both of which enhance quality of life. It is possible that central to these reported benefits is a changing view of the physical self—from a physical self that is compromised by the need to monitor food intake and blood sugar levels to one that is coping with exercise and feeling improvements in physical condition. There is a clear need for researchers to establish the psychological benefits from exercise and the motivations and barriers to exercise perceived by this patient group.

ARTHRITIS

Sharratt and Sharratt (1994) present an excellent summary of the role of exercise in both rheumatoid arthritis (inflammation of membrane surrounding the joint) and osteoarthritis (degeneration of cartilage within the joint). It would seem that for these particular diseases there is a consensus that exercise can enhance the quality of life by maintaining range of movement and functional capacities connected with daily living. As with diabetes, the literature contains anecdotal mention of the psychological gain from exercise in coping with the stress of this chronic illness (Gordon 1993a), but it is difficult to find experimental studies that have addressed either the psychological outcomes of exercise or strategies to enhance initiation and maintenance of exercise for this population. The problems of maintenance are particularly difficult because pain is often associated with movement, and this of course will not reinforce continued activity. Very specific instructions are required to avoid overstressing the arthritic joints, and it may well be that special educational classes are required to introduce arthritic patients to exercise. Gordon (1993a) has written an excellent guide to exercise for those suffering from arthritis; it deals directly with the issue of pain and is essential reading for anyone constructing exercise opportunities for this patient group.

OSTEOPOROSIS

Osteoporosis is the medical term for a condition in which there is a decrease in absolute amount of bone that renders the skeleton susceptible to breakages and fractures. Osteoporosis can affect both sexes, as there is a gradual decline in bone density with age. However, the loss of bone mass accelerates for women when ovarian function decreases during and after menopause. Thus, postmenopausal women are more susceptible to osteoporosis than any other sector of the population (Kanis et al. 1990). In addition, osteoporosis sufferers often have to contend with pain, disability, depression, and decreased confidence in their physical abilities (Rickli and McManus 1990; Vaughn 1976).

Several reviews have suggested that physical activity can enhance bone density and therefore should be considered part of the treatment for osteoporosis (Gannon 1988; Marcus et al. 1992). Clinical trials suggest that appropriate, weight-bearing activity can enhance bone density by around 4%, which is the amount of improvement noted from drug therapies (Chow, Harrison, and Notarius 1987; Simkin, Ayalon, and Leichter 1987; Smith, Smith, and Gilligan 1990).

Kriska et al. (1986) have noted that adherence to exercise programs has been the major problem in most studies evaluating the effect of exercise on bone, but very few studies have directly addressed this problem. Very little is known about exercise behavior, including patients' motives and perceptions of barriers to exercise, the way patients view activity and the benefits it may provide, or what strategies the medical professions might adopt to increase adherence.

One study in the United Kingdom attempted to shed light on this issue and used a postal questionnaire to a local branch of the National Osteoporosis Society to establish current activity patterns and attitudes toward activity (Paton 1993). A response rate of 55% was achieved (74 out of 140), but no follow-up of nonrespondents was possible because the society required that responses be anonymous. Thus the results may not be representative of the larger group of osteoporotic patients. All the respondents had been diagnosed as osteoporotic for at least five years. Of this group 26% were sedentary, and of the 74% who reported that they were physically active, more than half were participating in three exercise bouts each week. The most popular activity was walking. The three most commonly mentioned motivations for exercise were "to feel better physically," "to prevent further osteoporosis," and "to feel better mentally." The three most commonly perceived barriers to exercise were "no facilities nearby," "no knowledge of how to exercise," and "not fit enough." It is interesting to note that only 24% of these respondents reported that they had been advised to begin exercise on diagnosis of the condition. Clearly, further studies on this population are required to enhance our understanding of motivations and barriers to exercise, but on the basis of these results it would seem that exercise is perceived to have benefits and that barriers could be overcome by education about exercise techniques and strategies. No literature examining the psychological benefits of exercise for this patient group could be found, but as with diabetes and arthritis it is reasonable to speculate that the self will be centrally implicated.

ASTHMA

As many as 10% of the world's population suffer from asthma with incidence increasing, particularly for children. In the United Kingdom, asthma is the most frequent medical reason which prevents children from attending school and for repeated visits to their general practitioner (Holgate 1993). Exercise for asthmatics is a double-edged sword. On the one hand it can improve overall functional capacity and reduce breathlessness, but on the other hand it can also induce an asthmatic attack (Belman 1989). Special advice on how and when to use medication in conjunction with exercise is usually required (Gordon 1993b).

Adherence to exercise programs for people with chronic obstructive pulmonary disorders (a term that includes asthma, chronic bronchitis, and emphysema; Higgins 1989) has certainly been studied (Atkins et al. 1984), and the results have enhanced knowledge on the effectiveness of various adherence strategies. The psychological outcomes from exercise have usually been implied rather than scientifically demonstrated. For example, Gordon (1993b) suggests, "Several studies have shown that chronic disease patients who exercise faithfully have less stress, anxiety, and depression; sleep better; and have enhanced self-esteem" (22). However, the reference used to support this claim (Sidney and Jerome 1990) does not specifically address patients with chronic obstructive pulmonary disease.

The conclusions that can be drawn from this selected review are consistent for people across a range of chronic conditions. The potential for exercise to have a significant impact on how patients cope with their illness is frequently stated, but there is little sound scientific evidence to back such statements up or to guide strategies for the initiation and maintenance of exercise for specific populations. There is enormous scope for exercise psychologists to contribute, either as researchers establishing sound information and explanations or as practitioners providing program advice. Coping with a chronic condition certainly presents a challenge, and the role of exercise in providing a sense of confidence in a medically compromised body, a sense of achievement in overcoming the difficulties of the condition, and a sense of control in one's life assuredly deserves further attention.

COPING WITH LIFE EVENTS

There may be several areas in the course of normal life in which exercise could have a positive influence on the physical self. Two examples of such areas, namely, events in women's lives and aging, will be briefly addressed here.

EVENTS IN WOMEN'S LIVES

Several reviews have suggested that exercise can have a particularly beneficial role for women in helping them cope with issues faced in their reproductive lives (Choi and Mutrie 1996; Gannon 1988; Mutrie and Choi 1993). There have been, for some time now, anecdotal indications that physical exercise is particularly beneficial for women (Berger 1984; Harris 1981).

Recent empirical evidence suggests that this is indeed the case. Four surveys, carried out in Canada and the United States, found level of physical activity to be positively associated with general well-being, lower levels of anxiety and depression, and more positive mood; and these associations were found to be particularly strong for women (Stephens 1988). Also, women in westernized societies tend to report lower self-esteem than men, are more critical of their bodies (see Davis, chapter 6), and are more likely to be prescribed medication for depression and anxiety. The potential for exercise to provide a sense of fulfillment, achievement, coping, and empowerment may therefore be greater than for men.

However, there is almost universal agreement that women take part in regular activity less than men. In the United Kingdom, for example, the Sports Council and Health Education Authority (1992) has shown that up to 91% of young women do not take sufficient exercise to obtain optimal health benefits. There is a massive task to be undertaken by physical education teachers and health promoters if this statistic is to be improved. It is interesting to speculate that exercise is often promoted for what may be (wrongly) seen as male health benefits (e.g., reduction in coronary risk factors) and that this might be one of the contributing factors explanatory of the discrepancy between levels of participation for men and women of all ages. However, it is likely that socialization processes and the cultural climate play an important role. It may be more appealing for women to hear about how exercise can benefit them during the uniquely female events in their lives. In the next section the psychological aspects of exercise as it relates to menstruation, pregnancy, and the menopause will be reviewed.

Menstruation

Exercise as a treatment for menstrual cycle symptomatology is not a new idea. It has been advocated in the lay literature for some time now (Cowart 1989), but such recommendations have lacked theoretical rationale and empirical support. Only two intervention studies have been carried out, one to assess the effects of exercise on dysmenorrhea (Israel, Sutton, and O'Brien 1985) and the other to assess the effects on premenstrual syndrome (Prior and Vigna 1987). Israel, Sutton, and O'Brien (1985) found that after a 12-week aerobic training program, the exercise group reported significantly less severe symptoms during menstruation than the no-exercise control group. In the second study, after a six-month running program, Prior and

Vigna (1987) reported a significant decrease in breast tenderness and fluid retention premenstrually for the previously sedentary exercising group but no change for the control group. The results of both these studies need to be treated with caution because of their small subject numbers, but the findings are suggestive of positive effects for exercise in alleviating premenstrual syndrome or dysmenorrhea. Unfortunately neither study measured psychological states.

Further data from cross-sectional studies indicate strong associations between physical exercise and positive psychological states during the menstrual cycle. Choi and Salmon (1995) prospectively monitored women who exercised at different levels for a whole month. The women, who had regular menstrual cycles, completed a specially devised mood adjective checklist every day. There were three groups: 33 high exercisers (those who regularly exercised more than three times a week), 36 low exercisers (those who regularly exercised less than three times a week), and 39 sedentary women. The results showed that positive mood and negative mood were related to cycle phase in all groups, and in addition that high exercisers experienced the most positive mood and the least negative mood throughout the cycle. In addition, a significant interaction showed that not only did the high exercisers feel better emotionally than the other two groups over the whole cycle, they also did not experience a decline in positive mood from midcycle to the premenstrual phase. A similar trend was seen in negative mood, although this only approached significance. Similar results did not emerge for the menstrual phase of the cycle, perhaps reflecting different mechanisms for the lowering of mood premenstrually and menstrually. For example, acute pain that is often present during menstruation, but not premenstrually, suggests one obvious way in which the sources of distress and discomfort may be different. Furthermore, it is not clear how self-perceptions influence either the reporting of menstrual discomfort or the role of exercise in alleviating discomfort. Cultural influences passed from mother to daughter may lead to the view for some women that menstruation is a time of incapacity; participation in exercise runs counter to this view and may therefore operate to influence feelings of strength and empowerment rather than incapacity. This viewpoint is reflected in the current advertising trend for sanitary products to be associated with women who lead physically active lives.

Choi and Salmon (1995) suggest that their findings indicate a possible protection from premenstrual deterioration in women who routinely engage in high levels of exercise. This is, of course, a very tentative suggestion because of the cross-sectional design of the study and also because it is unknown why the sedentary women were sedentary. It is conceivable that the high exercisers might have less severe premenstrual symptoms or perceive less incapacity during menstruation. Nonetheless, the study does support the notion that women who exercise have fewer premenstrual problems. Since almost all women menstruate and since it has been suggested that as many as 50% report discomfort and negative moods at some point in the menstrual cycle (Richardson 1990), this is an area in which exercise could play an important role. There is a clear need for further experimental research to follow up the promising results from the cross-sectional data.

Pregnancy

In comparison to the literature available on the physiological issues of exercise during pregnancy (Lokey et al. 1991), the literature on psychological issues is sparse. The transition to parenthood can be seen as a developmental crisis, and emotional and social changes take place during pregnancy. The pregnant woman may feel that she is perceived by others only as a "pregnancy" and that her own identity becomes submerged (Alder 1994). In addition, a woman's perception of her pregnancy may be influenced by both peer and cultural pressures. Strang and Sullivan (1985) reported that pregnancy resulted in negative changes in body image for many women. Wallace et al. (1986) conducted a cross-sectional study of pregnant women who participated in aerobic exercise and pregnant women who were sedentary and found that the exercising women had higher self-esteem scores and lower discomfort scores than the sedentary women. Hall and Kaufmann (1987) reported that pregnant women who had exercised during pregnancy retrospectively reported improved self-image, reduced tension, and decreased discomfort during the time of participation. Using a cross-sectional but prospective study, Slavin et al. (1988) found that exercise allowed women to feel more in control of their bodies and helped them maintain a positive self-image during pregnancy. These authors suggest that one of the most consistent benefits of exercise during pregnancy is psychological, because exercise allows women to feel control over their bodies at a time when many bodily changes occur that are biologically driven. In addition, postnatal depression may respond to exercise, since the effects of exercise on mild and moderate depression are well established (Martinsen 1989; North, McCullagh, and Vu Tran 1990). To date, however, no specific studies on the effects of exercise on postnatal depression have been carried out.

To summarize, moderate physical exercise may be psychologically beneficial to pregnant women, but there is clearly a need for randomized controlled trials on the psychological effects of exercise during pregnancy as well as on the psychological responses to labor before any firm conclusions can be drawn.

Menopause

The psychosocial challenges of the transitional years during which women gradually lose their reproductive function (medically termed the climacteric, but more commonly known as the menopause) include coming to terms with the end of reproductive years; changing roles in the family as children mature and leave home; potential increases in health problems of parents, self, and partner; and opportunities for dedicating more time to career, self-development, or both. Many women report that the climacteric is a positive time of change and an opportunity to experience more independence (Musgrave and Menell 1980). However, some women may experience a certain amount of physical and psychological distress during the climacteric. Vasomotor symptoms such as nocturnal sweating and hot flushes are the most commonly reported physical symptoms and are related to hormonal changes (Hunter, Battersby, and Whitehead 1986). There is also evidence of nonclinical psychological symptoms with loss of self-confidence, depression, and anxiety being the most frequently reported (Barlow et al. 1989; Hunter and Whitehead 1989). Greene (1980, 1988) has suggested that loss of self-esteem is the most general climacteric symptom with several factors contributing, such as low socioeconomic status, negative attitude toward the menopause and its consequences, limited social networks, poor marital relationships, and stressful life events.

As exercise has the potential to alleviate depression and anxiety and has been associated with positive moods and stress reduction, Gannon (1988) has noted that exercise might help women cope better with the climacteric. However, there is very little research to support this suggestion. Bachman et al. (1985) randomly assigned postmenopausal women to either an exercise group (n = 12) or a control group (n = 10) and noted improvements in fitness and psychological well-being, with no change in sexual vitality, after 13 weeks for the exercise group. Crammer, Neiman, and Lee (1991) obtained similar results from a 10-week exercise program for premenopausal women. In this study the women were randomly assigned to either a walking program or a sedentary control group. The exercise group showed improvements in cardiovascular function and psychological well-being but no change in percentage body fat after the 10-week program.

No other experimental studies on women during the climacteric years could be found in a search of the literature. A qualitative study by Harris, Rohaly, and Dailey (1993) examined why middle-aged, menopausal women exercise. From their qualitative analysis of interviews with their sample, they identified five primary motives for exercise:

1. *Personal power/control*—"I really like being in shape . . . there's a certain element of personal power that's involved in it"; "I feel fairly good about myself, and confident in the things that I can do."

2. *Reclaiming the body*—"When I look in the mirror, I want to see a fit body"; "Exercise has probably enabled me to look better in my clothes and feel better about myself."

3. *Well-being*—"It relieves me of a lot of tension"; "I think the main reward in exercising is just feeling good. I know how much better I feel when I exercise regularly."

4. *Enjoyment*—"I really love the walk"; "I enjoy having fun."

5. *Adjusting to the years*—"This is the way I want to grow old—active and thin"; "I guess I want to be independent. I want to feel stronger"; "[As I get older I want to] look the way I want to look and feel about myself the way I want to feel."

It is evident from the examples of responses that the high self-esteem and happiness and satisfaction of these women with the process of aging is being attributed to physical exercise.

Further evidence on the association between exercise and menopausal status is available from cross-sectional studies. In one such study of women attending a hospital clinic for menopausal symptoms, 38 of the women were interviewed as they waited for their appointment (Cox 1992). They also completed a questionnaire on exercise habits, the Climacteric Symptoms Scale (Greene 1991), and the Physical Self-Perception Profile (Fox and Corbin 1989). On the basis of their responses, the group were divided into those who were exercising for health or leisure purposes for at least 60 minutes per week ($n = 17$) and those who were sedentary ($n = 21$). The exercisers reported a higher estimation of their physical self-worth and physical condition than the nonexercisers ($p < .05$) and a trend to experience less anxiety than the nonexercisers ($p = .053$). These data suggest either that those women who exercise experience positive psychological advantages over nonexercisers, or that more positive psychological dispositions allow women to exercise. The next generation of research must disentangle the nature of cause and effect in this relationship. However, this was a clinical sample, and in view of the indications that reduction of self-esteem is the most general symptom of the climacteric, it is suggested that exercise could be used as an adjunctive and/or alternative treatment for this population of women.

Together the studies that have been surveyed in this section suggest that exercise may be a useful self-help and clinical treatment for menopausal symptoms and may be particularly important in promoting positive changes in body image and physical self-perceptions. Future experimental research must establish the effectiveness of such a treatment.

AGING

As we grow older there is a decline in our physical capacities. Research suggests that physical activity may have particular health benefits for older adults, but little is known about how self-perceptions may influence physical activity levels. This section addresses these issues.

Health Benefits of Exercise for Older Adults

The Allied Dunbar National Fitness Survey (Sports Council and Health Education Authority 1992) concludes, "The physiological evidence supports the view that with proper regular exercise the deterioration that occurs with increasing age beyond mid-forties can be marginalised" (131). For older people, physical abilities are central to everyday functioning. As people age, a gap tends to open up between potential and actual physical capacity. Younger people have sufficient resources to cope with the demands of everyday life. In contrast, the older person whose actual capacity might have declined, through a combination of aging and inactivity, may find the shortfall tips the balance between integration and isolation, independence and dependence. In addition to physical and functional gains, regular activity has been associated in older adults with positive psychological outcomes such as improved mood (McMurdo and Burnett 1992), self-esteem (Chase 1991), and cognitive functioning (Chodzko-Zajko 1991). However, Brown (1992), in reviewing the evidence for an association between physical activity, aging, and well-being, concluded that there are insufficient data from well-controlled studies at the present time to show that activity *causes* enhanced psychological well-being in this age group. The most important outcome of such physiological and psychological changes may well be an improvement in quality of life (Berger 1989).

Self-Perceptions, Initiation of Exercise, and Adherence to Exercise

A question that has not been fully answered is how to promote activity to a group of the population who may see sport and physical activity as socially unacceptable, who may fear that they will injure themselves, or who may be hesitant to try new activities (Belmont, Henderer, and Bennet 1990). There is evidence in Scotland of successful classes run for older adults with very high levels of adherence (83%) to an exercise prescription of three classes per week for 32 weeks (McMurdo 1992; McMurdo and Burnett 1992). To date there have been no analyses of the characteristics of the people attending such classes, although McMurdo and Burnett (1992) do acknowledge that the sample attracted to their research project were unlikely to be similar to the general population. In addition, there has been little evaluation of opportunities to exercise from home. Home-based programs have been shown to be successful in creating regular activity for U.S. citizens (King et al. 1991), and many older adults may not have the time, money, or inclination to attend class-based programs. In the United Kingdom, Mutrie et al. (1994) compared adherence rates over six months for participants aged over 55 in home-based and class-based exercise programs. At the six-month follow-up, 66% of the home-based and 71% of the class-based participants were exercising on average 60 minutes per week. It was concluded that home-based exercise programs could be a successful method of promoting increased activity in this age group. The physical self-perceptions of these subjects were monitored over time using an adaptation of the Physical Self Perception Profile for older adults (Chase 1991). The participants in the class-based groups had higher levels of physical self-worth than those attracted to the home-based program, although both groups increased their scores on this domain after six months of regular exercise (Mutrie and Davison 1994). These results have two implications. First, some people may not feel comfortable enough with their physical self to want to attend an exercise class. Home-based programs are a method of helping such people into activity. Second, exercise has the potential to favorably alter physical self-worth in older adults, although the causal relationship cannot be established from these data. This may be a critically important aspect of quality of life in older adults.

Other researchers (most notably McAuley) have proposed exercise self-efficacy as a possible determinant of adoption and maintenance of exercise for middle-aged and older adults. The links between self-efficacy and other elements of self-perceptions have been discussed in previous chapters (see Sonstroem, chapter 1, and Biddle, chapter 3). Exercise self-efficacy has been conceptualized as perceived physical ability (McAuley 1992), perceived ability to maintain exercise in the face of known barriers (McAuley 1992), and perceived ability to comply with the prescribed program (Duncan and McAuley 1993). Self-efficacy appears to represent an important interface between the individual and his or her behaviors. It is therefore critical that future research focus on techniques and strategies that are effective in the promotion of self-efficacy judgments.

CONCLUSIONS AND FUTURE DIRECTIONS

From this review it is clear that most of the populations who are either undergoing rehabilitation for a medical condition, coping with a chronic illness, dealing with reproductive events, or dealing with the processes of aging might benefit psychologically from involvement in regular programs of exercise. There are many other chronic conditions/illnesses not dealt with in this review, such as back pain, obesity, hypertension, cancer, and epilepsy, for which there is some support for the positive role of exercise in treatment. However, it is also clear that in most of the areas, further well-controlled research is required to establish whether or not the populations really can benefit psychologically. The best evidence lies in the area of the use of exercise for the treatment of clinical depression; here, both meta-analytic and narrative reviews provide favorable conclusions. In most other areas, the evidence is based on cross-sectional, descriptive reports, some of which are anecdotal. The role of exercise in positively enhancing self-perceptions and self-esteem seems particularly important to investigate because all these conditions provide a challenge to the patient's sense of physical self either through limited capacities or unfavorable body image. This may have a serious affect on global self-esteem. The potential for exercise as a medium for redefining the physical self for people suffering chronic conditions or experiencing difficult life events is evident. Finally, the underlying mechanisms involved in psychological change as a result of exercise need further exploration. There is sufficient evidence to warrant more serious consideration of the idea that self-perceptions play a mediating role in perceived psychological benefit and ultimately the quality of life.

A major issue in discussion of the effects of exercise on health is that of maintaining a pattern of activity over the life span. In some areas (e.g., cardiac rehabilitation) a great deal is known about adherence to exercise for these special populations, but in other areas (e.g., diabetes) there is no knowledge base. It may well be that adherence strategies will differ in relation to each population and the perception they might have about exercise. There is a need for replications of the kind of studies conducted by Martin et al. (1984), who investigated a variety of adherence strategies, on each of these patient populations. Furthermore, reporting adherence rates over the course of one year and the provision of detailed reasons for dropout (the procedure adopted by Chow, Harrison, and Notarius [1987] for osteoporotic patients) is to be commended and could serve as a model for other researchers.

Rejeski and Hobson (1994) point out that for some people, even when they know that exercise offers them potential health benefits the demands of becoming involved are perceived as stressful. Clearly, the study of situational self-perceptions such as confidence, self-efficacy, and physique anxiety (see Biddle, chapter 3) is particularly important in understanding patients who are physically compromised and perhaps more reluctant than others to approach exercise settings. A clearer understanding of such perceptions could underpin better treatment strategies.

Qualitative research may provide a crucial starting point because many treatment situations do not lend themselves to standard clinical trials. For example, the variety of responses to withdrawal from drugs and the small number of patients available at any one time make experimental work on the role of exercise for this group very difficult. In addition, qualitative research may hold the key to a better understanding of the mechanisms underlying the effect of exercise on life quality. A richer, more informed view can also be achieved through approaches using multidimensional models and instruments. These require continual development and fine-tuning to match special populations and treatment settings.

If the potential of exercise in the use of therapy is to be realized, researchers and academics should try to form stronger links with medical teams dealing with specific conditions. The topics of psychological outcomes and initiation and maintenance of exercise are open for wider investigation, and there is scope for training patients and the medical team in appropriate exercise prescription and counseling (Loughlan and Mutrie 1995). The financial assistance for programs will appear all the more quickly if the research community demonstrates a cost-benefit advantage (Shephard 1990). Such advances will benefit both the specific population and the more general field of exercise psychology.

ACKNOWLEDGMENTS

My thanks to June Adamson, Precilla Choi, Katherine Cox, Marie Donaghy, Liz Marsden, Lori Paton, and Jean Rankin for posing interesting research questions and to Dorothy Harris for putting some of these ideas in my head all those years ago. I would also like to thank Ken Fox for his vision in putting this book together and his guidance and helpful comments on drafts of this chapter. Two anonymous reviewers also helped clarity by posing questions and providing helpful insights.

REFERENCES

Abramson, L.Y., Seligman, M.E.P., and Teasdale, J.D. 1978. Learned helplessness in humans: Critique and reformulation. *Journal of Abnormal Psychology* 87: 49-74.

Adamson, M.J. 1991. *The role of exercise as an adjunct to the treatment of substance abuse*. Master's thesis, University of Glasgow.

Alder, B. 1994. Postnatal sexuality. In *Female sexuality: Psychology, biology and social context*, ed. P.Y.L. Choi and P. Nicolson, 83-99. London: Harvester Wheatsheaf.

Arif, A., and Westermeyer, J. 1988. *Manual of drug and alcohol abuse guidelines for teaching in medical and health institutions*. New York: Plenum Press.

Atkins, C.J., Kaplan, R.M., Timms, R.M., Reinsch, S., and Lofback, K. 1984. Behavioral exercise programs in the management of chronic obstructive pulmonary disease. *Journal of Consulting and Clinical Psychology* 52: 591-603.

Bachman, G., Leiblum, S., Sandler, B., Ainsley, W., Narcissioan, R., Sheldon, R., and Nakajima, H. 1985. Correlates of sexual desire in post menopausal women. *Maturitas* 7: 211-16.

Banks, A., and Waller, T.A.N. 1988. *Drug misuse. A practical handbook for GP's*. London: Blackwell Scientific.

Barlow, D.H., Grosset, K.H., Hart, H., and Hart, D.M. 1989. A study of the experience of Glasgow women in the climacteric years. *British Journal of Obstetrics and Gynaecology* 96: 1192-97.

Beck, A.T., Weissman, M., and Kovacs, M. 1976. Alcoholism, hopelessness and suicidal behavior. *Journal of Studies on Alcohol* 37: 66-77.

Belman, M.J. 1989. Exercise in chronic obstructive pulmonary disease. In *Exercise in modern medicine*, ed. B.A. Franklin, G. Seymour, and G.C. Timmis, 175-91. Baltimore: Williams & Wilkins.

Belmont, M.F., Henderer, K., and Bennet, J. 1990. Health promotion for the elderly. In *Aging: The health care challenge*, ed. C.B. Lewis, 241-52. Philadelphia: Davis.

Berger, B.G. 1984. Running away from anxiety and depression: A female as well as a male race. In *Running as therapy*, ed. M.L. Sachs and G.W. Buffone, 138-71. Omaha: University of Nebraska.

—. 1989. The role of physical activity in the life quality of older adults. *American Academy of Physical Education Papers*, 42-58. Champaign, IL: Human Kinetics.

Berger, M., and Kemmer, F.W. 1990. Discussion: Exercise, fitness and diabetes. In *Exercise, fitness and health*, ed. C. Bouchard, R.J. Shephard, T. Stephens, J.R. Sutton, and B.D. McPherson, 491-95. Champaign, IL: Human Kinetics.

Biddle, S.J.H., and Mutrie, N. 1991. *Psychology of physical activity and exercise*. London: Springer-Verlag.

Bouchard, C., Shephard, R.J., Stephens, T., Sutton, J.R., and McPherson, B.D., eds. 1990. *Exercise, fitness and health*. Champaign, IL: Human Kinetics.

Brown, D.R. 1992. Physical activity, ageing and psychological well-being: An overview of the research. *Canadian Journal of Sports Sciences* 17 (3): 185-92.

Cacioppo, J.T., and Tassinary, L.G. 1990. Inferring psychological significance from physiological signals. *American Psychologist* 45: 16-28.

Carson, P., Phillips, R., Lloyd, M., Turker, H., Heophytou, M., Buch, N.J., Gelson, A., and Lawton, A. 1982. Exercise after myocardial infarction: A controlled trial. *Journal of the Royal College of Physicians of London* 16: 147-51.

Chamove, A.S. 1988. Exercise effects in psychiatric patients: A review. In *Sport, health, psychology and exercise. Symposium Proceedings*, 8-48. London: Sports Council and Health Education Authority.

Chase, L. 1991. Physical self-perceptions and activity involvement in the older population. Ph.D. diss., Arizona State University.

Chodzko-Zajko, W.J. 1991. Physical fitness, cognitive performance, and aging. *Medicine and Science in Sports and Exercise* 23 (7): 868-72.

Choi, P.Y.L., and Mutrie, N. 1996. Psychological benefits of exercise for women: Improving employee quality of life. In *Workplace health: Employee fitness and physical exercise*, ed. J. Kerr, J. Cox, and A. Griffith, 83-100. London: Taylor Francis.

Choi, P.Y.L., and Salmon, P. 1995. Symptom changes across the menstrual cycle in competitive sportswomen, exercisers, and sedentary women. *British Journal of Clinical Psychology* 34:447-60.

Chow, R., Harrison, J.E., and Notarius, C. 1987. Effect of two randomized exercise programmes on bone mass of healthy postmenopausal women. *British Medical Journal* 295: 1441-44.

Cowart, V.S. 1989. Can exercise help women with PMS? *The Physician and Sportsmedicine* 17 (4): 169-78.

Cowles, E. 1898. Gymnastics in the treatment of inebriety. *American Physical Education Review* 3: 107-10.

Cox, K.J.S. 1992. Exercise, physical self-perception and climacteric symptoms. Master's thesis, Glasgow University.

Crammer, S.R., Neiman, D., and Lee, J. 1991. The effects of moderate exercise training on psychological mood state in women. *Journal of Psychosomatic Research* 35: 437-49.

Donaghy, M.E., Mutrie, N., and Smith, I. 1993. *The investigation of exercise as an adjunct to the treatment and rehabilitation of the problem drinker*. Edinburgh: Scottish Home and Health Department Research Grant Chief Scientist Office.

Donaghy, M.E., Ralston, G., and Mutrie, N. 1991. Exercise as a therapeutic adjunct for problem drinkers. *Journal of Sports Sciences* 9 (4): 440.

Dugmore, D. 1992. Exercise and heart disease. In *The community prevention of coronary heart disease*, ed. K. Williams, 43-58. London: Her Majesty's Stationery Office.

Duncan, T.E., and McAuley, E. 1993. Social support and efficacy cognitions in exercise adherence: A latent growth curve analysis. *Journal of Behavioral Medicine* 16: 199-218.

Dunn, S.W. 1993. Psychological aspects of diabetes in adults. In *International review of health psychology*, ed. S. Maes, H. Leventhal, and M. Johnston, 175-97. London: Wiley.

Fox, K.R., and Corbin, C.B. 1989. The Physical Self-Perception Profile: Development and preliminary validation. *Journal of Sport and Exercise Psychology* 11: 408-30.

Frankel, A., and Murphy, J. 1974. Physical fitness and personality in alcoholism: Canonical analysis of measures before and after treatment. *Quarterly Journal of Studies on Alcohol* 35: 1271-78.

Gannon, L. 1988. The potential role of exercise in the alleviation of menstrual disorders and menopausal symptoms: A theoretical synthesis of recent research. *Women and Health* 14 (2): 105-27.

Gary, V., and Guthrie, D. 1972. The effects of jogging on physical fitness and self-concept in hospitalized alcoholics. *Quarterly Journal of Studies on Alcoholism* 33: 1073-78.

Gloag, D. 1985. Rehabilitation of patients with cardiac conditions. *British Medical Journal* 290: 617-20.

Gordon, N.F. 1993a. *Arthritis: Your complete exercise guide.* Champaign, IL: Human Kinetics.

—. 1993b. *Breathing disorders: Your complete exercise guide.* Champaign, IL: Human Kinetics.

—. 1993c. *Diabetes: Your complete exercise guide.* Champaign, IL: Human Kinetics.

Greene, J.G. 1980. Life stress and symptoms of the climaterium. *British Journal of Psychiatry* 136: 486-91.

—. 1988. *A biosocial model of the climacteric syndrome.* Paper presented at the 3rd Congreso de la Societa Italiana per La Menopausa, 16-19 November, Bologne.

—. 1991. *Guide to the Greene climacteric scale.* Glasgow: University of Glasgow.

Greist, J.H., Klein, M.H., Eischens, R.R., Faris, J.W., Gurman, A.S., and Morgan, W.P. 1981. Running through your mind. In *Psychology of running*, ed. M.H. Sacks and M.L. Sachs, 5-31. Champaign, IL: Human Kinetics.

Hall, D.C., and Kaufmann, D.A. 1987. Effects of aerobic and strength conditioning on pregnancy outcomes. *American Journal of Obstetrics and Gynecology* 157: 1199-1203.

Harris, B., Rohaly, K., and Dailey, J. 1993. *Mid-life women and exercise--A qualitative study.* Paper presented at the XIIth Congress of the International Association of Physical Education and Sport for Girls and Women, July, Melbourne.

Harris, M.B. 1981. Women runners' views of running. *Perceptual Motor Skills* 53: 295-402.

Heather, N., Robertson, I., and Davies, P. 1985. *The misuse of alcohol: Crucial issues in dependence treatment and prevention.* London: Croom Helm.

Higgins, M.W. 1989. Chronic airway disease in the United States: Trends and determinants. *Chest* 96:328s-34s.

Holgate, S.T. 1993. Asthma: Past, present, and future. *European Respiratory Journal* 6: 1507-20.

Holmes, D.S. 1993. Aerobic fitness and the response to psychosocial stress. In *Exercise psychology: The influence of physical exercise on psychological processes*, ed. P. Seraganian, 39-63. New York: Wiley.

Hunter, M., Battersby, R., and Whitehead, M. 1986. Relationships between psychological symptoms, somatic complaints and menopausal status. *Maturitas* 8: 217-88.

Hunter, M., and Whitehead, M. 1989. Psychological experience of the climacteric and post menopause. *Progress in Clinical and Biological Research* 320: 211-24.

Hyman, G.P. 1987. *The role of exercise in the treatment of substance abuse*. Master's thesis, The Pennsylvania State University.

International Society of Sport Psychology. 1992. Physical activity and psychological benefits: A position statement from the International Society of Sport Psychology. *Journal of Applied Sport Psychology* 4: 94-98.

Israel, R.G., Sutton, M., and O'Brien, K.F. 1985. Effects of aerobic training on primary dysmenorrhea symptomatology in college females. *Journal of the American College of Health* 33: 241-44.

Johnstone, D.W. 1985. Invited review of psychological interventions in cardiovascular disease. *Journal of Psychosomatic Research* 29: 447-56.

Kallio, V., and Hamalainen, H. 1979. Reduction in sudden deaths by a multifactorial intervention programme after acute myocardial infarction. *Lancet* 24: 1019-94.

Kanis, J., Aaron, J., Thavarajah, M., McClusky, E.V., O'Doherty, D., Hamdy, N.A.T., and Bickerstaff, D. 1990. Osteoporosis: Causes and therapeutic implications. In *Osteoporosis*, ed. R. Smith. London: Royal College of Physicians Osteoporosis.

Kaplan, R.M. 1994. The Ziggy Theorem: Toward an outcome-focused health psychology. *Health Psychology* 13 (6): 451-60.

King, A.C., Haskell, W.L., Taylor, B., Kraemer, H.C., and DeBusk, R.F. 1991. Group vs home-based exercise training in healthy older men and women. *Journal of the American Medical Association* 266: 1535-42.

Kriska, A.M., Bayles, C., Cauley, J.A., Laporte, R.E., Sandler, R.B., Pambianco, G. 1986. A randomized exercise trial in older women: Increased activity over two years and the factors associated with compliance. *Medicine and Science in Sports and Exercise* 18 (5): 557-62.

Langosch, W. 1988. Psychological effects of training in coronary patients: A critical review of the literature. *European Heart Journal* 9: 37-42.

Lewin, B., Robertson, I.H., Cay, E.L., Irving, J.B., and Campbell, M. 1992. Effects of self-help post-myocardial-infarction rehabilitation on psychological adjustment and use of health services. *Lancet* 339: 1036-40.

Lokey, E.A., Tran, Z.V., Wells, C.L., Myers, B.C., and Tran, A.C. 1991. Effects of exercise on pregnancy outcomes: A meta-analytic review. *Medicine and Science in Sports and Exercise* 23 (11): 1234-39.

Loughlan, C., and Mutrie, N. 1995. Conducting an exercise consultation: Guidelines for health professionals. *Journal of the Institute of Health Education* 33 (3): 78-82.

Marcus, B.H., Albrecht, A.E., Niaura, R.S., Abrams, D.B., and Thompson, P.D. 1991. Usefulness of physical exercise for maintaining smoking cessation in women. *American Journal of Cardiology* 68: 406-7.

Marcus, R., Drinkwater, B., Dalsky, G., Dufek, J., Raab, D., Slemenda C., and Snow-Harter, C. 1992. Osteoporosis and exercise in women. *Medicine and Science in Sports and Exercise* 24 (6): s301-s307.

Marlatt, G.A., and Gordon, G.R. 1985. *Relapse prevention*. New York: Guilford Press.

Martin, J.E., Dubbert, P.M., Katell, A.D., Thomson, J.K., Raczynski J.R., and Lake, M. 1984. Behavioral control of exercise: Studies 1 through 6. *Journal of Consulting and Clinical Psychology* 52: 795-811.

Martinsen, E.W. 1989. The role of aerobic exercise in the treatment of depression. *Stress Medicine* 3: 93-100.

Martinsen, E.W., Hoffart, A., and Solberg, O. 1989a. Comparing aerobic and non-aerobic forms of exercise in the treatment of anxiety disorders: A randomized trial. *Stress Medicine* 5: 115-20.

—. 1989b. Comparing aerobic and non-aerobic forms of exercise in the treatment of clinical depression: A randomized trial. *Comprehensive Psychiatry* 30: 324-31.

McAuley, E. 1992. The role of efficacy cognitions in the prediction of exercise behavior in middle-aged adults. *Journal of Behavioral Medicine* 15: 65-88.

McDonald, D.G., and Hodgdon, J.A. 1991. *Psychological effects of aerobic fitness training.* New York: Springer-Verlag.

McMurdo, M.E.T. 1992. Exercise and the elderly. *Scottish Medical Journal* 11: 6-7.

McMurdo, M.E.T., and Burnett, L. 1992. Randomized controlled trial of exercise in the elderly. *Gerontology* 38: 292-98.

Morgan, W.P. 1985. Affective beneficence of vigorous physical activity. *Medicine and Science in Sports and Exercise* 17: 94-100.

Morgan, W.P., and Goldston, S.E., eds. 1987. *Exercise and mental health.* Washington, DC: Hemisphere.

Murdoch, F.A. 1988. Short term intervention for withdrawal from benzodiazepines: A comparative study of group therapy plus exercise vs group therapy. MBChB diss., University of Glasgow.

Murphy, T.J., Pagano, R.R., and Marlatt, G.A. 1986. Lifestyle modification with heavy alcohol drinkers: Effects of aerobic exercise and meditation *Addictive Behaviors* 11: 175-86.

Musgrave, B., and Menell, Z. 1980. *Change and choice. Women and middle-age.* London: Peter Owen.

Mutrie, N., and Biddle, S.J.H. 1995. Effects of exercise on non-clinical populations. In *Exercise and sport psychology: A European perspective*, ed. S.J.H. Biddle, 50-70. Leeds: Human Kinetics.

Mutrie, N., Blamey, A., Davison, R., and Kelly, M. 1994. Adherence to home-based and class-based exercise programmes for older adults. In *Proceedings of the 10th Commonwealth and International Scientific Congress*, ed. F.I. Bell and G.H. Van Gyn, 262-65. Vancouver, BC: University of Victoria.

Mutrie, N., and Choi, P. 1993. Psychological benefits of physical activity for specific populations. In *Proceedings of the 7th Conference of the European Health Psychology Society*, 98. Brussels: European Health Psychology Society.

Mutrie, N., and Davison, R. 1994. Physical self-perception in exercising older adults. *Journal of Sports Sciences* 12 (2): 203.

Naughton, J. 1985. Role of physical activity as a secondary intervention for healed mycocardial infarction. *American Journal of Cardiology* 55: 210-60.

Newton, M., Mutrie, N., and McArthur, J.D. 1991. The effects of exercise in a coronary rehabilitation programme. *Scottish Medical Journal* 36: 38-41.

Norstrom, J. 1988. Get fit while you sit. Exercise and fitness options for diabetics. *Caring* (November), 52-58.

North, T.C., McCullagh, P., and Vu Tran, Z.V. 1990. The effect of exercise on depression. *Exercise and Sports Science Reviews* 19: 379-415.

Oldridge, N.B., Guyatt, G.H., Fischer, M.E., and Rimm, A.A. 1988. Cardiac rehabilitation after myocardial infarction. Combined experience of randomized clinical trials. *Journal of the American Medical Association* 260: 945-50.

Orwin, A. 1981. The running treatment: A preliminary communication on a new use for an old therapy (physical activity) in the agorophobic syndrome. In *Psychology of running*, ed. M.H. Sacks and M. Sachs, 32-39. Champaign, IL: Human Kinetics.

Ossip-Klein, D.J., Doyne, E.J., Bowman, E.D., Osborn, K.M., McDougall-Wilson, I.B., and Neimeyer, R.A. 1989. Effects of running and weight lifting on self-concept in clinically depressed women. *Journal of Consulting and Clinical Psychology* 57: 158-61.

Palmer, J., Vacc, N., and Epstein, J. 1988. Adult inpatient alcoholics: Physical exercise as a treatment intervention. *Journal of Studies on Alcohol* 49: 5.

Paton, L. 1993. Barriers and motivations to exercise in osteoporotic post-menopausal women. Master's thesis, University of Glasgow.

Petruzzello, S.J., Landers, D.M., Hatfield, B.D., Kubitz, K.A., and Salazar, W. 1991. A meta-anlysis on the anxiety reducing effects of acute and chronic exercise: Outcomes and mechanisms. *Sports Medicine* 11: 143-180.

Plante, T.G. 1993. Aerobic exercise in prevention and treatment of psychopathology. In *Exercise psychology. The influence of physical exercise on psychological processes*, ed. P. Seraganian, 358-79. New York: Wiley.

Prior, J.C., and Vigna, Y. 1987. Conditioning exercise decreases premenstrual symptoms: A prospective controlled 6 month trial. *Fertility and Sterility* 47 (3): 402-8.

Rejeski, W.J., and Hobson, M. 1994. A framework for enhancing exercise motivation in rehabilitative medicine. In *Toward active living*, ed. H.A. Quinney, L. Gauvin, and A.E.T. Wall, 107-14. Champaign, IL: Human Kinetics.

Rejeski, W.J., and Thompson, A. 1993. Historical and conceptual roots of exercise psychology. In *Exercise psychology. The influence of physical exercise on psychological processes*, ed. P. Seraganian, 3-35. New York: Wiley.

Richardson, J. 1990. Questionnaire studies of paramenstrual symptoms. *Psychology of Women Quarterly* 14: 15-42.

Rickli, R.E., and McManus, R. 1990. The effect of exercise on bone mineral content in post menopausal women. *Research Quarterly of Exercise and Sport* 61 (3): 243-49.

Rovario, S., Holmes, D.S., and Holmsten, D. 1984. Influence of a cardiac rehabilitation program on the cardiovascular, psychological, and social functioning of cardiac patients. *Journal of Behavioral Medicine* 7: 61-81.

Seligman, M.E.P. 1975. *Helplessness: On depression, development and death*. San Francisco: Freeman.

Sharratt, M.T., and Sharratt, J.K. 1994. Potential health benefits of active living for persons with chronic conditions. In *Toward active living*, ed. H.A. Quinney, L. Gauvin, and A.E.T. Wall, 39-45. Champaign, IL: Human Kinetics.

Shephard, R.J. 1990. Costs and benefits of an exercising versus a non-exercising society. In *Exercise, fitness and health*, ed. C. Bouchard, R.J. Shephard, T. Stephens, J.R. Sutton, and B.D. McPherson, 49-60. Champaign, IL: Human Kinetics.

Sidney, K.H., and Jerome, W.C. 1990. Anxiety and depression. In *Current therapy in sports medicine*, ed. J.S. Torg, 159-65. Toronto, ON: Decker.

Simkin, A.J., Ayalon, J., and Leichter, I. 1987. Increased trabecular bone density due to bone-loading exercises on postmenopausal osteoporotic women. *Calcified Tissue International* 40: 59-63.

Sinyor, D., Brown, T., Rostant, L., and Seraganian, P. 1982. The role of physical exercise in the treatment of alcoholism. *Journal of Studies on Alcohol* 43: 380-86.

Slavin, J.L., Lutter, J.M., Cushman, S., and Lee, V. 1988. Pregnancy and exercise. In *Sport science perspectives for women*, ed. J. Puhl, C.H. Brown, and R.O. Voy, 151-60. Champaign, IL: Human Kinetics.

Smith, E., Smith, K.A., and Gilligan, C. 1990. Exercise, fitness, osteoarthritis and osteoporosis. In *Exercise, fitness and health*, ed. C. Bouchard, R.J. Shephard, T. Stephens, J.R. Sutton, and B.D. McPherson, 517-24. Champaign, IL: Human Kinetics.

Sports Council and Health Education Authority. 1992. *Allied Dunbar National Fitness Survey*. London: Sports Council and Health Education Authority.

Stephens, T. 1988. Physical activity and mental health in the United States and Canada: Evidence from four population surveys. *Preventive Medicine* 17: 35-47.

Strang, V.R., and Sullivan, P.L. 1985. Body image attitudes during pregnancy and the post-partum period. *Journal of Obstetrics and Gynecology and Neonatal Nursing* (July/August): 332-37.

Tsukue, I., and Shohoji, T. 1981. Movement therapy for alcoholic patients. *Journal of Studies on Alcohol* 42: 144-49.

Tunstall-Pedoe, H., Smith, W.C.S., and Crombie, I.K. 1986. Levels and trends of CHD mortality in Scotland compared with other countries. *Health Bulletin* 44: 153-61.

Vasterling, J.J., Sementilli, M.E., and Burish, T.G. 1988. The role of aerobic exercise in reducing stress in diabetic patients. *Diabetic Education* 14 (3): 197-201.

Vaughn, C.C. 1976. Rehabilitation of post-menopausal osteoporosis. *Israeli Journal of Medical Sciences* 12: 652-59.

Vranic, M., and Wasserman, D. 1990. Exercise, fitness and diabetes. In *Exercise, fitness and health*, ed. C. Bouchard, R.J. Shephard, T. Stephens, J.R. Sutton, and B.D. McPherson, 467-90. Champaign, IL: Human Kinetics.

Wallace, A.M., Boyer, D.B., Dan, A., and Holm, K. 1986. Aerobic exercise, maternal self-esteem, and physical discomforts during pregnancy. *Journal of Nurse-Midwifery* 31: 255-62.

Wing, R.R., Epstein, L.H., Nowalk, M.P., and Lamparski, D.M. 1986. Behavioral self-regulation in the treatment of patients with diabetes mellitus. *Psychological Bulletin* 99: 78.

INDEX

A

ability-oriented motivation 65
Academic Self-Description Questionnaire 36
achievement goal theory 124
achievement motivation 65
Adamson, M.J. 294, 295
adolescents
    and development tasks 209-210
    and dieting 233, 245
    and eating disorders 245-247
    and health perceptions 215-216
    and inactive leisure pursuits 221
    and lifestyle 223-225
    and physical self-concept 213- 214
    and self-esteem promotion 197-198
adolescent weight management xiii
    and body image 240-241
    and centrality of appearance 241-245
    and decision making 233-245, 251
    and exercise 247-248, 250-251
    and fatness, size, and shape 235-238
    gender effects on 236-237, 246-248
    and health promotion 248-253
    and individual profiles 249-250
    methods of 245-248
    need for 230-233
    and the physical self 229-252
    and sexual maturation 238-240
age
    and body image 150-152
    and perceived physical competence 187-188
    and physical self-concept 214
aged
    exercise effects on 304-306
    home-based vs. class-based exercise programs
        for 305-306
Ahonen, T.P. 278
Albrecht, G.L. 264
alcohol rehabilitation, exercise effects on 292-293
Alibhai, N. 153
Allan, J.D. 153
Allied Dunbar National Fitness Survey 72, 305
Altabe, M. 146, 151, 158
ambivalence, toward individuals with disabilities
    264-265
American Alliance for Health, Physical Education,
    Recreation and Dance (AAHPERD) 191
American Psychological Association, disability
    terminology of 258
Ames, C. 66-67
Andersen, A.E. 144, 152, 155
anorexia. See eating disorders
Anshel, M.H. 190
Arif, A. 295
Armstrong, J. 157
Armstrong, N. 147, 148, 231, 236, 243, 249
Arnold, P. 269
arthritis, exercise effects on 297
aschematics 69
asthma, exercise effects on 299

Atha, B. 264
athletes with disabilities
    and self-actualization 277-278
    and sport participation impact on self-esteem
        275-279
athletes. See athletes with disabilities; female
    athletes; injured athletes; wheelchair
    athletes
Atkins, C.J. 299
Attaway, J.R. 196
Attie, I. 239, 240, 246
attraction 39
    defined 4
Australian Health and Fitness Survey 37, 45

B

Babladelis, G. 150
Bachman, G. 303
Baguma, P. 153
Bailey, J. 261, 264
Bailey, S.M. 147
Bandura, Albert 7, 62-63, 71-73, 74
Banks, A. 294-295
Bar-Eli, M. 269, 275
Barnes, J. 37, 44
Bartky, S. 95, 96, 98
Barton, L. 259
Baudrillard, J. 85
Baumeister, R.F. 113, 115, 116, 118, 181
Baur, J. 216
Bausell, R.B. 151
Beales, S. 159, 245
Beck, A.T. 293
Beck Depression Inventory (BDI) 292
Beck, U. 212
Becque, M.D. 232
behavioral intensity 60-61
Belman, M.J. 299
Belmont, M.F. 305
Benson, E. 275
Berger, B.G. 112, 119, 300, 305
Berger, M. 296
Berman, P.W. 150
Betterton, R. 98
between-network studies of construct validation
    28, 55
Beumont, P.J.V. 156, 164-165
Bickenbach, J.E. 262, 263
Biddle, Stuart J.H. x, 61-63, 66-8, 71, 73, 77, 124,
    130, 189, 192, 248, 288-290
Biocca, F.A. 156, 158
Blacher, J. 266
Black, D.R. 162
Blackman, L. 190
Black, S.J. 188
Blaine, B. 114, 117, 119
Blinde, E.M. 162
Blustein, D.L. 207
bodily attractiveness, cultural derivation of 122-123

body. *See also* gendered-sexual body; mechanical
     body; performing body
  and identity, individual, self 83-86
  sociological constructs of x, 86-88
body beautiful 87
bodybuilding, gender differences in 99-101
Body Cathexis Scale 38
body composition 146-148
body concept, role in identity development 207-208
body dissatisfaction. *See* body image
body esteem 145
  defined xii
Body Esteem Scale 38
body image. *See also* female body image; male
     body image
  and adolescent weight management 240-241
  and age 150-152
  assessment of 145-146
  and body composition 146-148
  and body size 146-148
  cultural conformity to 146, 152-154
  defined xii, 145
  distortion of 145
  and eating behaviors 143-165
  endogenous influences on 146-156
  and ethnic groups 152-154
  and exercise 159-165
  and fitness 159-165
  and gender-role orientation 154-156
  and health promotion 159-160
  measurement of 38
  media influence on 144, 156-157
  and menstrual cycle 158
  and personality 148-150
  and sexual preference 154-156
  stability of 156-158
body maintenance, media influence on 89-90
body shape
  ideal vs. perceived 146
  importance of 89
  role in weight management 236
  and women 95
body size 146-148
  and body image 146-148
  role in weight management 236
  gender differences in 95
Bordo, S. 95-96
Borgen, J.S. 246
Bouchard, C. 159, 197, 248, 287, 294
Bourdieu, Pierre 89, 94-95, 208, 212
Boutcher, S. 112
Bovey, S. 93, 95
Bowe, F. 260-261
Boyle, G.J. 35
Bracken, B.A. 31, 32, 40
Brackenridge, C. 98
Brame, D.L. 267
Brand, P. 155
Braskamp, L.A. 59-61, 65, 116
Bräutigam, M. 213, 218, 223
Brawley, L.R. 74, 78-79
Brenner, J.B 143, 148
Brettschneider, Wolf-Dietrich xiii, 184, 213, 216,
    218, 223
Brewer, B.W. 127
Brinkhoff, K.P. 213
Brock, S. 103, 104
Brodie, D.A. 147
Bronfenbrenner, U. 208

Brooks-Gunn, J. 239-240, 246
Brown, C. 175
Brown, D.R. 305
Brownell, K.D. 130, 158, 162, 230
Brown, J.D. 116, 117, 119, 126
Brown, M. 261
Brown, S.W. 190
Bruch, H. 164
Brumberg, J. 154
Bruner, J. 101, 102
Bryan, T.H. 271
bulimia. *See* eating disorders
Burckes-Miller, M.E. 162
Burkhart, B. 198
Burnett, L. 305
Bushakra, F.B. 266, 270, 278
Butler, A. 269
Butler Research Associates, Inc. 191
Butters, J.W. 157
Button, E.J. 233, 246
Byrne, B.M. 30, 35-36, 43

C
Cacioppo, J.T. 288
Cameron, J. 76
Campbell, D.T. 51
Campbell, E. 277
Campbell, J.D. 118
Campbell, M. 269
Campbell, R.N. viii-xii, 115-116, 116
Campbell's First Law of Human Behavior viii
Canada Fitness Award 191
Canadian Active Living Challenge 191
Cannon, G. 248
Cantell, M.H. 278
cardiac rehabilitation, exercise effects on 291-292
Carroll, L. 150
Carson, P. 292
Cash, D.W. 157
Cash, T.F. 145, 148, 149, 153, 157, 158
Cassidy, R. 175
categorization, of individuals with disabilities
    262-263
centrality, in individuals with disabilities 272
Chamove, A.S. 290
Chang, J.L. 163
Chapman, J.W. 271
Chapman, M. 269
Charmaz, K. 103
Chase, L. 121, 132-133, 305, 306
children, and self-esteem xi, 176-185, 189-199
Children's Self-Concept Scale 37-38
Chinn, S. 230
Chodzko-Zajko, W.J. 305
Choi, P. 288, 300-301
Chow, R. 298, 307
chronic bronchitis, exercise effects on 299
chronic illness, and identity dilemmas 103
Clarke, L. 269
Clifford, E. 241
climacteric. *See* menopause
Climacteric Symptoms Scale 304
*The Cloak of Competence: Stigma in the Lives of the
    Mentally Retarded* 274-275
Coakley, J. 96-97
Coen, S.P. 164
cognitive evaluation theory. *See* self-determination
    theory (SDT)
cognitive motivation theories 59-79

and future research 78-79
history of 61-63
Cohen, J. 20
Cohn, L.D. 238
Colditz, G.A. 230
Collins, I.T. 16, 122
Colquhoun, D. 90
Combs, R.H. 267
competence motivation theory 63-64, 179-182, 278-279
compulsive exercise 163
Connell, J.P. 179
Conn, V.S. 20
Conrad, C.C. 151
construct validation
classification of 28
and future research 42, 43
known group differences approach to 36
for physical self-concept measurement 27-55
consumer culture
and individualized bodies 88-90
and narcissism 92-93
contingent self-esteem 129-130
defined 182
continuing motivation 60
Cooley, C.H. 84, 114, 181, 205
Cooper Institute for Aerobics Research 191
Cooper, M.J. 233, 246
Cooper, P.J. 143, 146, 148, 246
Coopersmith, S. 17, 30, 37, 128, 145
Cooper, T. 143, 148
Corbin, C.B. 240, 246, 279, 304
Corbin, Charles B. xi, 3, 5, 7, 11, 13, 15, 40-43, 112, 121, 175, 184, 191, 195, 198, 213
correlated factor model of self-concept 31
Couldrey, W.H. 5, 7
Cowart, V.W. 300
Cowles, E. 293
Cowles, M. 144, 149, 151, 159, 160, 162
Cox, K.J.S. 304
Craft, D.H. 272
Craik, J. 98
Crammer, S.R. 303
Crawford, R. 90
Crocker, J. 114, 117, 119, 261
Crocker, P.R.E. 124, 274, 275, 276
Crowne-Marlow Social Desirability Scale. See Social Desirability Scale
Csikszentmihalyi, M. 61
Cuddihy, T.F. 191, 195
cultural dominance, and physical appearance 125
culture, and body image 152-154
Cunningham, J.G. 143, 148
Curby, D. 121
cyberculture, and identity 85

D
Dacey, C.M. 245
Damhorst, M.L. 239
Davies, E. 147, 239, 240
Davis, Caroline xi, 144, 147-148, 149, 150, 151, 159, 160, 161, 162, 163, 164, 165, 236
Davison, R. 124, 306
Debus, R. 18
DeCharms, R. 75-76, 176
Deci, E.L. 75, 76-77, 114, 116, 129, 130, 133-134, 176-179, 182, 183, 189, 192
De Coverley Veale, D. 163
defensiveness, and self-esteem preservation in

individuals with disabilities 274-275
denial, and self-esteem preservation in individuals with disabilities 274-275
Denniston, C. 149
Department of Defense Dependent Schools 198
Department for Health 230
DePauw, K.P. 264, 267
depression, exercise effects on 290
development tasks 208-211
in adolescents 209-210
characteristics of 209-210
defined 209
gender differences of 210
importance of 210-211
types of 209
Dhaliwal, J.S. 147, 151-152
diabetes, exercise effects on 296-297
Diener, E. 116
dieting
in adolescents 233, 245
adverse effects of 233
and body image 158-159
and exercise 161-162
gender differences in 95-96
Dietz, W. 231-232
DiNicola, V.F. 240
Dionne, M. 149, 151, 155, 160
direction 60
Directory of Psychological Tests in the Sport and Exercise Sciences 38
disability. See also athletes with disabilities; individuals with disabilities; learning disabilities; mental retardation; physical disability
congenital vs. acquired 265
cultural view of 88, 93
defined 257-258, 259-260
and physical education xiii
social constructs of 260-265
terminology of 258-259
discounting 125
discrimination, toward individuals with disabilities 260-261
Dishman, R.K. 5, 19
diversion, and lifestyle 92
Doka, K.J. 150
Dolan, B. 152
domain-general self-perception, and motivation 63-70
domain-specific self-perception, and motivation 70-78
dominant body order, challenges to 99-101
dominant heterosexuality 97
Donaghy, M.E. 294-295
Donovan, R.J. 73
Downs, P. 264, 267
Dreher, E. 209, 210, 211
Dreher, M. 209, 210, 211
drug rehabilitation, exercise effects on 293-296
Drummer, G.M. 162
Dubas, J.S. 238
Duda, J.L. 64-65, 68, 124, 133, 188
Dugmore, D. 292
Duncan, M. 97-98
Duncan, T.E. 306
Dunn, J.L. 278
Dunn, L.M. 267
Dunn, S.W. 296
Durnin, J.V.G.A. 147-148, 149, 236

Duval, R.J. 261
Dweck, C. 67-68
Dwyer, J.T. 236, 240, 245
dysmenorrhea, exercise effects on 300-301

E
eating behaviors, and body image 143-165
Eating Disorder Inventory 16
eating disorders
    in adolescents 245-247
    in female athletes 162-163
    gender differences of 246-247
    incidence of 233
    and low self-esteem 148-150
    and neuroticism 150
    and overexercising 164-165
Ebbeck, V. 122
Edgerton, R.B. 269, 274-275
effectance (competence) motivation theory 63-64, 75
effectance motivation. See intrinsic motivation
efficacy expectation, vs. outcome expectations 71
Egleston, S.A. 20
ego orientation, vs. task orientation 188-189
Eisenberg, M.G. 261
Eklund, R.C. 184
Elias, Norbert 89
elite sports, and self-concept 217-221
emotional reactivity. See neuroticism
emphysema, exercise effects on 299
enlightenment subject, and the sociological self
    84-85
Epling, W.F. 164, 165
Epstein, S. 114, 117, 128
Erikson, Erik H. 114, 117, 180, 205-206, 208
Escober, A. 85
essential center (self) 84
estimation 39
    as a mediator between fitness and self-esteem
    3-4
Estimation scale 3-4, 5, 8, 9, 11
ethnic groups
    and lifestyle 223-225
    and physical self-concept 213-214
Ewart, C.K. 73
excessive exercise. See overexercise
exercise. See also compulsive exercise; overexercise
    and body image 159-165
    and dieting 161-162
    effects on mental illness 289-291
    and future research 306-308
    gender differences in 96-97
    motivational models of x
    and perceived physical attractiveness 16-17
    psychological therapeutic effects 287-308
    psychological vs. physiological impact of 287-
    288
    and self-efficacy theory of motivation 70-74
    and self-esteem 3-26
    and self-esteem in children and adolescents
    189-192
    and weight management 247-248, 250-251
exercise dependence 60, 163
exercise models, summary of associations 19-20
exercise prediction
    role of importance ratings 17
    role of perceived physical competence 21
    role of self-efficacy 17-19, 73-74
    role of self-esteem 19-20

Exercise and Self-Esteem Model (EXSEM) 5-23, 78,
    290-291
    associations with degree and type of exercise
    14-15
    associations with exercise dichotomy 13
    structure of 6-7, 15-16
exercise self-schemata 69-70
exploratory factor analysis 33
EXSEM. See Exercise and Self-Esteem Model
    (EXSEM)
external regulation 177
extrinsic motivation 194
    types of 177-179
Eysenck, H.J. 149
Eysenck, S.B.G. 149

F
Fahlberg, L.A. 131
Fahlberg, L.L. 131
Fallon, A. 144, 151
fatness. See also obesity
    cultural view of 88, 93
    gender differences in 95-96
    role in weight management 235-238
    and socioeconomic status 152
Fava, J.L. 11, 13, 14, 42, 121
Featherstone, M. 89-90, 92, 94
feedback 194
    and perceived physical competence 187-188
Feinberg, R. 76
Felson, R.B. 19
Feltz, D.L. 73
female athletes
    and eating disorders 162-163
    lesbian stereotypes of 97
female body image 143, 146-148
    and age 150-152
female self-esteem
    promotion of 198-199
    vs. male self-esteem 184-185
Fewell, R.R. 266
Fichten, C.S. 263
Fischer, C. 222
Fiske, D.W. 51
Fiske, S.T. 60, 69
fitness. See physical fitness
Fitness for Life program 191, 198
fitnessgram 191
Fitts, W.H. 31, 32, 40, 274
Fleischman, F.A. 45
Fleming, J.S. 40
Flintoff, M. 279
Foley, E. 157
food consumption, and body image 157
Fortier, M.S. 77
Foucault, M. 88, 90
Fowler, B.A. 232
Fox, J. 149, 160, 161, 163, 164
Fox, Kenneth R. 3, 5, 7, 11, 13, 15-17, 31, 40-43, 63, 66,
    73, 74, 77, 112, 115, 121-122, 125-127, 130,
    147-149, 183-184, 188-190, 192, 195-196, 213-
    214, 236-237, 243-244, 247, 249, 279, 304
Frankel, A. 294
Franzoi, S.L. 38, 145, 146
Freedson, P.S. 196
French, R. 273
Fuchs, W. 222
Furnham, A. 147, 153, 239-240

G

Gannon, L. 298, 300, 303
Gardner, R.M. 145
Garfinkel, P.E. 163
Garlow, G. 269
Garner, D.M. 16, 143, 146, 160, 162-163
Garrow, J. 230, 232
Gary, V. 294
gay men, and body image 155-160
gender
    and adolescent weight management 236-237,
        246-248
    and eating disorders 246-247
    and health perceptions 215
    and obesity 232
    and perceived physical appearance 243-244
    and physical self-concept 214, 218, 220-221
    and self-esteem 243, 244, 267, 271-272
    and sexual maturation 238-240
gendered scripts, media impact on 97-98
gendered-sexual body 95-99
gender-role orientation, and body image 154-156
General Self-Worth subscales 116
Gergen, K. 85, 102, 104
Gergen, M. 102, 104
Gerhardt, C. 231-32
Gibbons, S.L. 266, 270, 278
Gibney, M. 231
Giddens, A. 83-84, 92-93, 101, 117
Gill, D.L. 28, 187
Gillett, J. 100
Gilman, S. 92
Gilroy, F. 149
Gliedman, J. 257, 262
Gloag, D. 291
Global Self-Worth Scale (Messer and Harter) 8, 11
goal perspectives theory of motivation 64-69
    and ability concepts 67-68
    and competence perceptions assessment 68-69
    individual differences in 65-66
    and situational factors 66-67
God-like metaphor of motivation 61-62
Goffman, E. 93, 261-262, 275
Gordon, N.F. 296-297, 299
Gordon, W.A. 261
Gorlow, L. 269
Gortmaker, S.L. 230-231
Gottschalk, S. 85
Goudas, M. 66, 67, 77, 189, 192
Gould, D. 187
Graber, J.A. 238
Green, B.C. 269, 273, 274, 276
Greene, J.G. 303-304
Greenwood, C.M. 272
Greist, J.H. 290
Griffin, P. 97
Grigsby, T.E. 269, 273, 274, 276
Gross, J.B. 187
growth through adversity 130
    in individuals with disabilities 273-274
Gruber, J.J. 119, 189-190
Guidano, V.F. 114, 117
Guilford, J.P. 31
Gull, W.W. 164
Gupta, M.A. 147, 151-152
Guthrie, D. 294
Guthrie, G. 269
Guttmann, L. 266

H

Haimovitz, D. 157-158
Hall, D.C. 302
Hall, S. 84, 85, 114
Hamalainen, H. 291
Hamilton, K. 156
handicap. *See* disability
Hargreaves, J. 96, 97, 99-100
Harlow, L.L. 3, 5, 8, 11, 12, 15, 17, 20, 42, 122
Harner, D.E. 144
Harper, J.L. 267
Harris, B. 303
Harris, M.B. 153, 300
Hart, E.A. 72, 115
Harter, Susan 6, 8, 11, 13, 22, 23, 40, 41, 42, 63-64, 66,
        112, 113, 115, 116, 117, 119, 122, 123, 124, 125,
        127, 129, 132, 179-182, 183, 184, 187, 195, 197,
        206, 207, 238, 240-243, 270-271
Hartmann, I. 217
Hattie, J. 28, 30, 31, 35, 40, 42, 54
Hauck, E.R. 163
Havighurst, R.J. 205, 208, 209
health perceptions, of adolescents 215-216
health promotion
    and adolescent weight management 248-253
    and body image 159-160
    and individualism 91
Heather, N. 293
Hedrick, B. 273
Heim, Rüdiger xi, 184
Heinberg, L.J. 157
Herzog, D.B. 155
Heunemann, R.L. 245, 247
Higgins, M.W. 299
high self-esteem 119
Hill, A.J. 151, 240, 245
Hill, J. 98
Hobbs, N. 267
Hocevar, D. 43, 51
Hodgdon, J.A. 289
Hoek, S. 164
Hofstetter, C.R. 19, 73
Holgate, S.T. 299
Holmes, D.S. 292
Hooker, K. 20
Hopper, C. 266, 274, 276
Horne, M. 258
Horn, T.S. 130, 187-188
How I See Myself Scale 37-38
Hubner, J.J. ix, 15, 33-36, 37, 41, 42, 49, 54, 145, 207
Huddleston, S. 187
Hurrelmann, K. 209
Hyland, T. 91
Hyman, G.P. 294

I

ideal body shape 146
identified regulation 179
identity. *See also* stigmatized identity
    and body, individual, self 83-86
    and chronic illness 103
    and cyberculture 85
    defined xii, 206, 207
    and injured athletes 103-104
    and life history research 105-106
    personal vs. social 206
    and self-concept 205-208
    sociological construct of 84-85

identity formation
  in adolescence 205-206
  role of body concept in 207-208
Imm, P.S. 160
impairment. *See* disability
importance-competence, and self-esteem 126-127
importance-competence discrepancies 125
importance ratings, role in exercise prediction 17
inactive leisure pursuits, in adolescents 221
Inches, P. 164
independent model of self concept 31
individual, and body, identify, self 83-86
individualism 90-92, 211-212
  and consumer culture 88-90
  and health promotion 91
  and lifestyle 92
  and self 120-121
  and self-regulation 91
individuals with disabilities
  ambivalence toward 264-265
  attitudinal hierarchies toward 263-264
  characteristics of 260-261
  discrimination and prejudice toward 260-261
  and self-esteem development 265-272
  stigmatization of 261-262
  uniqueness vs. categorization of 262-263
Ingham, A. 92
injured athletes, and identity dilemmas 103-104
integrated regulation 179
International Federation of Body Builders 99-100
International Federation of Body Builders Constitution
  and Rule Book for Judges, Athletes and
  Officials 99-100
International Paralympic Committee (IPC) 271
International Sports Federation for Persons with
  Mental Handicaps 271
intervention hypothesis viii
intrinsic motivation 176, 195
  and self-determination 75-78
introjected regulation 177-178
Israel, R.G. 300

J
Jackson, B.K. 179
Jackson, D.N. 9
Jackson, L.A. 150
Jackson, S. 36
James, William 17, 114, 115, 116, 121, 124, 181, 205,
  230
Janis, I.L. 145
Jarvis, W.T. 196
Jasnoski, M.L. 10
Jenkins, J. 267
Jerome, W.C. 299
Johnson, A.W. 212
Johnstone, D.W. 292
Jones, G. 275, 277
Josephs, L. 3, 11, 12, 15, 17, 42, 122
Josephs, R.A. 119
Jourard, S.M. 38, 146

K
Kallen, E. 263
Kallio, V. 291
Kampper, K.P. 5, 11, 20
Kaplan, R.M. 289
Karabenick, S.A. 238
Kaskisaari, M. 101
Katz, I. 261, 264

Katz, J.L. 150, 165
Kaus, C.R. 20
Keelan, J.P.R. 149
Kelly, G.A. 115, 124, 127-128
Kemper, H.C. 232
Kendzierski, D. 69-70, 127
Kennedy, M.J. 266
Kennedy, S.H. 163, 165
Kiernan, M. 161
Killen, J.D. 238
King, G.A. 269, 278
Kin, M.M. 246
Kirby, B.J. 147, 148, 236, 243, 249
Kirk, D. 89-90, 248, 250
Kissling, E. 96
Kleiber, D. 103, 104
Klein, A. 99
Kleinman, A. 104
Klein, T. 266
known group differences approach, to construct
  validation 36
Kopec-Schrader, E.M. 156
Kornbrust, A.M. 164
Kosonen, U. 101
Koteskey, R.L. 212
Kovacs, M. 203
Kowal, D.M. 5
Kreisel, P.S.J. 187
Krejci, R.C. 163, 164
Kriska, A.M. 298
Kron, L. 165
Kuldau, J.M. 153
Kurz, D. 213
Kuznesof, A.W. 164

L
Langosch, W. 292
Lansky, L.M. 157-158
La Ronde, C. 117
Lasch, A. 92
Lasch, C. 144
Laurelton Self-Concept Scale 269
Laurie, D.R. 195
Lazarus, R.S. 273
learning disabilities
  effect on self-esteem development 271-272
  gender differences in self-esteem development
  271-272
Leary, M.R. 61, 72, 115, 122, 234, 248
Lecky, P. 117
Leehey, K. 163
Lefevre, J. 232
Leggett, E. 67-68
Le Grange, D. 163
Lenskyj, H. 96, 97
Lerner, R.M. 149, 208, 238
lesbians, and body image 155-156
lesbian stereotypes, of female athletes 97
Leveillee, C.M. 16, 17
Lewin, B. 292
Lewis, L. 121, 184
Lewthwaite, R. 187
Lieberman, L.S. 143, 152
life adjustment, and physical self 20-21
life history research, and identity, self 105-106
lifestyle
  defined 221-222
  and diversion 92

of German adolescents 223-225
and individualism 92
and physical self 221-225
and victim blaming 92
Lightsey, D.M. 196
Lillie, T. 266
Linder, D.E. 127
Lintunen, T. 238, 240, 279
Linville, P.W. 119
Lloyd, J. 190
Lockhart, B.D. 128-129
Lohman, T.G. 230
Lokey, E.A. 302
"the look" 89, 98
looking glass self 206
Loughlan, C. 307
Lovejoy, P.Y. 191
low self-esteem 118-120
    and body image 149
    characteristics of 118
    and eating disorders 148-149
    and weight 149-150
Lucas, A.R. 246
Lupton, D. 91

M
machine metaphor 61, 90
MacKinnon, J.R. 164
MacNeill, M. 100
Maddux, J.E. 78-79
Maehr, M.L. 59-61, 64, 65, 116
Magill, J. 267
male body image 143-144
    and age 151-152
    cultural attitudes toward 159
male self-esteem, vs. female self-esteem 184-185
Maloney, M.J. 245
Mangan, J. 96
Mansfield, A. 99
Marcia, J. 114, 205, 206
Marcus, B.H. 19, 61, 296
Marcus, R. 298
Markland, D. 161
Markus, H. 114, 115, 124, 127
Marlatt, G.A. 293-4
Marold, D.B. 127, 129
Marsh, Herbert W. xii, 3-4, 17-18, 20, 21, 22, 28, 30,
    31, 32, 35, 36, 37, 40-47, 49-51, 54-55, 63,
    112, 114-115, 116, 123, 127, 183-184, 190,
    206, 210, 213, 214, 218, 219, 220, 270
Marsh/Shavelson theoretical model of selfconcept
    33-34
Marsland, J. 247
Martens, R. 192, 197
Martin, J.E. 307
Martino, S. 276
Martinsen, E.W. 288, 302
Marwell, G. 6, 23, 33
Marx, R.W. 30
Maslow, A. 116, 273
mastery challenge, in individuals with disabilities
    272-273
mastery class climate 67
Mastro, J.V. 263
Mathes, E.W. 148
Maude, D. 159
Maxwell, K. 161
Mayer, J. 236, 240, 245
Mayo, K. 153

Mazur, A. 143, 146, 148, 155
McAdams, D. 101
McAuley, E. 71, 73, 74, 306
McCauley, M.L. 149
McDavid, J.W. 258
McDonald, D.G. 289
McDonald, K. 161
McDonald, R.P. 46
McGinn, B. 99
McManus, R. 298
McMurdo, M.E.T. 305
McTeer, W. 103
Mead, G.H. 84, 205
mechanical body 87
media
    impact on gendered scripts 97-98
    influence on body image 144, 156-157
    influence on body maintenance 89-90
menopause, exercise effects on 302-304
menstruation
    and body image 158
    exercise effects on 300-302
mental illness, exercise effects on 289-291
mental retardation, effect on self-esteem
    development 269-271
Messer, B. 8, 11
Michel, Y. 153
Miller, L. 98, 101
Miller, W.C. 231
Miller, W.R. 131
Ministry of Agriculture, Food, and Fisheries 231
minority, defined 263
Mintz, L. 148, 246
Mishkind, M.E. 143, 144, 154, 159-160
modeling, and self-efficacy 72-73
Montada, L. 209
Moore, D.C. 240, 246
Morgan, D. 88
Morgan, W.P. 5-6, 9, 70-71, 78, 131-132, 163, 289-290
Morris, A. 143, 148
Morris, J. 93, 196
motivation. See also cognitive motivation theories;
        specific motivation type and theories
    continuum categories of 177-178
    and domain-general self-perception 63-70
    and domain-specific self-perception 70-78
    extrinsic vs. intrinsic 130
    indicators of 59-61
    and school fitness testing 191-192
    stages of 61
    task vs. ego orientation 188-189
motivational climate 66-67
motivation and self-esteem
    of children 176-183
    theory vs. reality 186-192
Mrazek, J. 213, 214, 217
Muller, D. 190
multidimensional hierarchial factor model of self-
        concept 32
multidimensional self-concept instruments
    development of 40-48
    with physical scales 39-40
Multidimensional Self Concept Scale 31, 40
Multitrait-Multimethod (MTMM) analysis,
        comparing PSPP, PSD, and PSDQ 48-54
Murdoch, F.A. 294-295
Murphy, G. 114
Murphy, T.J. 294
Musgrave, B. 303

Must, A. 232
Mutrie, N., xi-xii, 112, 124, 248, 288-290, 300, 305-
306
Myers, P. 156, 158

N
Naidoo, J. 90
naive theory 207
narcissism 144
and consumer culture 92-93
and weight preoccupation 150, 248
National Children's Youth Fitness Survey of 1985,
230
National Health Examination Survey 230
National Institute of Mental Health 289
Naughton, J. 291
Nead, L. 100
negative addiction 163
Nelkin, D. 92
Nelson, J.K. 27
Nelson, M. 269
neuroticism
and body image 149
and eating disorders 150
and weight 149-150
Nicholls, J.G. 64-65
Noles, S.W. 148, 149
Norstrom, J. 297
North, T.C. 289, 302
Notarius, C. 298, 307
Nudelman, S. 161, 163-164

O
obesity
cause of 230-231
complications of 230
cost of 230
gender differences in 232
Odom, S. 267
Oerter, R. 209
Ogles, B.M. 164
Ohzeki, T. 152
Oke, L. 240
Oldridge, N.B. 291
Olmsted, M.A. 146
O'Reilly, P. 157, 158
organismic integration 114
organizing self 113
Orwin, A. 290
Ossip-Klein, D.J. 290
osteoporosis, exercise effects on 297-299
Ostrow, A.C. 27, 28, 38, 39, 40, 54, 151
O'Toole, L.C. 163
outcome expectations, vs. efficacy expectations 71
overexercise 163-165
overweight. See obesity
Owen, Johnny 60
Owens, V.L. 190

P
Page, Angela xi, 121 ,122, 124, 127, 147, 148, 214,
236-237, 243, 247, 249
Palladino, D.E. 207
Palmer, J. 294
Pangrazi, R.P. 175, 195
Papaioannou, A. 67, 189
parents, effect on self-esteem development in indi-
viduals with disabilities 266-267
Pasman, L. 163

Pate, R.P. 196
Paton, L. 296
Patrick, D.R. 277
Patrick, G.D. 276
Patrick, K. 231
Patton, G.C. 246
Patton, J.F. 5
Peart, N.D. 36, 190
peers, effect on self-esteem development in
individuals with disabilities 267
Penner, L.A. 146
Penz, O. 98, 101
perceived ability, defined xii
perceived body shape 146
perceived competence
and athletes with disabilities 278-279
defined xii
perceived importance 244
and self-esteem 124-128
perceived locus of causality (PLOC) 75-76
perceived physical attractiveness
gender differences in 243-244
multicultural study of 16-17
as a predictor of exercise 16-17
and self-esteem 17
perceived physical competence
and age 187-188
assessment of 68-69
defined 7
as exercise predictor 21
and feedback 187-188
relationship to self-efficacies 7
Perceived Physical Competence Scale 279
perceived sport importance 127
perceived weight, and body image 158
Perceived Importance Profile (PIP) 16, 42, 125, 127
performance 61
performing body
and the self 92-95
and social class differences 94-95
persistence 60
personal identity, vs. social identity 206
personal investment theory of motivation 65
personality, and body image 148-150
personality characteristics, and self-esteem 120
personalized hierarchial model of self-concept 42
Personal Orientation Inventory (POI) 132, 277
person as judge (motivation) 62
Peters, D.M. 147, 148
Peterson, A.C. 238
Peterson, C.C. 150
Peterson, J.L. 150
Petrie, T.A. 162
Petruzzello, S.J. 289
physical self, and adolescent weight management
229-252
physical activity. See exercise
physical appearance. See also bodily attractiveness
and cultural dominance 125
perceptions of vii, 242-245
and self-esteem 13, 122-123, 242
physical competence
measurement of 39
and self-esteem 123-124
physical disability, effect on self-esteem
development 268-269
physical education, and disability xi
physical educators, effect on self-esteem
development in individuals with

disabilities 267
Physical Estimation and Attraction Scales (PEAS) 39
physical fitness
    and body image 159-165
    and self-esteem 3-4
physical self. *See also* physical self-concept;
        socially constructed physical self
    of adolescents xi
    and cognitive motivation theories 59-79
    cross-cultural differences xi
    investigation of vii-x
    and life adjustment 20-21
    and lifestyle 221-225
    and public self 112-113, 115
    and self-esteem 111-135
    social-psychological approach to ix
physical self-concept vii
    and elite sports 218-219
    gender differences in 218, 220-221
    in German adolescents 213-214
    and sports 216-217
    vs. academic self-concept 37
physical self-concept measurement
    criteria for 54
    and future research 54-55
    history of 37-40
    MTMM analysis of 48-54
    multidimensional instrument development
        40-48
    through construct validation 27-55
Physical Self-Concept Scales (PSC) 40, 43-45
    PSDQ and PSPP compared to 48-54
Physical Self-Description Questionnaire (PSDQ)
        22-23, 40, 45-48
    Australian adolescent scores on 186
    confirmatory factor analysis 46-47
    on physical competence 123, 124
    PSC and PSPP compared to 48-54
    relations to external criteria 47-48
Physical Self-Efficacy Scale 74
physical self-esteem of children and adolescents
    content and structure of 183-185
    promotion of 193-199
    sports vs. exercise 193
Physical Self-Perception Profile (PSPP) 5, 11, 13, 15,
        18, 20, 22-23, 31, 40-43, 121, 279, 304, 306
    Children and Youth scales 184-185
    Harter's work and validation of 64
    with older population 132-133
    Perceived Importance Profile (PIP) used with
        42, 125, 127
    on physical appearance 122
    on physical competence 123, 124
    PSC and PSDQ compared to 48-54
    self-efficacy theory/research and 74
    Whitehead and Corbin's work with 184
physical self-system 3-26. *See also* physical self
physical self-worth, and importance-competence
    126
Physical Self-Worth Scale (PSW) 11-13
Pierce, W.D. 76, 164-165
Piers, E.V. 267, 269
Piers-Harris Children's Self-Concept Scale 269
Pike, R. 270, 278
Plante, T.G. 288, 290
Pliner, P. 151
Plummer, K. 105
pluralization 211-212
Podosek, H.A. 267, 271, 278

Polivy, J. 16
postmodern self 85-86
Pratt, C.C. 269, 273, 274, 276
pregnancy, exercise effects on 302
prejudice, toward individuals with disabilities
    260-261
premenstrual syndrome, exercise effects on 301-302
The Presentation of Self in Everyday Life 93
principle of reciprocal determinism, defined 7
Prior, J.C. 300
Probast, C.K. 143, 152
Prochaska, J.O. 61
Profile of Mood States 292
Prohaska, T.R. 151
Prout, H. 271
Pruitt, J. 160
Pruzinsky, T. 145, 151
Psychological Model for Physical Activity
        Participation 4-5, 64
    dynamic associations validation 8-11
    internal structure and association validation 8
    validity testing of 5
public self vii, 123
    and physical self 112-113, 115

R
race. *See* ethnic groups
Radke-Sharpe, N. 147
Rand, C.S.W. 153
rationalization, and self-esteem preservation in
        individuals with disabilities 274-275
Ratusny, D. 161, 162, 164
realization, of self-worth 128-129
reciprocity 117-118
Redmayne, R.S. 42, 45, 213
reflected appraisal, in individuals with disabilities
    272
reflexivity of the self 84, 101, 117-118
Rejeski, W.A. 115
Rejeski, W.J. 72, 287, 288
relatedness, defined 177
Renick, M.J. 271, 278
Richards, G. 37, 40, 43-44
Richardson, J. 302
Rickli, R.E. 298
Riddoch, C. 231
Riebe, D. 16-17
Riessman, C. 101
Rigby, C.S. 177, 179
Riggen, K. 266, 278, 279
Riordan, J. 232, 245
Rizzo, T.L. 264, 267
Roberts, N. 240
Robinson, A. 240, 245
Rodgers, W.M. 74
Rodin, J. 147-148, 158, 159, 162, 233, 245, 246, 248
Rogers, Carl R. 128, 131, 273
Rollnick, S. 131
Rona, R.J. 230
Rosenberg, M. 8, 17, 116, 124, 161, 272, 273, 274
Rosenberg Self-Esteem Scale 8-9, 116, 276
Rosen, J.C. 161, 163
Rosin, P. 144
Ross, J.G. 196
Rothblum, E. 155
Roth, D. 149, 157
Roth, W. 257, 262
Rotter, J.B. 118
Routtenberg, A. 164

Rovario, S. 292
Royal College of Physicians 230-231
Rozin, P. 151
Rucker, C.E. 153
Rummel, A. 76
Russell, G.F. 233
Russell, J.C. 164
Ryan, R.M. 75, 76-77, 114, 116, 129, 130, 133-134,
    176-179, 182, 189, 192
Ryckman, R.M. 74

S
Sack, H.G. 222
Sacks, M.H. 150
Safilios-Rothschild, C. 264
Salisbury, K.S. 5, 8, 20
Sallis, J.F. 5, 19, 61, 73, 198, 231
Salmon, P. 301
Sarrazin, P. 68
Scanlan, T.K. 187
schema, defined 69
schizophrenia, exercise effects on 290
Schmidt-Gotz, E. 261, 264, 267
school fitness testing, motivational outcomes of
    181-192
Schork, N.J. 147, 151-152
Schulsinger, F. 47
Schulze, G. 212
Schwalbe, M. 85-86, 271
Schwarzer, R. 7, 74
Scott, S. 88
Scraton, S. 96, 98
Secord, P.F. 38, 146
Sefton, J.M. 187
self. See also postmodern self
    and body, identity, individual 83-86
    and individualism 120-121
    and life history research 105-106
    and the performing body 92-95
    social constraints of 120-121
self-acceptance 131-132
    defined 131
    and self-description 131-132
self-actualization
    in athletes with disabilities 277-278
    defined 277
self-attribution, in individuals with disabilities 272
self-based theory of motivation 63
self-concept
    academic vs. physical 36-37
    in athletes vs. nonathletes 219-220
    defined xii, 34-35
    and elite sports 217-221
    and identity 205-208
    multidimensional model of xiii
    origin of 207
    and sports 213-221
    structural models of 28-33
    theoretical models of x, 33-34
Self-Concept of Ability Scale 37-38
Self-Concept Inventory 37-38
self-confidence, defined xiii
self-consistency 117, 126
self-description, and self-acceptance 131-132
Self-Description Questionnaire (SDQ) instruments
    35-37, 39, 43, 44, 45, 46, 116
self-determination theory (SDT) 76-77, 130-131,
    176-179, 194

and intrinsic motivation 75-78
    and self-esteem 182-183
self-development hypothesis. See self-enhance-
    ment hypothesis
self director 113-115
    tasks of 116-117
self-efficacy 70-75
    defined xiii, 7, 71
    development of 71-73
    as exercise predictor 17-19, 73-74
    and future research 73
    and modeling 72-73
    relationship with self-perceptions and
        motivation 74-75
    relationship to perceived physical competence 7
self-enhancement hypothesis viii, 5, 59, 116-117, 126
self-esteem. See also body esteem; high self-
        esteem; low self-esteem
    in adolescents 189-192
    alternative contributions to 128-132
    in athletes with disabilities 275-279
    in children xi, 176-183
    defined xii, 4, 115-116
    and exercise 19-20, 189-192
    and future research 21-23, 132-134
    gender differences in 244
    high vs. low 118-120
    and motivational applications 186-192
    and perceived importance 124-128
    and perceived physical attractiveness 17
    and personality characteristics 120
    phases of 111-112
    and physical appearance 13, 122-123
    and physical competence 123-124
    and physical fitness 3-4
    and physical self 111-135
    prediction of 127
    preservation in individuals with disabilities
        274-275
    and self-determined motivation 182-183
    and self-system 113-121
    true vs. contingent 129-130
    unconditional vs. conditional support 182
    variance 12
self-esteem development in individuals with
        disabilities 265-272
    causes and correlates of individual differences
        275
    effect of age at onset 265-266
    effect of disability type 267-272
    and gender discrimination 267
    parental effect on 266-267
    principles of 272-273
Self-Esteem Inventory 37-38
Self-Perception Profile for Children 40
self-perceptions
    defined xii
    and self-efficacy 74-75
Self-Presentation (Leary) 72
self-presentation 115
Self-Rating Scale 40
self-regulation, and individualism 91
self-schemata 114-115
self-system x
    and self-esteem 113-121
self-theory 114
self-worth. See also unconditional self-worth
    defined xii

gender differences in 243
realization of 128-129
and sexual maturation 239-240
sexual maturation
and adolescent weight management 238-240
gender differences in 238-240
and self-worth 239-240
sexual preference, and body image 145-156
Shalin, D. 85
Shapiro, C.M. 147, 149, 151, 159, 161
Shapiro, J.P. 261, 262, 265
Sharratt, J.K. 297
Sharratt, M.T. 297
Shavelson, Hubner, and Stanton model of self-
concept 33-34
Shavelson, R.J. ix, 15, 30, 31, 33-36, 37, 41, 42, 43,
45, 49, 54, 145, 207
Shear, C.L. 230
Shepard, L.A. 131
Shephard, R.J. 159, 307
Sherrill, A. 198
Sherrill, C. xi, 130, 131-132, 261, 262, 264, 266, 267,
269, 272, 273, 275, 277, 278
Shields, S.A. 38, 145-146
Shilling, C. 83, 87, 89, 92, 94-95, 101, 208, 212
Shisslak, C. 163
Shontz, F.C. 268
Shostrom, E. 277
Shotter, J. 86
Sidney, K.H. 299
Siedentop, D. 175
Sieghart, M.A. 250
Siever, M.D. 155-156
Sigelman, C.I. 270
Silberstein, L.R. 155, 159, 160, 161, 233, 245, 246, 248
Siller, J. 267
Silon, E. 270
Silvennoinen, M. 101
Silverstein, B. 143, 144, 154
Simkin, A.J. 298
Singh, D. 147
Sinyor, D. 294
size-estimation accuracy 145
skill development hypothesis of self-esteem 4, 5, 71
skill-enhancement hypothesis viii
Slade, P.D. 147
Slava, S. 195
Slavin, J.L. 302
Smart, B. 88
Smith, E. 298
Smith, J.E. 152
Smith, K. 91
Smyth, M.M. 278
Soares, A.T. 31
Soares, L.M. 31
Sobal, J. 152
social approval-oriented motivation 65
social cognitive perspective 62
social cognitive theory 7
social comparison, in individuals with disabilities
272
social desirability 9, 11
Social Desirability Scale 41
social identity, vs. personal identity 206
social identity theory of motivation 60
socially constructed body 86-88
and future research 104-105
historical development of 87

inequalities of 88
socially constructed physical self 83-106
socioeconomic status, and fatness 152
sociological self, and the enlightenment subject
84-85
Solomon, L. 150, 155
Song and Hattie test 40
Sonstroem, Robert J. ix, 3, 4, 5, 6, 7, 8, 10, 11, 12, 13,
14, 15, 16, 17, 20, 39, 41, 42, 70-71, 78, 112,
120, 121, 122, 127, 131, 132
Sorenson, T. 47
Spanier, G. 208
Sparkes, Andrew x, 60, 90, 91, 97, 101, 103, 104,
105, 113
Spears, W.D. 19
Special Olympics 265-266
Speliotis, E.D. 11, 13, 14, 42, 121
Speltz, M. 267
Spencer, S.J. 119
sports. See also elite sports
motivation for participation in 187
and self-concept 213-221
Sports Council and Health Education Authority
(Great Britain) 72, 300
spread phenomenon 264
Stanton, G.C. ix, 15, 33-36, 37, 41, 42, 49, 54, 145, 207
Steele, C.M. 119
Steinberg, L. 240
Steiner-Adair, C. 155
Stephens, T. 159, 300
stereotyping. See categorization
Stewart, D.A. 259
stigmatization
defined 261
of individuals with disabilities 261-262
stigmatized identity 93
Stone, L. 91
Story, M. 231, 246
Strang, V.R. 302
Strauman, T.J. 147
Striegel-Moore, R.H. 148, 155, 158, 159, 233, 245,
246, 248
Stroebe, W. 62
structural modeling analysis, EXSEM 15-16
structural model of self-concept, and instrument
development 33
Stryker, S. 114, 115, 117
Stuart, J.L. 238
Stunkard, A.J. 47, 152
Summer Paralympics 266
Sundgot-Borgen, J. 162
Super, J.T. 269, 276
Swann, W.B., Jr. 117
Sweeting, A. 250
Synnott, A. 83, 86-87, 89
Szmuckler, G. 163, 233, 245, 246
Szyman, R.J. 276

T
Tajfel, H. 60
task mastery 193
task orientation, vs. ego orientation 188-189
task-oriented motivation 65
Tassinary, L.G. 288
Taub, D.E. 162
taxonomic model of self-concept 31-32
Taylor, M.J. 246
Taylor, S.E. 60, 69

Tchividjian, L.R. 61, 122, 234, 248
Tennessee Self Concept Scale 31, 40, 276
terminology xii-xiii, 258-259
Tesser, A. 116, 124
Thelan, M. 151
Therberge, N. 96
Thompson, A. 287, 288
Thompson, J.K. 146, 151, 157-158, 161, 163
Tibbs, J. 163
Tice, D.M. 117
Tiihonen, A. 101
Timko, C. 155
Tinning, R. 90-91, 96, 233, 248
Tockerman, Y.R. 145
Touyz, S.W. 156, 164
Transtheoretical Model of Stages of Change 19, 61
Trieschmann, R.B. 266, 274
true self-esteem 129
    defined 182
Tsukue, I. 294
Tucker, L.A. 161
Tunstall-Pedoe, H. 291
Turner, B. 88

U
Ulrich, D.A. 270, 279
unconditional self-worth 128-129
unidimensional model of self-concept 30
uniqueness, of individuals with disabilities 262-263

V
Vallerand, R.J. 177, 195
Valliant, P.M. 276
Van Raalte, J.L. 127
Vasterling, J.J. 297
Vaughn, C.C. 298
Veale, D. 60
Vealey, R.S. 27-28
victim blaming 91-92
Vigna, Y. 300-301
Vogel, J.A. 5
Vranic, M. 296

W
Wadden, T.A. 242, 246
Walker, A.R.P. 231, 232
Walker, R. 18
Wallace, A.M. 302
Waller, G. 156
Walter, J.S. 212
Walters, L.C. 153
Walton, W.E. 258
Wankel, L.M. 187
Wardle, J. 153-154, 157, 159, 245, 247
Warrick, R. 96
Waschull, S. 153
Waterman, A.S. 207
Watkinson, J. 278
Watson, E.R. 198
Weigand, B. 198
weight
    and low self-esteem 149-150

and narcissism 150
and neuroticism 149-150
Weight, L.M. 161, 164
weight management. *See also* adolescent weight
    management
    and body shape 236
    and body size 236
    and exercise 161, 247-248, 250-251
    and fatness 235-238
Weinberg, N. 259, 267-268
Weiner, B. 59, 61-62
Weiss, M. 266
Weissman, M. 293
Weiss, M.R. 64, 130, 176, 187-188, 192
Welk, G.J. 121, 184, 195
Wells, L.E. 6, 23, 33
Werner, E.E. 120
Wertheim, E.H. 246
West, P.C. 262
West, R. 230
wheelchair athletes, and self-esteem 276
Whitehead, Hannah 180
Whitehead, James R. xi, 65, 77, 112, 121, 184, 191
White, P. 100, 103
White, Robert W. 63, 75, 76, 116, 176, 183
Whitesell, N.R. 127, 129
whole-body procedures 145
Widaman, K.F. 270, 271
Widdershoven, G. 101
Wiersma, U.J. 76
Wilfley, D.E. 130, 230
Williams. G.J. 148
Williams, J.F. 175
Williamson, D.A. 150
Williams, T. 259, 261, 264, 267, 275
Wing, R.R. 296
Winne, P.H. 30
Wiseman, C.V. 143, 148, 161
within-network studies of construct validation 28
women athletes. *See* female athletes
Woods, S. 97
World Health Organization, and disability
    terminology 258
Wright, B.A. 259, 262, 263, 264, 274
Wright, J. 266
Wuerch, G. 277
Wyeth, D.O. 264
Wylie, R.C. 33, 35, 37, 38, 39-40, 41, 42, 48-49, 54,
    111, 131

Y
Yates, A. 162, 163, 164
Young, K. 103
You Stay Active program 191
Yuker, H. 261, 263, 268, 274

Z
Zellner, D.A. 144
Zigler, E. 270
Zinnecker, J. 208, 212
Zoerink, D.A. 275

ABOUT THE CONTRIBUTORS

Stuart Biddle is currently Reader in Exercise and Sport Psychology and programme leader of the MSc and MSc (European) Exercise and Sport Psychology programmes at the University of Exeter, United Kingdom. He is also president of the European Federation of Sport Psychology, psychology editor for the *Journal of Sports Sciences,* and International Associate Editor for *The Sport Psychologist.* Biddle has written, coauthored, or edited two textbooks on exercise and sport psychology and five textbooks on physical education and sport.

Wolf-Dietrich Brettschneider, PhD, is professor and chair at the Institute for Sport Sciences at the Free University of Berlin, Germany. He is the author, coauthor, editor, or coeditor of eight books and 80 articles in national and international journals on major issues of sport sociology and sport pedagogy. His research interests include sport and youth culture, cross-cultural studies in adolescent sport and lifestyle, and the development of sport culture and its pedagogical implications. He is also a member of several national and international scientific committees related to sport.

Charles B. (Chuck) Corbin is a professor of exercise science and physical education at Arizona State University. He has authored several widely used texts, including *Fitness for Life* and *Concepts of Physical Fitness* (with Ruth Lindsey). His recent research has focused on intrinsic motivation in physical activity, physical self-esteem in children and youth, and physical activity patterns in people of all ages. A past president of the American Academy of Kinesiology and Physical Education, Corbin was recently named Distinguished Scholar of the National Association for Physical Education in Higher Education.

Caroline Davis, PhD in experimental psychology, is an associate professor both in the Department of Kinesiology and Health Science and in the Graduate Programme in Psychology at York University, Canada. Caroline also has an adjunct appointment as associate professor in the Department of Psychiatry at the Toronto Hospital and on the Faculty of Medicine at the University of Toronto. She has published extensively in the areas of eating disorders, dietary restraint, body image, and exercise.

Rüdiger Heim, PhD, after qualifying in 1986 as a teacher of German language and physical education, went on to complete his doctorate at the University of Münster in 1991. He is a research assistant at the Free University in Berlin, with special interest in adolescent development and elite sport involvement. Dr. Heim has published four books and several articles in national journals.

Herbert W. Marsh is Dean of Graduate Research Studies and Professor of Education at the University of Western Sydney, Macarthur, and a Fellow of the Australian Academy of Social Sciences. He is a prolific researcher in the fields of education and psychology, and his research spans an array of methodological, statistical, and substantive concerns. He has reviewed submissions for more than 70 journals and is on the editorial board of six journals. Dr. Marsh is author of the teaching-effectiveness instrument and several widely used self-concept instruments, which include the Physical Self-Description Questionnaire.

Nanette Mutrie coauthored (with Stuart Biddle) one of the first textbooks in exercise psychology and has since contributed to two other texts in this area. Her research interest in exercise psychology stems from her doctoral work (funded by a

Fulbright scholarship and supervised by Dorothy Harris at Penn State) on the role of exercise as a treatment for depression. A member of the physical activity task force of the Health Education Board for Scotland, she is a senior lecturer in the Institute of Biomedical and Life Sciences, University of Glasgow.

Angie Page recently completed her PhD at the University of Exeter and is a lecturer in exercise and health sciences at the University of Bristol. Her main research interests are in adolescent health behaviors, with a particular focus on issues of weight management, dietary restraint, self-perceptions, and various aspects of physical activity promotion.

Claudine Sherrill, EdD, is a professor of kinesiology at Texas Woman's University in Denton, Texas. She received her bachelor's degree from Texas Woman's University and her master's and doctoral degrees from Teachers College, Columbia University, New York. A Fellow in the American Academy of Kinesiology and Physical Education, Dr. Sherrill is active in many organizations related to disability and sport and serves as Vice President of the International Federation of Adapted Physical Activity (IFAPA). She has published six books on aspects of adapted physical activity, disability sport, creative arts, and leadership, and more than 50 research studies on the psychosocial dimensions of disability. Dr. Sherrill is editor of the *Adapted Physical Activity Quarterly.*

Bob Sonstroem earned a PhD in educational psychology at the University of Minnesota. He has been active in research for 29 years, publishing research primarily about self-esteem, the physical self, exercise participation and adherence, and anxiety. Dr. Sonstroem is a Fellow of the American College of Sports Medicine and was a member of the program committee for six years (1991-1996). He is also a fellow of Division 47 of the American Psychological Association, the Research Consortium of AAHPERD, and is on the Editorial Board of the *Journal of Sport and Exercise Psychology.*

Andrew C. Sparkes, PhD, is a Reader in Social Theory at the University of Exeter. Since earning his doctorate from Loughborough University in 1987, Dr. Sparkes has been instrumental in promoting qualitative forms of inquiry, and in particular life history research within the domains of physical education, sport, and health. Current research interests revolve around the changing nature of body-self relationships over time, including a narrative analysis of chronic back pain, and a life history study of elite athletes with career-ending injuries or illness.

Jim Whitehead spent 13 years teaching physical education in England before completing his MS and EdD degrees at Arizona State University. Now an associate professor in the Department of Health, Physical Education, and Recreation of the University of North Dakota, he specializes in exercise psychology and fitness education. Dr. Whitehead is a Fellow of the Research Consortium of AAHPERD and of the American College of Sports Medicine. His research interests concern fitness education, physical self-perceptions, and motivation.

ABOUT THE EDITOR

Kenneth R. Fox, PhD, is senior lecturer and program leader in the Department of Exercise and Sport Sciences at the University of Exeter.

Dr. Fox has written more than 100 research and professional publications, including 25 book chapters. He is the author of the *Physical Self-Perception Profile and Manual*, a psychological instrument translated into several languages and recently featured in a review volume of self-concept instruments (Byrne 1996), published by the American Psychological Association.

He has presented his research at more than 50 conferences around the world, including the American College of Sports Medicine Annual Conferences, and he reviews regularly for several psychology and sport science journals. Fox also has consulted in the UK on topics related to exercise, health, and weight management for the Food and Drink Federation, National Dairy Council, British Nutrition Foundation, and Health Education Authority.

Dr. Fox is a member of the American College of Sports Medicine, the British Association of Sport and Exercise Sciences, the Association for the Study of Obesity, and a Fellow of the Physical Education Association of Great Britain.

Dr. Fox lives in Exeter with his wife, Linda, and their two sons, Robbie and Gregory. He enjoys cycling, jogging, and playing jazz music.

More Sport Psychology Textbooks

Advances in Exercise Adherence

ROD K. DISHMAN
EDITOR

1994 • Cloth • 416 pp
Item BDIS0664
ISBN 0-87322-664-X
$42.00 ($62.95 Canadian)

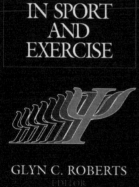

MOTIVATION IN SPORT AND EXERCISE

GLYN C. ROBERTS
EDITOR

1992 • Paper • 288 pp
Item BROB0876
ISBN 0-87322-876-6
$25.00 ($37.50 Canadian)

European Perspectives on Exercise and Sport Psychology

Stuart J. H. Biddle
EDITOR

1995 • Cloth • 360 pp
Item BBID0826
ISBN 0-87322-826-X
$42.00 ($62.95 Canadian)

Human Kinetics
The Premier Publisher for Sports & Fitness
http://www.humankinetics.com/
2335

To request more information or to place
your order, U.S. customers call
TOLL-FREE 1-800-747-4457.
Customers outside the U.S. use appropriate
telephone number/address shown
in the front of this book.